The American Elections of 1984

The American Elections of 1984

EDITED BY AUSTIN RANNEY

An American Enterprise Institute Book,
Published by Duke University Press
1985

Contents

Tables and Figures

FIGURES

Preface

AUSTIN RANNEY

————This book is the third in the American Enterprise Institute's continuing series on America's biennial national elections.[1] It is the first to be published by the Duke University Press in collaboration with AEI.

Its structure is similar to that of the book on the 1980 elections, but there are some differences. It begins, as in 1980, with my summary of main events of the preceding administration, in this case Ronald W. Reagan's first term, as they appeared to have consequences for Reagan's popularity and prospects for reelection. Next comes a chapter by Nelson W. Polsby on the struggle—the most protracted in history in either party—for the Democratic party's presidential nomination, which ended in the selection of Walter F. Mondale and in his choice of Geraldine Ferraro as his running mate, the first woman in history to run on a major party's national ticket. It is followed by Charles O. Jones's chapter, which covers not only President Reagan's decision to run for reelection, but also how the Republicans turned the absence of a contest for their nomination into an asset in preparing for the general election campaign—and how the first moves in the campaign for the Republicans' 1988 presidential nomination took place at the party's national convention in 1984, suggesting that presidential nominating politics in the United States now operates continually, with no time off whatever for good behavior of any kind. Next comes a chapter by Thomas E. Mann on the high expectations some held for the role of the new "superdelegates" at the Democratic national convention and how their actual performance matched up to those expectations.

The next section focuses on the general election campaign. Albert R. Hunt describes the main strategies, issues, and events of the campaign from the conventions to the election. Michael J. Robinson reports the main findings, some quite surprising, from the George Washington University–AEI study of the role of the mass communications media in the campaign.

William Schneider follows with his analysis of the voting in the November 6 presidential election, with special attention to the question of whether Reagan's big victory was mainly a tribute to his personal popularity, an endorsement of his policies, a simple response to peace and prosperity, another milestone in a basic realignment of American politics—or some mixture of all four. Norman J. Ornstein describes the Republicans' striking failure to match the presidential landslide with comparable gains in elections for the Senate, the House, and state governors and legislatures.

Although they focus mainly on other topics, the book's first eight chapters frequently touch on what the 1984 results tell us about the question of whether the United States is in the midst of a fundamental party realignment comparable to those that took place in the 1830s, 1850s, and 1930s. The final two chapters concentrate on that question. Raymond E. Wolfinger argues that, contrary to the views of many commentators, there has not been a major weakening of party identification in recent years; and he adds that the South is the only part of the country in which a significant long-term shift of loyalties from the Democrats to the Republicans is taking place. James Q. Wilson argues that there has been and continues to be a significant realignment of ideologies and loyalties among political elites accompanied by an equally significant weakening of party loyalties and party-influenced voting among the mass electorate.

The appendixes update for 1984 all the items of information provided for 1980 and 1982 by the preceding volumes. Our hope continues to be that future students of American elections will find in this book all of the most important facts about *what* happened in 1984 and some illuminating explanations of *why* they happened that way and what it means for the future.

Washington, D.C.
July 1985

Reagan's First Term

AUSTIN RANNEY

─────────In the American presidential election of 1984 the Republican incumbent, Ronald W. Reagan, defeated the Democratic challenger, Walter F. Mondale, with 54,455,074 popular votes (58.8 percent) to Mondale's 37,577,137 votes (40.6 percent). The remaining 620,582 votes (0.6 percent) were divided among fourteen other candidates.[1] The total of 92,652,793 votes constituted a turnout of 53.3 percent of the voting-age population, which was 0.7 points higher than the 52.6 percent who voted in 1980. It was a modest increase, but nevertheless the first uptick in presidential voting turnout since 1960.

Mondale carried only his home state of Minnesota and the District of Columbia, for a total of 13 electoral votes. Reagan carried the other forty-nine states, for a total of 525 electoral votes.

Depending on the measure used, it was either the second, fifth, or seventh greatest landslide in an American presidential election since the Civil War.[2] Moreover, it was the first election since 1972 in which an incumbent president was reelected.

The results in the congressional elections, however, were disappointing for the Republicans. In the Senate the preelection party division was fifty-five Republicans and forty-five Democrats; the Democrats made a net gain of two seats, but the Republicans retained control. In the House of Representatives the preelection party division was 266 Democrats, 167 Republicans, and 2 vacancies. In the elections the Republicans made a net gain of 14 seats, but the Democrats continued to control the House, as they have ever since the election of 1954.[3]

Some observers saw these mixed results as a phenomenon unique to 1984— a magnificent personal triumph for Ronald Reagan that established him as the most popular and successful president since Franklin Roosevelt. That may be an accurate appraisal of Reagan's place in history, but the 1984 results do not prove it. Rather they continued one of the most striking patterns in American politics since the end of World War II: Republican strength in presidential elections paralleled by Democratic strength in congressional elections. The record is clear: Ten presidential elections have been held from 1948 to 1984, the Republicans have won six, and their candidates have accumulated 369 million votes (53 percent) to the Democratic candidates' 329 million. Moreover, the last *northern* Democratic presidential candidate to win as much as 50 percent of the popular votes was Franklin Roosevelt in 1944!

In contrast, there have been twenty elections for Congress since 1946 and thus forty chances for each party to win control of a chamber. The Democrats have won thirty-three times and the Republicans seven—a rate of success even greater than that of the Republicans in presidential politics.

To say there was nothing unusual about the mixed results of the 1984 elections, however, is not to say there was nothing unusual about Reagan's first term. Quite the contrary. In some respects it was as radical a departure from the presidencies since Franklin Roosevelt's as Roosevelt's presidency was from those of Harding, Coolidge, and Hoover. Thus it seems appropriate to begin this book with a review of Reagan's first term from his inauguration in 1981 to the formal declaration of his candidacy for a second term in early 1984.

Reaganism: History and Ideas

Let us begin our review of Ronald Reagan's first term by remembering who he was when he took office on January 20, 1981, and why he had defeated Jimmy Carter. The first thing to note is that he had won the Republican nomination in 1980 not so much as a successful political entrepreneur in the mold of John Kennedy or Jimmy Carter, or as a veteran Washington insider like Lyndon Johnson, Richard Nixon, and Gerald Ford, but as the longtime leader of a political *movement*. As Hugh Heclo and Rudolph Penner point out, "Reagan's candidacy [in 1980] represented the culmination of almost fifteen years of grassroots political agitation and organization across the nation."[4]

In 1980, then, Reagan was Mr. Conservative more than Mr. Republican, but that is not why he defeated Carter. In the study of the 1980 election by the American Enterprise Institute (AEI), William Schneider concluded that the election was essentially a referendum on the Carter administration, not on conservatism, and the verdict was thumbs down. Schneider added, however, that if the election outcome did not constitute a ringing mandate for conservatism it certainly gave Reagan full power and justification to adopt conservative policies if he thought they would do the job:

> The voters were voting for a *change*, and they were certainly aware that the type of change Reagan was offering was going to take the country in a

more conservative direction. They were willing to go along with that, not because they were convinced of the essential merits of the conservative program, but because they were willing to give conservatism a chance. It is as if, having got nowhere for the past four years with Jimmy Carter at the wheel, the voters turned to Ronald Reagan and said, "O.K.—you drive."[5]

And drive he did, right from the start. In its first term the Reagan administration attempted a more thoroughgoing change in the direction of public policy than any administration since Franklin Roosevelt's first term (1933–37). And, in its determined effort to design and implement its measures according to an explicit and controversial political philosophy, the "Reagan revolution" was an even more radical departure from the prevailing ways than the "Roosevelt revolution" had been forty-eight years earlier.

The Rise of Conservatism and Reagan

In its early years Roosevelt's New Deal was not informed by any particular guiding philosophy, except perhaps good old American pragmatism. Roosevelt's approach was simplicity itself: The house is collapsing about our ears, and any action is better than no action; so let's try a lot of new policies, stick with what works, and replace what doesn't with something else. In later years, to be sure, some analysts have teased out of Roosevelt's actions and speeches a kind of implicit public philosophy with these main principles: (1) All Americans are equally entitled to at least the minimum conditions of the good life; (2) It is the obligation of government to provide those conditions for people who cannot provide them for themselves; and (3) The basic responsibility for honoring that obligation lies with the federal government, not with the state and local governments. From the late 1930s on this philosophy was called, loosely but widely, "liberalism."[6]

Since the 1930s every administration has, explicitly or implicitly, proceeded on the basis of that philosophy, without thinking or talking about it very much. There were, to be sure, variations of interpretation and emphasis. The Republican administrations of Eisenhower, Nixon, and Ford emphasized encouraging business and balancing the federal budget, while the Democratic administrations of Truman, Kennedy, Johnson, and Carter emphasized raising the level of the federal government's guarantees and extending them to more people. But the general direction of policy changed only a little from one administration to the next, even when Republicans succeeded Democrats in the White House.

New Deal liberalism did not go entirely unchallenged, of course. From its earliest days a few politicians like Robert Taft and Barry Goldwater, and a few intellectuals like Russell Kirk, Willmoore Kendall, and William F. Buckley, Jr., kept alive a counterphilosophy, which they called "conservatism," in their unceasing attacks on the liberal Democrats and their "me-too" fellow travelers among the liberal/moderate Republicans. They had one brief shining moment in 1964 when Goldwater won the Republican presidential nomination over the liberal/moderates Nelson Rockefeller and William Scranton. But Goldwater's overwhelming loss to Lyndon Johnson and his Great Society programs led most observers to conclude that New Deal liberalism had become America's mainstream political philosophy and could not be successfully challenged by an "extremist" like Goldwater or a reversionary philosophy like conservatism.

In hindsight, it is clear that one of the most significant events of 1964 was Reagan's emergence as the most popular and successful political leader of the conservative movement. We cannot retell his history in detail here,[7] but we should note that as a second-banana movie actor in the 1930s and 1940s Reagan was an ardent New Deal Democrat and the president of a labor union, the Screen Actors Guild. As late as 1948 he enthusiastically supported Harry Truman and Hubert Humphrey, but in the 1950s he grew increasingly disillusioned with New Deal liberalism, and, as touring spokesman and television host for General Electric from 1954 to 1962, he made hundreds of speeches expounding his new conservative views. In 1962 he reregistered as a Republican, and on October 27, 1964, he gave a nationally televised speech for Goldwater officially called "A Time for Choosing," but afterward better known to Reagan-watchers as "The Speech." With minor variations he delivered it hundreds of times over the next twenty years—during his two terms as governor of California (1967–73), in his nearly successful attempt to take the Republican presidential nomination away from moderate incumbent Gerald Ford in 1976, in his successful effort to win the nomination over moderate George Bush in 1980, in his campaign against Jimmy Carter, and throughout his first term as president.

The Main Principles of Reagan's Conservatism

Whether or not Ronald Reagan's conservatism qualifies as a full-fledged ideology or philosophy, it certainly contains principles that Reagan and his colleagues constantly relied on in deciding what to do and what not to do. In that sense, at least, his first term was the most ideological administration in this century, and its underlying principles must be borne in mind by anyone who seeks to understand what his administration attempted.

1. Government Nonintervention in the Economy   The core principle in Reagan's conservativism holds that the most creative and dynamic force in the

American (or in any) economy is the desire of talented and energetic people for material gain. When that force is allowed to work freely, such people will design, produce, and sell more and better goods and services because they know they will make money; and in the process they will create jobs and prosperity for others. But when they are constricted by government regulations, and when high, progressive tax rates keep economic achievers from enjoying the full rewards of their achievements, investment dwindles, production drops, jobs vanish, and the economy slumps. Accordingly, the first goal of a conservative administration must be to "get the government off the people's backs"—to reduce government intervention in the economy to a minimum and let economic decisions be made by business operators in free markets rather than by bureaucrats in government agencies.

Reagan expounded this view in many speeches from the mid-1950s on, but at the beginning of his first term in 1981 its newest version was the "supply side" school of economics pressed by, among others, economist Arthur Laffer, journalist Jude Wanniski, and New York Republican Congressman Jack Kemp. Their view was that the key to low inflation, high economic growth, high employment, and a balanced federal budget is cutting personal and corporate income taxes. If we do that, they argued, the economy will boom and many more people and businesses will pay taxes; hence, even at lower marginal rates, revenues will grow sufficiently to both support increased military spending and permit a balanced budget. Of all the policies Reagan pressed in his first term, he gave the highest priority to cutting taxes and keeping them cut.

2. *Reducing the Size of Government*   For decades before he took office Reagan argued that many domestic spending programs, especially the sort installed by Johnson's Great Society, should be drastically reduced or eliminated altogether. These programs, he said, are expensive and lead to high taxes and unbalanced budgets. Even worse, they swell the size of government; make government the master, not the servant, of the people; and make large numbers of people wards of society rather than contributors to it.

From the 1950s on Reagan made an important distinction between types of social welfare programs, and this distinction became fundamental to his budget-cutting strategy as president. We must, he said, maintain an adequate "safety net" for the "truly needy"—people who really cannot support themselves at all. But we must stop coddling the "working poor"—people who *can* support themselves and their families if they want to but see no reason to make the effort as long as the government supports them with income-maintenance and life-style-enhancement programs. Government has an obligation to see that no one starves, Reagan said; but it has no obligation to guarantee that an able-bodied but lazy "welfare cheat" has a car and a TV.

3. The New Federalism   First as governor and then as president, Reagan believed that the federal government has grabbed far too much power from the states and that it is time to return a sizable chunk of that power to the states, where it belongs and where it will be better used. Note that Reagan regarded the states, not the cities or the counties, as the proper units to take back powers usurped by Washington.

4. Government Intervention in Moral and Religious Matters   Reagan-style conservatives do not, like Libertarians, oppose all forms of government intervention in all aspects of people's lives. They believe that government has an obligation to promote morality and religion even if that entails considerable government intervention in private affairs. For instance, they see abortion as something close to murder, and they do not agree with Libertarians that government should leave the choice of abortion to the consciences of individual women. They believe that government should prohibit abortion, or allow the states to prohibit it, by a constitutional amendment if need be. They also believe that religious values, enhanced by the habit of prayer, are important for the nation's moral health and that government has an obligation to ensure that those values are inculcated in children even if their parents don't believe in them or don't want to bother. Hence they favor a constitutional amendment allowing state and local school systems to hold prayers as part of the educational process, and they are not impressed by arguments that religion is a private matter and that only parents should be responsible for their children's religious education.

5. Anti-Communism as the Key to Foreign Policy   Reagan has long believed that the basic cleavage in world affairs is the gulf between the "evil empire" of Soviet communism and the countries who resist it. In his view the leaders of the Soviet Union have a master plan to impose communism everywhere in the world. They foment subversion and revolution wherever they can. And where, as in Central America, there is a serious challenge to the stability and legitimacy of a noncommunist government, the root cause is seldom poverty, ignorance, or the authoritarian traditions of the country (as Democrats are prone to believe); it is the machinations of the Soviet Union and its vassal states, such as Cuba and Nicaragua. Because of its strength and its dedication to democracy and free enterprise, the United States has a responsibility to help noncommunist governments resist Soviet aggression wherever it can. And the closer to home that aggression comes, as in Central America, the more urgent is the need to take whatever measures are required to stop it in its tracks.

6. Military Strength as the Basis for Effective Foreign Policy   In its relations with other countries, Reagan has often said, America should always stand openly and proudly for American interests first. It should never apologize to its friends or enemies for doing so. And it should aim not at being liked but at being respected. Candor, firmness, and consistency in our statements and actions will help to achieve that respect; but the foundation of a strong and effective foreign policy is a defense second to none. If all nations, friends and foes alike, know that we have great military strength and that we can and will back up the commitments we make, our friends will trust us and our enemies will negotiate seriously with us. Thus the indispensable prerequisite for any fruitful arms control discussion with the Soviets is a military capability at least equal to theirs.

Those six principles have been strongly held and forcefully advocated by Ronald Reagan ever since the 1950s. But philosophical principles are one thing and running a government is quite another. What policies did he actually pursue in his first term?

The Game Plan

Every new American administration begins with its version of what football coaches call "the game plan"—a general strategy of action based upon a conception of what the nation needs and wants, and a set of tactical notions about the people and policies that will meet those needs and wants. Even the Carter administration in 1977 began with such a plan; but, by comparison, in its depth and reach the Reagan administration's 1981 game plan was a master strategy worthy of Knute Rockne and the Gipper themselves. It was explicitly rooted in the conservative philosophy outlined above, and the new team was determined that all major decisions—appointments, legislative proposals, administrative actions—would be made in accordance with that philosophy.

Personnel

For some time now each new administration has taken longer than its predecessors to fill the 2,500 or so "political" positions readily available to it. The Reagan administration took even longer, in part because of the more demanding preappointment investigations required by the new ethics-in-government laws. The main cause of delays, though, were the administration's special efforts to make sure that every appointee at every level was "on board"—that is, committed to Reagan's philosophy.

For such an ideological administration, however, many of the cabinet appointments were surprisingly pragmatic. For example, Alexander Haig at State, Richard Schweiker at Health and Human Services, Drew Lewis at Transportation, and William Brock as U.S. Trade Representative were not longtime "Reaganauts." On the other hand, James Watt at Interior, William

French Smith at Justice, James Edwards at Energy, and Richard Allen as national security adviser were all Reagan-style conservatives, and Jeane Kirkpatrick at the United Nations, the only Democrat appointed to the cabinet, was a well-known advocate of views congenial to Reagan on foreign and defense policy.

In the appointment of subcabinet officers Reagan made his intentions explicit. In a 1980 campaign speech he said:

> Crucial to my strategy of spending control will be the appointment to top government positions of men and women who share my economic philosophy. We will have an administration in which the word from the top isn't lost or hidden in the bureaucracy. That voice will be heard because it is the voice of the people.[8]

He meant what he said. Most appointees to subcabinet policymaking positions were carefully screened to make sure they were dedicated to Reagan's policies and goals. His immediate team of advisers consisted of the "troika" of Edwin Meese III and Michael Deaver, both of whom had been with him since his Sacramento days, and James Baker, who had been high in George Bush's campaign opposing Reagan for the Republican nomination. (Throughout the first term many true-blue conservatives grumbled about what they regarded as Baker's efforts to lead Reagan away from resolute conservatism to wishy-washy pragmatism, but Reagan relied heavily on Baker's political skills and advice, and his influence grew steadily.)

Most other initial appointments in the executive departments and regulatory agencies were made by a personnel office headed by E. Pendleton James, a college classmate of Meese's, and Lyn Nofziger, a conservative political operator who had been with Reagan since the 1960s and now served as chief political adviser to the president. The success of their efforts was described in a story by Howell Raines of the *New York Times*, who reported in midsummer 1981 that the regulatory jobs important to business had been filled first, while key positions in agencies responsible for guaranteeing the rights of minorities, consumers, workers, and union members had been filled later, or, in many instances, had not yet been filled. Most appointees to the regulatory agencies were either former employees or financial beneficiaries of the enterprises whose activities they were supposed to police. Stewardship of natural resources on federal lands was turned over to former employees of mining, timber, and oil companies; and jobs that concerned environmental quality went to advocates of the increased use of coal and nuclear power and of lower water and air quality standards for industry.[9]

This procedure was nothing new or shameful. Every administration tries to put people in office who sympathize with its views. The only difference in 1981 was that Reagan's views were stronger, more explicit, better known, and involved more changes from the immediate past; and the members of his transition team worked harder than their predecessors to make sure that only people who agreed with those views got policymaking jobs.

This aspect of the game plan did not, however, draw nearly as much attention as its budgetary and legislative initiatives.

The Top Priorities

In many respects the Carter administration's first months in office served the Reagan administration as a model of what *not* to do. Reagan's team believed that Carter's greatest mistake had been to begin with a laundry list of dozens of different proposals, with no particular priorities, rather than concentrating on a few high priority measures. They believed that Carter had thereby squandered the goodwill and power that a new administration enjoys only in its honeymoon period, and they resolved to avoid this mistake by focusing their efforts, at least at the outset, on four main areas.

1. Budgetary Policy As Hugh Heclo and Rudolph Penner make clear, the Reagan administration began with a crystal-clear idea of what it wanted to do first:

> The economy was Reagan's first, second, and third priority. It was here that Ronald Reagan engaged in sustained struggles with Congress, launched his major public appeals, and put his personal reputation on the line. . . .
> The presidential priority in economic affairs was to reduce the role of government—its taxes, spending, and regulations—and then stand aside for an economic revival in the private sector.[10]

The first economic priority was to alter the budget, particularly in two respects. First, the administration proposed cutting personal income tax rates 10 percent each year for the next three years—a proposal that closely followed the Kemp-Roth bill first introduced in 1978 and praised by Reagan. Allied to the rate cuts were proposals to improve the tax situation for businesses and individuals by, for example, improving depreciation allowances and indexing income taxes to prevent "bracket creep." Second, the administration planned to cut the rate of increase in domestic spending. Note that they did not propose to cut the absolute amounts being spent, but to cut the rate of increase. Thereby the financial burden would be considerably lighter than it would have been if spending had risen at the rate proposed in Carter's last budget. The "safety net" programs were by and large to be left alone, but the programs benefiting the working poor were to be slowed down sharply.

2. Defense Spending   Reagan's second priority was to increase military spending vastly. In 1979 the Soviet invasion of Afghanistan had led Carter to propose increases of 5 percent in real (that is, inflation-corrected) defense spending for each of the next five years. Reagan proposed increases of over 13 percent per year, with the new money going to just about every aspect of defense — stockpiling more of the existing weapons, producing new weapons such as the B-1 bomber and the MX missile, developing even newer weapons, raising military pay, providing more spare parts and "consumables," and so on. Some critics challenged the administration to set forth its master strategic plan so that the new spending would be related to the nation's military mission and needs, but the administration said that could wait; the urgent need was to close the "window of vulnerability" by restoring the nation's ability to defend itself against a possible attack by the Soviet Union.

3. Deregulation   Nine days after his inauguration, Reagan ordered a sixty-day freeze on all pending new regulations on business until their impact could be assayed further. He appointed a special task force on deregulation, chaired by Vice-President George Bush, to review all existing regulations to see how the burdens they placed on business could be lightened. He subsequently appointed as heads of the major regulatory agencies persons he knew were strongly committed to deregulation, notably: James C. Miller III to the Federal Trade Commission, Anne Gorsuch to the Environmental Protection Agency, and Mark Fowler to the Federal Communications Commission.

4. Stopping Communism in Central America   During his first months in office Reagan gave most of his attention to budgetary initiatives and had little to say about foreign affairs. Secretary Haig and Ambassador Kirkpatrick, however, made a fast start on his behalf. Their first priority was stopping what they saw as a clear and present danger to American security posed by the increasing strength of Castroite governments in the Caribbean and Central America, especially Cuba's and Nicaragua's, and their escalating assaults on noncommunist governments in the area, especially El Salvador's. On January 23, 1981, economic aid to Nicaragua was stopped because of Nicaragua's support of the guerrillas trying to overthrow the government of El Salvador; and, on March 2, military assistance to El Salvador was stepped up and more U.S. military advisers were sent to help train the Salvadoran army.

Measures Deferred

Various administration spokespersons were at some pains to justify these priorities to their more conservative supporters, especially the acolytes of the Moral Majority, who were eager for the administration to start fulfilling its campaign promises to restore prayer to the public schools and allow the states to outlaw abortions. We are in favor of these measures, the administration responded, and we will get to them in due time; but our first priorities have to be saving the economy and closing the window of military vulnerability. Some conservatives were not delighted at having *their* top priorities relegated to the back burner, but most were willing to play along—for a while.

That was the game plan, and the administration began to put it into effect shortly after noon on January 20, 1981. The rest of this chapter will outline what happened to the plan from then until Reagan declared his candidacy for reelection on January 29, 1984. Much of the story is succinctly told in table 1.1 and figure 1.1. Table 1.1 lists in chronological order the main events between the two dates, and figure 1.1 traces the ups and downs of Reagan's presidential approval rating as measured by the percentage of respondents replying "approve" to the Gallup Poll's periodic question, "Do you approve or disapprove of the way Ronald Reagan is handling his job as president?"

Table 1.1   Chronology of Reagan's first term

Date	Event
1980	
November 4	Election results, presidential contest:
	Reagan-Bush, 43,899,248 popular votes (50.8 percent); 489 electoral votes
	Carter-Mondale, 35,481,435 popular votes (41.0 percent); 49 electoral votes
	Anderson-Lucey, 5,719, 437 popular votes (6.6 percent); no electoral votes
	Others, 1,395,558 popular votes (1.6 percent), no electoral votes
	Election results, congressional contests:
	House: 243 Democrats, 192 Republicans
	Senate: 53 Republicans, 46 Democrats
December 11	First cabinet appointments announced
1981	
January 7	All cabinet appointments announced
January 20	Reagan inaugurated fortieth president; as first official act, orders temporary federal hiring freeze
January 23	Reagan orders suspension of aid to Nicaragua because of support of guerrillas in El Salvador

Table 1.1   (*continued*)

Date	Event
January 29	Reagan orders sixty-day freeze on pending regulations of business
February 5	In his first national TV speech as president, Reagan calls for 10 percent cut in income taxes for each of next three years; tax indexing; major cuts in domestic spending; major increase in defense spending
February 18	In his first State of the Union address, Reagan focuses on budget matters, urging same measures as in Feb. 5 speech, and pledges to maintain the "social safety net"
March 2	Military assistance to El Salvador is increased and more U.S. military advisers are sent
March 30	Reagan is wounded in an assassination attempt by John Hinckley, Jr.; life saved by emergency team of George Washington University hospital
April 24	Carter-imposed embargo on grain sales to USSR lifted by Reagan
April 28	In first major public appearance after assassination attempt, Reagan makes televised speech to Congress urging adoption of cuts in domestic spending and taxes called for in his budget
May 7	Democrat-controlled House votes 253–176 to approve Gramm-Latta (Reagan) budget
July 7	Reagan nominates Sandra Day O'Connor to be the first woman associate justice of the U.S. Supreme Court
August 3	Air-controllers' union (PATCO) goes on strike; Reagan declares all will be fired for violating the no-strike provision of their contracts
August 19	U.S. Navy jet fighters down two Libyan, Soviet-made fighters over Libyan gulf
December 1	In *Atlantic Monthly* interview, OMB director David Stockman expresses doubts about wisdom of Reagan's budgetary approach; in face of widespread Republican criticism Stockman offers resignation, but Reagan declines
December 14	Israel announces annexation of Golan Heights; U.S. voices strong criticisms; Israeli premier Menachem Begin retorts that U.S. is treating Israel like a "vassal state," "a banana republic"
December 16	Reagan announces appointment of fifteen-member Na-

Table 1.1   (*continued*)

Date	Event
	tional Bipartisan Commission on Social Security Reform, chaired by Alan Greenspan
1982	
January 4	Richard V. Allen resigns as national security adviser after being investigated for alleged receipt of $1,000 from Japanese newsmen for arranging an interview with Nancy Reagan
January 26	In his second State of the Union address Reagan calls for a "new federalism" in which the states will take over food stamps and AFDC, while the federal government takes full responsibility for federal programs in education, transportation, social services, and community development
February 6	Reagan presents budget for FY 1983, with more cuts in domestic spending, further increases in defense spending, and a projected deficit of $91.5 billion
April 5–30	Argentina seizes Falkland Islands; Great Britain sends a military expedition to recapture them; Secretary of State Alexander Haig shuttles between Buenos Aires and London seeking a diplomatic solution
April 30	U.S. announces failure of mediation efforts, declares support for Great Britain, imposes economic sanctions on Argentina
June 6	Israel invades southern Lebanon to destroy PLO strongholds
June 25	Alexander Haig resigns as secretary of state and is replaced by George P. Shultz
June 25–27	Democrats hold mid-term conference in Philadelphia
July 22	Murray L. Weidenbaum resigns as chairman of the Council of Economic Advisers and is replaced by Martin S. Feldstein
August 16	Reagan makes televised speech urging passage of the $98.5 million "revenue enhancement" measure crafted by Senator Robert Dole; says it is mostly tax reform, not tax increase
August 17	U.S. and Peoples Republic of China issue joint communiqué in which U.S. promises gradual reduction in arms sales to Taiwan, and PRC promises to seek a peaceful solution to Taiwan problem; many conservatives object to "sellout of Taiwan"

Table 1.1   (*continued*)

Date	Event
November 2	In mid-term elections Democrats gain a net of twenty-six seats in the House; no net change in the Senate; Democrats gain a net of seven governorships; nuclear freeze referendums win in eight states, lose in one
November 13	Reagan announces lifting of sanctions on firms selling U.S.–developed technology for building Siberia-Europe pipe-line
December 16	House votes contempt of Congress citation against Anne M. Gorsuch, head of Environmental Protection Agency, for her refusal to deliver documents to House committee investigating use of "superfund" for cleaning up toxic waste dumps
1983	
January 3	House Democrats strip Phil Gramm (D-Tex.), a leading "boll weevil," of membership on House Budget Committee for his support of Reagan's budget over Democrats' proposals; Gramm resigns his seat and says he will run for the vacancy as a Republican
January 3	Reagan appoints a seven-member commission headed by Brent Scowcroft to recommend new deployment options for the MX missile
January 12	Reagan removes Eugene Rostow as director of the Arms Control and Disarmament Agency, and nominates Kenneth Adelman as his successor
January 15	The National Commission on Social Security Reform reports a number of recommendations to bring the system back to solvency
January 31	Reagan presents proposed budget for FY 1984, with a freeze on or cuts in domestic spending, further increases in defense spending, and a projected deficit of $188.8 billion
February 2	Senator Alan Cranston (D-Calif.) becomes first formally declared presidential candidate for 1984
February 28	Reagan asks for increase of $60 million in military aid to El Salvador, sends more military advisers
March 9	Anne McGill Burford (formerly Anne Gorsuch) resigns under fire as head of EPA; on March 21 Reagan names William Ruckelshaus as her successor
March 25	Congress passes Social Security reform legislation implementing most of commission's reforms

Table 1.1   (*continued*)

Date	Event
March 30	Reagan makes televised address on nuclear arms reduction, advocating "zero option," but offering to reduce the number of U.S. intermediate-range missiles in Europe if USSR will reduce theirs; Soviets reject the proposal
April 18	A car-bomb explosion demolishes most of U.S. embassy building in Beirut, killing over fifty persons
April 27	Reagan addresses a joint session of Congress urging approval of his package of increased military and economic assistance to Central America, his first special address to Congress on a foreign policy issue
May 4	House votes 278–149 for nonbinding resolution urging a "mutual and verifiable freeze on and reductions in nuclear weapons" by the U.S. and USSR
May 19	Senate votes 50–49 for a compromise budget resolution including a tax increase not approved by Reagan; presidential aides say vetoes of overspending appropriations are likely
May 25	Reagan dismisses three liberal Democratic members of the U.S. Civil Rights Commission (Mary Frances Berry, Blandino Cardenas Ramirez, and Rabbi Murray Saltzman) and names three conservative Democrats (Morris Abram, John Bunzel, and Robert Destro) to replace them
June 23	Both houses of Congress pass compromise budget resolution for FY 1984
July 18	Reagan announces appointment of twelve-member bipartisan commission headed by Henry Kissinger to make recommendations for U.S. policy in Central America
July 28	House votes to ban all covert aid to *Contras* (Nicaraguans trying to overthrow Sandinista government)
September 1	Soviet fighters shoot down Korean Airlines Flight 007 over Sea of Japan, killing 240 passengers and 29 crew; U.S. leads denunciation of act in UN Security Council; USSR vetoes resolution condemning the shooting
October 9	James Watt resigns as Secretary of the Interior after widespread criticism of his remarks about having an advisory board composed of "a black, a woman, two Jews, and a cripple"; William C. Clark is named to replace Watt, and Robert C. McFarlane is named to replace Clark as national security adviser

Table 1.1   (*continued*)

Date	Event
October 23	Over two hundred marines and sailors, members of the multinational peacekeeping force in Beirut, are killed when a truck-bomb crashes into the compound at Beirut airport and explodes; Reagan says he will not waver from his determination to keep troops in Beirut until their mission is accomplished
October 25	U.S. marines and rangers land on Caribbean island of Grenada with announced purpose of saving U.S. lives under threat from island's new hard-left government
November 2	U.S. declares Grenada hostilities ended, starts withdrawing troops
November 23	Soviet Union withdraws from Geneva talks with U.S. on reducing number of intermediate-range missiles in Europe
November 30	Reagan signs bill reconstituting U.S. Commission on Civil Rights and names as his four presidential appointees Clarence M. Pendleton, Jr., as chairman, and Morris Abram, John Bunzel, and Esther Gonzales-Arroyo Buckley
December 28	U.S. gives notice that it will withdraw from UNESCO at the end of 1984
1984	
January 11	Kissinger commission issues report recommending increase in military and economic aid to El Salvador, but tying it to progress on human rights
January 29	Reagan formally announces his candidacy for reelection, ending rumors that he will not run again
February 1	House Democratic caucus calls for the prompt and orderly withdrawal of marines from Lebanon; White House aides say the resolution "aids and abets the enemies of the peace process" and will be ignored
February 1	Reagan presents his budget for FY 1985, with a further increase in defense spending, a freeze on most domestic spending, and a projected deficit of $180.4 billion
February 7	In a surprise move, Reagan orders marines in Beirut to withdraw to ships offshore; Great Britain, France, and Italy announce that they will withdraw their forces

Source: Compiled by the author.

17

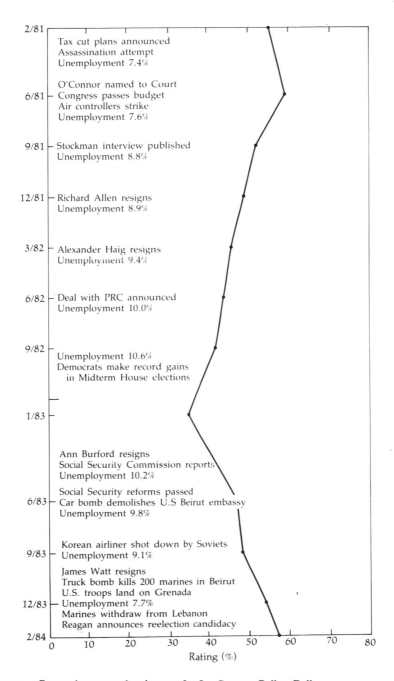

Figure 1.1 Reagan's approval ratings, 1981–84. *Source:* Gallup Poll.

The Four Phases of the First Term

When the ups and downs of Reagan's approval rating in figure 1.1 are related to the events listed in table 1.1, the story of Reagan's first term falls readily into four phases:

1. The Honeymoon, January to September 1981

The first six to twelve months of every new administration has traditionally been a "honeymoon" period, in which the prevailing mood in the press and the public is to give the new president and his team a fair chance to install their people and policies and show what they can do. Thus during the honeymoon period a new administration is given the maximum opportunity to make whatever major policy shifts it wants to make. As we have seen, Reagan's people were acutely aware of this opportunity and determined not to waste it. They decided to go all-out on economic policy, and the result was the greatest success for radically new policy initiatives by a new administration since Lyndon Johnson's Great Society measures in 1965—some observers said the greatest success ever.

A prime reason for the Reagan administration's astonishing achievement of getting its new budget policies through Congress, especially through the Democratic majority in the House of Representatives, was its imaginative use of the reconciliation process, which up to then had been a little-understood and little-used device established by a Congressional Budget Act of 1974. The story's details are a bit technical, but its main outline is clear.[11]

The administration knew that if its proposals for cutting domestic spending, increasing defense spending, and cutting taxes were considered one by one, the new budget would end up being much like its predecessors. Each committee and subcommittee had a strong inclination to preserve and expand the programs under its jurisdiction, and their individual actions, aggregated by the familiar process of logrolling, would make a significant overall cut in the domestic budget impossible. The reconciliation process, however, offered the chance of getting the Congress to vote on the administration's overall budget *package* rather than having it nibbled to death as this or that specific program cut was discussed, voted on, and probably rejected.

Thus on February 5, 1981, in the first nationally televised address of his administration, Reagan declared that his forthcoming budget proposals were the heart of his economic recovery program, which was desperately needed to avoid an impending economic calamity. He made the same appeal in his first address to a joint session of Congress on February 18, and on March 10 he submitted his budget proposal. It had five parts: (1) sharp reductions in the rates of increase in spending that Carter's last budget had proposed for many domestic programs—most sharply reduced were those programs that aided the "working poor," such as aid to families with dependent children, food stamps, Medicaid, housing aid, energy aid, and social services; (2) a major increase in defense spending; (3) a cut of 10 percent in individual income tax rates for each of the following three years; (4) the indexing of those tax rates to the rate of inflation; and (5) accelerated depreciation and other tax breaks for businesses.

During March the Republican-controlled Senate defeated many amendments to increase domestic spending and reduce the tax cuts, and, on April 2, it adopted the whole Reagan package. But many observers felt that it was bound to be altered drastically by the Democratic majority in the House of Representatives.

The House Budget Committee recommended a reconciliation bill with $18 billion more in domestic spending and $21 billion less in tax cuts than Reagan had proposed, but conservative Democrat Phil Gramm (a "boll weevil" in Washington's new bestiary) and Reaganaut Republican Delbert Latta proposed a substitute reconciliation bill that was very close to Reagan's proposal and to the bill the Senate had approved. The Democratic House leadership proposed a compromise that was quite similar to the Republicans' bill, but Reagan determined to fight for his original proposal. The key vote came on May 7 when the House, by a vote of 253 to 176, approved the Gramm–Latta substitute. In a rare display of cohesion worthy of European parties, the Republicans voted 190–0 in favor of it. The Democrats voted 63–176 against it, but *Southern* Democrats voted 46–32 in favor.

The House vote was a stunning victory for the administration. It was accomplished against great odds and confounded the predictions of most pundits. More than any other event, it won for Reagan the reputation he never quite lost of being a leader of Congress in the class of Franklin Roosevelt and Lyndon Johnson.

Other major events in the honeymoon period also contributed to the administration's fast start. Perhaps the most important was the tragedy that became a triumph. On March 30, Reagan addressed a group of labor unionists at the Washington Hilton hotel. On leaving, he and his entourage were attacked by pistol shots from a mentally unbalanced drifter named John W. Hinckley, Jr. Reagan and several others were wounded, and Reagan was rushed to the George Washington University Hospital, where an emergency medical team saved his life. The country was appalled by this dreadful act, but Reagan's courage, humor, and concern for others made it a kind of victory. He joked with his doctors ("Please tell me that you're Republicans"), his wife ("Honey, I forgot to duck"), and his attendants ("All in all, I'd rather be in Philadelphia"). In a few perilous hours he became, even to his political and ideological opponents, much more than an overaged conservative ideologue and ex-movie actor. As his leading chronicler put it:

Reagan's grace under pressure destroyed forever any lingering doubts that the President was a cardboard man whose aspirations and emotions were as synthetic as a celluloid screen. The heroism reflected in Reagan's humor was genuine, and everyone knew it. *Forever afterward, criticisms of Reagan's policies would be separated from an evaluation of the man.*[12]

None of the other events in the honeymoon period were as salient as the assassination attempt and the budget victory, but some further boosted Reagan's popularity. On July 7 he nominated Sandra Day O'Connor to be the first woman justice of the Supreme Court. His action was enthusiastically hailed by just about everyone except a few extreme conservatives who objected to her views on abortion, and it added substantially to his growing reputation as a strong, innovative leader who got things done.

On August 3, the Professional Air Traffic Controllers union (PATCO) went on strike in violation of its contract pledging it not to strike. Reagan announced immediately that the striking controllers would all be fired because they had broken the law, and he made his decision stick. The episode further reinforced his image as a strong leader who did not dither in tough situations but acted promptly and vigorously, and the union received little sympathy from other unions or from the general public. Then on August 19 U.S. Navy jet fighters shot down two Soviet-made Libyan fighters that had attacked them over the Libyan Gulf, and most Americans applauded the act as an appropriate "don't-tread-on-us" rebuke to Libyan dictator Muammar al-Quadaffi.

On the whole Reagan's eight-month honeymoon featured one outstanding legislative achievement, a considerable rise in his personal popularity, and some good economic news. Only a few presidents before him had had as much legislative success, although most had ridden higher in the polls (see table 1.2).

Table 1.2   Approval ratings[a] of elected first-term presidents, 1952–84

Period	Eisenhower	Kennedy	Nixon	Carter	Reagan
End of four months	74	75	62	64	68
End of first year	68	79	63	52	47
End of eighteen months	61	66	61	39	42
End of two years	70	74	57	43	35
End of thirty months	72	61	50	29	42
January of next election year	77	—	50	58	54

Source: Public Opinion; February–March 1984, 34.
[a] Percent replying "approve" to Gallup Poll's question, "Do you approve or disapprove of the way [president's name] is handling his job as president?"

It was a good honeymoon, but, like all presidential honeymoons, it was bound to end.

2. The Midterm Slump, September 1981 to February 1983

Since World War II, all new administrations have begun with honeymoons and then fallen into slumps lasting for one to two years. Reagan's slump started in September 1981 and continued until February 1983. As figure 1.1 shows, his Gallup Poll approval ratings fell from 60 in August 1981 to 52 in September and then to 49 in December. They stayed in the 43–49 range during the last half of 1982, and reached a low point of 35 in January 1983.

Reagan's slump appears to have resulted, not from any single great failure, but from several medium-sized setbacks. The most important was the deterioration of the economy, which, as table 1.3 shows, began to become apparent in September 1981. Real economic growth started to slow down, and it was a *negative* 2.1 percent for all of 1982. Unemployment rose steadily, from 7.3 percent at the end of the Carter administration to 8.0 in October 1981, 8.4 percent that November, and finally 10.6 percent in December 1982—the highest level since the Great Depression of the 1930s.

There was also some good news: the inflation rate declined sharply, just as orthodox economists had said it would if the economy cooled and unemployment rose. From an annualized rate of 12.0 percent when Carter left office, inflation fell to 10.4 percent for 1981 and 6.1 percent for 1982.

This good news, however, was soon overshadowed by more bad news. Reagan and his supply-side economic advisers counted on the 1981 tax cuts to stimulate a boom in the economy great enough to enable the administration to increase defense spending sharply and still balance the budget by 1984, as Reagan had promised. But 1982 saw a major slump, not a boom. The slump meant fewer people paid taxes and they paid them at lower rates, and unemployment payments rose rapidly as well. Hence the federal budget deficits grew larger and larger: By early 1982 administration economists forecast deficits of $109 billion for fiscal 1983 and $152 billion for fiscal 1984—the largest peacetime deficits in history.

This produced an ironic switch of party positions. Ever since the early 1930s Republicans and conservatives had argued that the deficits incurred by liberal Democratic administrations were outrageous and would bankrupt the country, and the Democrats had replied that the deficits didn't really matter as long as the economy was performing well and unemployment was low. Now the Democrats began to argue that the Republican deficits were ruinous and had to be drastically reduced. Reagan and the supply-siders replied that the deficits were not bad in themselves so long as they were not an increasing percentage of the Gross National Product (GNP); moreover, the worst possible way to deal

Table 1.3   Quarterly Economic Indexes, 1980–1984

Quarter Ending	Consumer Price Index[a]	Unemploy- ment Rate[a]	Change, Real GNP[b]	Prime Rate	Dow-Jones
December 1980	12.0	7.3	5.0	21.5	960.58
March 1981	7.2	7.3	10.0	18.0	1,003.87
June 1981	8.4	7.4	−0.5	20.0	976.88
September 1981	13.2	7.6	2.8	16.5	849.98
December 1981	4.8	8.8	−5.4	15.7	875.00
All 1981	10.4	—	2.5	—	—
March 1982	0.0	8.9	−4.6	16.5	822.77
June 1982	13.2	9.4	−0.8	16.5	811.93
September 1982	1.2	10.0	−0.9	13.5	896.25
December 1982	−3.6	10.6	0.5	11.5	1,046.54
All 1982	6.1	—	−2.1	—	—
March 1983	1.2	10.2	3.3	11.0	1,130.03
June 1983	2.4	9.8	9.4	10.5	1,221.96
September 1983	6.0	9.1	6.8	11.0	1,231.30
December 1983	3.6	8.1	5.9	11.0	1,258.64
All 1983	3.2	—	7.6	—	—
March 1984	2.4	7.7	10.1	11.5	1,164.89

Sources: Consumer price index and unemployment data for 1980 and 1981 are from *Economic Report of the President, February 1982* (1982), table B-55, p. 295, table B-33, p. 271. Data for 1981 and 1983 are from *Economic Report of the President, February 1984* (1984), table B-55, p. 283, table B-33, p. 259. GNP data are from Bureau of Economic Analysis, *U.S. Department of Commerce News*, July 23, 1984, table 6. Figures on the prime rate and the Dow-Jones stock average are from *Facts on File*, various issues.
[a]Seasonally adjusted.
[b]Constant dollars.

with them would be to raise taxes, which would make economic recovery impossible. The Democrats asked, "What recovery?" and the Reaganauts replied that a recovery would come if only the nation would "stay the course" with Reagan's policies. They were both right: The deficits kept on getting larger and larger, and the economy recovered impressively in 1983–84. But the argument over the deficits continued and became one of the major issues in the 1984 election campaign (see chapter 5).

Although, in his budget message of January 1982, Reagan proposed further domestic spending cuts and no tax increases some powerful Senate Republicans, notably Robert Dole and Pete Domenici, proposed a package of "revenue enhancement" measures (few Republicans could swallow "tax increases" so soon). It was strongly opposed by resolute supply-siders like Jack Kemp, but Reagan, after a long silence, reluctantly accepted it on the advice of most of his economic boffins. In August he even made a speech on national television recommending it, and it eventually passed. About the only good economic news in this period came in August 1982 when the stock market began a sharp rise that continued unabated through 1983. Some economists took this to be a sign of eventual economic recovery, but it helped the administration's popularity very little in 1982–83.

Not only did the continuing slump make many people lose faith in the "Reaganomics" that was so popular in 1981, but other events raised even more questions. The December 1981 issue of the *Atlantic Monthly* published an article by William Greider entitled "The Education of David Stockman," which was based on interviews with the bright and energetic young director of the Office of Management and Budget, who was widely regarded as one of the key architects of the 1981 budget miracle. Stockman made a number of damaging statements to the effect that the people who had drawn up the budget in fact had been guessing and gambling about its effects. But his most embarrassing contribution was his statement that supply-side economics is really just the old-fashioned Republican "trickle-down" approach (make things easy for the rich and they will make jobs for the poor) warmed over. The article quoted Stockman as saying:

> It's kind of hard to sell "trickle-down," so the supply-side formula was the only way to get a tax policy that was really "trickle-down." . . . The hard part of the supply-side tax cut is dropping the top rate from 70 to 50 percent—the rest of it is a secondary matter. The original argument was that the top bracket was too high, and that's having the most devastating effect on the economy. Then, the general argument was that, in order to make this palatable as a political matter, you had to bring down all the brackets. But, I mean, Kemp-Roth [the 30-percent, across-the-board cut proposal] was always a Trojan horse to bring down the top rate.[13]

Democrats chortled and some Republicans called for Stockman's dismissal. After dressing him down, however, Reagan decided to keep him on at OMB because of his encyclopedic knowledge of the budget's complexities.

Problems with other members of the administration also began to proliferate. Richard Allen, never thought to be a great success as national security adviser, came under a cloud when it was charged that he had accepted presents from Japanese journalists. An investigation was begun, Allen took administrative leave, and finally resigned in January 1982; he was replaced by William P.

Clark. Sharp and sometimes acrimonious disagreements between Secretary of State Alexander Haig and Secretary of Defense Caspar Weinberger surfaced, particularly over Middle Eastern policy, and Haig resigned in June 1982.

Moreover, the administration did not seem much better than the Carter administration at making events in the world go as they wished. On December 14, 1981, Israel annexed the Golan Heights, and when Secretary Haig and Secretary Weinberger publicly criticized the move, Israeli prime minister Menachem Begin replied angrily that the United States was treating Israel like a "vassal state" or a "banana republic" and he would not stand for it. These were some of the harshest words ever directed by an Israeli leader at an American administration, and they sounded especially harsh to an administration that claimed to be a stronger supporter of Israel than its predecessor had been.

Also in December 1981 General Wojciech Jaruzelski, Poland's Communist party leader and premier, declared martial law and outlawed Lech Walesa's Solidarity labor union. Many Americans, and particularly many of Reagan's strongest conservative supporters, urged strong action against Jaruzelski and against the Soviet Union for ordering the crackdown. The administration responded by suspending flights by Soviet and Polish airlines to the United States, imposing an embargo on the sale and shipment of certain strategic goods to the two countries, and making a number of speeches attacking the Communist leaders. But that was all. The administration did not, as many conservatives urged, declare Poland in default of its debts, and it did not impose a Carter-style embargo on the sale of grain to the Soviets—indeed, it had earlier lifted the embargo Carter had imposed. Some conservatives grumbled that Reagan was following the opposite of Theodore Roosevelt's famous advice: He was, they said, "talking loudly and carrying a limp noodle!"

In April 1982 Argentine troops invaded the British-held Falkland Islands in the South Atlantic, and Britain prepared a military expedition to retake them. The administration had a stake in retaining the friendship of both countries and sent Haig on a series of shuttle-diplomacy visits to London and Buenos Aires trying to work out a compromise, but he failed. At the end of April the administration announced the end of its peacemaking efforts and declared its full support for Britain, thereby evoking angry protests from many Latin Americans.

In June 1982 Israeli troops invaded southern Lebanon with the avowed purpose of wiping out the guerrilla bases of the Palestine Liberation Organization (PLO), and then advanced to the capital of Beirut. The administration was caught by surprise but agreed to send American marines to participate in a multinational peacekeeping force while the PLO forces were evacuated. It seemed reasonable enough at the time, but it eventually led to the greatest foreign policy failure of Reagan's first term.

Throughout much of 1982 the administration tried to persuade the Western

European countries not to cooperate with the Soviets in the construction of a pipeline to carry natural gas from Siberia to customers in the West. None of the Europeans showed much inclination to go along and the French openly defied the United States. The administration finally lifted its sanctions because, spokesmen said, they were no longer necessary. Construction of the pipeline began.

Of all the administration's early foreign-policy initiatives, it was its policies toward the People's Republic of China (PRC) and Taiwan that deviated most sharply from the statements Reagan had made in his years on the lecture circuit. For decades Reagan and his conservative supporters had called the PRC every bit as great an enemy as the USSR, and had praised the anticommunist Taiwan regime as "our China." Reagan frequently denounced the Nixon-Ford-Kissinger reestablishment of relations with the PRC in the early 1970s, and warned against a "sellout" of Taiwan. But as president he came to believe that the PRC was a valuable counterfoil to the Soviet Union in Asia as well as a market of enormous potential for American goods. So, to the disappointment and anger of many veteran Reaganauts, in August 1982 he made a deal with the PRC in which the United States promised a gradual reduction in arms sales to Taiwan and the PRC promised to seek a peaceful solution to "the Taiwan problem." In 1984 Reagan went even further when, after returning from a state visit to the PRC, he proclaimed that the "so-called Communist regime" in China was one with which the United States could and should work.

Reagan gave the "social issues" of outlawing abortion and restoring school prayers more attention in 1982–83 than in 1981, but he confined his support to making occasional speeches and did not put on anything like the full-court press he had put on for his budgetary policies. Many conservatives were disappointed by his relative quiescence on *their* issues, but they hoped that their time would come soon.

The most damaging evidence of Reagan's mid-term slump came not from his declining approval ratings in the public opinion polls (see figure 1.1 and table 1.2), but from the Republicans' subpar performance in the mid-term congressional elections of November 1982. In the heady days of late 1980, immediately after winning the presidency and also (unexpectedly) gaining control of the Senate, a number of Reagan conservatives believed that 1980 was the mirror image of 1932—that it signaled a massive and permanent switch of voters from the Democratic party to the Republican party and from liberalism to conservatism. Cooler heads said that it was too soon to tell, and that we would find out in the 1982 elections whether a realignment comparable to that of the 1930s was taking place in the 1980s, for it had been the Democrats' unprecedented gains in the mid-term elections of 1934 that showed that a major realignment had in fact taken place. If the Republicans were to match that performance, it would indeed be a new day. And even if they merely performed better than par, it would show that they were on their way.

What was par? If we judge by the performance of the parties of previous, newly elected postwar presidents in the mid-term elections of their first terms (Eisenhower, 1954; Kennedy, 1962; Nixon, 1970; and Carter, 1978), par was the net loss of 12 seats in the House.[14] By that standard, the Republicans' performance in 1982 was very poor: Their net loss was 26 seats, over twice the average loss and the poorest showing of any first-term president's party since World War II. The Republicans managed only a draw in the Senate elections despite the fact that twice as many Democratic as Republican seats were contested, and suffered a net loss of 7 governorships.

Moreover, the Gallup Poll's "trial heats" for the next presidential election taken at the time showed Walter Mondale defeating Reagan by 52 percent to 40 percent, and John Glenn winning with 54 percent to Reagan's 39 percent. Thus it is not unreasonable to suppose that if the presidential election had been held in November 1982 rather than two years later, Reagan might well have lost to either Mondale or Glenn. Speculation aside, however, the 1982 congressional elections clearly showed that the Republicans were still a long way from displacing the Democrats as the majority party.

Thus the Reagan administration's mid-term slump was long and deep, and its electoral performance was poor—a point worth bearing in mind when, as below, we consider Reagan's term-long popularity in the light of his great success in 1984. Nonetheless, previous administrations had emerged from their slumps sometime in their third years—and so did the Reagan administration in 1983.

3. The Recovery, February to October 1983

Reagan's approval rating in the Gallup Poll reached its nadir of 35 percent in January 1983. It recovered to 40 percent in February, inched into the 40–46 range, and stayed in the high forties until the end of October, when it rose to 53 percent, the first time it had been over 50 percent since November 1981. That was good news, and it reflected other good news.

First and foremost among the good news items was the economic recovery. As table 1.3 shows, the recovery began in the first quarter of 1983 and continued steadily to the end of the year. On February 4, the Labor Department announced that the unemployment rate had dropped from 10.8 percent in December 1982 to 10.4 percent in January 1983—the first drop since July 1981. The rate continued to drop for the rest of 1983—to 10.2 in the first quarter, 9.8 in the second, 9.1 in the third, and 8.1 in the fourth.

At the same time the GNP started to grow at an impressive rate—3.3 percent in the first quarter, 9.4 in the second, 6.8 in the third, and 5.9 in the fourth—for a rate of 7.6 percent growth for the whole of 1983, one of the highest rates of growth since World War II. Clearly the economy was recovering, as Reagan had promised in the 1982 campaign.

Even better was the news that the economic recovery did not bring renewed inflation: The Consumer Price Index stayed steady throughout 1983, with an annual increase of 3.2 percent. And on Wall Street the bull market continued: The Dow-Jones average went over 1,000 in late 1982 and climbed steadily in 1983, finishing at 1,259 in December 1983. So, just as the recession of 1981–82 had damaged the administration's popularity and led to the mid-term election losses, so the recovery of 1983 played the leading role in sending its approval rating back up.

On top of all this good news, the administration had another visible and widely praised legislative success. The financial status of the Social Security system had been worrying observers for a long time, but some felt the problems were too politically dangerous ever to be solved. However, the fifteen-member bipartisan National Commission on Social Security, appointed in 1981 and chaired by Alan Greenspan, made its report on January 15, 1983. The report was praised highly by almost everyone, including House speaker "Tip" O'Neill and the president, and on March 25 Congress passed legislation adopting most of its proposals. Almost every commentator said that disaster had been averted, and achieving bipartisan support for remedial legislation was a minor political miracle. This was the first talk of a Reagan-inspired legislative miracle since the great days of 1981.

Foreign affairs became more prominent in 1983 than in the previous two years, and they too provided more good news than bad. The infighting and disarray that had marked Haig's tenure at the State Department was gone, and Shultz, Clark, and Kirkpatrick reserved their disagreements for private discussions and in public presented a solid front of unity and cooperation.

Reagan undertook several initiatives that made him look both firm and peaceloving. He made several proposals for new arms control agreements and arms reductions in Western Europe, but the Soviets rejected them. Whatever the consequences for peace, it became harder for Reagan's critics to call him a warmonger and the Soviets peacelovers. The USSR mounted a major propaganda campaign in Western Europe against the deployment of cruise and Pershing II missiles in the NATO countries; but, despite many antinuclear demonstrations, the installation of the missiles began in the fall, and the U.S. policy was counted a success.

The controversy over U.S. military aid to the government of El Salvador and over clandestine U.S. support for the *Contras* trying to overthrow the Castroite Sandinista government of Nicaragua heated up considerably, but on July 18 Reagan appointed a bipartisan commission chaired by Henry Kissinger to make recommendations about Central American policy. In January he had appointed another bipartisan commission chaired by Brent Scowcroft to make recommendations about the basing of the controversial MX missile. Both commissions were modeled on the Greenspan commission, and the reports of both were generally hailed as statesmanlike efforts to resolve difficult problems rather than belittled as passing the political buck.

On September 1 Soviet fighter planes shot down a Korean Airlines civilian passenger plane that had strayed into Soviet airspace. The United States, joined by most noncommunist nations, vehemently denounced the act in the United Nations, forcing the Soviets to veto a condemnatory resolution—yet the administration took no action that seemed to increase the danger of war. Thus at the end of 1983 more than at any previous time in his presidency, Reagan looked like a leader who really understood how treacherous and dangerous the Soviets are, who stood up to them, but who did not risk war.

Almost the only bad news in foreign policy came from Beirut. On April 18, 1983, a truck loaded with high explosives and driven by Arab terrorists crashed into the American embassy compound and exploded, killing over fifty people. On August 26, two U.S. marines serving in the multinational peacekeeping force were killed by mortar fire. The administration nevertheless declared that it would not withdraw the troops until the multinational force had completed its mission, but the episodes were early warnings of what was to become the first term's greatest foreign policy failure.

Some other events in 1983 were not such good news. There were several more mini-storms over prominent administration officials. In January Reagan dismissed Eugene Rostow as director of the Arms Control and Disarmament Agency and replaced him with Kenneth Adelman, who had little experience in the field. The Senate Foreign Relations Committee recommended that Adelman not be confirmed, but the Senate as a whole confirmed him anyway. The director of the Environmental Protection Agency, Anne Gorsuch (who had married and changed her name to Anne Burford), came under increasing fire for what critics called her failure to enforce the antipollution laws. Her deputy, Rita Lavelle, was convicted of misappropriating the special "superfund" for cleaning up toxic wastes, and eventually Burford herself resigned under fire. But Reagan's appointment of William Ruckelshaus as her successor was widely praised, and none of these affairs damaged Reagan's rising personal popularity.

The most publicized of all the controversies concerned Secretary of the Interior James Watt. From the beginning Watt was the administration's most outspoken and unyielding conservative ideologue, given to saying things like there are "two kinds of people—liberals and Americans." He drew heavy fire from environmentalist groups for his declared plans to encourage more commercial development of the country's public lands. What finally brought him down, however, was an offhand remark to a breakfast meeting of lobbyists at the U.S. Chamber of Commerce: Speaking of a new commission he had just appointed to study Interior's coal-leasing policies, he said that the commission had "three Democrats, two Republicans, every kind of mix you can have. I have a black, a woman, two Jews, and a cripple." This remark touched off a storm of protest, and within a week fourteen Republican senators were calling for his resignation. Reagan publicly stood by him as a loyal and effective public servant, but on October 9 Watt resigned. Reagan adroitly replaced him with William P. Clark, who had begun as Haig's Undersecretary of State, had become national security adviser when Richard Allen resigned, and had developed a reputation for being both reasonable and a loyal Reaganaut. So the Watt affair, like the Allen, Haig, Adelman, Gorsuch, and Lavelle affairs, damaged Reagan's reputation very little — so little, indeed, that commentators began to call him "the Teflon president" because "nothing bad sticks to him."

Reagan's recovery in the third year of his administration was similar to those enjoyed by Eisenhower, Nixon, and Carter at comparable points in their administrations. As table 1.2 shows, by January of Reagan's fourth year his approval rating stood at 54 percent, compared with 58 percent for Carter, 77 percent for Eisenhower, and 50 percent for Nixon. Reagan's recovery then took a considerable jump at the end of October 1983, and the final phase of his first term was launched.

4. Upswing to the Second Candidacy, November 1983 to February 1984

In a seventy-two-hour period in October 1983 two events took place that constituted, successively, the greatest foreign policy failure and the greatest foreign policy triumph of Reagan's first term, the net result being a major rise in his approval ratings which carried him to the announcement in late January 1984 of his candidacy for a second term.

On October 23, 1983, a truck packed with explosives and driven by Arab terrorists crashed into the U.S. military compound at Beirut airport and blew up, killing over 200 U.S. marines and sailors stationed there as part of the multinational peacekeeping force. The tragedy dismayed and angered many. Some contenders for the 1984 Democratic presidential nomination charged that the United States had no clear policy in Lebanon, that our forces there were protecting no vital national interest, and that they should be withdrawn before any more tragedies occurred. But, in a national television address four days later, Reagan firmly declared that he would not withdraw the troops until their mission was accomplished. Chiding his critics, especially House speaker O'Neill, for being so faint of heart, he said:

> Let me ask those who say we should get out of Lebanon: If we were to leave Lebanon now, what message would that send to those who foment

instability and terrorism? If America were to walk away from Lebanon, what chance would there be for a negotiated settlement producing a unified democratic Lebanon? If we turned our backs on Lebanon now, what would be the future of Israel?[15]

To some observers this sounded ominously reminiscent of Lyndon Johnson's statements in the 1960s declaring that the United States would stand firm in Vietnam, and some wondered if Reagan's similar commitment to Lebanon would have similar consequences for his reelection hopes.

In the end, though, Reagan showed that he was more prudent and pragmatic than Lyndon Johnson. On February 7, 1984, he ordered the U.S. troops to abandon the airport and withdraw to ships anchored offshore. It was a sudden and precipitous retreat, and it was contrary to all his previous declarations. Yet it did not damage his reviving approval ratings.

There were several reasons for this. First, the announcement was not made at a presidential press conference where Reagan himself would be subjected on live television to reporters' sharp questioning concerning his about-face; announcement was made by the White House communications office while Reagan was on vacation in Santa Barbara and was not immediately available for questions—a good illustration of the administration's news management skills and how they contributed significantly to the "Teflon" character of Reagan's presidency. Second, in withdrawing he did what most Americans wanted him to do. Third, he abandoned the commitment before there were any more casualties which would have made it even more unpopular. And, most important of all, an event that took place just two days after the Beirut bombing had so firmly established his reputation as a strong and resolute leader that abandoning the Lebanon commitment, even after his Churchillian rhetoric about standing firm, could not tarnish him.

On October 19, 1983, Maurice Bishop's Castroite government of the eastern Caribbean island of Grenada was overthrown in a coup engineered by his deputy, Bernard Coard. Bishop was killed, and Coard declared his determination to work even more closely with Cuba, the Sandinista regime in Nicaragua, and the Soviet Union. On October 25 a force of U.S. Marines and Rangers landed on Grenada and secured the island within a few days. The action was condemned as an unwarranted invasion by a number of U.S. allies in Europe and Latin America, even including Margaret Thatcher. Many of the Democratic presidential contenders immediately condemned it as "gunboat diplomacy" that proved Reagan was every bit as "trigger-happy" as they had previously warned.

But, in a televised address to the nation, Reagan said that he had ordered the operation for two reasons. First, the Organization of Eastern Caribbean States (Antigua, Barbados, Dominica, Jamaica, Saint Lucia, and Saint Vincent) had asked him to intervene to forestall Castroite attacks on their governments. Second, hundreds of Americans on Grenada, including a number of students at a medical school, were in imminent danger of being taken hostage or worse by Coard's revolutionary regime.

As on previous occasions, public opinion backed Reagan, not his critics. After his speech the polls showed that, by margins of 70 to 75 percentage points, the public accepted Reagan's explanation of the reasons for the operation and approved of his actions. Moreover, the weakening faith of some of his more conservative supporters was restored. Terry Dolan of the National Conservative Political Action Committee said later: "Grenada is a dirty word to liberals [but it] is as important as the Panama Canal to the average American. It's the most important foreign policy achievement of the last ten years. For the first time we took away a Soviet satellite." [16]

In hindsight it is clear that the Grenada operation satisfied what have evidently become the requirements for a popular presidential use of military force in the post-Vietnam era. The casualties were light (18 Americans killed and 115 wounded), the combat was brief (the troops began to withdraw on November 2, just a week after they had landed), and, above all, the operation was successful—our forces won quickly and overwhelmingly.

The proof was in the approval ratings. Much as in the preceding three months, in interviews taken on October 26–27, immediately after the Grenada landing, Reagan's handling of the presidency was endorsed by 48 percent of those polled. But in interviews taken between October 28 and November 13— after he had made his speech, the battle had been won, and the troops were withdrawing—the president's approval rating jumped to 53 percent, the first time it had been over 50 percent since the height of his budget triumphs in November 1981. His rating continued to rise—to 54 percent in December and January.

On January 29, 1984, Reagan formally announced his candidacy for a second term, thereby ending rumors that he would not run again. Beginning with that event the story moves on to the election period itself, which is the concern of the rest of this book. It seems appropriate, however, to end this survey of his first term with an analysis of the popularity of Ronald Reagan the president and of Ronald Reagan's conservative philosophy and policies. As we will see, they were not the same.

The Popularity of Reagan and Reaganism

Many analysts believe that Reagan's landslide reelection in 1984 confirmed that he is a phenomenally popular president, perhaps the most popular since Dwight Eisenhower or even Franklin Roosevelt. Some go further: The 1984 results, they say, show that most Americans have become, or are about to become, Reagan-style conservatives, and consequently the 1984 election was a historic "realigning election," like the elections of 1860 and 1932, in which a minority party overtakes a majority party and dominates elections for decades thereafter.

That may or may not be an accurate assessment of the meaning and future consequences of the 1984 elections (several chapters in this book deal with that question), but an effort such as this to assess Reagan's first term must recognize that he was *not* an unusually popular president during most of that term.

Compared with Other First-Term Presidents

The most appropriate way to assess Reagan's popularity in his first term is to compare him with other newly-elected presidents in theirs. Since we have reliable survey data for such presidents only since World War II, the proper comparisons are with Dwight Eisenhower (1953–56), John Kennedy (1961 to his assassination in 1963), Richard Nixon (1969–72), and Jimmy Carter (1977–80).[17] Their approval ratings at successive stages in their first terms are shown, along with Reagan's, in table 1.2.

The figures in table 1.2 show that for the first two years of his first term Ronald Reagan was the *least* popular of the five first-term presidents elected since the war, although Jimmy Carter was only a bit more popular. Reagan recovered enough to pass Carter on his third year, but in January of his fourth, reelection year he was less popular than Carter or Eisenhower, though more popular than Nixon (who, let us remember, eventually won reelection by an even greater landslide than Reagan's).

In January 1984, though, Reagan had no reason to be alarmed. His approval rating was over 50 percent, it was rising, and in any case he would not be running for reelection against John Kennedy or Jimmy Carter. It looked as though his opponent would be either Walter Mondale or John Glenn (Gary Hart did not emerge until well after January). What did the polls say about his chances against them?

Compared with Mondale and Glenn

The Gallup Poll and other national polling organizations regularly run "trial heats" well in advance of presidential elections by asking people how they would vote if the choice were between the incumbent president and this or that contender for the opposition party's nomination. Most analysts think that the results of these pairings tell more about the incumbent's popularity than anything else, because the incumbent is sure to be much better known than any potential challenger. Even so, it is interesting to recall the results of the sixteen trial heats run by the Gallup Poll from April 1982 to February 1984. In the first eight of those polls Glenn defeated Reagan every time, by margins ranging from 4 to 17 points. The ninth poll (November 1983) produced a 47–47 tie. Reagan took the lead (49–45) for the first time in the tenth poll (December 1983), tied (45–45) in the eleventh poll (January 1984), and retook the lead for good (51–36) in the February poll.

Mondale did not do as well as Glenn in the trial heats, but he defeated Reagan in six of the first eight, by margins ranging from 5 to 12 points. Reagan edged ahead, by margins ranging from 1 to 3 points in the next three polls, Mondale recaptured the lead in the next two, there was a 45–45 tie in the January 1984 poll, and Reagan did not pull away (53–43) until the poll of early February 1984.[18]

For the rest of 1984 candidate Reagan's lead in the polls over candidate Mondale rose, with a few slips, to the 15–20 point range and remained there through the election. In assessing Reagan's popularity *as president*, however, it is important to remember that his performance in the polls was not impressive until people saw that the only likely alternative was Walter Mondale.

Reagan and Reaganism

To assess the full meaning of the 1984 election we need to know how much of Reagan's sweep was due to his personal popularity and how much was due to the popularity of his philosophy and policies. The other chapters in the book deal with different facets of this question, but I can shed some light on it here by noting that during most of his first term Reagan was considerably more popular than his policies. That is made clear by the answers to a question that the ABC News/ *Washington Post* poll asked its respondents on six occasions between 1982 and 1984:

> Which of these statements comes closest to your opinion?
> (A) I like Reagan personally and approve of most of his policies.
> (B) I like Reagan personally but I disapprove of most of his policies.
> (C) I don't like Reagan personally but I approve of most of his policies.
> (D) I don't like Reagan personally and I disapprove of most of his policies.

The answers given at various stages of Reagan's first term are set forth in table 1.4. There are a number of instructive findings in this table. For one, the first "net" line at the bottom of the table shows clearly that Reagan was liked *personally* throughout his first term by remarkably consistent majorities, ranging from 65 to 69 percent. On the other hand, the proportion approving his *policies* averaged 48 percent, never rose above 53 percent, and fell below 50 percent in two of the five polls.[19] Table 1.4 also shows that the largest single portion of the respondents (averaging 39 percent) liked both Reagan and Reaganism, but the second-largest portion (averaging 29 percent) liked Reagan

Table 1.4   Popularity of Reagan and his policies, 1982–1984 (percent)

Position	April 1982	September 1982	August 1983	January 1984	May 1984
Like Reagan personally, approve policies	41	35	38	40	39
Like Reagan personally, disapprove policies	28	33	30	25	28
Don't like Reagan personally, approve policies	9	7	9	13	11
Don't like Reagan personally, disapprove policies	20	23	21	18	18
No opinion	3	2	2	4	4
Net—like Reagan personally	69	68	68	65	67
Net—approve Reagan policies	50	42	47	53	50

Source: ABC News/ *Washington Post* polls.
Note: Percentages may not add to 100 because of rounding.

but disapproved of his policies, while only a handful disliked Reagan but approved of his policies (averaging 10 percent). The third-largest group (averaging 20 percent) disapproved of both man and policies.

Ronald Reagan, Man and Leader

Whatever they may have thought of him in the past,[20] in 1984 just about every political analyst was saying that Ronald Reagan was one of the best-liked men to occupy the White House in this century—right up there with John Kennedy, Dwight Eisenhower, and maybe even Franklin Roosevelt. Certainly he was much better liked than Jimmy Carter, Gerald Ford, Richard Nixon, Lyndon Johnson, or Harry Truman. Some ascribed Reagan's popularity mainly to the professional skills as a television performer that made him "the great communicator"; others stressed the way his aides made him "the Teflon president" by insulating him from everything that went wrong; still others said that the man was simply very lucky. Analysts more sympathetic to Reagan said that, if his liberal critics took off their ideologically (pink) colored glasses, they would see that Ronald Reagan was not a phony creation of public-relations hype but a great human being and a great leader dedicated to a sound and ascendant political philosophy.

The pollsters, of course, are interested in the general public's perceptions of all presidents as men and as leaders, and they have frequently asked their respondents what they particularly like and dislike about each incumbent. The answers have made quite clear what the public likes about Reagan. One of their most frequent comments is that Reagan is a strong leader: He is decisive; he keeps his cool in a crisis; and he cannot be pushed around by the Russians or by his political adversaries at home. Closely related is the frequent comment that Reagan says what he means and means what he says; he does not trim his sails to placate his critics. A third frequent comment is that he is a likeable human being—cheerful, humorous, upbeat, optimistic, warm, and not mean or spiteful. Finally, people see him as a religious person with strong moral values.

The public does not think he is perfect, for he has consistently drawn negative comments as well. The most frequent is that he understands and sympathizes with the needs of the rich better than with those of poor people and the middle class. Another frequent comment is that he does not always keep his promises, in particular he hasn't kept his promise to cut the deficits and balance the budget. Still another is that "he seems to appoint too many people to high posts who get into trouble and end up embarrassing the president." And the public is about evenly divided on the question of whether he is too bellicose in his dealings with the Soviet Union and other foreign nations.[21]

Conclusion

Four years ago I ended my sketch of Carter's first (and only) term by noting that, according to the polls, most Americans in 1980 thought that Jimmy Carter was a man of high moral principles, a likeable person, and a man who sympathized with the poor and put the country's interests ahead of politics. But they also thought he was indecisive and ineffective—in short, a decent man but not a strong leader. And I suggested that this perception of Carter— along with double-digit inflation and the continuing captivity of the American hostages in Iran—accounted for his failure to win reelection.[22]

It therefore seems appropriate to end this sketch of Ronald Reagan's first term by noting that in 1984 most Americans thought he was a man of high moral principles, a likeable person, *and* a strong and decisive leader. Moreover, Walter Mondale was clearly not so formidable an opponent for Reagan in 1984 as Reagan was for Carter in 1980. Perhaps that—together with the peace, prosperity, and low inflation the nation was enjoying in the months before the election—and not popular enthusiasm for all the principles of "Reaganism" explains why Reagan was so successful in his bid for reelection in 1984.

The Democratic Nomination and the Evolution of the Party System

NELSON W. POLSBY

Our own politics are running true to form under Republican administration. The Democrats are engaged in bitter internecine strife; the Republicans wallowing in inane banality. — Dean Acheson to Robert Menzies, April 20, 1956, *Among Friends*, 116

Democratic Dominance: Stability and Erosion

————In the wake of the overwhelming defeat of the Democratic nominees for president and vice-president in 1984 many observers were ready to argue that a new party system was evolving, one which reflected fundamental changes in voting behavior and party allegiances. This has been a theme in American political commentary at least since 1952, when Dwight Eisenhower won the first of his two decisive triumphs over what even then was the "old" New Deal coalition.[1] With every passing year, the plausibility of the case for realignment grows stronger. Otherwise, how to explain repeated Republican victories in presidential elections, which now have occurred in four out of the last five elections, and six times in the last 30 years — twice as often as Democratic wins? Recent converts to the realignment hypothesis include not merely cheerleaders for the idea of a Republican "mandate" like George Will and the editorial page of the *Wall Street Journal* but also such mandarins of liberal chic as NBC News commentator Ken Bode (former research director of the Democratic party's own McGovern Commission) and columnist Max Lerner. The latter, in a cascade of glittering phrases, pronounced the election of 1984 "a historic election because it changed the climate of the political culture and shifted the center of political gravity."[2] Such circumstances, if true, would greatly change the value of the Democratic nomination. They would suggest that Democrats can expect an uphill battle in every presidential election henceforth, and that the election of 1984 might therefore be regarded as something of a prototype, not merely a forerunner, of presidential elections to come.

There are three major indications of long-term stability, however, which suggest that realignment has not yet occurred. The first of these has to do with party allegiance: There is only spotty and inconclusive evidence of any great change in popular political attitudes such as would be necessary to underwrite a massive nationwide party realignment. To be sure party identifications and party registrations undergo seasonal fluctuations, and to some degree follow the headlines, but—even in the face of Republican presidential landslides and of strong evidence of party realignment in the southern states—at the national level Democratic majorities have been maintained over a remarkably long span of time.

Here a sense of history is helpful. Consider some old numbers and some very new numbers on party identification, as shown in table 2.1. The last, most recent figures in the table show Democrats and Republicans about as close together as they were in the middle of the Roosevelt era. I have seen exactly one reputable tabulation in which Republicans came out ahead of Democrats in party identification—and it is important to say that it occurred directly after the 1984 election. The CBS News/*New York Times* poll for November 8–14 is shown in table 2.2. This distribution did not persist. The next poll taken under the same auspices (January 14–17, 1985) had the Democrats back on top again (see table 2.3).

Table 2.1 Party identification: historical perspective

	Democratic (%)	Independent (%)	Republican (%)	R/D difference
Gallup Polls				
1940	42	20	38	4D
1950	45	22	33	12D
August 1984	42	22	28	14D
Exit polls, 1984[a]				
ABC	38	27	32	6D
NBC	33	37	32	1D
CBS	38	26	35	3D

[a]Evidently the leaners are not distributed here. The argument for distributing people who say they "lean" toward one party or another although they do not claim to "belong" to either party into the ranks of the party toward which they lean is given in two papers delivered at annual meetings of the American Political Science Association by Raymond E. Wolfinger, Bruce E. Keith, David B. Magleby, Candice J. Nelson, Elizabeth Orr, and Mark C. Westlye: "The Myth of the Independent Voter" (1977); and "Further Evidence on the Partisan Affinities of Independent 'Leaners'" (1983).

Table 2.2   Party identification: a Republican blip, 1984

	Democratic (%)	Independent (%)	Republican (%)	R/D difference
All respondents	32	36	32	—
When "leaners" are distributed	44	8	47	3R

Source: CBS News/*New York Times* poll conducted November 8–14, 1984.

Table 2.3   Party identification: a Democratic restoration, 1985

	Democratic (%)	Republican (%)	R/D difference
Among all adults	47	44	3D
Among registered voters	49	45	4D

Source: CBS News/*New York Times* poll conducted January 14–17, 1985.

Table 2.4   Party registration 1984

	Democratic (%)	Independent (%)	Republican (%)	R/D difference
Gallup, April	43	27	30	13D
ABC/*Post* October	37	32	26	11D

Source: Gallup Poll, April 1984, and ABC News/*Washington Post* poll, October 1984. Adam Clymer, "Americans in Poll View Government More Confidently," *New York Times*, November 19, 1984.

Consider party registration—what people say about how they are registered to vote. Gallup's numbers in April 1984 and the ABC News/*Washington Post* poll in October 1984 are shown in table 2.4. The October poll presumably reflects the results of the big party registration drives. All together these polls show that the Republican party has, in a decade, recovered from the highly destructive aftermath of Watergate. Whether it has become the majority party, or positioned itself to capture the majority, is quite another matter.

The second indication of stability is the electoral results. At the beginning of 1984 there were 7,363 state legislators of whom 4,624, or 63 percent, were Democrats. Newspaper reports said that the Republicans gained around 300 legislative seats in the elections of 1984. So, 4,324 out of 7,363 means the

Democrats held 59 percent of the seats after the Republican landslide. Or, to quote the outgoing Republican governor of Delaware, Pierre du Pont, "Of the 6,243 state legislative seats contested in 1984, Republicans lost 58 percent of them."[3] The Republicans now control 32 out of 98 legislative chambers, that is one-third. Before the landslide, there were 35 Democratic governors, 15 Republican governors. After the landslide, there were 34 Democratic governors, 16 Republican governors. Over the last thirty-two years, from Dwight D. Eisenhower's first election until 1984, 7,392 congressional elections have been held, and the Democrats have won 4,372 of them, or 59 percent. Over the same period, 1952–84, 1,540 senatorial elections have taken place. There have been 901 Democratic winners, or 58.5 percent.[4]

Even in the election of 1980, when the Republicans took control of the Senate for the first time in twenty-six years, there were actually over three million more votes cast for Democratic than for Republican senatorial candidates. The pattern more or less repeated itself in 1982. As table 2.5 shows, taking all the 33 Senate races and ranking them by the margin of victory of the winners, one finds 13 Democrats at the top of the chart before getting to the first Republican, and three Republicans at the bottom of the chart moving upward before the first Democrat, then six Republicans before the next Democrat. In 1984 the Republicans won by more respectable margins, on the whole (see table 2.6), but Democrats registered a net gain of two seats.

Thus, consistently over the last thirty, forty or fifty years, the Democratic party has been the majority party in this country by the measures of party allegiance and success at the polls, and by those measures the Democrats are the majority party in the nation today.

The third bit of evidence that works against the realignment hypothesis is the strong possibility that the election of 1984, far from constituting a sharp break with the past, actually followed a rather stable pattern that has been more or less well established over the last fifty years. During these last five decades we have had fourteen presidential elections. Ten of them—two-thirds—have been part of what we could call a "landslide sequence" (see table 2.7). In the first election in the sequence a candidate is elected president. The second time around he wins a resounding personal triumph, in a great big landslide. This happened to Roosevelt in 1936, to Eisenhower in 1956, to Johnson, standing in for Kennedy, in 1964, to Nixon in 1972, and to Reagan in 1984. Seen in this light, 1984 does not seem so unusual. It is also interesting to note that when these landslide sequences happen to Democrats, big things occur farther down the ticket.[5]

It is a little hard to see this pattern in 1936, because Roosevelt came into the election with 69 Democrats out of 96 Senators, and 333 Democrats out of 435 House members. This was the result of the 1934 election, the only mid-term election in the twentieth century when the president's party gained seats. Even

Table 2.5   Winners of the Senate elections of 1982 (ranked by percentage of vote)

Democrats	Republicans	Winner's percentage of vote
Matsunaga* (Hawaii)		82
Jackson* (Wash.)		69
Byrd* (W. Va.)		69
Zorinsky* (Nebr.)		67
Burdick* (N. Dak.)		65
Moynihan* (N.Y)		65
Stennis* (Miss.)		64
Proxmire* (Wis.)		64
Sarbanes* (Md.)		63
Chiles* (Fla.)		62
Sasser* (Tenn.)		62
Mitchell* (Maine)		61
Kennedy* (Mass.)		61
	Heinz* (Pa.)	60
DeConcini* (Ariz.)		59
Bentsen* (Tex.)		59
	Hatch* (Utah)	58
Riegle* (Mich.)		58
	Wallop* (Wyo.)	57
Metzenbaum* (Ohio)		57
	Roth* (Del.)	56
Bingaman (N. Mex.)		54
Melcher* (Mont.)		54
	Lugar* (Ind.)	54
	Durenberger* (Minn.)	53
	Wilson (Calif.)	53
	Trible (Va.)	51
	Stafford* (Vt.)	51
	Chafee* (R.I.)	51
Lautenberg (N.J.)		51
	Weicker* (Conn.)	51
	Danforth* (Mo.)	51
	Hecht (Nev.)	50

Source: Nelson W. Polsby, "Party Realignment in the 1980 Election," *The Yale Review*, 72 (Autumn 1982), 46.
*Indicates incumbent

Table 2.6 Winners of the Senate elections of 1984 (ranked by percentage of vote)

Democrats	Republicans	Winner's percentage of vote
Nunn* (Ga.)		80
	Kassebaum* (Kans.)	78
	Simpson* (Wyo.)	78
Boren* (Okla.)		76
	Cohen* (Maine)	74
	Pressler* (S. Dak.)	74
Pell* (R.I.)		73
	McClure* (Idaho)	72
	Domenici* (N. Mex.)	72
	Stevens* (Alaska)	71
	Warner* (Va.)	70
	Thurmond* (S.C.)	67
	Hatfield* (Ore.)	66
Bradley* (N.J.)		65
	Armstrong* (Colo.)	64
Heflin* (Ala.)		62
Gore (Tenn.)		61
	Cochran* (Miss.)	61
Biden* (Del.)		60
	Humphrey* (N.H.)	59
	Gramm (Tex.)	59
	Boschwitz* (Minn.)	58
Baucus* (Mont.)		57
Pryor* (Ark.)		57
Harkin (Iowa)		56
Kerry (Mass.)		55
Levin* (Mich.)		53
Exon* (Nebr.)		53
Rockefeller (W. Va.)		52
	Helms* (N.C.)	52
Simon (Ill.)		50
	McConnell (Ky.)	50

Source: National Journal, November 10, 1984, 2136.
*Indicates incumbent

Table 2.7   Landslide Sequences: Presidential landslides and congressional outcomes

Year	Winner of presidency	Percentage margin in two-party vote	Electoral vote margin	Net result in Congress compared with last mid-term	
				House	Senate
		Democratic			
1932	Roosevelt	+18	+413	+92D	+12D
1936	Roosevelt	+24	+515	+11D	+6D
1960	Kennedy	+0.7	+84	+21R	+2R
1964	Johnson	+23	+434	+37D	+2D
		Republican			
1952	Eisenhower	+11	+353	+22R	+1R
1956	Eisenhower	+15	+384	+2D	0
1968	Nixon	+0.7	+110	+3R	+5R
1972	Nixon	+23	+503	+7R	+2D
1980	Reagan	+10	+440	+33R	+12R
1984	Reagan	+18	+512	+14R	+2D

Source: Richard M. Scammon, ed., *America Votes, 15* (Washington, D.C.: Congressional Quarterly, 1983). Data for 1984 are from appendixes A, B, and G in this volume.

so, in 1936 the Democrats bumped up against the ceiling of possibility, winning 11 more House seats and 6 more Senate seats to go with Roosevelt's advantage of 515 more electoral votes and 24 percent more of the popular vote. In 1964, Johnson's margin over Barry Goldwater was 23 percent of the popular vote and 434 of the electoral votes. Democrats picked up 2 Senate and 37 House seats. This is what Democratic landslide sequences look like: When the Presidential candidate does well, the party does well.

Republican sequences follow a different pattern. Eisenhower's great popular victory in 1956 gave him a net advantage of 384 electoral votes and a 15 percent popular vote margin over Adlai Stevenson. There were no net gains for Republicans in the Senate and a net loss of 2 Republican seats in the House. In 1972 Nixon's margin was 503 electoral votes and 23 percent of the popular vote, yet Republicans only picked up 7 seats in the House and Democrats gained 2 Senate seats.

Reagan's 1984 victory was like that: an 18 percent margin in the popular vote, and 512 in electoral votes, and yet the Democrats gained 2 Senate seats and suffered a net loss of only 14 seats in the House. In 1980, when Reagan's personal margin was only 10 percent, the Republicans picked up 12 seats in the Senate (mostly by very small margins) and 33 House seats. But there was no realignment, nor even much of a mandate, as we all discovered at the midterm election when the Democrats bounced back with a net gain of 26 House seats.

How is it possible to maintain a political system in which Republicans do extremely well in presidential elections and Democrats do extremely well otherwise? Such a phenomenon is clearly impossible in a system lacking a separation of powers, giving voters no chance to make the disparate choices that add up to this peculiar pattern of results. But the separation of powers, long ballots, and a large array of electoral choices all exist in the American political system. And Americans take advantage of the opportunity to diversify their political portfolios. Rock-ribbed Republican states of the mountain region have in recent years overwhelmingly preferred Democrats for governor. A Republican governor of California faces a phalanx of Democratic state constitutional officers elected statewide: lieutenant governor, secretary of state, controller, treasurer, attorney general. Nationally, Democrats run the House while Republicans run the Senate. And so on. But the fact that a formal opportunity exists for voters to split their tickets does not require them to do so. Presumably this is the fact—that they do so—that needs explaining.

There seem to be three types of explanations that might account for all this, and all have their advocates. (1) massive autonomous changes in the electorate itself, changes that are making people more Republican than they used to be; (2) Republican strength at the top of the ticket—the magical influence of Ronald Reagan and other charismatic Republican presidential candidates; (3) Democratic weaknesses at the presidential level.

As to the first, there is a problem of simple logic: If people are becoming more Republican, why does this show up decisively only in the voting for president? Is there any reason why grassroots realignments should start at the top of the ticket? Perhaps there is a reason: the great visibility of the presidential race as compared with other races on the ballot. But if this is how a modern realignment works, it works through a mechanism that focuses on candidates, not parties, and helps Republican presidential incumbents, not Republicans generally. The weight of evidence seems to be against the proposition that realignment has gone further than the presidency, except in the South. There I think we can see ample evidence of realignment as Northern migrants have combined with native converts to greatly strengthen the Republican party. As table 2.8 suggests, in a twenty-year period, the number of

Table 2.8   Republicans in the House of Representatives

Election year	National		Non-South		South[a]	
	Number of Republicans	Percentage of seats	Number of Republicans	Percentage of seats	Number of Republicans	Percentage of seats
1960	176	40	170	52	6	6
1970	180	41	154	47	26	25
1984	182	42	151	47	31	27

Source: Guide to U.S. Elections (Washington D.C.: Congressional Quarterly, 1975), 841–44, 866–70. The figures for 1984 are from appendix G.
[a]The states of the old Confederacy: Ala., Ark., Fla., Ga., La., Miss., N.C., S.C., Tenn., Tex., Va.

Republicans representing the old Confederacy in Congress has risen steeply. All this has been at the expense of conservative Democrats; the prospects of liberals in the Democratic parties of the South are at worst unchanged.[6]

But in the nation taken as a whole, as I have said, the evidence for a massive realignment of underlying attitudes and allegiances is not overwhelming.[7] In part this is true because the Democratic party is such a protean organism, capable of assimilating and espousing quite diverse doctrines in widely separated places. Continuing attempts to centralize the party, and to define more sharply the party along philosophical and doctrinal lines may in time result in a realignment of the electorate but so far this has not occurred.

In the aftermath of the 1984 landslide, the newspapers have been full of copy extolling Ronald Reagan and his magic bullet. And yet the president's popularity does not seem to extend to any of the baggage that a president normally carries with him—for example, approval of the way he is doing his job. Roughly on the occasion of his second inaugural, an ABC News/ *Washington Post* poll gave a national sample of Americans an opportunity to grade President Reagan's handling of eleven national problems. His overall score was mediocre, and, significantly, many of those giving him this score were people who had voted for him. In the words of the *Post*'s Barry Sussman, "People who gave Reagan only a C grade overall tended to vote for him last November . . . by a ratio of better than 2 to 1."[8]

Reagan's overall popularity has not been outstanding when compared with other postwar presidents. Throughout his presidency, his personal popularity has at best placed him somewhere in the middle of the pack.[9] On the whole he has espoused policies that have, on a one-by-one basis, achieved only indifferent levels of approval among surveyed Americans—in those cases when, indeed, majorities of Americans have not flatly disapproved of them. He is perceived by Americans as more conservative than they are.[10] And he has not brought large numbers of people into the Republican party. In January 1984, according to ABC News/*Washington Post* numbers, 27 percent of the American people thought of themselves as Republicans; by January 1985, following the landslide election, the number was 29 percent.[11]

Thus we turn to activities on the Democratic side, where 34 percent of the ABC/*Post* respondents claimed to be Democrats in early 1985, down from the 43 percent of a year earlier.[12] Estimates vary from poll to poll, but they appear to suggest a defection rate among Democrats in presidential voting in 1984 of about 25 percent, a figure consistent with the performance of Democrats in presidential voting on average since the reforms of the post-1968 era.[13]

The Democratic Nomination Process

What happened to the Democrats in 1984? Perhaps one short answer is that they lost the presidential election because—as the history of landslide sequences suggests—it is normally hard to beat an incumbent when there is peace and prosperity and there are no well-publicized overt annoyances to the public mood prominent on the horizon.[14] It has been argued—by me among others—that the rules and practices now governing the nomination process also hurt Democrats and non-incumbents far more than Republicans and incumbents.[15] I believe that this is still the case. Whether it was slightly more or less true in 1984 than in other recent years is impossible to determine because in 1984 Republican incumbency produced the same effect as the effects imputed to the Democratic rules—namely a situation favorable to the Republican incumbent.

Once again, in 1984 the Democratic party changed its nominating process, as it had for the last several presidential elections. This time efforts were directed toward taking a few small steps back from the brink of self-destruction. The chosen instrument of reform was, as usual, a party commission, on this occasion headed by North Carolina's governor, James Hunt.[16]

Among the changes the commission voted were the following:

(1) A few convention delegates—14 percent of the total—were snatched away from primary electorates and placed in the hands of party leaders—elected officials and state party functionaries.[17] As a condition of taking their seats these "super delegates" were not obliged, indeed they were not supposed, to commit themselves to any candidate in advance of the national convention.

(2) Primary elections and other delegate-selecting events were forced into a three-month, March to June "window."[18] Exceptions were given to Iowa and New Hampshire, thus vitiating the intended effect of damping down the impact of the publicity resulting from any one state's selection process.

Because the official selection of delegates began later in the election season, early—very early—unofficial straw polls took on a greatly distorted signifi-

Table 2.9   Proportion of delegates selected and committed in primaries

	Democrats	
	Selected (%)	Committed (%)
Mean 1952–68	48.2	30.6
1972	66	58
1976	75	66
1980	71	71
1984	55	virtually all

Source: Nelson W. Polsby; *Consequences of Party Reform* (New York: Oxford University Press; 1983), 64.

cance as the news media hungrily fixed on whatever they could find to gratify their need for information about the prospects of various candidates. A few state parties, seeking to draw candidates' attention and get public notice, encouraged this activity. "The later you start," said candidate Alan Cranston at the January 1983 California state Democratic party convention in Sacramento, "The more ground you have to make up."[19] By September 1983, the *Wall Street Journal* reported there had been "four statewide straw polls. Senator Cranston . . . won two, and Mr. Mondale and Senator Glenn one each. In addition, Senator Cranston won a straw poll among young Democrats in Alabama, and [former Florida governor Rubin] Askew swept two picnics in New Hampshire."[20]

Cranston made something of a specialty of straw-poll campaigning, establishing a publicity beachhead in the Wisconsin mini-sweepstakes in June 1983 by busing in supporters to the state caucus and winning by 789 votes to 727 for Mondale. This made headlines all over the country. The *Washington Post* said, "In a stunning upset, California Senator Alan Cranston defeated Democratic presidential front-runner Walter F. Mondale . . . significantly boosting Cranston's long-shot candidacy."[21]

The publicity given to these meaningless events would not have mattered except for the continued dominance in the delegate selection process of primary elections—and hence primary electorates. These electorates consist of individuals whose choices of delegates are mainly guided by publicity and name recognition. Fewer Democratic primaries were held in 1984 than in 1980 (twenty-five as compared with thirty-one),[22] but primaries still selected more than half the delegates, and virtually all but the super delegates were officially committed to one candidate or another far in advance of the national convention (see table 2.9).

(3) Direct-election primaries were restored to favor, which meant that winner-take-all delegate races within congressional districts became possible once again in those states adopting this method of aggregating votes.[23]

(4) Higher limits were set on the number of primary and caucus votes required of candidates before they were eligible to receive delegates. This formula was intended to clear minor candidates away expeditiously and to help frontrunners. Frontrunners were also aided by a regulation of the Federal Election Commission which withheld federal matching funds from candidates failing to receive at least 10 percent of the votes cast in two successive primary elections.[24]

The nominating process thus remained significantly "front-loaded," as several Hunt Commission advisers warned. Early decisions more or less determined what alternatives would be available later on. Early activity was therefore necessary for those actors seeking to play an important part in the process. Organized labor finally grasped this elementary fact of post-1968 politics and for the first time made an endorsement—of Walter Mondale—well in advance of the national convention. This action by the AFL-CIO executive council, on October 1, 1983, although much criticized by second-guessers, served to structure the field of candidates by producing an instant front-runner versus everyone else.[25]

The activities and results of the Hunt Commission, which completed its work on February 5, 1982, thus constituted the first major influence peculiar to 1984 on the 1984 Democratic nomination process. The second was the decision by Edward Kennedy, which he rendered in a timely fashion, to bow out of the race. In December 1982 Kennedy announced that for family reasons he would not be a candidate. This left Walter Mondale as the probable favorite, a position that was more or less universally conceded by the time the AFL-CIO endorsement came through.

Mondale was occasionally spoken of as a throwback to the politics of the pre-1968 era in that he was highly regarded by party leaders. It is a reasonable assumption that, under the mixed system that prevailed before the post-1968 reforms took hold, Mondale would have been a strong, even an overwhelmingly likely, nominee. Nevertheless, Mondale won the 1984 nomination playing by 1984 rules. He gathered an organization around him very early. Soon after leaving the vice-presidency in 1981, he established himself in the Washington office of a Chicago law firm and put together a campaign team. He traveled extensively throughout the country, working to set up personal alliances in all the key states, and campaigning for Democratic candidates in the Congressional elections of 1982. He raised enormous amounts of money, some of which was invested in a political action committee (PAC) of his own. And he reached out to major interest group constituencies of the Democratic party which he knew would be strongly represented at the national convention.

As John Glenn's campaign treasurer said: "Mondale began raising money with his own political action committee two weeks after Reagan was inaugurated. This allowed him to have a political base, it gave him money to travel, money to solicit for direct mail. He identified the 200 top fund-raisers in the party, he played tennis with them in Beverly Hills and had lunch with them in New York and Washington."[26]

By November 1983, according to the *New York Times*, the Mondale campaign had 175 staff workers in twenty-one states, with average salaries of $22,000 to $24,000, and a few salaries as high as $60,000.[27] Casting off, or at least setting aside, his former distaste for the nomadic existence of an inhabitant of anonymous hotel rooms, Mondale traveled everywhere—to meetings of teachers' groups and of course to labor unions, but also to black groups, youth groups, womens' groups, ethnic groups, and to rural Georgia to receive the blessing of Jimmy Carter.[28] "You know me," he told interest-group meetings from coast to coast, pointing out that for many years he had been a model mainstream Democrat supporting their goals, and now it was time for them to reciprocate.[29] Although Mondale was clearly comfortable making a public alliance with organized labor well in advance of the convention, the association did not come without cost to him. He had spent much of his career as a supporter of free trade, but he endorsed labor's view on the need for domestic-content legislation and other protectionist measures.[30]

Mondale did not restrict himself to appeals to interest groups on the ideological left wing of the party. He also made a pit stop at a meeting of the Coalition for a Democratic Majority, reminding them of his association with his "mentor," Hubert Humphrey, and that he "was an original sponsor of the Jackson amendment" on Soviet migration.[31]

And so, as the primary season began in February 1984, the question became: Which of the other seven announced Democratic candidates would emerge from the pack to become Mondale's principal challenger? A broad consensus thought this role would fall to Senator John Glenn of Ohio. Glenn, a former astronaut and marine, was the beneficiary of an extraordinary stroke of good luck when it appeared that *The Right Stuff*, a major motion picture glorifying the work of the first group of American astronauts, and especially his own role as the "Dudley Do-right" of the group, would be released in the summer of 1984. It was, to enormous publicity, but the movie—though it received some critical acclaim—flopped in the marketplace.[32] So, inexplicably, did Glenn's candidacy. He proved to a somewhat wooden campaigner, more popular with independent voters than with the Democrats who voted in early primaries and caucuses, and so the spotlight moved elsewhere.

Glenn's undoing came at the Iowa local caucuses on February 20, 1984, the first actual delegate-selecting events of the 1984 season. Mondale swept these, with almost as many votes as all the rest of his rivals put together. Glenn, by contrast, came in sixth with 5.3 percent of the vote (in fifth place at 7.5 percent were the uncommitted). He was "expected," to do better. Instead, Senator Gary Hart did better than "expected," placing second with 16.5 percent of the vote. Mondale, the winner, had 48.9 percent. From such unpromising material the news media fashioned a horse race.

During the weeks following the Iowa caucuses Hart blossomed as a news media figure.[33] His call for "new ideas" and his criticisms of "old arrangements" were sufficiently ambiguous to appeal to a broad spectrum of voters who, evidently, sought some alternative to Mondale. Hart's own candidacy was not without difficulties, however. As the news media focused on him, bits and pieces of his public persona began to come unstuck. It was discovered that the candidate of "new ideas" was shaving a year off his age for public consumption. His explanation for a change in the family name (from Hartpence)—in which he denied that it was done as a political maneuver—was disputed by family members.[34] It was noted that Hart's sometimes shaky marriage had mended just in time for the campaign, and that as a public speaker he had adopted body language that reminded observers of John Kennedy.[35] Questions therefore began to arise as to the extent to which he was restyling himself for public acceptance to a degree unusual even for American politicians.

Much in the politics of nominating American presidential candidates depends upon the judgments of mass electorates, of people remote from the leaders whose fortunes are held in their hands. Commentators who watch the exercise of power from seats closer to the action therefore occasionally worry over the problem of authenticity in public leaders, and over the extent to which the presentation of self that leaders show to electorates can serve as an accurate predictor of the ways in which politicians will behave as officeholders. To at least some observers, for at least part of the nominating process, Senator Hart came perilously close to flunking that rather amorphous test.

Nonetheless, immediately after Iowa Hart became a major news figure. William Adams of the George Washington University Media Project reported:

> In the week following his Iowa triumph, Mondale actually suffered a decline in his relative share of attention on CBS and NBC newscasts. . . . Hart gained and Mondale suffered most on NBC where Hart's airtime actually equaled that of Mondale. . . .
>
> Hart's relative share of coverage the week after Iowa was ten times on NBC and five times on CBS what it had been the week before.[36]

David Moore of the University of New Hampshire, a close observer of his state's primary, reports that, from March 1983 until mid-February 1984, polls showed Mondale leading Glenn in New Hampshire by a margin of about two to one, and Glenn leading Hart by about the same margin. "But during the last week before the primary," Moore says, "starting with the period right after

Table 2.10   Early Democratic results, 1984

| Date | State | Number of delegates | | | | Dropouts |
		Mondale	Hart	Jackson	Others	
2/20	Iowa*	34	18	0	1	
2/28	New Hampshire	11	10	0	1	
3/1–3						Askew
						Cranston
						Hollings
3/1–15	Wyoming*	7	8	0	0	
3/4	Maine*	12	13	0	2	
3/13	Alabama	37	13	9	3	
	Alaska*	9	4	1	0	
	Florida	77	51	1	14	
	Georgia	32	28	17	7	
	Hawaii*	27	0	0	0	
	Massachusetts	41	47	0	20	
	Nevada*	9	11	0	0	
	Oklahoma*	19	28	1	5	
	Rhode Island	12	12	0	2	
	Washington*	31	34	1	0	
3/14	Delaware*	13	5	0	0	
	North Dakota*	8	4	0	6	
3/15						Glenn
						McGovern

Source: New York Times, June 7, 1984.
*Caucus/convention states.

the Iowa caucuses, there is a significant shift in voter sentiment, as Mondale slips and Hart makes substantial gains in support from those who had been undecided or who had previously supported other candidates." Among that part of the primary electorate—about half—that made up their minds early, Mondale beat Hart in New Hampshire; but Hart beat Mondale decisively among the late deciders.[37]

The publicity made an immediate impact not only on Hart's campaign, which took on a new vigor, but also on the campaigns of the other candidates. In short order Hart won substantial victories not only in places like New Hampshire, Massachusetts, Florida, Maine, and Connecticut, where he had made a campaign effort, but also in such states as Oklahoma, Hawaii, and Nevada, where there were scarcely any traces of a Hart campaign (see table 2.10).[38] Others in the race began to drop out. Florida's former governor Rubin Askew, California senator Alan Cranston, and Senator Ernest Hollings of

South Carolina exited in early March, followed by former senator George McGovern and John Glenn after "Super-Tuesday" (March 13).

Only Hart, Mondale, and, the last "minor" candidate, Jesse Jackson, remained after March 15, 1984, thus propelling the Democratic nominating process into the classic paradox that since 1785 has been identified with the French philosopher Condorcet. Concretely, the situation was this: Jackson voters, by subtracting key elements of support from their overwhelming second choice, Mondale, kept their third choice, Hart, alive and in the race to the end. This considerably handicapped the eventual winner, Mondale, in his prospects for the general election.[39]

Among the three surviving candidates Mondale was the "Condorcet winner," the single candidate who, when compared with either of the other two individually, emerged as the clear favorite. The nominating process provided no such means of structuring the choices, however; despite increasing evidence of Mondale's general acceptability as the nominee, both Hart and Jackson decided to stay in the race all the way to the convention.[40] The pot of gold at the end of their rainbow was, at a minimum, a conspicuous role at the Democratic National Convention, a possible means of projecting their own political hopes into a future beyond 1984. Of all the ultimately unsuccessful candidates who started down the road toward the nomination only Hart and Jackson commanded one hour each of prime-time television coverage at the convention. They alone were permitted to advertise themselves in a conspicuous fashion as putative "runners-up" and as significant figures in the party second only to the nominee himself.

During the later weeks of the campaign, as Mondale scored major victories in Northern industrial states (table 2.11), Hart publicly persisted in portraying his candidacy as an active one, even though near the end he was told in no uncertain terms by party leaders in Washington that this pose was divisive. The effective coup de grace for the Hart candidacy came at the hands of the Democratic party's super delegates, a Hunt Commission innovation. These party leaders lined up for Mondale by a margin of nine to one. They did so, however, late in the day, and not before Mondale had outdistanced Hart and Jackson and all the other candidates in eleven primary elections out of twenty-five and thirteen caucuses out of twenty-seven.[41]

As black voters have become a significant fraction of the Democratic presidential electorate,[42] the importance of a black candidate devoted to mobilizing them has undoubtedly increased. Jesse Jackson claimed considerable success in this regard. Throughout the primary election season large numbers of votes by black voters were cast for Jackson, votes that almost certainly would have gone mostly to Mondale had a black candidate not been in the race.

In addition to holding the nomination in abeyance for a crucial period of time, Jackson's candidacy raised a number of issues that proved to be difficult

Table 2.11   Late Democratic results, 1984

Date	State	Number of delegates			
		Mondale	Hart	Jackson	Others
3/17	Arkansas*	24	9	7	2
	Latin. Am. Dems.*	1	0	0	4
	Kentucky*	19	3	6	27
	Michigan*	95	49	9	2
	Mississippi*	23	4	12	4
	South Carolina*	15	7	16	10
3/18	Puerto Rico	53	0	0	0
3/20	Illinois	114	42	6	32
	Minnesota*	51	3	2	22
3/24	Kansas*	24	16	0	4
3/24–26	Virginia*	31	13	22	12
3/25	Montana*	3	13	0	4
3/27	Connecticut	23	36	1	0
3/31	Wisconsin*	57	26	6	0
4/3	New York	155	77	51	2
4/7	Louisiana	16	21	24	8
4/14	Arizona*	19	19	1	1
4/16	Utah*	4	14	0	6
4/17	Missouri*	53	9	15	6
4/24	Pennsylvania	160	17	18	195
	Vermont*	5	8	3	1
	Guam*	6.25	0.75	0	0
5/1	District of Columbia	4	0	12	0
	Tennessee	35	21	15	5
5/5	Texas*	100	38	30	18
5/7	Colorado*	0	45	0	3
5/8	Indiana	31	38	7	4
	Maryland	47	3	17	3
	North Carolina	47	18	14	1
	Ohio	80	80	10	6
5/15	Nebraska	8	16	0	0
	Oregon	18	29	0	0
5/19	American Samoa*	6	0	0	0
5/22	Idaho*	6	11	0	3
6/5	California	91	207	30	5
	New Jersey	104	1	8	1
	New Mexico	13	14	0	0
	South Dakota	7	9	0	1
	West Virginia	22	16	0	0

Source: New York Times, June 7, 1984. *Caucus/convention states.

and even divisive for Democrats. Jackson gained publicity early in the campaign by leading a delegation to Syria with the intention of rescuing an American Navy pilot, Robert Goodman—a black American and a resident of New Hampshire—who was being held prisoner there. The mission was a success and gained Jackson much favorable publicity. But it could not have succeeded without the cooperation of the president of Syria, Hafez al-Assad, who thereby injected himself into the election campaign, presumably with the intention of embarrassing the Reagan administration. Assad had recently rebuffed Donald Rumsfeld, the president's official emissary, in his efforts to extricate Lieutenant Goodman, preferring to deal with Jackson. Assad missed his mark, however: By strengthening Jackson, Assad weakened Mondale, the main loser of votes from Jackson's candidacy. By weakening Mondale, he actually helped President Reagan, the presumed target of his machinations.

There was also the lurking problem of bigotry, never far from the surface of American politics. This problem cut in a number of directions. In the first place, there can be little doubt that fear of raising the issue of bigotry restrained public discussion of Jackson's qualifications for actually holding the presidential office. Normally one thinks of the presidency of the United States as a public position of sufficient complexity as to require serious contenders for it to have had some prior experience of public officeholding. Jackson did not meet this elementary criterion of seriousness and yet, by seeming tacit agreement, his candidacy was treated in the mass media as in some sense equivalent to that of the other Democratic aspirants. To do otherwise would have invited charges of racial prejudice.[43]

Then there was the issue as it was raised by the candidate himself in at least two actions. First, Jackson tied a part of his campaign to the efforts of Louis Farrakhan, an openly racist, anti-Semitic, Chicago clergyman who traveled in Jackson's entourage and supplied him with bodyguards.[44] Second, there was the unguarded utterance, widely interpreted as anti-Semitic, that Jackson made to a *Washington Post* reporter during the New Hampshire primary.[45] A very sizable controversy followed the publication of this remark. Jackson at first denied making it; it was revealed that a black reporter was responsible for communicating it to the *Post*; that reporter, and his wife, were threatened with dire consequences by Farrakhan; others came forward with evidence of various sorts purporting to show that Jackson was not on good terms with Jews; Jackson then admitted making the remark; he disavowed Farrakhan's threats against the reporter but refused to repudiate Farrakhan; questions were raised more generally about relations between blacks and Jews in the Democratic party; and so on.

This flap did no serious harm to Jackson's chances for the nomination, since he had no serious chance to begin with. Yet it may have galvanized elements of the electorate in various ways that were probably detrimental to the cam-

Table 2.12   Jackson primary voters in ten states, 1984, by ethnic composition

State	Turnout	Jackson percentage	Percentage of Jackson Vote			
			White	Black	Hispanic	Other
Alabama	428,283	19.6	2	96	1	1
California	2,724,248	19.6	38	50	7	5
Georgia	684,541	21.0	6	92	1	1
Illinois	1,659,425	21.0	10	88	0	1
Massachusetts	630,962	5.0	80	16	0	4
New Jersey	678,893	23.6	13	81	4	2
New York	1,387,950	25.6	14	78	6	2
North Carolina	960,857	25.4	8	89	1	2
Ohio	1,444,797	16.4	18	81	0	i
Pennsylvania	1,656,294	16.0	18	81	0	0

Source: CBS News/*New York Times* exit polls.

paign of the eventual Democratic nominee. It may, for example, have worried Jews—the targets of Jackson's and especially Farrakhan's hostilities—and loosened their commitment to the Democratic party.[46] It may also have helped to mobilize white southerners, traditionally hostile to black political participation,[47] and to propel them toward the Republican party. It drew attention to the fine line Walter Mondale needed to walk, deploring interethnic hostility on the one hand and trying not to antagonize Jackson and his followers on the other.

Who these followers were and how many there were of them remained a matter of intense interest. Jackson made two claims: one, that his candidacy was registering unprecedented numbers of black voters, and, two, that his was a "rainbow coalition" encompassing not only blacks, but other disadvantaged groups as well.

No impartial observer seems to have detected much evidence to support the second claim. Jackson attracted a significant number of non-black voters in a few primary elections, but apparently not in most of them. (see table 2.12). The manifest enthusiasm for a black candidate among many black voters makes the first claim more plausible. The Jackson candidacy did well, moreover, in black communities where black elected officials endorsed Mondale. And, in some communities, it was reported that black officials who preferred Mondale were deterred from campaigning for him because Jackson was so popular among their constituents.[48]

These important political facts could easily have been created without any significant expansion of the black electorate. The black share of the Democratic vote has expanded steadily over the past few presidential elections, but it did not change (from 22 percent) from 1980 to 1984. And before 1984 sizable increases in the black electorate do seem to have taken place among young people and in cities where black candidates have been nominated and elected to high public office.[49] Jackson was the first black candidate to take advantage of this expanded electorate in a presidential race. A preliminary look at the numbers seems to suggest that his electoral support came from this prior expansion rather than from voters registered in 1984.

The Morning After

Was Walter Mondale the strongest possible Democratic nominee? Ultimately this is an unanswerable question. Although history may occasionally repeat itself, it never does so in the form of a strictly-controlled experiment, and so we shall never know for certain. We do know, however, that, early and late, Mondale was the clear preference of the bulk of Democratic voters as well as of party leaders. Thus one possible effect of the post-1968 reforms, the selection of the wrong candidate, does not seem to have plagued Democrats in 1984. But a second effect of the revolution in rules changes does seem to have had an impact: the crippling of the eventual nominee by requiring him to campaign against Democrats long after common sense required a shift to a strategy tailored to the problems and opportunities of the general election campaign.

Could Mondale have run a better campaign? Perhaps under some circumstances. There is evidence of staff burnout and of Democratic self-destructiveness in the course of the campaign itself. Any presidential campaign held under the present rules must be structured in such a way as to cause candidates to rely very heavily upon their own inner circle of advisors and not on state and local party leaders. One persistent organizational consequence of this arrangement is to give immense potential value—perhaps too much value—to membership in a candidate's entourage and to reduce the incentives for those on the inside to share their access to the candidate. Insularity, jealousy, a seige mentality, internal power trips, the search for scapegoats when mishaps occur, overwork, and staff burnout during the general election campaign are the natural outcomes of a situation in which candidates and their organizations— and the interactions between these tight-knit organizations with primary electorates—dominate the delegate selection process.

The Mondale operation was clearly not free from such problems. One conspicuous example was the miscue at the Democratic National Convention itself when Mondale more or less stanched the rush of favorable comment that attended his choice of New York representative Geraldine Ferraro as his vice-presidential running mate by attempting the next day—after very little consultation—to maneuver Charles Manatt prematurely out of his job as national party chairman in favor of Jimmy Carter's former budget director, the Georgia state Democratic party chairman, Bert Lance. Manatt fought to stay on through the convention, as was customary. He had managed to promote a convention site in his home state, and so he was able to make his way around familiar territory in San Francisco at the various preconvention events, lining up support, and sowing discontent and bad publicity for the Democratic national campaign—while Mondale and his closest aides remained closeted in splendid isolation at Lake Tahoe.

Later, the Ferraro nomination itself endured some rough moments, and it became apparent that the Mondale entourage had inadequately checked into the business affairs of the vice-presidential nominee's husband, a New York real estate man. In mid-campaign Elizabeth Drew commented in the *New Yorker*:

> The effect of the Ferraro problem within the Mondale campaign has been deadly, especially coming, as it has, on top of a very long campaign year in which, it is now clear, a very few people were stretched too thin. John Reilly, Mondale's law partner, who spent much of the campaign on the plane and then headed the Vice-Presidential search, is described by friends as "burned out," and has been taking some time off. Michael Berman, an attorney and a longtime Mondale aide, who was also involved in the Vice-Presidential search and was supposed to be administering both the Mondale campaign and the Democratic National Committee, has been detailed for some time to deal with the Ferraro problem. This cost time in getting the campaign organized, staffed, and budgeted. Fundraising has been hurt—and continues to be, as the polls show Mondale far behind. Big givers want access to a President. James Johnson, the campaign chairman, was described by a close friend as nearly consumed with the problem—and also shaken by it, and exhausted. This, on top of the Lance matter, was hard for Johnson to take. Another Mondale aide says, "You get a little gun-shy after events like these." One key Mondale adviser has said to me, "We had too rough a year and we're too tired. There are too few of us trying to do it all."[50]

It is too early to make a definitive evaluation of the longer-term effects of the Ferraro candidacy. Trends in the education and employment of women in the society at large suggest that the nomination of a woman on a national ticket was scarcely premature. In recent times women have served as prime ministers in Israel, India, the United Kingdom, and Sri Lanka and have held responsible political positions in most other modern democracies. It is true that they have not been elected to high public office in the United States in anywhere near the numbers in which they are present in the population at large, but there seems to be no widespread prejudice against their leadership.

In 1984 Representative Ferraro appears to have contributed only slightly less to the Democratic ticket than vice-presidential candidates customarily do.[51] She made a vigorous platform appearance and campaigned energetically. Admittedly, as a third-term member of congress and former public prosecutor, her curriculum vitae compared unfavorably with the bloated résumé of Vice-President Bush, but her acquaintance with national and international affairs was surely no worse than that of candidate Ronald Reagan in 1980. Because the outcome of the election was not close, there could be no reason for the Mondale camp to regret having taken whatever electoral risks may have been associated with the innovative step of placing a woman on the ticket.

It is doubtful that any Democratic ticket in 1984 could have unseated the incumbents. If no challenger could have won in 1984, then we must ask what longer-term forces made Ronald Reagan, a Republican, the 1984 incumbent. Democrats have suffered disproportionately the unfortunate effects of the nominating-process reforms that they, in the main, instigated since 1968. Thus the 1984 election provides some mild vindication of the proposition that the rules of the presidential nominating process continue to have a strong impact on political outcomes. In particular the rules have proven to be highly influential in positioning the various Democratic candidates to compete in the general election. These rules helped Ronald Reagan get elected president in the first place, thus making him the incumbent in 1984. They also constrained the Mondale candidacy in important ways, although it seems reasonable to suppose that no Democrat could have beaten the incumbent in 1984. But that merely poses the further question: Why was a Republican the 1984 incumbent?

Journalistic accounts of the 1984 Democratic nomination process are thick with expressions of chagrin at the number of alleged judgment errors made by expert observers on a day-to-day basis as the events of 1984 unfolded. Hindsight prompts a different conclusion. Since 1972 or thereabouts a considerable band of analysts have argued that formal properties of the nominating process itself—and various waves of intervention by party leaders, and fixers flying under the flag of reform—have dominated the nomination cycle in presidential elections. This group of analysts seems, once again, to have been richly vindicated in its opinion. Just as Bill Cavala said in 1974, changing the rules changes the game.[52] This does not mean, of course, that those who changed the rules were fully aware of what they were doing, or have gotten what they wanted, or have enjoyed a 1984 free either from surprises or from unpleasant moments.

Table 2A.1 Proportions of votes and seats in the House of Representatives, 1952–84

Year	Democratic (%)		Republican (%)	
	Votes	Seats	Votes	Seats
1952	50	49	49	51
1954	53	53	47	47
1956	51	54	49	46
1958	56	65	43	35
1960	54	60	45	40
1962	52	59	47	40
1964	57	68	42	32
1966	51	57	48	43
1968	50	56	48	44
1970	53	59	45	41
1972	52	56	46	44
1974	58	67	41	33
1976	56	67	42	33
1978	54	63	45	37
1980	50	56	48	44
1982	55	62	45	38
1984	50	58	50	42

Sources: For 1952–71, U.S. Bureau of the Census, *Historical Abstract of the United States: Colonial Times to 1970*, Part 2 (Washington, D.C.: Bureau of the Census, 1975), 1084. For 1972–82, U.S. Bureau of the Census, *Statistical Abstract of the United States, 1984* (Washington, D. C.: Bureau of the Census, 1984). For 1984, *Congressional Quarterly Weekly Report*, November 10, 1984, 2923–30; *National Journal*, November 10, 1984, 2135.

Table 2A.2 Voters' self-identified ideology, 1976–84

	Percent of respondents calling themselves			
Year	Liberal	Conservative	Difference	Moderate or Neither
1976	22	30	8 (C)	48
1978	22	27	5 (C)	51
1980	21	30	9 (C)	49
1982	20	34	14 (C)	46
1984	16	34	18 (C)	50

Source: CBS News/*New York Times* poll.

Table 2A.3 Presidential approval ratings, 1945–85

	Percent approving the way the president is handling his job							
Stage of presidency	Truman	Eisenhower	Kennedy	Johnson	Nixon	Ford	Carter	Reagan
End of first year	50	68	79	70	63	46	52	47
End of second year	57	70	74	62	57	—	43	35
End of third year	36	77	—	49	50	—	58	54
Start of second term	69	73	—	—	51	—	—	62

Sources: Gallup Polls reported in *Public Opinion*, February–March 1984, 34. Gallup Poll released January 31, 1985.

Table 2A.4   Voters' perceptions of candidates' ideologies, 1984

		Percent of placements on scale			
Ideological scale		Mondale	Glenn	Reagan	Yourself
Liberal	0	4	2	5	2
	1	4	1	1	1
	2	6	3	2	2
	3	8	5	4	4
	4	13	10	6	6
Middle	5	17	24	14	22
	6	10	12	9	8
	7	8	9	13	9
	8	7	6	18	10
	9	4	3	10	2
Conservative	10	4	2	11	4
No ranking	—	14	24	7	31
Mean score	—	4.98	5.35	6.39	5.8

Source: National Journal, January 21, 1984, 138.

Table 2A.5   Rate of defections from party identification, 1984

	Percent of defecting identifiers, by exit polls			
Defections	CBS/ *N.Y. Times*	ABC/ *Washington Post*	NBC	*L.A. Times*
Democrats for Reagan	26	24	17	16
Republicans for Mondale	7	6	5	3

Source: Public Opinion, December–January 1985, 28–29.

Table 2A.6 Democratic "straw polls," 1983

State and date	Number partici-pating	Percent voting for						
		Askew	Cranston	Glenn	Hart	Hollings	Mondale	Others
California (1/15)	1,322	0.1	59.2	5.1	4.8	0.3	23.4	—
Massa-chusetts (4/9)	3,453	0.3	16.9	15.3	10.5	0.5	29.3	"Jobs" 25.6
Wisconsin (6/11)	2,035	0.7	38.8	1.9	21.8	0	35.7	—
Alabama (6/18)	124	1.6	52.4	6.5	0.8	14.5	7.3	Willis 10.5
New Jersey (9/13)	1,125	0.3	1.1	38.4	3.6	2.3	28.2	No pref. 16.6
Maine (10/1)	1,849	0.1	28.7	5.6	1.1	10.7	50.8	—
Iowa (10/8)	4,143	0.8	37.0	5.9	3.5	0.3	47.0	—
Florida (10/22)	2,325	45	0	18	0	0	35.0	—

Source: Congressional Quarterly Weekly Report, October 22, 1983, 2184.

Table 2A.7 Major changes in Democratic delegate selection procedures, by state, 1980–84

State	1980	1984	Number of 1984 delegates
Arkansas	primary	caucus	35
Kansas	primary	caucus	37
Kentucky	primary	caucus	53
Montana	primary	caucus	19
Nevada	primary	caucus	15
Wisconsin	primary	caucus	78
Total			237

Source: Appendix E.

Table 2A.8   New Hampshire Democratic primary
voters' choices and times of decision, 1984

Time of decision	All voters	Percentage of Voters voting for			
		Mondale	Hart	Glenn	Jackson
Day of election	15	19	44	8	7
Day before	8	9	63	11	3
Over weekend	12	10	67	7	2
During week before	14	12	57	11	6
Before Iowa caucuses	51	31	29	11	9

Source: David W. Moore, "Myths of the New Hampshire Primary" (Paper presented at the annual meeting of the American Political Science Association, Washington, D.C., August 29– September 2, 1984).

Table 2A.9   Second choices of Jackson voters in Democratic primaries, 1984

Primary and date	Percentage of respondents choosing			
	Mondale	Hart	McGovern	No second
New Hampshire (2/28)	11	41	13	22
Alabama (3/13)	61	11	1	11
Georgia (3/13)	48	21	4	14
Massachusetts (3/13)	22	30	24	19
New York (4/3)	38	24	—	29
Pennsylvania (4/24)	41	19	—	24

Source: CBS News/ *New York Times* exit polls.
Question asked was: "Which candidate was your second choice today?"

Table 2A.10 First choices of Democrats in Gallup Polls, 1981–84

Date	Mon-dale	Glenn	Hart	Jackson	McGovern	Cranston	Askew	Hollings	None, don't know
12/81	32	14	2	—	—	2	—	—	26
12/82	32	14	2	—	6	6	1	2	37
3/83	32	13	6	—	—	2	2	1	36
5/83	29	23	4	—	—	3	1	1	31
6/83	36	22	3	8	—	7	4	1	19
7/83	41	25	4	—	—	7	2	2	19
9/83	34	23	3	8	8	5	3	1	15
10/83	40	21	3	10	8	6	1	1	10
11/83	47	19	2	7	7	3	3	1	11
12/83	40	24	3	10	8	3	1	1	10
1/16/84	47	16	3	9	4	4	1	1	15
2/12/84	49	13	2	14	3	2	3	2	12
3/6/84	33	—	30	9	—	—	—	—	28
3/19/84	44	—	38	10	—	—	—	—	8
4/9/84	40	—	35	13	—	—	—	—	12
4/15/84	51	—	28	9	—	—	—	—	12
5/5/84	53	—	27	9	—	—	—	—	11
5/21/84	46	—	34	10	—	—	—	—	10
6/8/84	48	—	35	6	—	—	—	—	11

Source: Gallup Poll, releases of June 1983; November 1983; May 1984; and June 14, 1984.

Table 2A.11   Percentage contribution to Democratic coalition
of blacks and other non-whites, 1952–84

Year	Percentage contribution to Democratic votes
1952	7
1956	5
1960	7
1964	12
1968	19
1972	22
1976	16
1980	22
1984	22

Sources: Robert Axelrod, "Where the Votes Come From: An Analysis of Electoral Coalitions, 1952–1968," *American Political Science Review*, 66 (March 1972), 11–20; Axelrod, Letter to the Editor, *American Political Science Review*, 68 (June 1974), 727–30; Axelrod, Letter to the Editor, *American Political Science Review*, 72 (June 1978), 622–24; Axelrod, Letter to the Editor, *American Political Science Review*, 76 (June 1982), 393–96. Figure for 1984 is from CBS News/*New York Times* poll reported in the *New York Times*, June 17, 1984.

Table 2A.12   Registration and turnout, by race, 1974–84

	Percentage voting						Percentage registered			
	1974	1976	1978	1980	1982	1984	1978	1980	1982	1984
White	46.3	60.9	47.3	60.9	49.9	53.0	63.8	68.4	65.6	72.0
Black	33.8	48.7	37.2	47.5	43.0	55.8	57.1	60.0	59.1	73.0
Difference	12.5	12.2	10.1	13.4	6.9	−3.0	6.8	8.4	6.5	−1.0

Source: Voting figures are compiled from U.S. Bureau of the Census, *Current Population Reports*, for elections of 1974–84. Registration figures for 1978–82 were compiled from the U.S. Bureau of the Census, *Current Population Reports*, for elections of 1978–82. Registration figures for 1984 are taken from *The Gallup Report*, No. 224, May 1984, 11–12.

Table 2A.13 Turnout and registration, by race and age, 1978–84

Age	1978		1980		1982	
	White	Black	White	Black	White	Black
			Voting turnout			
18–20	21.1	14.9	37.7	25.3	20.4	17.5
21–24	26.7	24.6	45.0	34.0	28.2	31.5
25–34	39.2	33.0	56.4	47.1	41.4	39.7
35–44	51.5	41.9	65.8	58.9	53.3	49.3
45–54	57.6	45.7	69.1	58.6	61.6	53.6
55–64	62.4	51.9	72.4	64.4	66.0	55.0
65–74	61.5	48.6	70.1	64.9	66.2	54.4
75+	49.5	39.5	58.8	48.6	52.8	44.5
			Registration			
18–20	36.2	27.7	46.5	35.4	36.2	30.7
21–24	45.5	45.3	54.4	46.2	48.2	50.3
25–34	56.7	53.1	63.6	56.6	58.4	56.4
35–44	68.0	62.2	71.7	67.2	69.0	64.0
45–54	73.2	68.1	75.4	67.3	75.9	68.4
55–64	77.4	70.7	78.7	71.9	78.3	71.4
65–74	76.3	71.8	78.0	73.8	79.3	71.3
75+	69.0	59.1	71.0	62.7	71.3	63.2
			Turnout in 1984			
18–24			46	63		
25–29			59	65		
30–49			74	74		
50–64			84	86		
65+			84	79		

Sources: Figures for 1978–82 are taken from U.S. Bureau of the Census, *Current Population Reports.* Figures for 1984 are taken from *The Gallup Report*, No. 224, May 1984, 11–12.

Renominating Ronald Reagan:
The Compleat Politician at Work

CHARLES O. JONES

First and foremost, Ronald Reagan is a wonderful politician, with a politician's instinctive grasp of how hard and far to push an issue—and when to take a dive.—Rich Jaroslovsky[1]

————This chapter focuses on the renomination of Ronald Reagan in 1984. Understandably one may ask why such an account is warranted. It was all so automatic. Therein lies the story worth telling, however. The compleat politician makes it look easy, but a great deal of skill and preparation is required to create that impression. It is said that we learn from our mistakes. Surely there are also many lessons to be learned about American politics from doing it right.

No one doubted that, if he decided to run again, Ronald Reagan would be renominated as the Republican candidate for president in 1984. After all, he had carried his party to a smashing victory in 1980 and he was by far the most popular figure in the Republican party. The certainty of his renomination had the effect of concentrating attention on *whether* he would run. Naturally many observers were moved to advise the president in regard to his decision. Thus, for example, in late May 1983 the Democratic speaker of the house, Thomas P. O'Neill, Jr., predicted that the president would be in for an "extremely hard fight" should he seek reelection. "My personal opinion [is] . . . he couldn't win. The man will be 74. My political instincts are that it would be kind of foolish."[2] Others suggested various reasons for not running: the president's love of his ranch, his concern for his wife's health, the probability of difficult issues during a second term, the prospects of a strenuous reelection campaign,

I wish to acknowledge the assistance, first, of the White Burkett Miller Center of Public Affairs, University of Virginia, and of a John Simon Guggenheim Memorial Foundation Fellowship that aided me in the preparation of this chapter, and, second, of the Russell Sage Foundation that provided the financial support I needed to attend the Republican convention.

the possibility of a close election and the loss of Republican control of the Senate. As it happened, the president ignored this political advice and decided to seek reelection.[3]

I have described Reagan's 1980 run for the nomination as a "trifocal campaign," that is, one in which he concentrated "on creating party unity and winning the general election while seeking to become the Republican candidate."[4] I argued that "Ronald Reagan ran the most party-oriented nomination campaign in recent decades. . . ."[5] After observing him in office I now realize that what I described in 1980 is part of a larger phenomenon which I will refer to here as *the practice of multidimensional politics*. Ronald Reagan is the *compleat politician*, defined simply as one who is sensitive to all major political aspects of an issue or decision. He views most events through political lenses. Further, he is led to an understanding of how others are affected by an event, issue, or decision and how they are likely to react politically. The compleat politician is, in a sense, the ultimate role player and it is not surprising, therefore, that an actor assumes this posture.

For present purposes, what this perspective on Ronald Reagan suggests is that the renomination story of 1984 should be integrated into the larger narrative of the first Reagan administration. It involves the development of a record that is oriented toward future political goals and options. The compleat politician displays sensitivity to political timetables and to the interactive effects of all decisions. Mind you, at this point this characterization says nothing as regards the success of a particular individual as compleat politician. As in all role playing, some are good at it, some not so good. Nor does this characterization address the matter of "right" versus "wrong" decisions. The concept is used here primarily to focus attention on the Reagan style so as to orient the reader to the more comprehensive context within which the president and his aides viewed the 1984 election.

Are all presidents compleat politicians? Comparing Ronald Reagan with Jimmy Carter suggests not. President Carter was proud of being a *segmental politician* who tended to disconnect electoral politics from policymaking. Indeed, he viewed it as his mission to protect the policy process from the effects of the electoral connection on Capitol Hill. As he once said: "One branch of government must stand fast on a particular issue to prevent the triumph of self-interest at the expense of the public."[6] Members of Congress are "buffeted from all sides," in Carter's view, and find it almost impossible to resist the pressures of politics. For the segmental politician, the time for politics is during an election year. Even this arrangement did not altogether suit Carter, however. He was attracted to the single six-year term since it permitted the president to entirely disconnect himself from electoral considerations. As it happened for Jimmy Carter, the Iranian hostage situation provided a rationale for him to avoid direct campaigning for the nomination in 1980 against his challenger, Massachusetts senator Edward M. Kennedy. Unfortunately the initial electoral advantage offered by the crisis dissipated as the failure to resolve the issue created doubts about the president's leadership qualities.

This chapter will concentrate on the integrative politics of Ronald Reagan as directed toward the 1984 confirmation of his presidential leadership. The essay is organized to treat the following topics: the compleat politician's behavior, special factors associated with the Reagan renomination, and the organization and integration of the renomination campaign.

The Compleat Politician Model

Not surprisingly, the compleat politician seeks to maintain control so as to influence events. Sustaining one's advantage is more important than any one policy victory. Indeed, all contests are evaluated in terms of the full range of knowable political effects. Adjustments are continuously made to suit estimates of political advantage. In decision making neither ideology nor the correct policy option is permitted to outweigh these estimates.

An interactive model of behavior, in its rawest form, involves relationships and issues between one person or group and another. We can refer to these elements simply as "us," "them," and the "agenda." A few basic rules logically suggest themselves when thinking about a highly politically motivated "us" (the Reagan administration) facing a rather indeterminate "them" (a divided Congress and a leaderless Democratic party):

1. First and foremost, seek to control the agenda.
2. Protect the major sources of support.
3. Minimize the effects of setbacks through damage control.
4. Provide escape hatches—do not get boxed in.
5. Capitalize on divisions among "them."
6. Seek to establish a base for improvement in critical areas ("Are you better off . . . ?").

These commonplace advisories can be used as measures of success for presidents during their first term. Fred I. Greenstein's account of Eisenhower's "hidden-hand leadership" demonstrates how it was that the president followed these rules, though in a less public fashion than is common.[7] Kennedy's tenure was brief but there was evidence that he, too, was attentive to these rules—indeed, he was engaged in rebuilding support in Texas when he was assassinated. Johnson lost control of the agenda and found himself boxed in by the Vietnam War. What began as a brilliantly successful administration ended with the president hardly able to travel outside Washington, D.C. Nixon began with few advantages—having won by a very narrow margin and facing a Congress controlled by the Democrats. Still he had a successful first term by the measures cited above and was rewarded by being reelected in a landslide. His presidency collapsed as a result of the mismanagement of the Watergate affair. Ford had even fewer advantages than Nixon—not having been elected at all and having to face a post-Watergate Congress with huge Democratic majorities. Relatively speaking, he did well. Remarkably enough, a shift of less than 10,000 votes in Ohio and Hawaii would have elected him in 1980. As noted earlier, Carter eschewed the integrative political approach, preferring a more segmental style. Accordingly he did not endorse these rules stated above, nor was he likely to accept them as tests of his presidency. As for Ronald Reagan, the remainder of this essay will be devoted to demonstrating the extent and nature of his attentiveness to these rules of the compleat political model.

Major Factors Associated with Reagan's Renomination

Conventional wisdom more or less has it that an incumbent president will seek renomination and normally stands a good chance of being reelected. Table 3.1 suggests the need to modify that wisdom. There have been sixteen presidents in this century. Of these, nine have been renominated (one— Franklin D. Roosevelt—was renominated three times) and six reelected. Of those reelected, two died in office (though Roosevelt was in his fourth term when he died), one suffered a serious stroke, and one resigned. Truly, only two presidents, Franklin D. Roosevelt and Eisenhower, completed more than one term in sufficiently good health as to be in full command of the White House (Wilson having been virtually incapacitated during his last months in office). It is also interesting to note that no one of the four vice presidents who served as president—Theodore Roosevelt, Coolidge, Truman, or Johnson—sought renomination (though all four were elected on their own for one term). Even if he had been elected in 1976, Ford would not have been eligible for renomination since the twenty-second amendment prohibits a vice-president who assumes the presidency before the midpoint of an administration from seeking a second term (Ford took over from Nixon in August 1974).

It is entirely possible that Ronald Reagan would not have sought renomination had the election occurred in 1983. The president reached a low point in public approval of his performance in January 1983 (see figure 3.1). In fact, his approval rating was the lowest for any recent president at that point (though President Truman had experienced a lower score earlier in his tenure). Further, the Gallup Poll showed Reagan far behind both the major Democratic contenders—former Vice-President Walter F. Mondale of Minnesota and Senator John Glenn of Ohio (see figure 3.2). Glenn's prospective candidacy suggested real problems for the president but Mondale, too, held a strong, early lead in 1983.

Table 3.1 Renominations and presidential service in the twentieth century

President	Sought renomination	Elected	Served out second term
William McKinley	Yes	Yes	No
Theodore Roosevelt[a]	No[b]	—	—
William Howard Taft	Yes	No	—
Woodrow Wilson	Yes	Yes	Yes[c]
Warren G. Harding	Died in office	—	—
Calvin Coolidge	No	—	—
Herbert Hoover	Yes	No	—
Franklin D. Roosevelt	Yes (3 times)	Yes (3 times)	Yes[d]
Harry S. Truman	No	—	—
Dwight D. Eisenhower	Yes	Yes	Yes
John F. Kennedy	Died in office	—	—
Lyndon B. Johnson	No	—	—
Richard M. Nixon	Yes	Yes	No
Gerald R. Ford	No opportunity[e]	—	—
Jimmy Carter	Yes	No	—
Ronald Reagan	Yes	Yes	?

Source: Compiled by the author.

[a] Vice-presidents who became presidents are in italics. All sought an initial nomination—four of five won. None sought renomination.

[b] Theodore Roosevelt did seek the Republican nomination in 1912 and was defeated. He then ran for president as a Progressive.

[c] Wilson was severely ill for the last several months of his second term.

[d] Franklin Roosevelt died in 1945—having served more than three terms.

[e] Even if Ford had won in 1976 he could not have sought renomination since he became president before the midpoint of the second Nixon term.

The 1982 congressional elections were a further bad sign for the president. The Republicans retained their majority in the Senate—a not inconsiderable achievement in that they had not been the Senate majority party for two consecutive Congresses since 1930. But they had a net loss of twenty-six seats in the House of Representatives and thus slipped below 40 percent of the overall congressional membership. It seemed that forging bipartisan coalitions for the president's programs would prove extremely difficult and, therefore, frequent stalemate would occur.

Evaluations of Reagan's performance and prospects at the beginning of the ninety-eighth Congress in 1983 were uniformly bleak. That by *National Journal* reporter Dick Kirschten was typical:

> Heading into the second half of his term, Reagan is beset by charges of unfairness and insensitivity. His standing in the public opinion polls is sagging, and legislators on Capitol Hill are distancing themselves from

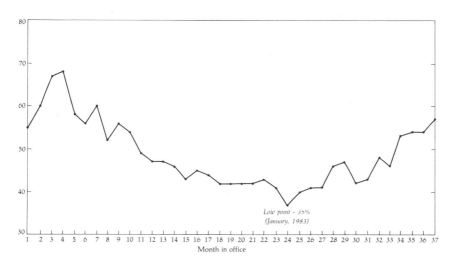

Figure 3.1 President Reagan's popularity, 1981–84
Source: "Opinion Roundup," *Public Opinion*, 7 (February–March 1984), 34.

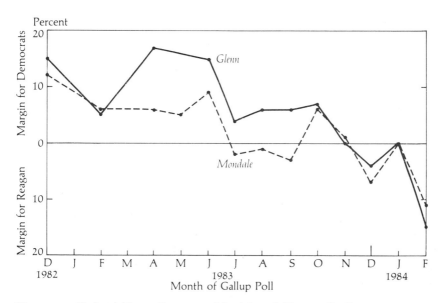

Figure 3.2 Early trial heats: Reagan vs. Mondale and Glenn, 1982–84
Source: "Opinion Roundup," *Public Opinion*, 7 (February–March 1984), 35.

the White House. Even before the new and clearly more independent 98th Congress is sworn in, the president's legislative mastery has begun to ebb. . . .

   The mood in Washington has changed vastly. . . . One no longer hears talk of a Reagan Revolution. . . .[8]

Thus the first major factor regarding renomination was simply whether the president was capable of leading the Republican party to victory in 1984. The state of the economy was unquestionably central to judgments about the president's political future. Inflation had been drastically cut but unemployment and interest rates remained high. The Reagan economic program was receiving mixed responses from the American public. Nearly 60 percent of the respondents in the Harris Poll taken at the end of 1982 judged the program a failure.[9] Yet the 1982 election-day polls taken for NBC found that a majority of voters were willing to give "Reaganomics" more time to work.[10] Further, according to political analyst Everett Carll Ladd, most Americans were "fairly optimistic about national leadership and direction, even with the economy in a deep recession."[11] As it happened, of course, the economy began to improve on almost all fronts during 1983. Accordingly the president's approval rating increased rather steadily (with some decline in the summer—see figure 3.1), and he improved in trial heats versus Mondale and Glenn (see figure 3.2).

   Obviously related to the president's performance was the matter of *agenda control*. The 1980 election was subjected to an incredible volume of analysis. Nothing quite like it had occurred before. A conservative Republican overwhelmingly defeated an incumbent Democratic president in the Electoral College—winning 91 percent of the vote. Equally stunning, however, was the Republican takeover of the Senate. No Republican president in the post–Civil War period had experienced such a large gain of Senate seats. And the thirty-three-seat gain for House Republicans was the greatest for them in a presidential election year since 1920. These significant shifts encouraged analysts to determine whether a more permanent shift away from the Democratic party might not be occurring. It is not important for present purposes to enter that debate. The more relevant matter is the effect of the sizable Republican victory on the national policy agenda.

   A shift in the agenda of domestic issues had been occurring for some time — at least since the late 1960s. The move was away from the expansive issues of the Great Society to more consolidative issues—i.e., those associated with making government work better, not more. The 1980 election brought to Washington a president with a contractive agenda—one designed to reduce the rate of government growth at first, followed by an attempt to shrink the size of the national government in the domestic sphere. While it is uncertain whether he had a public mandate to accomplish this goal, it is clear that political circumstances favored his effort to try. As Fred I. Greenstein observed, the combined results made the election look like a landslide. "Reagan's aides inevitably treated the outcome as a mandate for his specific policy proposals, and, with far less justification, much of the press and many members of Congress accepted this reading of the election results."[12] One result of interpreting the election as a mandate for Reagan's program was to confirm the shift to a consolidative/contractive agenda.

It was the nature of the Reagan policy formula, as applied in 1981, that a subsequent return to an expansive social welfare agenda was precluded. In other words, the Reagan adjustment, if we may call it that, was bound to affect national domestic decision making for at least a decade. And that is the principal point to be made here. Reagan's initial victories committed future congresses to a more consolidative agenda. The combination of a three-year tax reduction program and multi-year defense increases guaranteed deficits that were unimaginable in the past, deficits equal to the size of whole budgets of not that long ago, deficits so huge that policy conversation would address almost nothing else.

Thus, in regard to this second major factor affecting renomination—agenda control—President Reagan was triumphant. Despite growing deficits he did not seem inclined to alter the general direction of his program, and the economic recovery in 1983 appeared to support his decision. The combination of economic recovery and a growing public debt was not a happy one for the eventual Democratic presidential candidate. The first made it unlikely that the second would be acknowledged as serious by the American public. Finding a winning campaign theme would prove difficult for the Democrats.

There were a number of other factors to be evaluated and treated in preparing for a Reagan renomination. The first involved a possible violation of contemporary campaign ethics—the Carter briefing papers issue. Had it developed into a "briefinggate" matter, as some labeled it, the president might have suffered a serious political setback. The other problems were illustrative of the balancing act required for a president performing as the compleat politician. First was the task of reinforcing the support of the far right wing of the party. The ideologues of either party are bound to be dissatisfied with a president who practices politics in the Oval Office. Next was the difficulty the president experienced in satisfying the demands of women's organizations. The so-called gender gap was shorthand for several thorny issues—arms control, abortion, the Equal Rights Amendment. And, of course, managing these issues satisfactorily threatened Reagan's base of support on the right. Third was the standard set of complications involved in working with Congress. As noted before, this president faced a peculiar arrangement—a Republican majority in the Senate, a Democratic majority in the House. Such an arrangement was not unprecedented but the previous cases (in 1910 and 1930) occurred in the second half of the administration and were associated with a decline in the fortunes of the Republican party.

The "briefing papers" episode was somewhat unusual. David Stockman, then a Republican representative from Michigan, played the role of President Carter in a 1980 debate rehearsal. In preparing for the encounter, Stockman was able to rely on the very notes that had been gathered for Carter. Apparently, these notes or papers had been provided to the Reagan campaign organization by someone in the Carter campaign. Stockman had made this fact known on the very day of the debate in speaking to an Optimist Club luncheon in Casopolis, Michigan. At the time there even was an account of Stockman's revelation, which appeared in an Elkhart, Indiana, newspaper.[13] Further, Lawrence I. Barrett, a correspondent for *Time* magazine, filed a story on the matter but it was never used.[14]

When Barrett's book, *Gambling With History*, was published in 1983, the "briefing papers" episode gained national attention. With the prospect of Reagan seeking reelection, and in view of the post-Watergate morality, it was entirely predictable that investigations would be launched. Michigan Democrat, Donald J. Albosta, chairman of the Subcommittee on Human Resources of the Committee on Post Office and Civil Service, announced a probe, and a formal investigation by the FBI was initiated by the Department of Justice.[15] President Reagan denied knowledge of the briefing papers in a press conference on June 28, 1983. Neither probe resulted in specific charges of wrongdoing. News of the incident was limited to some apparent infighting within Reagan's staff—with different accounts of the event being offered by William J. Casey and James A. Baker III (both of whom had served Reagan during the campaign).[16] A potentially explosive issue simply fizzled out. It had little or no effect on the 1984 campaign.

In his comprehensive analysis of "conservatives in an age of change," A. James Reichley proposes a spectrum of Republican party identifiers from right to left as follows: fundamentalists, stalwarts, moderates, and progressives. Reichley observes that the strength of the fundamentalists is a relatively new development in the party. They are described as supporting

> rigorous (their critics claimed simplistic) versions of various beliefs and attitudes that are a part of modern ideational conservatism: nationalism in foreign policy, market capitalism, and moral and cultural traditionalism, among others. By pressing each of these beliefs and attitudes to rather extreme positions, however, the fundamentalists tended to bring them into conflict with one another and with the organic view of society that lies at the heart of ideational conservatism. The fundamentalists, moreover, often advanced their views with a stridency that seemed likely to produce the opposite of social harmony.[17]

The contemporary champion of fundamentalism within the Republican party is, of course, Ronald Reagan. Reagan's rise in politics more or less coincided with the emergence of the fundamentalists as a powerful force within the party. Their first victory in winning the presidential nomination for Barry Goldwater in 1964 ended in an electoral disaster for the Republican party and their influence waned. In 1976 conservatives demonstrated renewed strength in very nearly stealing the nomination from an incumbent president. In 1980 they finally triumphed with the nomination and election of Ronald Reagan.

Yet Reichley points out that "Reagan's political style is not revolutionary, and his record in California indicates that he is a pragmatic rather than an autocratic conservative. . . ."[18] A pragmatic president with a reasonably coherent ideological direction naturally establishes priorities. The four major policy themes of the fundamentalist, Reagan programs are supply-side economics, a more nationalistic foreign and defense policy, a new "old" state-centered federalism, and strengthened family and religious values (the moral issue).[19] As president, Reagan's two major priorities were clear: cut taxes and strengthen defense. Rearranging the federal system ran a distant third and lagging still further behind was the set of moral issues. What this meant as a practical matter was simply that the president would sacrifice the latter two if it was necessary in order to gain support for the first two.

In considering renomination, however, the president had to reaffirm his devotion to the moral issues that provided the litmus test for so many fundamentalist Republicans. He was heavily criticized by prominent conservatives for not acting more forcefully on such issues as abortion and school prayer early in the administration, before the president's initial advantage was dissipated by the mid-term elections. Two fundamentalist spokesmen, Richard A. Viguerie and Paul M. Weyrich, were especially critical of the president. Viguerie, who masterminded the impressive direct-mail fund raising techniques for right-wing groups, questioned the commitment of the White House. "The Republicans of 1984 claim that they deserve the support of the so-called religious right. But where were they in 1981 and '82 and '83 when these issues could have been brought to the floor of the House and Senate, when the White House staff could have burned the midnight oil working on these issues?"[20] Weyrich expressed doubt that 1984 would bring major gains, suggesting instead that the religious right was being used by the Reagan forces. "In the Carter years, and for that matter in the Nixon and Ford years, we were outside the gate watching the party going on inside. Now in the Reagan administration we have been let in the back door and we are enjoying the crumbs at the servants' table."[21]

The stakes were high for President Reagan and his supporters in reestablishing close contact and identification with the fundamentalists on social issues. Voter registration and turnout drives were important in 1980 and were

Percent voting for Republican candidate

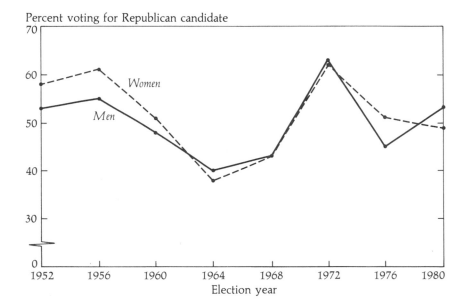

Figure 3.3   Republican vote among men and women, 1952–80
Source: Gallup Monthly Opinion Index, December 1976 and December 1980.

planned for 1984 as well. Many so-called Christian Right ministers were prepared to use their pulpits—in churches and on radio—to rally political support. Thus a strategy had to be developed to confirm the president's commitment to these groups (for details, see below).

The gender gap was an equally nettlesome problem for the White House. It
reflected growing political activism among women and thus was a volatile
issue. One could easily lose support either by standing firm or by shifting
position on questions of importance to women. The evidence for a gap begins
with the data presented in figure 3.3. Note that in four of the eight elections a
higher percentage of women than men supported Republican candidates, and
for one other election the percentages are equal. In 1964 and 1972, a slightly
lower percentage of women supported the Republican candidates. Note also
that the two trend lines follow the same basic pattern up until 1980. Though
the quantities differ, still the percentage of women voting Republican increased
and decreased along with that for men. In 1980, however, the two lines went in
opposite directions—there was a significant increase among men (8 percent)
and a slight decrease among women (2 percent)—thus the "gender gap."

Further cause for concern among Reagan supporters was to be found in turnout statistics. Since winning the right to vote in 1920 women have consistently had a lower turnout percentage than men.[22] But in recent elections the decline in turnout for women has been less than that for men, and in 1980 for the first time a higher percentage of women than men voted, and from 1976 to 1980 the percentage of women voting increased, while the percentage for men voting continued to decrease. The combination of the higher Democratic vote among women and the larger percentage of women becoming politically active had to be of concern to Republican strategists.[23]

Coping with the so-called gender gap required special political sensitivity for several reasons. First, many of the issues of concern to women were highly divisive in nature. Any effort to win over new women activists threatened the president's base of support among men and other women (not to mention the problem of maintaining credibility if major shifts were attempted). Second, for the Democrats the growing gender gap was of even greater proportions, and would increase even more during the campaign. Again, Republican strategists had to be careful not to lose support among men. Third, concentrating too heavily on one group inevitably invites criticism for ignoring others. Possibly more effective is a strategy to attract voters on a non-gender basis—e.g., through appeals to ethnic, occupational or religious groups—thus attracting both men and women. A particularly strong effort was made by Republicans to attract Hispanic-American voters, and, of course, the appeal to fundamentalist and family values cut across gender.

Poll results in 1983 suggested that the problem for the president in attracting the support of women was getting steadily worse. Wide disparities were revealed between male and female evaluations of the president's performance (58 to 37 percent positive among men; 47 to 51 percent negative among women according to the ABC News/*Washington Post* poll in late July 1983). In the match-ups between Reagan and Mondale/Glenn in this same poll, Reagan led among men but trailed badly among women (by as much as 17 points in the Reagan-Glenn match-up).[24] On August 21, 1983, the *Washington Post* published a statement by a special assistant to the deputy assistant attorney general for civil rights that accused the president of reneging on his commitments to the "civil rights of American women." In a rather bizarre incident, Barbara Honegger, a Reagan appointee, blasted the administration's record on women's issues ("Frankly, my dear, I don't think Ronald Reagan gives a damn."), and then resigned.[25] Women's organizations immediately provided a forum so that Honegger could continue speaking out. The principal effect of Honegger's action was to dramatize further the need for the Reagan administration to improve its standing with women.[26]

Still another balancing act required of Reagan as a candidate for renomination was that of maintaining decent relationships with Republican members of

Congress. The strength of Reagan's victory in 1980, combined with significant Republican gains in the Senate and House of Representatives, produced impressive support for the president's program during the ninety-seventh Congress. Presidential support and party unity scores among congressional Republicans were comparatively high—reminiscent of the Eisenhower years.[27] And the president certainly got most of what he wanted in 1981, primarily because of Republican unity.

Democratic success in the 1982 elections produced a very different political situation. In 1980 the Republicans gained 33 House seats, ending up with 192 representatives (44 percent of the total). Their leaders were thus in a position to fashion legislative majorities with the support of southern Democrats. In 1982 the Democratic gain of 26 House seats made it much more difficult to produce these majorities. Further, a more aggressive Democratic opposition in the House made it more difficult for Senate Republicans to support the president (despite a gain of one seat over the 1980 results).

Of even greater significance than the 1982 election for influencing support of the president by congressional Republicans was the upcoming 1984 elections. All House Republicans were, of course, up for reelection. And on the Senate side, 19 of the 33 seats being contested were held by Republicans. If he did seek reelection, it was clear that Ronald Reagan would be the major issue in the campaign. Thus all Republican candidates could be expected to be particularly attentive to Reagan's standing among American voters. His low ratings in the polls during the early part of 1983, therefore, had to be disconcerting to many congressional Republicans. Further, several Republican senators naturally began to evaluate their own chances for the presidential nomination should Reagan decide to retire.

Predictably, presidential support and party unity declined during the ninety-eighth Congress. Yet most of the president's program already had been set in place in 1981. And since it was a multiyear program, the subsequent congressional action mainly reacted to what had been done. The tax-cut program alone guaranteed that the ninety-eighth Congress would concentrate on budgetary questions. For his part, the president forwarded his budget to the Hill in 1984, then allowed the members of Congress to wrestle with the political problems created by huge deficits.

In summary, a Reagan renomination was by no means preordained. The president's low status in the polls, possible loss of control of the agenda with bad economic news, a potential campaign scandal left over from 1980, a serious gender gap, and questions about the president's support among far right groups and congressional Republicans—these were problems that required careful evaluation by the president and his political advisers. The president himself delayed his announcement until January 29, 1984, though he earlier authorized the creation of a campaign unit and confirmed that George Bush would again be his running mate if he decided to seek reelection. Meanwhile 1983, which had started as a difficult political year for the president, steadily improved. By December his approval rating had climbed to 54 percent and he had surpassed both Glenn and Mondale in trial heats (see figures 3.1 and 3.2). At the end, columnist Joseph Kraft could write convincingly: "1983 was Ronald Reagan's year."

> He is a blithe spirit. He beams all the time and likes nothing better than telling funny stories. He takes large amounts of time off from work and pays almost no attention to detail. Optimism comes naturally to him, and he regularly bucks the proposition that you can't have your cake and eat it too.[28]

The Renomination of Ronald Reagan

As is shown in figure 3.1, the low points in Reagan's approval ratings occurred in the months of December 1982 and January, February, March, and April 1983. Yet if the president were to seek reelection, plans had to be laid and organizational moves had to be made in the early months of 1983. The president did not have to make his decision at that point but if he wished to preserve the option to run, he had to organize as though he intended to run. In an unprecedented, but wholly Reaganesque, arrangement, Nevada senator Paul Laxalt was chosen in late January 1983 as a sort of Republican party overseer or superintendent to coordinate the many elements of the party. That is the point at which the renomination effort began in earnest. This review will begin with the Laxalt appointment and discuss five aspects of the renomination process: organization, the decision to run, issues, the role of the president throughout the period, and the convention.

Getting Organized

Organizing to reelect a president is much more complicated than one might suppose. The task is intricate and sensitive in large part because of the balkanized nature of the major parties' organizations. The many elements of these organizations include: a national committee and headquarters; congressional and senatorial campaign committees; individual candidate organizations (with campaign consultants); state and local organizations (which are seldom well-structured or well-coordinated even within a state); supportive, but independent, political action committees; pollsters; and a White House political advisory unit. These many entities vary in purpose and capability. They are frequently in competition for money and personnel. Personality conflicts are guaranteed. Here, then, was a supreme challenge to the political skills of the Reagan White House.

Recognizing the aforementioned problems, and determined to avoid Nixon's method in 1972 of separating the presidential campaign from the national Republican party, the Reagan strategists created a new position: general chairman of the Republican National Committee. This was the position given to Senator Laxalt. He was a sensible choice. Laxalt had managed Reagan's 1976 and 1980 campaigns. He was as close to the president as anyone in politics, yet he did not work for the president. No other person had such high status in the party and with Reagan. Laxalt could speak *to* and *for* the president. It is not surprising that on election night President Reagan thanked Laxalt first.

It was Laxalt's job to coordinate the major elements of Reagan's reelection drive and to integrate the presidential campaign with other party efforts. He was aided in this effort by the appointment of another Nevadan, Frank Fahrenkopf, to be chairman of the Republican National Committee. Fahrenkopf, who had served previously as Republican state chairman in Nevada, would manage the national party headquarters. He inherited an impressive party apparatus—one that was well-organized and financed as a result of effective management by a series of able party chairmen.

The president's chief of staff, James A. Baker III, was a key figure throughout the campaign. He managed all White House operations and maintained communication with the reelection committee. He worked closely with a small group of strategists in the White House: deputy chief of staff Michael Deaver, pollster Richard Wirthlin, campaign troubleshooter Stuart Spencer, and political adviser to the president Edward J. Rollins. Edward Meese played a less public role than in the past due to the fact that confirmation of his appointment as attorney general was still pending.

During the early months of 1983 the campaign strategy was developed within the White House and, of course, coordination was not a difficult matter. Rollins and his deputy, Lee Atwater, spent much of the summer of 1983 preparing an organization that would eventually separate from the White House. His mentor, Lyn Nofziger (former political aide to the president), was brought in as an outside consultant, as were Charles Black and pollster Robert Teeter. James Lake was designated as the campaign press secretary. Drew Lewis was initially assigned to run a National Strategy Committee.[29]

The actual creation of a reelection committee was a bit tricky since it was interlaced with the president's decision to run—a decision Reagan wished to delay as long as possible (see below). Senator Laxalt convinced the president that a committee had to be organized and begin to operate even before his announcement. On October 17, 1983, "Reagan-Bush '84," headed by Rollins, officially began its work. Meanwhile, President Reagan insisted that he had not yet made up his mind. In a press conference held just two days after the creation of his reelection committee, he refused again to confirm that he was running for reelection.

The first task for the new organization was to raise enough money for a yearlong campaign. Republicans have become very good at fund raising. They do it continuously. The Republican National Committee announced its budget of $52 million in early February 1983. Party Chairman Fahrenkopf noted, "We're in tremendous financial shape." He "called the budget, 'the largest in the history of American politics by any party.'"[30] The Reagan-Bush '84 Committee was likewise "in good shape." By one account:

> The money rolls in faster than the committee's volunteers can open the envelopes. Since early November, 2.8 million letters have been mailed to loyal Republicans, who have responded by sending $7.5 million to Washington.
>
> "We have 20,000 pieces of mail upstairs we haven't had a chance to open," says Jim Lake, the communications director. "We expect they contain another $500,000."[31]

With a well-financed organization in place, attention could be directed to reinforcing traditional Republican support and reaching out to potential voters among Democrats and independents. Work began on registering new voters, establishing state and local organizations (with a heavy concentration on key counties), identifying appeals to various voting blocs, and planning the most elaborate and expensive media campaign in history. Building on the West as a solid base, efforts were made to secure the South, then concentrate on the Midwest and Northeast during the actual campaign. A plan to use surrogate candidates permitted President Reagan to remain presidential even beyond his announcement.

> With cheerleader-in-chief Vice-President George Bush heading the list, Cabinet officers, Republican congressional notables and presidential daughter Maureen Reagan were out on the hustings competing for publicity with the Democratic primary contestants. And with each succeeding month, the surrogate schedule has expanded in both personnel and geographical reach.[32]

One should not get the impression that there were no foul ups in getting organized. The president's determination to delay his announcement caused concern within the campaign structure. Accommodating all those who had been active in previous campaigns but were not presently in government (e.g., Lyn Nofziger, Drew Lewis, and William Timmons) required creativity in organizational placement and the invention of new titles. And, of course, the management of an apparatus as disjointed and multifaceted as a presidential reelection organization simply cannot be error-free. Most problems were overcome, however. In fact, the 1984 Reagan-Bush organization likely will be the model by which subsequent renomination and reelection efforts will be measured.

The Decision to Run

Washington cocktail circuit talk during the fall of 1983 naturally focused on whether the president would seek reelection. Many of the most knowledgeable pundits were convinced that he would not. Yet it seems clear in retrospect that, barring some unforeseen event, the president intended from the start to seek a second term. One would hardly expect the compleat politician to act otherwise. *National Journal* reporter Dick Kirschten described these intentions as follows:

> Reagan gave early lip service to the lofty goal of doing "what's good for the nation and not politically beneficial." He told his newly selected Cabinet appointees at a preinaugural briefing in January 1981, "We want to operate as if there is no next election."
>
> Having said that, he then proceeded, upon taking office 12 days later, to set up a sophisticated White House network of political and communications operations that built steadily toward the goal of reelection to a second term.[33]

As the president made one move after another signaling his intention to run, speculation continued that he might retire. His appointment of women to cabinet posts (Elizabeth Dole to Transportation, Margaret Heckler to Health and Human Services), the replacement of the secretary of the interior James Watt and Environmental Protection Agency administrator Anne Burford, the authorization of a reelection committee, his confirmation that George Bush would be his running mate, the postponement of the appointment of Edward Meese as attorney general—these and other actions could be interpreted as showing he intended to run in the 1984 election.

Even the delay itself suggested the probability that the president would seek reelection. If he did *not* intend to run, then the delay would certainly cause problems within the Republican party. Candidates would be put in a very difficult position if they were not able to raise money or organize their forces until early 1984. The longer the president postponed his decision, therefore, the more likely it was that he would run. He was simply too party-oriented a politician to have done otherwise.

In fact, we don't have to speculate about his thinking in regard to this important matter. He openly expressed his belief that an early decision would adversely affect his presidency and that campaigns were too long. The president was quoted in May 1983:

If the answer would be one thing, I would become a lame duck. . . . And if the answer was the other way, yes, then everything I tried to do would be viewed by the opposition as part of a political campaign and maybe we couldn't get as much bipartisan cooperation as we need. We're not playing any games or anything. I know that it has to be done, but I don't think this is the time to do it.[34]

Here is a perfectly rational approach to a second-term announcement. Yet observers continued to speculate that a decision would be made in the fall, 1983. Often relying on hints from White House aides, some in the press first estimated that the president would announce after Labor Day, then by mid-October, then it was by late November or early December, and finally by early January. The passing of each date left the impression that the president was still undecided or uncertain about his political future. But to have announced during the early fall months would have been unprecedented. Even President Carter didn't announce until December 4, 1979, and he had a serious opponent in Senator Edward Kennedy. Other recent Republican incumbent presidents waited until the election year itself to make their announcements—Nixon on January 5, 1972; Eisenhower not until the end of February 1956.

Of course, teasers along the way kept the president in the center of political discussion while he was presumably making up his mind about whether to continue. It was classic Reagan dramaturgy—creating circumstances under which the media could not suppress their curiosity about a wholly predictable decision. At the time of the actual decision he first, on January 25, delivered an upbeat State of the Union message to Congress, stressing that "America is back—standing tall"—then went to Atlanta to kick off the campaign in the South, and on January 29, a Sunday, he announced: "I am a candidate and will seek reelection to the office I presently hold. Thank you for the trust you have placed in me." As is so often the case with Reagan, in retrospect no one could doubt that his timing was right. Patience, too, is an attribute of the compleat politician.

The Issues

It is commonly accepted now by students of voting behavior that voters make their choices "retrospectively"—they vote on the past, not the future. As stated by V. O. Key, Jr.:

[The electorate] judges retrospectively; it commands prospectively only insofar as it expresses either approval or disapproval of that which has happened before. Voters may reject what they have known; or they may approve what they have known. They are not likely to be attracted in great numbers by promises of the novel or unknown. Once innovation has occurred they may embrace it, even though they would have, earlier, hesitated to venture forth to welcome it.[35]

That judgments about the past may contain hopes for the future is, perhaps, indisputable. Still, when an incumbent is running for reelection, it seems axiomatic that voters will approve of a president associated with good times and disapprove of one associated with bad times. I am reminded of my conversation about elections some years ago with a person sitting next to me on an airline flight. He observed: "It's the old story in democracy. We don't elect anybody—we just throw the other guy out."

The point of this digression is simply that neither convention delegates nor voters are likely to "throw out" a president who is perceived as responsible for dramatic economic recovery. Other important issues would have to emerge to displace economic growth for that to happen. President Reagan himself prepared the test for his renomination and reelection when he asked voters in 1980 to judge whether they were better off than they were in 1976. They answered resoundingly in the negative in 1980. Meanwhile, all major economic indicators showed significant improvement during the first Reagan administration. The picture looked bleak early in 1983 but that was the low point. During 1983 low inflation rates were maintained, interest rates were lowered, and unemployment was reduced. The so-called misery index—the combined inflation and unemployment rates—was at its lowest point during the election year (just the opposite had occurred for Carter). And per capita disposable income was increasing dramatically. Edward R. Tufte has shown that growth in purchasing power is associated with a strong performance by the incumbent party. Thus, for example, in 1980 there was actually a decline in purchasing power (-0.6 percent). In 1984 the growth was projected at 5.6 percent—matching the highest rate in the post–World War II period.[36] In regard to the 1984 election Tufte was quoted as saying: "This has been almost a classic election year cycle for Reagan"—meaning simply that the president "took his medicine early in his four-year term" and was then in a position to benefit "from the upswing."[37]

What issues might displace that of a growing economy? Certainly the threat of a nuclear war being triggered by a hawkish president was one possibility. One Democratic presidential candidate, Senator Alan Cranston of California, based his campaign on that prospect. The possibility that record deficits and trade imbalances could destroy the economic progress that had been made was another. Walter Mondale stressed that prospect. Other possibilities included environmental disasters as a consequence of acid rain or toxic waste, potential Vietnams occurring in Lebanon or Central America, ethical improprieties by presidential aides or cabinet officials, and failure of the Reagan recovery program to improve the condition of poor people. The dramatic emergence of one of these issues, possibly associated with a catastrophe, or perhaps a combination of issues creating an alliance against the president, seemed necessary to discount the favorable effect of a robust economy.

From the perspective of the president and his campaign staff it was necessary to maintain the advantage implicit in the economic recovery by taking actions to ensure that displacement did not occur. The strategy for accomplishing this feat was simple and seemingly effective. As noted below, the president improved his image as world leader during the nomination period and he systematically countered efforts to establish other issues as preeminent, either by taking the initiative or through damage control. Meanwhile, the Democrats were more or less neutralized by an intensive and lengthy nomination fight.

There is another point to be made in regard to issues. Bear in mind that the president first had to be renominated and that he typically viewed one political event as linked to others. The renomination ultimately would be carried out by a party convention likely to be controlled by conservatives. Thus there were issues associated with that reality. No one doubted that Ronald Reagan would be renominated by the 1984 Republican convention. The question was whether that nomination would be made in a spirit that would then carry over to sustain an enthusiastic national campaign. The prospects of that happening were good but not guaranteed. President Reagan experienced bitter criticism from the far right for his appointment of Sandra Day O'Connor to the Supreme Court, his failure to offer more fervent support on the so-called social issues (anti-abortion, school prayer), his willingness to compromise on certain budgetary issues, and his identification with a deficit of historic proportions. There were fences to be mended on the way to Dallas. And an important test of success for the Republican convention was whether conservatives were reassured that Ronald Reagan was theirs. They were so reassured.

Ronald Reagan Doing Politics

Just as future party professionals will look back at the Reagan-Bush organization as a model for reelecting a president, so too will future politicians review the Reagan style for the lessons it teaches. To observe President Reagan's activities during the preconvention period is to witness a master at work. He emphasized his strengths, fortified his weaknesses, and took advantage wherever possible of the division among the Democrats. It is a story well worth recording.

Table 3.2 presents a sampling of presidential events, with the Democratic political calendar placed alongside. The sampling of events shows the president alternating between the roles of chief executive, ceremonial head of state, world leader, and candidate. As he moved closer to the nomination itself, he was more active as a pure candidate. But he was consistently attentive to the

Table 3.2 From the announcement to the Republican
National convention: Ronald Reagan doing politics

Date		Presidential event	Date	Democratic calendar
January	25	State of the Union message		
	29	Announcement		
February	1	Budget message		
	2	Economic report		
	7	Withdrawal from Lebanon announced		
	17	Congress urged to act on Kissinger Commission report		
	20	Campaigns in Iowa	20	Iowa caucus (Mondale)
	22	News conference (Lebanon, budget)		
	23	Justice Department report on Carter briefing papers		
			28	New Hampshire (Hart)
March	1	Hearings begin on Meese for attorney general		
	5	Senate debate begins on school prayer amendment		
	7	Ambassador to Vatican confirmed		
			13	Super Tuesday (Mondale wins 2; Hart wins 3)
	19	Meese hearings reopened		
	20	Senate rejects school prayer amendment	20	Illinois (Mondale)
			27	Connecticut (Hart)
	30	Participation in Lebanon multinational force ended		
April	2	Independent counsel for Meese; Smith stays on as attorney general		
			3	New York (Mondale); Wisconsin (Hart)

Table 3.2 (*continued*)

Date		Presidential event	Date	Democratic calendar
April				
	4	News conference (control of chemical weapons, budget, school prayer, foreign policy)		
	6	CIA participation in Nicaragua mining revealed		
			10	Pennsylvania (Mondale)
	26	China trip begins		
May	1	China trip concludes	1	District of Columbia (Jackson); Tennessee (Mondale)
	3	Defense budget cuts announced		
			5	Louisiana (Jackson)
			8	Indiana (Hart); Maryland (Mondale); North Carolina (Mondale); Ohio (Mondale)
	9	Feldstein resigns (effective July 10); televised speech on Central America		
	14	Mini news conference (Olympic boycott, foreign policy)		
			15	Nebraska (Hart); Oregon (Hart)
	22	News conference (foreign policy, trip to Europe)	22	Idaho (Hart)
	22	President-elect Duarte (El Salvador) visits Capitol Hill		
	23	Albosta subcommittee issues report on Carter briefing papers		
	31	Visit to Ireland, followed by Normandy D-Day commemoration and London economic summit (to June 9)		

Table 3.2   (*continued*)

Date	Presidential event	Date	Democratic calendar
June		9	California (Hart); New Jersey (Mondale); New Mexico (Hart); South Dakota (Hart); West Virginia (Mondale)
		12	North Dakota (Hart)
	14 News conference (summit with Soviets, politics, domestic issues)		
	27 Down payment on budget passes Congress		
July	10 Launches a proenvironment campaign		
		12	Mondale selects Ferraro as running mate
		19	Mondale and Ferraro accept Democratic nomination for president and vice-president
	23 Gallup Poll shows slight edge for Mondale-Ferraro		
	24 News conference (tax increase, politics, some foreign policy)		
	25 Launches campaign trip (Texas, Georgia, New Jersey)		
	28 Opens the Olympic games		
August	1 Burford resigns		
	11 Gaffe on "bombing Soviet Union"		
	13 GOP platform committee hearings begin		
	16 Ends 16-day vacation in California		

Table 3.2 *(continued)*

Date		Presidential event	Date	Democratic calendar
August				
	17	GOP platform committee adopts platform		
	23	Accepts Republican nomination		

Source: Compiled by the author.

politics of issues and appearances along the way, blending electoral and policy politics. Throughout the period he showed sensitivity to the need to manage potential campaign issues. The incumbent has the advantage of a lengthy preparation for the fall campaign. His opponents provide the free service of identifying major issues (in this case during a record number of debates), and he can then make the requisite adjustments.

Observe in table 3.2 how all of this worked in 1984. The following were among the difficult issues for President Reagan: the budget deficit, the president's standing as a world leader, Lebanon, Central America, the so-called sleaze factor, the failure to be more assertive on the social issues, and the administration's environmental record. Very briefly the record shows exactly that combination of taking initiative and controlling damage that we would expect from the compleat politician. In regard to the budget deficit, the president had the singular and impressive advantage of a growing economy (an advantage President Carter lacked in 1980). Thus, whereas the problem itself was unlikely to be resolved, it provided a limited edge to the Democrats. As long as the principal economic indicators were favorable, voters were unlikely to punish the president for the deficit. Further, an incumbent president can transfer the issue of the deficit from the White House to Capitol Hill by fulfilling his responsibility to produce a budget early in the election year. And with the House of Representatives controlled by the Democrats, President Reagan, too, was in a position to run against deficit spending—blaming past Democrats for reckless spending and present Democrats for failing to reduce future expenditures. The budget deficit was, perhaps, the principal domestic issue in 1984, but the Democrats were never able to establish this in the minds of the voters (despite Mondale's valiant try at the Democratic convention).

In regard to the major foreign-policy issues, White House actions were taken directly from the manual of multidimensional politics. The president traveled to China and Europe while the Democrats were locked in bitter debates over the future leadership of the party. Both trips were triumphs for the president. *Washington Post* columnist Richard Cohen's analysis was typical:

> Gary Hart went to San Diego, Walter Mondale went to San Bernardino, Jesse Jackson went to Washington and back, and Ronald Reagan is about to hit the beach at Normandy. In a time of hard traveling, the president has had the best week of all. . . .
>
> There is as much symbolism as nostalgia in Reagan's trip to Normandy. He is strong and triumphant, his enemies in disarray. . . . While they were fighting one another, Reagan took their beach.[38]

By June the president was dropping strong hints that he would not be adverse to a summit meeting with the Soviets. Indeed, he indicated that "quiet diplomacy" had been under way for some time, but the problem of frequent changes in Soviet leadership made it difficult to arrange a meeting. Further, on April 4, the president announced "a bold, American initiative for a comprehensive worldwide ban on chemical weapons."[39]

In regard to Lebanon it became apparent that a further terrorist incident like the bombing of the Marine barracks in the fall of 1982 would severely damage the administration. Therefore, the president sought a rationale for removing the marines. He found it in the deteriorating situation. "There was no way that we could really contribute to the original mission [of stabilization]."[40] The marines were "redeployed" to the ships, then withdrawn altogether. The president even blamed Congress in part for encouraging terrorist attacks by criticizing the presence of marines in Lebanon.[41]

The problems in Central America were not so easily finessed. They were bound to persist throughout the campaign. Still, the president had earlier appointed a National Bipartisan Commission on Central America, headed by Henry Kissinger, and was therefore in a position to refer to their report as representing credible support for his policy. In May, José Napoleón Duarte was elected president of El Salvador. Duarte visited Washington shortly after his election and made a very favorable impression on Capitol Hill. Again, the opposition to the president's policy was muted by events. Unquestionably, however, the situation was difficult for the administration. Revelations that the Central Intelligence Agency had participated in the mining of harbors in Nicaragua caused problems even within the Republican party. And questions about possible use of American military forces persisted. Still, at no point in the campaign was it likely that the Central American situation would override the positive effects of solid economic growth and thus defeat Reagan's bid for a second term.

Table 3.2 also shows the recurrence of ethical issues—the "sleaze factors." The president nominated his longtime associate Edwin Meese to be attorney general after William French Smith announced his resignation. Questions were raised about Meese's financial dealings. The White House resolved this matter by appointing an independent counsel and convincing Smith to remain as attorney general for the duration of the investigation. Here was true damage control. The effect was to defuse the issue and permit the president to avoid answering questions pending the results of the investigation. The controversy over the Carter briefing papers also dissipated during the early months of 1984.

A Senate debate on a school-prayer amendment provided the president with a perfect opportunity to restore his standing among right-wing fundamentalists —at relatively low cost. The president was an active supporter of the amendment. The amendment itself divided the two parties with a Republican senator, Lowell Weicker of Connecticut, leading the fight against and many Democrats voting in favor. The amendment failed to get the two-thirds vote required. The parties split with thirty-seven Republicans and nineteen Democrats voting in favor; eighteen Republicans and twenty-six Democrats voting against.

Finally, in what was viewed by many as a most audacious move by the president, criticism of the administration's record on the environment was tackled by a minicampaign to claim otherwise. On July 10, just after setting off another firestorm of protest for appointing former EPA administrator Anne Burford to an advisory environmental panel, President Reagan visited Chesapeake Bay, Theodore Roosevelt Island in the Potomac, and Mammoth Cave National Park in Kentucky. In speaking to campers at Mammoth Cave, the president claimed that the national parks had been vastly improved during his administration, and he endorsed greater public use of park facilities. *New York Times* reporter Steven Weisman concluded that:

> Few episodes more greatly demonstrate the President's boldness in image-related campaigning than his stumping on environmental issues last week.
>
> People who did not have time to read or listen to what he was saying got a subliminal message by seeing photographs or film of Mr. Reagan at a wildlife refuge on Chesapeake Bay, or in the green sanctuary of Theodore Roosevelt Island in the Potomac River, or exploring the limestone recesses of Mammoth Cave in Kentucky.
>
> Mr. Reagan's words and actions sent environmental groups into a sputtering rage.[42]

As a footnote to the management of this issue, on August 1 Anne Burford asked the president to withdraw her advisory panel appointment, which he did.

There is a danger that one may overstate the shrewdness of the Reagan reelection group. They were, unquestionably, very able. Yet mistakes were made (the Burford appointment was incomprehensible to many), the president committed a few major gaffes (most notably the warm-up joke he made before one of his radio broadcasts, saying, in reference to the Soviet Union, "We begin bombing in five minutes"), and certain issues could only be managed, not resolved (e.g., the mammoth deficit, Central America, arms control). Why was the president not more injured by these difficulties? Was he the "Teflon president" as was claimed by his adversaries? Hugh Sidey judged this characterization a "slick stump slogan" but one that vastly oversimplified reality.

> Reagan has made many blunders, from his tax and budget formulas to his press conference fictions to the tragedy in Lebanon, on through his insensitivity to blacks and women and the shady dealings of a host of his aides. Yet these so far simply do not outweigh the reductions in interest rates and inflation, dealing with the striking air-traffic controllers, restraining government spending, enhancing American power, emplacing new NATO missiles and fighting in Grenada.[43]

Another factor in Reagan's political success in 1984 renomination politics is revealed on the right side of table 3.2. Simply put, the Democrats were too preoccupied with their own campaign politics to produce a coordinated, concentrated attack on the presidency of Ronald Reagan. The media story tended to be what Mondale, Hart, and Jackson said about each other—not what they said about Reagan and his policies. This left the Reagan strategists relatively free to manage their candidate. Had Walter Mondale won the New Hampshire primary, the description of Ronald Reagan doing politics in 1984 might have read quite differently.

The Thirty-Third Republican National Convention

It was a mark of the press reaction to the Republican National Convention that the two candidates—Reagan and Bush—only made the righthand corner of the *Time* magazine cover for the week following the meeting in Dallas. "Ferraro Fights Back" was the big news and therefore her picture graced the full cover. The coverage inside the magazine typified journalists' reactions to the event: "Very little was left to chance. The proceedings were so carefully scripted that virtually the only suspense was whether all 50,000 balloons in the Dallas Convention Center would disgorge on cue when Ronald Reagan and George Bush appeared on the podium for their victory waves the final evening."[44] Never have so many reporters gathered in one place to cover so little. Efforts were made to uncover conflict and discontent from any source. As Tom Shales, television critic for the *Washington Post*, put it: "By Thursday night, network news personnel stationed in Dallas for the duration were exhausted from trying to find ways to make news out of a convention with virtually no surprises."[45]

A "no news" party convention is not purposeless, however. In fact, one might argue persuasively that no news was good news for a party seeking to present a united front for the fall campaign. There was a great deal going on in Dallas that was of importance to candidates and to the party. The principal task to be accomplished was well stated by Republican National Committee chairman, Frank Fahrenkopf: "The biggest fear I have is overconfidence on the part of the activists we depend on as a minority party to go out and do our missionary work. I hope the convention will serve as an energizer for them."[46]

The renominating convention is obviously more manageable than the convention that must nominate a new candidate. First and foremost, with a renomination the managers are in a position to control the party. They can orchestrate convention proceedings—coordinating activities among the national party headquarters, the candidate's reelection organization, and the many other satellite party units. Not only is planning possible, but there is a reasonable prospect that plans will be put into effect.

Dallas is a friendly city for Republicans and Texas was crucial for the reelection of the president. Dallas had other advantages too. It has several forests of modern hotel complexes connected by miles of freeways. Its modern convention center could easily accommodate the 4,470 delegates and alternates (2,235 of each), the estimated thirteen thousand news media personnel, and the estimated ten to fifteen thousand visitors and guests. The main exhibit hall consists of 200,000 square feet of space and an additional 300,000 square feet of space is available for news media operations. Finally, the physical layout of the city and its August climate make it inhospitable to protesters—the bane of the ceremonial convention. Events were scheduled throughout the city—in the luxury hotels that were located many miles apart. Only those protesters with cab fare could make most events. And the heat was intense—sometimes exceeding 110°. It is hard to produce a decent demonstration if your sign bearers are suffering heat prostration.

Like all political party operations, organizing a convention has a certain byzantine quality. Many units must be involved, yet someone has to be in charge to see that the event actually takes place. The two units most directly involved were the Republican National Committee (RNC) and the Reagan-Bush '84 Committee. The RNC had the formal responsibility for managing the convention. It worked through a Committee on Arrangements, chaired by the national committeeman from Texas, Ernest Angelo, Jr. The committee was organized into twelve subcommittees—decorations, entertainment, host, housing, news media operations, program planning, security, special events, tickets and badges, transportation, VIPs, and youth activities. The actual day-to-day management of the convention was the responsibility of Ronald H. Walker. It was Walker's job to transform the hall into a workable convention facility. As he described it:

> I have to come in and build this convention, secure it, give them the means in which to conduct their business, a place to stay, transportation to get them here, and give them nice cool accommodations, because it is going to be a little warm here in August. . . . My goal is to run this convention like a business. And in that context, for the first time, we will leave a paper trail of how we made decisions. . . . I have got a line-item budget. . . .[47]

Walker was the convention's administrative manager—the nuts and bolts man. But it was also necessary to have a political manager, someone who could handle all of the sensitive relationships among top party and government officials, as well as guarantee that the larger political goals of the convention were met. This task was given to William Timmons. Timmons previously served Republican presidents in congressional liaison capacities and participated in the management of several conventions. He is a well-known and respected figure in Republican party politics.[48] His formal role was that of convention director for the Reagan-Bush '84 Committee.

The convention was uniformly praised for being well managed. Actually the proceedings appeared to go so smoothly that the convention managers were occasionally ridiculed for their efficiency. Those in charge left no doubt that they wanted to project unity and control, however. As the Virginia delegation chairman put it in his state's caucus (attended by the author): "We will have an orderly convention. We will work to get it orderly. This train is going to run on time."

One noteworthy feature of the convention was the imaginative use of communications technology. Many of the speakers were introduced by videotapes projected on one huge screen and several smaller television monitors around the hall. At one point Nancy Reagan waved from the speaker's podium to her husband, whose image was projected on the screen above her head. He was watching her on a television set back in the hotel room. The RNC Network television service had ten cameras in the hall to record the entire convention. At its place in the hall each state delegation had a computer terminal, with a trained operator, for receiving messages. Further, each delegation hotel was provided with word-processing, graphic, and electronic mail capabilities for interdelegation communication. As one Reagan-Bush '84 regional coordinator said at a state caucus attended by the author: "This is the most high-tech convention I've been involved with."

The Platform   Turning now to specific convention activities, it was widely reported that the conservatives dominated the platform-writing process. Had it been otherwise, the news media would really have had a story. The Committee on Resolutions was chaired by Representative Trent Lott, a conservative from Mississippi; the seven subcommittees were chaired or co-chaired by other conservative members of Congress;[49] and the platform was being written for President Ronald Reagan to be approved by delegates selected to cheer him on to victory. There were minor disagreements between the committee leaders and the White House (particularly in regard to criticism of the Federal Reserve Board) and more serious conflicts with certain moderate Republicans, led by Connecticut senator Lowell Weicker and Maryland senator Charles McC. Mathias, Jr., and Iowa representative James Leach. Basically, however, the committee produced a document that had strong support from those attending the Republican convention. The seventy-four-page platform was approved without change by the delegates on Tuesday, August 21.

The platform and the writing of the rules for the next convention exposed certain traditional divisions within the Republican party. Reporter Robert W. Merry made reference to the party's "subterranean machinations" that "reflect the swirl of political forces and ideological divisions within the party."[50] The press searched for conflict during the week of the convention, but essentially, as one moderate put it to me, this was "Ron Reagan's convention." Yet another moderate wrote: "Nothing is forever. New opportunity is there. . . ."[51] Thus, the stories on party divisiveness were futuristic—focusing on the probable revival of old debates going back as far as the Progressive era.

State Caucuses The politics of an uncontested renomination convention permit political parties to compose delegation lists to suit a variety of national, state, and local purposes. For example, many party workers and contributors— persons who would not normally expect to attend a national convention— were rewarded by being selected as delegates and alternates. Under strong pressure from the national party, many women were selected as delegates or alternates (48.9 percent of the total). And though the number of blacks and Hispanics was small (4.4 and 4 percent, respectively), still an effort was made in certain delegations to appoint minority delegates (e.g., there were a number of Cuban-Americans in the Florida delegation).[52]

What do delegates do at a convention that is a foregone conclusion? The short answer is that they have a ball. But there is also business to conduct and, quite surprisingly, state delegations diligently caucused to fulfill their responsibilities. I attended eight caucuses—a sample from each region. As expected, these meetings served organizational and cheerleading functions. Delegates were instructed to be in their seats during the sessions, to give their seats to alternates when they had to leave, and to avoid "being a hero for twenty-four hours" when speaking to the press. The convention managers wanted a full house for every session and they wanted to display harmony, not conflict. The cheerleading was led by teams organized by the Reagan-Bush reelection committee. Meeting with state delegations, the teams typically included a member of the cabinet or subcabinet, one or two members of Congress, often a governor, and possibly someone from the White House. There were thirty-three such team presentations scheduled. Each team member would review the administration's record within an issue area. A question and answer period followed the presentations. For example, the Nevada delegation heard from EPA administrator William Ruckleshaus on environmental issues, Secretary of Agriculture John Block on farm policy, and New Mexico senator Pete Domenici on budgetary matters; the Illinois delegation heard from Secretary of the Treasury Donald Regan on the deficit and economic growth, Ohio representative Delbert Latta on taxes, and Tennessee governor Lamar Alexander on education. Vice-President George Bush also attended many of these caucuses as a kind of super cheerleader.

The caucuses were also used for state and local purposes. Voter registration and get-out-the-vote drives were topics discussed in most of the caucuses I attended. The Republican leaders of the Ohio delegation used the Dallas setting to level a blast on television at the tax rebate program of the Democratic governor of their state, Richard Celeste. And congressional and other candidates used local radio and television coverage of the convention to advantage. The news-starved media were more obliging than usual.

Sideshows   Those who have attended a national nominating convention are well aware that much more takes place outside than inside the convention hall. Each morning a daily calendar is made available to delegates. Though by no means listing all of the day's events, the schedule does provide a sampling of those events. For example, on Tuesday, August 21, there were eleven press conferences or briefings, two sponsored breakfasts, three sponsored luncheons, twelve state delegation caucuses, thirteen receptions, four appearances by Vice-President Bush, one youth rally, one fund-raising dinner, and five other miscellaneous events. The events are typically sponsored by interest groups, a political party unit, a state delegation, or an ideological group.

Various conservative groups were active in Dallas. Particularly in evidence were: the National Conservative Political Action Committee, Young Americans for Freedom, and a new group—Conservative Opportunity Society. The latter group was led by several junior members of the House of Representatives who had drawn attention to themselves by their use of the televised coverage of the House floor. Georgia representative Newt Gingrich is the best known of this group. He and his colleagues conducted several seminars for the delegates and the press, outlining their conservative philosophy and vision of the future. It is of interest that much of their rhetoric found its way into the platform and even into some of the president's campaign speeches.

Countering the Gingrich group was the Mainstream Committee—led by representative James Leach. This group held press conferences, sponsored receptions, and issued position statements. As noted in one of their press releases: "It is an issue salvo, a philosophical counter-charge, that we are attempting to launch with our activities at this convention." Though hardly a major force at the convention itself, the Mainstream Committee was successful in getting significant press coverage. In fact, Leach was one of the most frequently interviewed persons in Dallas, and countless news articles were written on the future of moderate Republicanism.

Also very much in evidence at the Republican convention was the so-called evangelical right. With the promise of using their pulpits to get Republicans registered and out to vote, ministers found that they had political influence. Led by Reverend Jerry Falwell of Virginia, founder of the Moral Majority, the group had a significant impact on the platform. They also had reason to be pleased with the president's remarks at a prayer breakfast in Dallas in which he stated, "Politics and morality are inseparable—and as morality's foundation is religion, religion and politics are necessarily related. . . . We need religion as a guide."[53] It was evident that the president and his advisers were anxious to do whatever was practical in order to take advantage of the fervor and organizational capability of the religious right.

Convention Floor Proceedings Perhaps among the least interesting events in Dallas were those that were covered by network television—four evenings filled with carefully structured and precisely timed political speeches. The major networks did not cover the morning sessions on Monday and Tuesday. Various party matters were scheduled for that time—including the presentation of selected senatorial, House, and gubernatorial candidates. The RNC Network filmed these sessions, making potentially useful campaign films for the candidates.

There were a few highlights in the evening sessions. The foreign-policy speech by Jeane Kirkpatrick, ambassador to the United Nations, was possibly the outstanding address of the convention. It overshadowed all the other speeches on Monday evening—including those by Tennessee senator Howard Baker and the keynote speaker, Katherine Ortega, treasurer of the United States. The audience response to the Kirkpatrick speech was extraordinary. In part this can be attributed to the fact that hers was the first major speech of the convention, but it must be acknowledged as well that she took advantage of this scheduling to establish certain basic themes for the convention. In particular, her aggressive assertion that the "San Francisco Democrats" had turned their backs on the traditional policies of their own party was to be repeated many times as a prelude to an invitation for Democrats to support Ronald Reagan. Her own political background as a "lifelong Democrat" contributed authenticity to her attack.

The highlight of the Tuesday evening session was a rousing partisan speech by former president Gerald R. Ford. All but a few speeches were cleared by the convention organizers. Ford's was one of those not cleared. Interestingly he was the only major speaker to mention Geraldine Ferraro. The approved pitch was clearly to link Walter Mondale's name with Carter, not Ferraro.

On Wednesday evening the most captivating speech was delivered by a black minister from Los Angeles—Reverend E. V. Hill who stressed reasons why blacks should support Reagan. But the television highlight was an appearance on the podium by Nancy Reagan who charged the convention "to win one more for the Gipper." Reagan and Bush were also nominated and selected as the nominees on Wednesday night.

Reagan and Bush delivered their acceptance speeches on Thursday. Both were introduced by slick movies which the convention managers hoped would be included in the television coverage. They were particularly anxious that the eighteen-minute Reagan film be run. Of the three networks, only NBC carried the film. The president's speech was not among his best performances. Essentially it was a disjointed collection of tried-and-true themes and phrases. But the delegates loved it, despite its length and discursiveness. They had come to Dallas to celebrate Ronald Reagan as president and his appearance before the convention was the principal occasion for demonstrating their support.

It is hard to fault the organizers of the Dallas convention for not producing a more interesting event. Essentially they were in charge of a coronation. Thus it was their job to provide pageantry, not cockfights. Unfortunately there was no way they could sustain audience interest for four days. Thus on Friday those who were there to observe and report on the pageantry, rather than participate in it, gratefully left Dallas, limp from boredom and the suffocating heat. For their part, the delegates left Dallas prepared to do what was necessary to reelect Ronald Reagan. For them, and for the convention managers, the meeting had been a huge success.

Concluding Comments

The renomination of Ronald Reagan in 1984 is a political success story. In retrospect, it is difficult to suggest how it might have been improved—particularly given Reagan's subsequent landslide victory. Throughout the period of decision, presidential posturing, and campaigning, he displayed all the characteristics of the compleat politician. He is a master of his craft. He is successful in getting Americans to identify with him and his efforts to govern. With this success comes a willingness by Americans to forgive mistakes and occasional excesses. Reagan appears to reassure the nation that things are going to be all right, even in the face of evidence to the contrary.

It is interesting to contemplate what Ronald Reagan's political legacy to the Republican party will be. By example, of course, he offers a method that was highly successful. But it is extremely difficult to separate the method from the man. It does seem evident, however, that his presidency has contributed to the strength of the Republican party. The national headquarters is stronger than ever before and many state and local organizations have been strengthened as well. The polls show that more Americans are identifying with the Republican party. And while relations between a president and his congressional party are never totally harmonious, President Reagan has worked closely with congressional Republican party leaders. Finally, one must not overlook money—the "mother's milk of politics." President Reagan has been responsible, either directly or through the party's use of his name, for raising more money than any person in the history of American politics. These funds have, in turn, contributed to building a more permanent Republican party organization throughout the country. What all of this suggests is that even if there is the "bloodletting" that many have predicted for 1988, a party structure will be there afterward to administer transfusions.

Elected Officials and the Politics
of Presidential Selection

THOMAS E. MANN

───No aspect of American presidential selection seems as peculiar to the foreign observer as the relatively insignificant role played by professional politicians. Anthony King, writing on "How Not to Select Presidential Candidates" shortly after the 1980 elections, offered a European view of the American system:

> Underlying both the lack of experience exhibited by recent presidential candidates, and also doubts about whether they have the requisite political skills, is the fact, all but unique to the modern American political system, that the elected officeholders of a party play almost no part in selecting the party's presidential nominee. . . .
>
> In most political systems, these national-level politicians act as a sort of screening device or filter between the political parties and the mass electorate; they provide, in the American jargon, an element of "peer review." This element is entirely missing in the United States today.[1]

In the aftermath of Ronald Reagan's 1980 electoral sweep and the Republican takeover of the Senate for the first time in a quarter century, this European view came to be shared by many Democratic party figures, including some who a decade earlier had succeeded in reforming national politicians out of the process.[2] The landslide defeat of George McGovern, who had used the new rules in 1972 to boost his factional candidacy, and the ineffectiveness in office of Jimmy Carter, who prided himself on his independence from the Democratic party and its officeholders, were seen from the vantage point of 1981 as signs that the party was incapable of winning elections and governing effectively. Although many factors were thought to contribute to this condition, the key factor was generally thought to be the absence of members of

Congress and other influential party officials from the nomination process and the convention.

What followed was the appointment of the fourth in a series of Democratic National Committee (DNC) commissions to revise the rules under which the party's nominee is chosen—this one called the Commission on Presidential Nomination and chaired by Governor James B. Hunt, Jr., of North Carolina. The Hunt Commission recommended a number of changes in the nominating rules that were subsequently adopted by the DNC and implemented in 1984, including a provision that reserved unpledged delegate slots for party leaders and elected officials. The task of this chapter is to trace the development of this rules change, to assess its consequences in 1984, and to explore the role in the presidential-selection process that elected officeholders might be expected to play in the future.

The chapter will begin by recounting how the reforms diminished the presence of elected officials at national Democratic conventions after 1968 and how an earlier attempt to deal with the problem failed. It will then describe the work of the Hunt Commission and the specific objectives the commissioners hoped to achieve by bringing key officials back into the process. Next it will weigh the impact of the rules change in 1984 on the selection of the presidential nominee, the development of the party platform, and the conduct of the national convention, and will contrast the role of Republican elected officeholders with that of the Democrats. The chapter will conclude with some thoughts on the role national politicians are likely to play in the presidential selection process in the years ahead.

The Reform Era

Byron Shafer has accurately described how Democratic party politics between 1968 and 1972 led to "a revolutionary change in the mechanics of presidential selection, the greatest systematically planned and centrally imposed shift in the institutions of delegate selection in all of American history."[3] Proposed by a party commission headed by Senator George McGovern of South Dakota and by Congressman Donald Fraser of Minnesota, new rules designed to promote widespread participation by rank-and-file Democrats, to represent traditionally disadvantaged groups, and to "fairly reflect" the candidate preferences of Democratic voters were adopted by the DNC and implemented in the states. The central consequence of these reforms, Shafer concludes, "was the diminution, the constriction, at times the elimination, of the regular party in the politics of presidential selection."[4]

The full story of the reforms and their consequences has been richly described by Shafer, Nelson Polsby, and Austin Ranney, among others, and will not be retold now.[5] Here, it is sufficient to note that the reforms succeeded, perhaps even beyond their proponents' expectations, in diminishing the influence of elected officials and state and local party leaders, who had dominated national party conventions since the 1830s. The shift from traditional party caucuses to participatory conventions and from delegate primaries, where local luminaries were elected under their own names, to candidate primaries, where the name of the presidential contender was dominant, together with the elimination of ex officio slots for party and public officials, contributed to this end. National politicians were discouraged from running for delegate slots by the requirement that they make an early declaration of preference for a presidential candidate and by the necessity of competing with their own constituents, both of which could lead to political problems for them at home. Moreover, the pressure on states to use at-large slots to balance their delegations demographically made it unlikely that the predominantly white, male elected officials would be appointed at the state level as delegates.

Data presented in 1977 to the DNC Commission on Presidential Nomination and Party Structure, chaired by Morley A. Winograd, confirmed a dramatic decline in the percentage of senators, representatives, and governors attending Democratic national conventions after 1968. The percentage of Democratic senators serving as delegates or alternates dropped from 68 percent in 1968 to 18 percent in 1976. Sharp declines were also experienced by the party's governors (from 83 percent to 47 percent) and House members (from 39 percent to 15 percent).[6]

While some members of the Winograd Commission expressed concern about the absence of the party's major politicians from its national convention, the sentiment underlying the McGovern-Fraser guidelines—that public officials and party leaders be given no preferred position in the delegate-selection process—continued to hold sway in 1977. A proposal to make all Democratic governors, senators, representatives, and state party chairs and vice-chairs automatic voting delegates, unbound by the candidate preferences expressed in their states' primaries or caucuses, was defeated decisively. Instead, the commission approved a provision increasing each state's delegation by 10 percent for party leaders and elected officials, but requiring them to declare their presidential preference and to be elected in accordance with the fair reflection rules.

The 10 percent "add-on" provision did little to restore participation by elected officeholders at the 1980 convention. While gubernatorial participation jumped back to 76 percent (with all of the twenty-three governors elected as part of the 10 percent add-on), congressional participation declined even further.[7] This occurred partly because there were not enough slots to cover the entire congressional delegation. But more important, because the pool of officials from which the 10 percent were to be chosen was so large, members of Congress had to compete for these slots with their party colleagues, and to do so with an early declaration of presidential preference. The disincentives to their participation in the nomination process remained strong.

The Hunt Commission

The Commission on Presidential Nomination was established in July 1981 to take yet another look at the rules and how they were affecting the party's presidential prospects. It was clear from the outset that Governor Hunt gave the highest priority to securing for party professionals and elected officials an enhanced role at the convention.[8] Statements made by DNC chairman Charles Manatt and by Hunt at the press conference announcing the appointment of the commission, interviews given by Hunt, presentations to the commission at its initial meeting, and the charge to the Commission's Technical Advisory Committee (TAC), all reflected the importance Hunt gave to achieving this enhanced role. The case for increasing the participation of elected officials centered on three main arguments.

The first addresses the representativeness of the party's convention. Hunt and others believed that the new dominance of candidate and issue activists had weakened the party's broad mainstream appeal. Evidence that convention delegates were ideologically unrepresentative of Democratic voters was widely available (though the phenomenon of mass-elite differences was neither new nor limited to the Democratic party). Elected officials, responsible to their own constituencies and naturally attuned to the interests of rank-and-file Democrats, could help moderate the image of the party among voters and thereby broaden its electoral appeal. This might be achieved by their simple presence at the convention, by their contributions to the party platform, and by their impact on the selection of a presidential nominee.

Second, elected officials might provide that missing element of peer review, whereby candidates for the presidency are screened by politicians who have dealt with them personally, instead of just observing them on television. Experienced politicians would bring seasoned and sensitive judgment to the selection of a nominee, weighing the requirements of the office, the strengths and weaknesses of the candidates, and the political realities of the November election.

Third, Hunt and others believed that greater participation in the convention by officeholders would create stronger ties between the party and its elected officials, promoting a unified campaign and teamwork in government. Their presence would force the candidates to negotiate before their nomination with the same officials whose support they would need to govern effectively.

These arguments were not persuasive to all members of the Hunt Commission. Opponents of the proposal to reserve unpledged delegate slots for party and elected officials argued that it would dilute popular preferences, damage the legitimacy of the process in a closely contested nomination fight, destroy the equal division (between men and women) and affirmative action guidelines of the party, create a separate and powerful class of delegates, and even threaten the separation of powers principle in American politics by making presidents dependent upon members of Congress for their nomination. The perspective of these critics was that automatic uncommitted delegates would become a powerful counterforce to the open and participatory system then in place.

Other, less vocal critics viewed the proposed change from just the opposite vantage point—that the new delegates would not be sufficiently strong and independent to alter the existing scheme. "Ex officio delegates . . . not so much introduced into the process of presidential selection as tacked onto the end . . . are not as likely to shape the course of presidential politics as they are to affirm its outcome. Only intransigent participants would overthrow an evolving consensus on the emerging winner at the final moment; party and public office-holders are the least likely aspirants for the role of intransigent." [9]

Of course, Hunt's success in achieving his primary goal was determined as much by the composition of the commission and the short-term political calculations of its members as the persuasiveness of these arguments. The seventy-member commission included four major voting blocs—the state parties, labor, loyalists of former vice-president Walter Mondale, and those of Senator Edward Kennedy—whose negotiations with Hunt and several other key figures shaped the compromise proposals ultimately approved by the commission. [10] The Kennedy bloc was the only one of the four at the outset of the commission's work to oppose uncommitted delegate status for elected officials. Representatives of the state chairs and labor each separately testified in favor of setting aside at least 30 percent of convention seats for uncommitted elected and party officials. Mondale representatives, believing that elected officials would most likely favor their candidate ("We aren't sure that it's true, but we certainly aren't going to act like we don't *think* they'll be with us!") [11], agreed to support whatever proposal Hunt endorsed.

Democratic members of Congress also pressed their case for uncommitted status with the commission. Senate Democratic whip Alan Cranston and House Democratic Caucus chairman Gillis Long both testified on behalf of unpledged delegate slots for elected officials. Long reported that the caucus had adopted a resolution asking "that at least two-thirds of the Democratic members of the House, upon election by our caucus, become uncommitted, voting delegates" to the 1984 convention. [12]

Controversy centered on the size of the uncommitted bloc, the method of appointment (whether congressional delegates would be appointed by their state parties or elected by House and Senate caucuses), and the applicability of equal division to the uncommitted bloc. At the end, a compromise proposal was crafted by Congresswoman Geraldine Ferraro, a member of the commission and secretary of the House Democratic Caucus, and TAC co-chairman Mark Siegel. It was revised in two important respects by party chairman Charles Manatt and was agreed to by the major blocs and adopted by the commission.

A total of 568 delegate slots (14.4 percent of the convention) were allocated for unpledged party and elected officials, who became known as "superdelegates." Two positions for each state were reserved for its party chair and vice-chair. The House and Senate caucuses would elect up to three-fifths of their members as delegates. The balance of the unpledged delegates would be chosen by the state parties, with priority given to governors and large city mayors. Another 305 delegate slots (corresponding to the 10 percent add-on initially approved by the Winograd Commission) were allocated for pledged party and elected officials, and state parties were allowed to set up later and less formal procedures for pledging and for candidate approval for these delegate positions.

In adopting these provisions and in promoting its larger goal of party renewal, the commission nonetheless felt obliged to stress its "determination to preserve the gains made in recent years in broadening participation and maintaining a fair and open process." No mere "tinkering" with the party rules, but "no wholesale departures from the rules-writing efforts of the past."[13] What are the likely consequences of this balanced effort to preserve the major thrust of the reform era but also to bring elected and party officials more effectively into the nomination process? The 1984 election provides the first bits of evidence.

The Democratic Nomination

Walter Mondale captured 2,191 votes (55 percent of the total) on the first ballot at the Democratic national convention in San Francisco, 224 more than the number needed to secure the nomination. The final CBS News survey of delegates completed before the convention revealed the following first ballot support among pledged delegates and unpledged party and elected officials:[14]

	Pledged	Unpledged	Total
Mondale	1,708	384	2,092
Hart	1,198	58	1,256
Jackson	364	25	389
Uncommitted or other	95	101	196

It is perfectly clear from these figures that the unpledged delegates overwhelmingly supported Mondale leading most observers to attribute his margin of victory to them. It would be a mistake, however, to infer that Mondale's success can be attributed solely or even primarily to the support he enjoyed among elected and party officials. These same figures show that Mondale went into the convention with 51 percent of the pledged delegates in his camp, compared with only 36 percent committed to Senator Gary Hart. By this reckoning, Mondale would have captured the nomination even without the rules change establishing unpledged delegate slots for Democratic officeholders. His victory stemmed more from his ability to build a substantial delegate lead in the primaries and caucuses. In this instance, another important set of Hunt Commission recommendations worked to Mondale's benefit.

Although in 1980 delegates were allocated almost entirely by proportional representation to "fairly reflect" candidate strength in primaries and caucuses, the 1984 rules permitted: the direct election of delegates at the district level (labeled by critics a "loophole" primary, because it allows a candidate to win all of the delegates in a district with only a plurality of the vote); a bonus delegate system, in which the winner of each district's primary or caucus is awarded one extra delegate; and thresholds ranging as high as 30 percent that candidates had to reach to win delegates.

On the one hand, Mondale's primary victories were concentrated in states with direct-election systems (Illinois, Maryland, New Jersey, Pennsylvania, and West Virginia) or bonus delegate systems (Georgia, New York, North Carolina, and Puerto Rico). Hart, on the other hand, won only one direct-election primary (California) and one bonus primary (Ohio), with fourteen of his victories in states with proportional representation or nonbinding primaries. As a consequence, Mondale won 49 percent of the pledged delegates in primary states with only 39 percent of the vote. Hart's 36 percent of the primary vote garnered him 36 percent of the delegates. And Jesse Jackson's 18 percent of the vote in primary states netted him just 10 percent of the delegates.[15]

Mondale also fared well in caucus states, where he built a 175-delegate lead over Hart by winning the six largest—Texas, Michigan, Minnesota, Missouri, Virginia and Wisconsin.[16] While Hart won more states than Mondale, his. caucus victories, like his primary victories, were concentrated in states whose small size and Republican voting tendencies in general elections produced a small number of delegates.

To emphasize the critical importance of Mondale's showing in the large states, particularly in the industrial frost belt, is not to deny that the unpledged delegates made a significant indirect contribution to his nomination. The appointment and commitment of the unpledged delegates were key factors at several stages in the 1984 nominating struggle. This can be seen by looking more closely at the 568 unpledged delegates—who they were, when and how

Table 4.1 Public and party officeholders serving as unpledged delegates at the 1984 Democratic National Convention

Position	Number
Public Office	(411)
U.S. Senator	27
U.S. Representative	175
Governor	24
Lieutenant governor	8
Attorney general	11
State legislator	71
Other state office	37
Mayor	30
Other local office	28
Party office[a]	(157)
State chair	57
State vice-chair	57
Other party office	43
Total	568

Source: CBS News.

[a] Those who held both public and party office are included only in the public office totals.

they were selected, which presidential candidate they committed themselves to, and when they did so.

Table 4.1 lists the number of public and party officials who served as unpledged delegates at the 1984 Democratic convention. Over a third of the delegates were members of Congress, one in five was a state-party chair or vice-chair, and the rest were mostly elected state and local government officials.

The delegate selection rules for the 1984 Democratic National Convention provided for three modes of selection for the unpledged delegates: (1) a certification by each state Democratic party of its chair and vice-chair; (2) election on or before May 1, 1984, by the House Democratic Caucus and by the Senate Democratic Conference of up to three-fifths of their respective memberships; and (3) selection of the balance of the party and elected officials by a state party organization (convention, committee of district-level delegates, or state Democratic committee) after that state's presidential primary or caucus. Another party rule specifying that no delegate-selection events be held before the second Tuesday in March (with exceptions for Iowa and New Hampshire) was not explicitly applied to the unpledged delegates, and the House Democratic Caucus reacted by scheduling the election of its delegation during the week of January 23, more than three weeks before the Iowa caucuses.

Although the rationale for the early selection of the House delegates was to allow members who failed to be elected by the caucus sufficient time to seek election in their respective states, its actual consequence was to provide Mondale with an early delegate lead that helped cushion his jarring losses to Gary Hart in the New Hampshire primary and in the primaries and caucuses that immediately followed.

Early in 1983 the Mondale campaign recognized the opportunity presented by the election of unpledged delegates from the Congress, both as an early test of Mondale's strength and as one of the largest delegate pools up for grabs. With a team of twenty volunteer lobbyists, Mondale campaign adviser Richard Moe led a yearlong effort to win commitments from House members. Mondale was able to build on personal friendships with House members, his reputation as a mainstream Democrat whose centrist positions and strong organization would help (or at least not hurt) other Democratic candidates in November, and the perception that he was the frontrunner and might wrap up the nomination early in the primary season.

Senator John Glenn also waged a serious drive for support among House members, enlisting Washington lobbyist Thomas H. Boggs, Jr., to lead the effort. His late start, more limited personal ties, and less than impressive performance in a presentation to the House Democratic Caucus, however, left him far behind Mondale. Candidates Hart, Alan Cranston, and Ernest Hollings largely conceded the contest to Mondale. On January 25, 1984, 110 delegates were nominated in twelve regional caucuses, by lottery, seniority, or presidential preference. The next day the Democratic Steering and Policy Committee named 54 at-large delegates, including 7 House leaders and substantial numbers of women and minorities. The preferences of these 164 delegates, who were ratified by the full Democratic Caucus on February 1, were recorded in an unofficial tally as follows:[17]

Mondale	70
Glenn	19
Cranston	13
Jackson	8
Hart	5
Askew	4
Hollings	3
Uncommitted	42

Although the House delegates were technically uncommitted and able to change their minds at any time, their public expressions of support were included in the widely publicized delegate counts that constitute a key barometer of candidate strength. And Mondale's continuing delegate lead between the New Hampshire primary and the March 13 "Super Tuesday," when he suffered numerous primary and caucus setbacks and saw his commanding margin in the national polls evaporate, helped sustain his faltering campaign. As one Democratic party campaign official put it: "I don't think Mondale would have survived if he had not had the super delegates. . . . They were one of his anchors at a time he was close to adrift. They allowed him to keep his credibility and his frontrunner status."[18] Richard Moe reached a similar conclusion: "The Congressional base sustained us in shaky times. . . . There's no question it helped us survive."[19]

The key point, however, is that Mondale's support among House Democrats could not have kept his candidacy afloat had he failed to salvage "Super Tuesday" primary victories in Alabama and Georgia. Mondale aides have acknowledged that their candidate was prepared to withdraw from the contest had Hart won a clean sweep on March 13. One might even make a case that Mondale's overwhelming endorsement by his party's officeholders was a double-edged sword: it raised expectations for Mondale's performance, thus further setting the stage for New Hampshire and emphasizing the drop-off thereafter, and it contributed to his difficulties with New Hampshire voters by reinforcing his campaign's tendency to play it safe and Mondale's reputation as the establishment candidate. Certainly, Mondale was helped by two factors unrelated to his support among House Democrats: the two-week break between New Hampshire and "Super Tuesday," which gave him time to marshal his resources and launch a counterattack on Hart,[20] and Hart's failure to file a full slate of delegates in the Florida primary, which gave Mondale a sizable delegate victory in spite of his loss to Hart in the nonbinding preference primary.

What one can safely conclude is that Mondale's candidacy came very close to ending in the first two weeks of March and that the early selection of delegates from the House Democratic Caucus, formally unpledged but publicly committed to Mondale, contributed however modestly to his ability to carry on to the Michigan caucuses and Illinois primary.

During the months following the election of delegates from the House Democratic Caucus, including the period immediately after the New Hampshire primary when his candidacy seemed on the verge of collapse, Mondale's strength among the House delegates continued to grow. When Cranston, Hollings, Askew, and Glenn withdrew from the race, their congressional supporters moved disproportionately to Mondale. On the eve of the final round of primaries, there were ninety House delegates supporting Mondale, nine behind Hart, seven backing Jackson, and fifty-eight who were publicly uncommitted.[21]

Mondale's tepid performance in these June 5 primaries (losing three of five states and a net of thirty delegates to Hart), was brightened by his ability to claim the 1,967 delegates needed for the nomination, and that was made possible only after a frantic drive to enlist the support of unpledged delegates. Among the prominent new converts announced by the Mondale campaign the day after the June 5 primary was Representative Gillis Long, chairman of the House Democratic Caucus. Long, Speaker Thomas P. O'Neill, Jr., and Majority Leader Jim Wright all declared Mondale the winner and urged that the party close ranks behind him. Soon thereafter, Mondale's public supporters in the House numbered 106.

Mondale's final drive for delegates was not limited to the House delegation. He also sought the Senate Democratic Conference's twenty-five delegates, who were elected on March 20 (a late date designed to placate fellow senator Hart who had objected to the House's early delegate selection). Although the number of these delegates was small, Mondale valued their prominence. Nine of the Senate delegates initially supported Mondale, two favored Hart. After the final round of primaries, the number of Mondale supporters grew to fifteen.[22]

The bulk of the unpledged delegates were not in Washington, but in the fifty states and in the territories. Mondale's final drive for a majority of delegates at the close of the primary season was successful because his support among state and local elected and party officials was as lopsided as it was among his former colleagues in the Congress. For example, of the 114 state party chairs and vice-chairs, 81 supported Mondale, 13 Hart, 1 Jackson, and 19 remained uncommitted one week before the convention.[23] Even in the states in which he won primary or first-tier caucuses, Hart attracted the allegiance of only five state chairs compared with eleven for Mondale and ten uncommitted. Similarly, only two of the thirty governors who served as delegates at the Democratic convention (twenty-four as unpledged delegates) supported Hart, while eighteen were identified with Mondale as the convention opened. From the early lead in the delegate count provided by the House Democrats to the last commitments from state party and elected officials needed to secure a bare majority of delegates, Mondale enjoyed unswerving support from the new class of unpledged delegates.

In the aftermath of Mondale's crushing defeat in the November election, some of his supporters on Capitol Hill began to have second thoughts about the early support they gave to his candidacy. By committing themselves early to Mondale, they felt that they had lost their opportunity to respond effectively to the concerns about Mondale and the traditional Democratic party registered by voters throughout the primary season. They would have increased their influence over the party by remaining uncommitted until they reached the convention. Others responded that the elected officials had acted as the Hunt Commission had intended—they supported a mainstream candidate who they knew personally to be qualified for the presidency. In either case, by inaction or action, the unpledged delegates played a significant role in the 1984 Democratic presidential nomination.

The Democratic Platform

As discussed earlier, the Hunt Commission's interests were not limited to the selection of the presidential nominee, but extended to the development of the party's platform. Party officials hoped to avoid a repeat of the 1980 platform process, in which delegates committed to Senator Edward Kennedy and disgruntled Carter issue activists collaborated to deal President Carter a series of political embarrassments and saddle him with a platform not well suited to the fall campaign. Michael Malbin has described how the new delegate selection rules reduced the influence of elected officials and increased the leverage of issue groups, leading to platforms that were both "more explicit and more extreme."[24] Malbin made clear that the 1980 platform process was shaped decisively by Carter's special vulnerability among Democrats and most importantly by Kennedy's decision to continue contesting the nomination after his defeat was all but sealed. But his analysis also suggested more fundamental problems with the process, problems that some Democrats thought might be corrected by the involvement of more elected officials.

Although the Hunt Commission proposed no specific remedy, the creation of the new bloc of unpledged delegates was thought relevant to the platform process in two key respects: It would ensure increased representation of elected officials on the Platform Committee (only four members of Congress had served on the 158-member 1980 committee) and it would alter the climate that had in recent years discouraged major public figures from taking an active role in putting the platform together. More public officials, especially members of Congress, should in turn mean a moderate platform geared to the needs of campaigning and governing, the quest for party unity, and the avoidance of actions at the convention that might weaken the party's nominee.

A superficial recounting of the highlights of the 1984 Democratic platform process supports the view that these hopes were largely realized. First, elected officials did assume a more prominent role. The final call for the 1984 Democratic convention provided for the appointment of twenty-five party leaders and elected officials to the Platform Committee (14 percent of its membership). Twelve members of Congress served on the committee, including its chair, congresswoman Geraldine Ferraro. Five of the fifteen members of the drafting committee were from the Congress, and critical negotiations on the draft platform were conducted by Congressman Michael Barnes (representing Mondale), Congressman Timothy Wirth and Senator Christopher Dodd (representing Hart), and Delegate Walter Fauntroy (representing Jackson). They worked from a staff draft that drew heavily on the House Democratic Caucus report, "Renewing America's Promise: A Democratic Blueprint for Our Nation's Future." Ferraro actively solicited the views of her colleagues in Congress and well over fifty members of Congress testified before the committee, many for the first time. The reaction of Senator Patrick J. Leahy was not atypical: "This is the first time, in the 10 years I've been in the Senate, that anyone has seemed at all interested in what members of Congress were thinking about in the platform." In the past, Leahy said, "I had no idea what was in the platform, nor did I care. The party also didn't care what I thought. This year it's entirely different, and there's an effort to get elected officials involved. There's a general realization that we're in this together." [25]

Second, the platform was developed without the rancorous debate that in 1980 continued from the platform committee to the convention floor. Although Mondale forces controlled eight of the fifteen seats on the drafting committee and a clear majority on the full committee, compromise was the much more typical response to differences among the candidates than divided votes. Much of the language proposed by the Hart campaign as an alternative to the committee staff draft was accepted by the drafting committee, leading Hart representatives to embrace the final document with an obvious pride of authorship. Ferraro and other close observers of the drafting committee concluded that its work was helped considerably by the fact that Hart representatives Wirth and Dodd knew and trusted chief Mondale spokesman Michael Barnes, their colleague in the Congress (although one key Mondale staffer privately criticized Wirth for making the negotiations more difficult by being less willing to compromise than Hart).

Only five minority reports were filed after the full platform committee completed its work, compared with twenty-three in 1980, and four of these were Jackson planks that surfaced only after the Mondale camp provided the necessary signatures. At the convention a compromise was reached on an affirmative action plank, leading to its adoption by a voice vote, and Mondale forces dropped their opposition to the Hart language on military force restrictions. The convention overwhelmingly rejected the Jackson planks on runoff primaries, "no first use" of nuclear weapons, and a defense-spending cut, and Mondale emerged from the platform skirmish with the image of a nominee fully in control of the convention and presiding over a reasonably united Democratic party.

Finally, the party appeared to succeed in writing a platform that was "less explicit and less extreme" than in 1980. Determined to avoid a repetition of 1980, Ferraro announced at the outset of the committee's work her goal of producing a "thematic" platform that emphasized Democratic principles and objectives and avoided specific legislative proposals. Ferraro and her staff were sensitive to the charge that the party and its likely nominee were too beholden to special interest groups. Thus, they sought to unify the party not by accommodating every particular interest but rather by first criticizing the Reagan record and then outlining a broad Democratic alternative in three broad areas: "Jobs, Economic Growth, and Prosperity," "Justice," and "Peace and Security."

Although Ferraro's goal of a lean document "that can be read in one day" [26] eluded the committee as the fifty-six page staff proposal doubled in size by the end of the drafting process, drafters succeeded in avoiding mention of specific pieces of legislation by name and in taking a more fiscally responsible economic stance. Press accounts stressed that the platform made far fewer commitments to sweeping social programs and was considerably more conservative than those adopted by the party in recent years. [27]

This reconstruction of events leading to the 1984 platform exaggerates both the centrality of elected officials to the process and the degree to which the platform differs in character from its recent predecessor. The relative harmony of the platform process in 1984 compared with 1980 was due largely to the altered political context. In 1980 Jimmy Carter's renomination, while never seriously in doubt, was not ensured until he won a fight on the rule binding delegates' votes on the nomination. [28] Carter's low standing in the polls, his lack of enthusiastic supporters within the Democratic party, and his more conservative fiscal policies made him especially vulnerable to Kennedy's decision to press his candidacy on the basis of his domestic-policy differences with the administration.

In 1984 the presumptive nominee, Walter Mondale, was "Mr. Democrat," not, like Carter, an outsider within his own party. The Reagan presidency had left the Democrats less ideologically divided and more inclined to do what was necessary to regain the presidency. While Hart, like Kennedy in 1980, continued to contest the nomination after his opponent claimed a majority of the delegates, his challenge had no concrete focus comparable to the 1980 "open convention" fight. He also had serious aspirations for the vice-presidential nomination. Moreover, Mondale could accommodate Hart's substantive interests in the platform without harming—indeed very likely even helping— his fall campaign.

What Carter in 1980 and Mondale in 1984 had in common was a desperate need, after a bruising and protracted nomination struggle, to unify their party at the convention and launch their fall campaign. The differences in their situations made the platform a nightmare for Carter in 1980 but an opportunity for reconciliation among Democrats in 1984.

The Mondale campaign seized that opportunity and directed its supporters on the drafting committee and the full platform committee to accept the bulk of Hart's language and to make much more limited concessions to Jackson. While certain elected officials were involved in these negotiations, they were not the major brokers. The shots were called by the candidates, based on their own calculations of political benefit. Geraldine Ferraro presided over the platform; she did not direct it. At most, members of Congress reinforced the spirit of compromise struck initially by the candidates. Had the context been different, like that of 1980, it is difficult to believe that the modest increase in the number of elected officials involved in the platform could have prevented a more divisive process or a more troublesome product.

It is also easy to overstate the success of the Democrats in 1984 in resisting the importunings of issue groups and in crafting a platform with broad political appeal. There were clear limits to a "thematic" document. Feminists reacted sharply to a suggestion by Ferraro that the platform might call for equal rights for women without endorsing the Equal Rights Amendment and extracted within hours a firm pledge regarding the ERA. Gay rights activists succeeded in adding new language on legal rights for homosexuals in employment, immigration, and the military. Environmentalists hailed their success in strengthening the platform's acid rain plank. Among the interest groups that successfully lobbied for inclusion of a favored paragraph were Japanese-Americans, single homemakers, federal employees, American Indians, illegal aliens, black colleges, and victims of sickle-cell anemia.

In their effort to unify the party, the Mondale forces chose to avoid controversy by accepting many of the proposals advanced by issue groups. The format of the platform, with its attack on President Reagan and its avoidance of specific legislative proposals, and the harmony with which the public negotiations were conducted, combined to create an impression that the party had broken with its past practice of making countless promises to special interest groups. In fact, the platform contained more detailed promises to groups than party officials or candidates desired. These additions were not widely reported in the press, however, and caused Mondale and the party little political damage.

Elected officials also appear to have had little success in crafting national security planks with broad political appeal. The foreign and defense policy section was perceived by those identified with Senator Henry Jackson's wing of the Democratic party as far to the left of the party mainstream. While the Mondale campaign rejected several proposals submitted by allies of Jesse Jackson—defense spending cuts and a Palestinian state—a rough consensus among the candidates was achieved by blaming President Reagan for most of the world's ills and avoiding any of the hawkish rhetoric preferred by the party's right wing.

This part of the Democratic platform was the focus of UN ambassador Jeane J. Kirkpatrick's well-publicized speech to the Republican National Convention in Dallas.[30] Kirkpatrick repeatedly referred to "the San Francisco Democrats" in charging that the Democratic party had abandoned the strong national defense tradition of Franklin Roosevelt, Harry Truman, and John

Kennedy and had instead taken to "blaming America first" for problems in world politics.

The foreign policy posture of the Democratic platform was dictated partly by perceptions of Reagan's political vulnerability on arms control and Central America. In this context, significant pressure from strong-defense advocates in the party may not have produced a very different stance. The more active involvement of elected officials in 1984, however, failed to generate any such pressure for a less dovish foreign policy stance. Only an occasional demurral from Mondale delegate Senator Daniel P. Moynihan raised such views on the drafting committee ("Do we really want to halt 'all' military exercises in Central America and the Caribbean? We've been doing this since Thomas Jefferson."[31]) With those candidates representing a strong-defense posture (Askew, Glenn, and Hollings) dropping out of the race, the platform process was dominated by candidates and issue groups whose views on foreign policy did not encompass the range that existed among rank-and-file Democrats. Like other delegates, the elected officials acted largely on behalf of the presidential candidates still in the race.

The Democratic Convention

The architects of the rules change providing unpledged delegate status for party leaders and elected officials expected their presence at the convention to have beneficial effects on the party beyond their role in selecting the nominees and shaping the platform. Since national party conventions in the modern era have come to ratify rather than select the nominee, the most important business of the convention is launching the general election campaign. The impressions a party and its presidential nominee make on the public through television coverage of its convention can boost a candidacy or damage it, and parties have every incentive to orchestrate the proceedings for public consumption. Elected and party officials, more than issue activists and enthusiasts of losing candidates, could be expected to place a high priority on unifying the party and showing it in the most favorable light on national television.

Walter Mondale, in spite of formidable obstacles, succeeded in using the 1984 Democratic convention to showcase a unified party rallying behind its national ticket and with its sights trained on Ronald Reagan. What accounted for this Democratic success? Did the presence of many major Democratic officeholders contribute in any significant way to the success?

In no sense was a unified convention foreordained. Mondale faced serious problems in the weeks after he claimed the nomination. Gary Hart and Jesse Jackson both vowed to stay in the race and indicated they would pursue their candidacies through the convention's platform, rules and credentials committees. The Hart campaign weighed a possible challenge to six hundred Mondale delegates who were elected with the help of money from independent Mondale delegate committees (the so-called tainted delegates), while Jackson pressed his claim that the delegate selection rules should be changed to award him his proportional share of the delegates.

At the same time numerous interest groups within the Democratic coalition began to position themselves for the San Francisco convention.[32] At its June 30 annual convention, the National Organization of Women confronted Mondale with a demand for a female running mate and hinted at the possibility of a floor fight on the issue. The gay and lesbian lobby sensed a unique opportunity to pitch its political agenda in the host city, with its large homosexual population. The group announced a large gay parade and rally for Sunday, July 15, the day before the opening of the convention, as well as an ambitious set of proposals for the platform and party charter. The labor movement, in a similar effort to demonstrate its political clout and attract media attention, scheduled a rally for the same day. Hispanic groups announced plans to stage protests in opposition to immigration legislation pending in the Congress. Environmental and peace groups made plans for a visible and active presence in San Francisco.

Mondale's prospects for the convention were further clouded by the ideological makeup of the delegates. While on the eve of the convention not a single delegate pledged to Mondale said he or she would fail to vote for him on the first ballot (in spite of the much-discussed elimination of the harsh 1980 binding rule), their loyalty to Mondale on other convention issues was less certain.[33] The delegates were, as in other recent Democratic conventions, a decidedly liberal group. Only 4 percent called themselves conservatives, compared with one-quarter of all registered Democrats. Almost three-quarters of the delegates favored a military withdrawal from Central America and a plurality agreed with Jackson's call for the elimination of runoff primaries, issues on which minority platform planks would be brought to a vote.

Finally, Mondale approached the convention with an aura of pessimism around his candidacy. His long and often bitter battle with Hart and Jackson had left him bloodied—perceived as a captive of special interests, caught in the middle of passionate disputes between blacks and Jews, unable to shed his reputation as a political journeyman tied to the past.

The Mondale campaign, believing that their success in the general election depended upon a fully successful national party convention—a 1976-style convention rather than 1972 or 1980—made a series of moves in the weeks before the convention to improve prospects for its success. Mondale moved quickly at the end of the primary season to claim the necessary support for the nomination and to create a sense of finality about it. As noted earlier, support from elected and party officials was central to that effort. He also directed the conciliatory platform-drafting process, and, as outlined above, members of Congress played an important, though not determinative, part in that process. Two additional actions taken by the Mondale camp were vital to the success of the convention—averting a credentials challenge by Hart and Jackson and choosing Geraldine Ferraro as the vice-presidential nominee.

Hart ended his threatened challenge to the Mondale delegates he claimed were "tainted" in return for Mondale's agreement to Hart's "democracy package" of changes in the delegate selection rules. The agreement was hammered out in five days of intensive negotiations between Mondale and Hart staff members and finally resolved with the intercession of Senator Edward Kennedy, who used his late endorsement of Mondale to promote a public reconciliation between the two leading contenders. Hart's decision not to challenge the credentials of any delegates to the 1984 convention effectively killed Jackson's campaign to claim his proportional share of the delegates, since he could not muster the 25 percent support in committee needed to bring a minority report to the floor. Although neither Hart nor Jackson formally withdrew from the contest (Hart indicated he would continue a low-key campaign that focused its fire on President Reagan, not Mondale), the agreement between Mondale and Hart virtually guaranteed that Mondale's nomination would not be marred by a major brawl over the rules. Mondale aide Tom Donilon, after concluding the marathon talks, said the unity agreement meant the convention floor would "be clear to do what we wanted to do on television and that was our main goal."[34]

While the Mondale camp was elated with the deal it had struck, many of Mondale's representatives on the Rules Committee were appalled by the concessions he had made to secure the agreement. The Hart package called on the Rules Committee to establish a new commission and mandate that it make a number of specific changes in the rules for 1988, including: cutting the number of unpledged party and elected-official delegates in half and requiring that they be selected after the primary and caucus season begins; reducing the thresholds, the percentage of popular votes candidates must have before being awarded any delegates; and prohibiting direct election and bonus delegate plans during the first half of the primary season. The proposed changes reflected the views of key Hart staffers John M. Quinn and Carol Casey, both prominent activists within the party's reform movement and outspoken opponents of the Hunt Commission recommendations, and addressed every aspect of the rules that in 1984 worked to Mondale's advantage.

Mondale's willingness to throw away the key elements of the Hunt revisions demonstrated how "the fundamental rules of the game have fallen hostage to the shortest-run calculations of temporary candidates."[35] Vocal opposition by Democratic public officials, state party chairs and spokesmen for organized labor forced the Mondale camp to renegotiate the terms of the agreement, an effort actually facilitated by the Jackson supporters on the Rules Committee, who hoped to make even more drastic changes in the rules. In the end Hart's "mandates" were changed to "recommendations" by modifying the language to read that the commission "should" rather than "shall" make the revisions proposed by Hart. Nonetheless, the resolution adopted by the Rules Committee retained the proviso, "It is the sense of the Convention that the provisions described below in the form of recommendations would be improvements over the present delegate-selection process, and, as such, the direction of those recommendations should not be reversed."[36] Moreover, the new Fairness Commission was given a double mandate, including a review and revision of the rules urged by Jesse Jackson "in an effort to establish equitable rules as they relate to the full participation in the party process of Blacks, Hispanics, Asian/ Pacifics, Native Americans, women, persons of all sexual preference and other members of the Rainbow Coalition."[37] Jackson's language directs the commission to consider eliminating caucuses, thresholds, direct election of delegates, bonus delegate plans, and unpledged official delegates.

Opponents of the call for a new rules commission failed to kill the agreement or even to reshape its substantive thrust. They did succeed in keeping the issue open, however, ensuring themselves an opportunity to do battle with the proposed changes in the future. The composition and mandate of the Fairness Commission became a major focus of attention for elected and party officials at the convention and in the weeks following the November election.

While Mondale's concession to Hart and Jackson on party rules headed off any possible convention dispute over credentials, his selection of Geraldine Ferraro as his running mate set the stage for an emotional outpouring of support for the ticket in San Francisco. Whatever the doubts about Ferraro's ability to help the ticket in the general election (she was, after all, a liberal, three-term member of Congress with no national campaign experience), her nomination rekindled the fires of hope for the Democrats in the fall campaign, created a sense of excitement among the delegates about the historic significance of the convention, and took the edge off those groups and individuals pressing their own agendas. The Ferraro nomination made it extremely difficult for the losing candidates and activist groups to act in ways that would embarrass the ticket.

On the eve of the convention the stage was set for a nationally televised display of a united and energized Democratic party. Whether or not Mondale paid too great a price to achieve that appearance of unity, in his concessions on the platform and rules, with his high-risk choice of a running mate, Mondale himself made the significant moves. The new rule providing for a vastly increased role for members of Congress and other officeholders had a bearing on Mondale's actions—Ferraro's rapid rise was directly tied to the effort to bring major politicians back into the nominating process and her candidacy was pushed by House Speaker Thomas P. O'Neill—but the contribution of these officials to the success of the convention was clearly secondary to the nominee's contribution.

However carefully scripted in advance, a convention can always take unanticipated and unwanted turns. The unpledged delegates were expected to play a stabilizing role at the convention, dealing with any emergencies that might arise, dampening conflicts before they damaged the party and its nominee, trying to keep public attention focused on the central purpose of the convention—the successful launching of the general election campaign. Those expectations were largely met at the Democratic convention in San Francisco.

The composition of the unpledged delegate bloc made them likely candidates to assume this stabilizing role at the convention. As a group of prominent national and state politicians, they were older, more experienced in party affairs, more moderate, and more loyal to the party than the delegates chosen by primaries and caucuses.[38] For example, 85 percent of the unpledged delegates said they supported the party every year, no matter which candidates were running, as against two-thirds of the pledged delegates.

No sooner had the delegates begun arriving in San Francisco than the politicians were called upon to put out a fire. In a move widely criticized by his own supporters as well as everyone else, Mondale asked Charles Manatt to step aside as chairman of the Democratic National Committee (DNC) and signaled that his replacement would be Georgia State Chairman Bert Lance, who had resigned under fire as director of the Office of Management and Budget in the Carter administration. The plan to depose Manatt was not without precedent in the Democratic party, in which presidential nominees traditionally call the shots on key personnel. But Mondale failed to consult with his key allies, his opponents, or party officials; embarrassed Manatt, who had brought the convention to his home state and was scheduled to preside at its opening session; made the mistake of selecting Lance, whose popularity among Southern party officials was clearly overestimated. Thereby, he created a flap that diverted attention from the Ferraro nomination and called into question the readiness of the Mondale camp for the fall campaign.

Members of Congress and state party officials played constructive roles in containing the damage and resolving the crisis. House Speaker O'Neill, who weeks earlier had urged Mondale to keep Manatt through the election, sent word to the principals that the issue had to be settled immediately. Representative Tony Coelho, chairman of the Democratic Congressional Campaign Committee, held a series of meetings with Manatt, Lance, and Mondale aides that ultimately led to a compromise. Lance was named as general chairman of the Mondale campaign, Manatt retained his position as DNC chairman, and key Mondale staffer Michael Berman was installed as DNC director. Coelho then put the best possible face on the agreement: "Mondale, as the nominee, wanted to set the overall political direction of the party. He's done that. The only thing that's changed is some titles . . . No one lost. Mondale won."[39] In statements to the press other elected officials did what they could to minimize the importance of the Lance-Manatt affair and turn attention back to the Mondale-Ferraro ticket and the case against Reagan.

When House delegates gathered Monday morning in the only scheduled caucus of the unpledged contingent, they heard House Majority Leader Jim Wright outline two major responsibilities of elected officials at the convention—to work within the state delegations to avoid distractions from the main purpose of the convention and to convey to the public upbeat themes for the general election. He reminded the delegates, "We can get more press this week than we can all year." Wright's admonition to his House colleagues outlined the two most significant activities of Democratic officeholders at the convention. All of the unpledged delegates, including those elected by the House caucus and the Senate conference, sat with their state delegations and had an opportunity to play a moderating role in delegation meetings. Moreover, as the most prominent members of the state delegations, they were able to shape the press coverage of the convention back home, conveying images in interviews with local media of a moderate party ready to do battle with the Republicans in the fall campaign.

This does not mean that all of the unpledged delegates actively carried out Wright's charge within their delegations. As a diverse group of politicians, they pursued many agendas during the convention. Representative Edward R. Roybal worked with Hispanic delegates to pressure House leaders to oppose the Simpson-Mazzoli immigration bill and to extract from Mondale a promise to work vigorously against the measure. And much of Representative Norm Mineta's time at the convention was consumed by his chairmanship of the Asian-Pacific caucus. Yet when the Hispanic and Asian-American delegates proposed a boycott of the presidential-nominating ballot, none of the Asian or Hispanic members of Congress at the convention went along with it, and, one of Hart's leading Hispanic supporters, Denver mayor Federico Pena, after initially backing the boycott, changed his mind. In the end the boycott fizzled as only 40 of the 361 Hispanic and Asian delegates abstained.[40]

Congressman Ted Weiss spoke from the podium in support of the minority plank on the "no first use" of nuclear weapons, in spite of his strong support of the Mondale-Ferraro ticket, while Congressman Ron Dellums vigorously endorsed the minority report on cutting defense spending. Several members of Congress were involved in negotiations during the convention to extract further platform concessions from Mondale. In this respect, and in others, some of the officeholders worked to push the party to the left.

More typically, members of Congress used the opportunity to raise campaign money, meet with lobbyists, mend fences with state and local party leaders and activists, and publicize their own candidacies through interviews with local television stations. Many were indifferent attenders—they thought the convention was boring and pointless. Enough of the members were sufficiently distracted from the main business of the convention that House leaders felt obliged to deliver a letter to each of them noting the large number of absences among the unpledged delegates for the platform votes and urging attendance during that evening's votes on the nomination. Had the need arisen, House leaders were prepared to put in place a whip system among members on the convention floor. Members of Congress would have almost certainly played a more central role if the convention had taken an unexpected turn.

As it was, the nationally televised portion of the convention went according to Mondale's script. The major prime-time speakers—Mario Cuomo, Tip O'Neill, Jesse Jackson, Gary Hart, George McGovern, Jimmy Carter, Geraldine Ferraro, Edward Kennedy, and Walter Mondale—created a festival of unity that was reinforced in the hours of network interviews, interpretations, and commentary. As William Adams has demonstrated, the networks' idea of Democratic party unity was harmony among Walter Mondale, Jesse Jackson and Gary Hart; they largely ignored the absence at the convention of centrist and conservative figures that might have appealed to Democratic regulars.[41]

The Democrats' successful scripting of the prime-time coverage was helped by the networks' decision to abandon gavel-to-gavel coverage. Podium slots could be used to reward or appease activists without affecting what viewers saw on their screens. One House leader observed that many members of Congress were appalled by the choice of podium speakers, which they saw as dominated by minority and issue activists, and worried about the image of the party these speakers conveyed to the public. They noted that the political rhetoric from the podium was almost entirely left of center and wondered whether a moderately conservative Democrat could speak honestly without being booed. The infrequent references to traditional concerns about crime and personal safety, for example, were not well received by the delegates. New York mayor Ed Koch's ringing call for a war on drugs was clearly out of place in the convention hall—the most generous reaction from the delegates was one of bemusement. And while the delegates responded tepidly to Geraldine Ferraro's claim that "I put my share of criminals behind bars," her charge that "it isn't right that a woman should get paid fifty-nine cents on the dollar for the same work as a man" brought down the house. Nonetheless, the impressions of the party formed through the more-limited national television coverage were, fortunately from the perspective of members of Congress, very different from those created by the gavel-to-gavel proceedings of the convention.

Behind the scenes a contingent of elected and party officials worked diligently to head off a wholesale revision of party rules by the new Fairness Commission. At the Monday morning meeting of House delegates, Representative Gillis Long asked for and received authorization to set up an ad hoc executive committee representing the various groups of elected officials to lead opposition to any retrenchment on unpledged delegates. He noted that while no public opposition to the Rules Committee report would be raised in the convention hall, strong pressure would be brought to bear on Mondale and DNC officials to do two things. First, appoint members of the Fairness Commission sympathetic to an expanded role for elected and party officials. And, second, to confirm that the commission was not bound in any way by the sections of its charter that had been written to placate the Hart and Jackson camps. Virginia Governor Charles Robb, representing the Democratic governors, voiced his strong support for active participation at the convention by elected officials and called on the governors, senators, representatives, state party chairs, and state legislative leaders to resist any change in the rules that would discourage such participation. Representatives from the State Legislative Leaders group and the Association of State Chairs seconded Robb's remarks and pledged their support of Long's proposal.

By the next day these efforts took on a sense of immediacy as word spread that Mondale had agreed to demands by Hart and Jackson that each candidate be alloted 25 percent of the seats on the Fairness Commission and that the appointments be made at the Friday DNC meeting. Mondale reportedly agreed to this in spite of his pledge to labor and party representatives during the Rules Committee negotiations to delay appointments to the commission until 1985. Once again the Mondale camp was prepared to make concessions to the losing candidates on the fundamental rules of the game in order to preserve the appearance of party harmony.

In the end, following countless meetings and lobbying initiatives, the elected and party officials were successful. On Wednesday evening, House leaders O'Neill, Wright, Foley, and Long extracted from DNC chairman Manatt a pledge to delay appointments to the commission until 1985 and to reconfirm that the commission was not bound by the language of the resolution adopted by the convention. Mondale endorsed the agreement and Representative Timothy Wirth delivered a letter of support from Hart. At the DNC meeting on Friday, when Manatt announced that he was seeking advice on appointments to the Fairness Commission, it was obvious that the composition of the commission and the struggle to write the rules for 1988 would turn on the outcome of the November election.

Republican Differences

The national rules governing the presidential nominating system in the Republican party, by contrast, are seldom shaped by the short-term calculations of candidates or by the outcome of the general election. All proposed changes in Republican party rules, including those supported by a majority of convention delegates, must first be approved by the Republican National Committee, where party leaders are in control, before being submitted to the next convention's Rules Committee for action. Since final approval requires adoption by the national convention, the Republicans have two formal bulwarks against candidate-inspired changes in the rules of the game.

Perhaps an even more important difference between the parties in this respect is the Republican emphasis on local control and discretion. According to Robert Huckshorn and John Bibby, "The Republicans believe that the state parties are independent sovereign units and that the national committee and the national convention are merely collections of these state party officers and delegates. Republican rules, therefore, permit state parties wide latitude in delegate-selection procedures and maintain the essentially confederate character of the party."[42] The national party has no rules requiring either delegate declaration of candidate preference, proportional representation, equal division between men and women, or affirmative action plans and goals.[43] States are largely free to adapt "their processes to the realities of local life, a matter of no small consequence for a party (any party) which includes Pennsylvania, South Carolina, Wyoming, and California."[44]

Moreover, as a process that proved permeable to conservatives as far back as 1964, and one that, since 1968, has produced presidential nominees who have run strongly in the general election, the Republican rules, unlike the Democrats', have not been the target of factions within the party seeking greater influence. The single exception has been the periodic effort of party moderates and liberals to gain a larger allocation of delegates for the most populous states. The norm within the Republican party is that the rules should be candidate neutral, a norm strongly reinforced by formal procedures and recent experience.

Of course, the Republicans have not been unscathed by the reforms that swept through the Democratic party. In response to mandates from the national Democratic party, Democrat-controlled legislatures made statutory changes that had a direct influence on Republican nominating procedures. For example, the increase in the number of presidential primaries in both parties can be traced to the McGovern-Fraser Commission recommendations. Some states have even required a proportional allocation of delegates in their primaries, which runs directly counter to the traditional Republican affinity for Electoral College–inspired winner-take-all systems. These and other societal forces have conspired to move the Republican party in a plebiscitary direction, in spite of its rules, to the point where many observers see little need for distinguishing between the two systems of presidential selection. Anthony King's argument on how not to select presidential candidates, which began this chapter, was directed very explicitly at the American, not the Democratic, nominating system.

Table 4.2   Percentage of governors and members of Congress
serving as voting delegates in national conventions, 1968–84

	Democratic			Republican		
Year	Governors	Senators	Repre-sentatives	Governors	Senators	Repre-sentatives
1968	96	61	32	92	58	31
1972	59	28	12	80	50	18
1976	44	18	14	69	60	36
1980	72	15	13	72	63	41
1984	86	62	68	87	53	44

Source: Computed from CBS News data 1968–80 by David E. Price, *Bringing Back the Parties* (Washington, D.C.: CQ Press, 1984), 202, and for 1984 by author.

Yet one curious difference between the parties, especially relevant for this discussion, is the relative prominence of national politicians at their conventions, as delegates and on the platform committee. As table 4.2 shows, the participation as voting delegates of top Democratic officials dropped sharply after 1968 in the aftermath of party reforms, rising only in 1984 with the Hunt Commission changes. At the same time Republican officeholders have maintained, with some fluctuation, a consistently high level of participation in GOP conventions. Although Republican rules prohibit automatic delegate status for party and elected officials, more lenient rules regulating other aspects of the delegate selection process make it relatively easy for officials to run as delegates and to be appointed by state parties. The disincentives to participation by top party officeholders that were so clearly present at the 1972, 1976, and 1980 Democratic conventions did not materialize in anywhere near the same proportion within the Republican party.

Determining what consequences have followed from this greater participation by Republican officials is no easy matter. One would be hard-pressed to make a case that top Republican officeholders have played a consistent and decisive role in the politics of Republican presidential selection. In 1976, by most accounts, Republican officials supported President Gerald Ford in his nomination struggle with Ronald Reagan, and they were active on his behalf in their state delegations, on the rules and platform committees, and on the convention floor. Although Ford won the nomination, he and his supporters were unable to prevent the convention from adopting a Reagan-backed amendment implicitly rebuking his administration's foreign policy.[45] In 1980 major Republican party and elected officials had little influence over the choice of the nominee—Ronald Reagan ensured his own victory by winning twenty-eight of thirty-four primaries, overwhelming candidates with extensive Washington experience. Members of Congress introduced an element of moderation on the platform committee, thereby contributing to the successful display of party harmony in Detroit, although they were ineffectual in resisting controversial language on abortion and the ERA.[46] Certainly, the presence at the convention of many Republican members of Congress contributed to the extraordinary coordination between the Reagan-Bush ticket and congressional candidates in the fall campaign and to the unusually high levels of support President Reagan received in 1981 from Republicans in the Senate and House.

In 1984 President Reagan's lock on the nomination proved no deterrent, perhaps it was even an incentive, to widespread participation at the convention by Republican members of Congress. But it would be a mistake to characterize their role in Dallas as moderating the public image of the Republican party. Congressmen Jack Kemp, Newt Gingrich, and Vin Weber successfully fought the administration to include in the platform several basic tenents of the "conservative opportunity society"—unequivocal opposition to tax increases, harsh criticism of the Federal Reserve Board, and praise for the gold standard.[47] Other members did press for moderation on the platform—Senate Finance Committee chairman Robert Dole urged flexibility on the tax issue and maverick Senator Lowell Weicker, Jr., a member of the platform committee, sought (mostly without success) to liberalize the social and domestic policy planks. With conservatives firmly in control of the platform committee and the convention (60 percent of the delegates described themselves as conservatives, barely 1 percent liberals),[48] the changes proposed by Kemp and his House colleagues received a more sympathetic hearing in Dallas than in Republican circles in Washington. The end result was seen by Gingrich as a positive force for the GOP. "This is a year almost like 1896. The country faces two very radical choices. We are moving toward a consciously polarized election."[49]

Conclusion

Architects of the Democratic party's proposal to involve elected officials more actively in presidential selection argued that the party's top officeholders would moderate the image of the party among voters, provide an element of peer review, and promote a party-based campaign and teamwork in government. This chapter has demonstrated that in some important respects their hopes and expectations were realized in the 1984 campaign. But since the party's failure to compete effectively in presidential elections was the most important factor leading to the Hunt Commission changes, it is not surprising that the outcome of the fall campaign colors any assessment of their consequences.

Walter Mondale's crushing defeat in the November election directly challenged the assumption underlying the latest round of reform, namely, that the Democratic party would become competitive once again in presidential elections if it nominated mainstream candidates well connected to its core constituencies. The key changes in the nominating process during 1984—the use of direct-election primaries in large, industrial states, the involvement of elected and party officials as unpledged delegates, and the preprimary endorsement by organized labor—were predicated upon that assumption, and most of the principal players viewed the nomination of Mondale as the desired and expected result of those changes.

One line of defense in the face of Mondale's landslide loss, adopted by organized labor and some major party officials, was that the election was a referendum on a popular incumbent at a time of peace and prosperity, conditions under which no Democratic candidate could have succeeded. There is a good deal of evidence elsewhere in this book substantiating the centrality of Reagan's record to the choices made by voters. The election was overwhelmingly a positive vote for Reagan rather than a negative vote against Mondale. And yet the magnitude of the loss and the widespread defection among the party's traditional constituencies suggest the need for a fuller explanation.

A second reaction to the November election outcome was that Mondale was damaged beyond repair by his struggle for the nomination. According to this argument, the changes in the nominating process, while saluatory and vital to Mondale's victory in San Francisco, did not alter the fundamental character of the system. Mondale was bloodied in his seesaw battle with Hart, damaged by the racial polarization Jackson's candidacy occasioned, portrayed as a captive of special interests by opponents seeking to dent his frontrunner status, drawn to the left on issues by the collapse of more conservative candidates Glenn, Hollings, and Askew and by the prominence of liberal activists, forced to appeal to his core Democratic base instead of expanding his support among loosely attached Democrats and independents. Had Mondale won the New Hampshire primary, thereby making his nomination a virtual certainty, he could have concentrated all his fire on Reagan and built a clear and consistent case for his candidacy.

At one level this argument is compelling. Mondale probably would have been a more formidable candidate against Reagan had he been the consensus choice of his party. But it strains credibility to argue that his problems wrapping up the nomination were due mainly to factors stemming from the rules such as the publicity accorded to the atypical New Hampshire primary, the media's tendency to be hard on frontrunners, or the unrepresentativeness of primary electorates. Large numbers of voters had doubts about Mondale—his independence, his leadership abilities, his ties to a failed administration, his vision of the future. A different nominating system—a national primary or a sequential process kicked off by Pennsylvania or New York instead of New

Hampshire—might well have blocked Gary Hart's ability to exploit those doubts, but it would not have removed them from the public's consciousness.

While the referendum on Reagan and the nature of the Democratic nomination struggle each provide a partial explanation for the landslide dimension of the November outcome, a third perspective is that mainstream Democratic candidates can no longer build a presidential majority based on the party's traditional coalition. This is not a novel observation; Republicans have dominated presidential elections since 1952 and have won four of the last five, three by landslides. But the idea has persisted that presidential elections are the majority Democratic party's to lose—if they avoid nominating candidates on the ideological extreme and keep their own house in order, they remain the odds-on favorite. In fact, the shrinkage of some groups in the Democratic coalition (the poor, union members, and city dwellers) and the long-term erosion of party loyalty among others (Catholics, Southerners, blue-collar workers) have so watered down the traditional Democratic coalition that it can no longer be presumed the majority in presidential elections.[50] By this line of reasoning, Democratic misfortunes go well beyond its presidential nominating system, and efforts to revive the party's presidential prospects through rules changes designed to strengthen the traditional coalition's influence are doomed to failure.

The limits and possibilities of rules changes are suggested by the Democratic experience with elected and party officials during 1984 and by the response of the national Democratic party to the defeat of the Mondale-Ferraro ticket. The new class of superdelegates played an important supporting role in the politics of presidential selection. They gave Walter Mondale their overwhelming endorsement because they knew and liked him, and thought him the likely nominee. Moreover, in the immediate aftermath of the 1982 elections, when the Democrats scored with traditional themes of jobs and fairness, Mondale seemed to them the right kind of candidate to lead the charge against the president. Had the economic context been different or had Senator Edward Kennedy entered the race, the party's major officeholders might not have been so supportive of Mondale.

Yet even under these special circumstances, the unpledged delegates played a supporting, not a leading role. Their early endorsement could not ward off, indeed, it may have helped bring on, Mondale's upset loss in New Hampshire; nor could it guarantee victory in the critical Alabama and Georgia primaries. Mondale's nomination was helped by the loyal support of elected and party officials, but it was won in the big state primaries and caucuses, by appealing, with the help of organized labor, to core Democratic voters. Similarly, on the platform and at the convention, Democratic officeholders played a constructive role in presenting the party and its presidential ticket in a favorable light, but their efforts were secondary to steps taken by Mondale and to the political context within which he operated.

Bringing major Democratic officials back into the national convention has neither revolutionized the nominating process nor helped the party win the presidential sweepstakes. In no serious sense has Anthony King's call for peer review, in which national politicians act as a screening device or filter between political parties and the mass electorate, been satisfied. The system remains plebiscitary in character—responsive to populist appeals, dominated by the media, vulnerable to outsiders. This should come as no surprise: The continuing involvement of Republican officials in presidential selection has not been the decisive factor in who the Republican nominee is and how he wins the nomination.

Early in 1985 the Democratic National Committee passed resolutions guaranteeing that the Fairness Commission would be dominated by DNC members and that the number of unpledged delegates would not be reduced. As the party struggled to regain its identity and direction following its second landslide defeat in a row, it turned quite naturally to its successful governors, state legislators, members of Congress. At the same time a group of elected officials led by Virginia governor Charles Robb and Representative Richard Gephardt, frustrated at what they saw as a domination of the DNC by special-interest caucuses, moved to establish a separate organization of elected Democratic officials charged with developing a new party manifesto.

These developments point to a significant role for Democratic officeholders in the 1988 presidential nomination. But the experience of 1984 combined with the wide-open nature of the contest (in both parties) makes it unlikely that the officeholders' participation will be decisive. Moreover, the party's success in building a new majority coalition will turn more on the performance of the economy during Reagan's second term and on the quality and vision of the Democratic and Republican nominees than on any collective actions to remold the party's image.

In any case, recent experience cautions against relying too much on a party's top officeholders to chart its future. Democratic members of Congress have not always been the best judges of which of their colleagues have what it takes to be elected president. And Ronald Reagan, the most successful president in recent decades, forced himself on the Republican establishment and held to an economic program against the advice of many senior Republicans in Congress. In American politics the skills and personal qualities that contribute to a successful presidency may be different from and not always recognizable by other party officeholders.

The Campaign and the Issues

ALBERT R. HUNT

──────To understand the 1984 Presidential campaign, a good starting point is the basketball clashes during the 1960s between Bill Russell, the great Boston Celtics center, and Wilt Chamberlain, the towering center for Philadelphia and San Francisco. Chamberlain was an amazing basketball player, but he simply didn't match up well against Russell. The Celtics won championships nine of the ten years they faced each other, and Russell invariably dominated Chamberlain.

Political contests, like basketball or marriage, often are a matter of match-ups. And a simple reality of 1984 was that Walter F. Mondale—no political Wilt Chamberlain but a seasoned politician—didn't match up well against Ronald W. Reagan. Conceivably another Democrat might have given the president a tougher challenge. The only way to run against Reagan was to make it a contest over the future, a race not of ideology but of ideas.

But as Jimmy Carter's vice-president and one of the remaining standard-bearers of the New Deal–Great Society liberal legacy of the Democratic party, Mondale was uniquely unable to escape either the past or ideology. Perhaps matched up against Senator Howard Baker—where the central question might be experience—or against George Bush—with the debate over who was the most able vice-president—Fritz Mondale would have been a good Democratic nominee. But not against Ronald Reagan, a man who in his field possessed some of Bill Russell's awesome abilities to dominate the game.

The Campaign's Strategic Situation

The State of Affairs

Reagan enjoyed enormous advantages against any opponent. He was the first presidential candidate to capture an uncontested nomination since Dwight

Eisenhower in 1956. None of Reagan's political energies or personal popularity were drained by a divisive primary struggle. Politically, the Reagan forces could aim all their efforts at the fall campaign; since spring it had been evident to them that Mondale would be their opponent.

Prosperity at home was a powerful plus for the incumbent. When Reagan took over in 1981, unemployment stood at 7.5 percent, while inflation was raging at better than 12 percent and interest rates were soaring. The new Republican administration successfully pushed through massive tax cuts and spending cutbacks in 1981. The Federal Reserve Board pursued a very tight monetary policy. In 1982, the result was the worst recession in half a century with joblessness soaring to more than 10 percent. But a buoyant recovery began in late 1982 and by 1984 the economy was booming. Record numbers of Americans held jobs, declining industries seemed to be struggling back, while inflation and interest rates moderated significantly. One of the best politico-economic indicators is the "misery index," a phrase first coined in the 1960s by the Democratic economist Arthur Okun. This index combines the rates of unemployment and inflation; back in the 1960s Okun suggested that when it reached double digits the party in power would be miserable. The "misery index" had skyrocketed to more than twenty points under President Carter but had dropped to less than twelve under Reagan. (Inflation was running at about a 4 percent rate, while unemployment was at 7.5 percent.) That was double digits, but the dramatic change in direction was good news for Ronald Reagan.

In foreign affairs, although 270 American Marines were killed by terrorists in Beirut during the Reagan years, American boys were not in direct combat anywhere as the general election began. Moreover, the Republicans pointed out that not an inch of territory had been seized by the Communists during the Reagan administration. Support for Reagan's huge defense budget and more bellicose foreign policies was eroding, but memories persisted of the humiliation of the 52 Americans held hostage in Iran during the last year of the Carter administration.

One simple maxim of American political history is that when an incumbent president enjoys party unity, prosperity, and peace, he wins reelection. In this century, fifteen times an incumbent president has run, eleven times successfully. The failures were William Howard Taft in 1912, when opposition from Theodore Roosevelt split the Republican party; Herbert Hoover in 1932 in the middle of the Great Depression; and Gerald Ford in 1976 following Watergate and a divisive primary challenge from Ronald Reagan. The final loser, Jimmy Carter in 1980, faced all three obstacles: a primary challenge from Ted Kennedy; a massive "misery index"; and the Iranian hostage humiliation. History was with Ronald Reagan.

The Pollsters' Estimates

Two men with special insight on the 1984 election prospects were among the country's best political pollsters, Robert Teeter, a Republican, and Peter Hart, a Democrat. Both men had huge stakes in the election. Hart was Walter Mondale's polltaker and surveyed for fifteen Democratic Senate and House candidates, more than any other Democratic pollster. Teeter did extensive polling for the Reagan campaign, sat in on the high-level Reagan strategy sessions, and surveyed for more than thirty other Republican aspirants.

These highly competent professionals—good friends off the political field—saw some similarities in the unfolding 1984 election despite their natural inclination to shade their perspectives to their partisan interests.

As 1983 drew to a close, Teeter was finding very encouraging signs in his surveys. "Most people think the recession is ending and the recovery is under way. The fact that this recovery has been in place for a year is of interest to economists. Politically, it's great for Republicans that most people think the recovery is now starting." He also saw an upswing of optimism in the country and a swelling of pride in American foreign policy in general despite misgivings about some particulars.

Hart saw some of the same signs in the economy. He thought Reagan was vulnerable in some areas—the question of whether Reaganomics treated lower- and middle-income people as well as better-paid Americans (the so-called fairness issue) was at the top of Hart's list. But he knew that the apparent health of the economy would work to Reagan's advantage. However, the president had more problems on foreign policy, according to the Democratic polltaker. "Ronald Reagan is going to have a harder time answering the question, Is America more secure than she was three years ago, are we closer to peace today?" Hart observed at the end of 1983.

Both pollsters agreed that the Democrats' only hope was to portray the race as a contest between the future and the present; a choice between the present and the past redounded to President Reagan's advantage. "Reagan's greatest strength may be the question of leadership and consistency of purpose," noted Hart. "People still contrast him to Jimmy Carter and that works very much to [Reagan's] advantage."

By the early summer of 1984, before the conventions, Hart was hopeful, but Teeter was positively exuberant. "Reagan has a very strong approval rating . . . he's viewed as someone who changed the country from going in the wrong direction to the right direction," Teeter declared in early July. The economy, he thought, was an overwhelming plus, and even in foreign policy, Reagan's negatives were softening in Teeter's surveys: "The war/peace issue has gone from being a fear (among the public) to an apprehension." Teeter—and other GOP strategists—were salivating when they started to survey the perception of their

November foe. "The best of all worlds for Reagan is to run against essentially a New Dealer and Mondale is viewed as a caricature of that," Teeter claimed. "This whole special-interest, over-promising thing, our polls show, has hurt Mondale a lot. Among working-class people, for example, he is seen as an old-timer who isn't strong enough."

Hart was not nearly so sanguine. But he saw possible openings. "On some important economic issues like fairness and unemployment the Democrats still enjoy an advantage, not as much as in 1982, but it's still there. And on foreign policy when we ask people if they think the Reagan policies have brought us closer to peace or closer to war, or safer or less safe, majorities respond closer to war or less safe." Nevertheless, inside the campaign, Hart was arguing that Mondale had to position himself more as the candidate of creative change and the future and less a proponent of a return to the salad days of yesteryear.

By early July another respected public opinion expert, William Schneider of the American Enterprise Institute, ventured, "At this stage I think Mondale is behind in every single state." Neither Teeter nor Hart disagreed.

The Conventions

The Reagan forces had used their free time during the primary season well. They assembled a top campaign team, headed by Ed Rollins, but with long-time Reagan strategist Stuart Spencer and top White House aide James Baker omnipresent. They launched advertising extolling the upsurge in the economy and the general confidence of the public during the Reagan years. And they targeted about $8 million in a massive effort to register two million new Republican voters, using the most sophisticated techniques available.

The GOP convention in Dallas was at best a mixed success. Much of the time was spent Mondale-bashing, and the Reaganites ceded the platform to the New Right forces who insisted on heavier emphasis on social issues and a more emphatic pledge against taxes than the president actually advocated. The president's acceptance speech (accompanied by a highly effective, eighteen-minute documentary that was aired in its entirety only by NBC), wasn't one of Ronald Reagan's more uplifting moments.

Moreover, Reagan started making more of his celebrated gaffes, perhaps because he was rusty, having not campaigned during the spring. He alluded to the Democrats as "leftists" on a couple of occasions, made a couple of minor miscues, and, at Dallas, seemed to embrace the religious right.

None of this worried top Republican strategists much. Reagan invariably made mistakes early in his campaigns—"There's always a shakedown cruise," observed one longtime Reagan strategist during this period. He also habitually throws some red meat to the true believers and then promptly ignores the more peripheral issues and hits his major themes and topics. (His religious observations paled compared to his start four years earlier when he began addressing religious fundamentalists and expressing doubts about the theory of evolution.)

By midsummer the Reagan forces had only one potential worry: the effect of Geraldine Ferraro's selection by Walter Mondale as the first female vice-presidential candidate of a major party in history. "Ferraro is a phenomenon . . . what we're going to have to do is wait and see," Edward Rollins said weeks after her selection. "If this turns out to be a much closer race than I and others anticipated, a lot of it's going to be this Ferraro factor."

But Rollins and others thought that unlikely. All indications, they believed, were that the election would be exceedingly tough to lose or even come close to losing. Reagan's positives and Mondale's negatives as a liberal, they felt, were too dramatic. Rollins saw an Achilles' heel for the president, saying, "There is a significant proportion of the public and some of our supporters that think the president's programs have helped the rich and not supported the poor and middle class. There's a divide along class lines (roughly at about $25,000 to $30,000 in annual income) though I'm not sure it'll remain through the election."

Still, he claimed Reagan was showing gains among low-income, blue-collar Southern whites—probably as a reaction to Jesse Jackson—and among working-class voters in all sections, reflecting a "tremendous backlash against homosexual rights in the Democratic platform." (The Democrats did decide that gays should be treated like women, blacks, and other minorities, and at future conventions the proportion of gay delegates should approximate the percentage of gays in society. How this would be determined wasn't specified.)

On balance, though, the Democrats' San Francisco convention was a success. The selection of Ferraro was hailed by many; the Reverend Jesse Jackson gave a dynamic and conciliatory speech; the acceptance speech of Ferraro was momentous and moving, and Mondale made the most cogent speech of his career in accepting the nomination. Immediately after San Francisco, both the Gallup and Harris polls indicated the presidential race was a toss-up.

Democratic euphoria was short-lived, the decline starting with the Bert Lance affair. Lance, who had to resign as Jimmy Carter's budget chief because of controversies over his banking practices, was an old friend of Mondale's who had stuck with the candidate in tough times. Mondale appreciated this loyalty and genuinely liked Lance. Also, after shunning Southerners as running mates, the Mondale camp thought it was good politics to put a prominent Southerner in a visible position.

They wanted Lance as national Democratic party chairman, but that backfired at the convention and Mondale was forced to stick with Charles Manatt. Instead, Lance was named general chairman of the Mondale-Ferraro campaign. But, within weeks, as controversy boiled over Lance's past, that appointment too had to be withdrawn. The upshot: Southern politicians were miffed at their lack of access to Mondale's high command, politicians elsewhere were stunned at the campaign's ineptitude, and precious time was lost.

Next came the Ferraro problem. Immediately after her selection, ethical problems surfaced. She had not filed her husband's financial statements during her six years as a member of Congress, claiming an exemption from the House rule that required her to do so; the exemption, House experts agreed, was unwarranted. She first promised to release all of her and her husband's tax returns, but, on August 12, she said that she wouldn't be releasing her husband John Zaccaro's returns after all. At a brief airport press conference she said that he had objected and flippantly added, "You people married to Italian men, you know what it's like."

This was one of the major mistakes of the 1984 campaign. It unleashed a barrage of investigative reporting and scrutiny from which Ferraro never quite recovered. The careless comment reflected her inexperience and naiveté in national politics where every utterance is recorded and carefully examined. A congressional candidate can make dozens of small mistakes and nobody notices; a national candidate makes one minor miscue and it can last for days. And this wasn't a minor miscue. It also reflected the initial unwillingness of the Mondale camp to provide her with staff familiar with these pitfalls.

Predictably, Zaccaro and Ferraro backed down days later and released both returns. She then held a ninety-minute press conference by herself, on their financial situation. The former Queens housewife and her real estate developer husband proved to be millionaires several times over. Ferraro's performance was impressive, as she parried hostile questions, demonstrated a command of the facts, and was cool and articulate. By then, however, much of the damage was done, and questions about Ferraro and her husband's business dealings and associations would plague the campaign until election day.

The Issues

The Candidates as Issues

As Labor Day approached, Reagan had a few problems. Republican campaign pollster Richard Wirthlin showed the president's lead dropping to nine points in the aftermath of negative reactions to the right-wing flavor of the Dallas GOP convention. Surveys also showed concerns over Reagan's flip remark (which he thought was off the record) made prior to a radio show. When testing the microphone he said, "I am pleased to tell you that I've signed legislation that will outlaw Russia forever. We begin bombing in five minutes."

Surveys also showed that on some important issues, ranging from abortion to arms control, the public was closer to Mondale's stance than to Reagan's.

But the Lance and Ferraro flaps took their toll, as Mondale's negatives were pronounced. A late summer Harris survey asked if Mondale had "an attractive, forceful personality and is a real leader?" The poll reported a 56–40 percent negative response. By 60 to 28 percent these respondents said he was "too cautious and vague," and by 60 to 31 percent they found that he "tries to appeal to too many special interest groups." The question of whether Mondale represented the "past more than the future" provided a 48–36 percent yes, and when asked if he was "too tied to the old, entrenched power centers in the Democratic party," Harris found that 53 percent of the public answered affirmatively.

Conversely, polls showed the American people saw Reagan as a strong, forceful president. On the issue of leadership he trounced Mondale, as he did on some other important issues. Ronald Reagan "owes his political fortunes more to an improving economy than to any other single factor," Andrew Kohut, president of the Gallup public opinion organization wrote in September. "The president's political recovery from recession began just about a year ago. Prior to that his approval ratings were in the forties and he trailed or at best tied most Democratic challengers in test elections throughout 1983."

By Labor Day Walter Mondale's task wasn't impossible—he didn't trail by more than thirty points as Barry Goldwater and George McGovern had at a comparable stage—but it was decidedly difficult. In nine weeks he had to convince the American people that their good feelings about the economy and the country were ephemeral, that he possessed a carefully conceived idea of how and where to lead the country, and that all the negative perceptions formed of him during the primaries were mistaken.

Campaign pollster Peter Hart wrote the candidate a memo shortly before the traditional Labor Day kickoff: "My advice is simple. Let 'er rip. Reach inside your soul and tell the voters why you are running and what this election is all about. Everyone has been telling you to 'let your hair down,' 'be tough and show leadership,' etc. You did not get this far by trying to be someone other than who you really are, and you will not get to the White House by inventing a new Walter Mondale for the next nine weeks." While Hart tried to be upbeat, he tossed out an undeniable but sobering thought: "For all the kudos you received for the selection of Geraldine Ferraro and your superb acceptance speech at the Democratic convention in July, you are just about where you were at the end of the primary season."

And the first week was a disaster for Mondale. On Labor Day, Reagan went to his native California to address enthusiastic crowds; the rest of the week produced more of the same. Mondale started at a labor rally in New York City. The crowds for the early morning event were small and such prominent local politicians as Mayor Edward Koch didn't even show up. The rest of his week produced more of the same for him, too. The next week he went to Green Bay, Wisconsin, to greet employees during a shift change at a Proctor & Gamble plant. Only a handful of workers greeted Mondale and the highlight was when they presented him with the plant's principal product: a four-pack of Charmin toilet paper.

Much more important than the mechanical or logistical problems was the fuzziness of Mondale's message. This very bright man grew up in Minnesota as a practitioner of interest-group politics when that not only made for good politics but also for good government. For all of his experience and intelligence, however, he couldn't change with the times. During the primaries, the *Washington Post*'s Dan Balz wrote that Mondale "ran for president by presenting himself as the ultimate Congressman for the nation—or for the nation's 435 congressional districts." Mondale's appeal to Democratic voters represented a kind of balkanization of America," Balz wrote. The candidate "divided the country into regions, states, and even small sections of states and found, as best he could, the issues that appealed most directly to the voters of each area."[1] Thus, in New England, he talked about oil imports; in North Carolina he extolled tobacco price supports; in New York about moving the Israeli capital to Jerusalem; and in industrial Michigan and Pennsylvania about his support for massive government assistance for Chrysler and the steel industry. Such retail politics may work in primaries, but every general election is very much a wholesale campaign.

Mondale offered no clear wholesale message. Four days after Labor Day, Democratic pollster Irwin Harrison worried: "Mondale still hasn't enunciated his basic view of America. He has failed to come up with any credible alternative." The campaign lacked political boldness and the once-vaunted Mondale campaign organization was increasingly under attack from nervous Democrats. The upshot, the *Wall Street Journal* concluded, was "a campaign sketched in earth tones rather than in brilliant colors, and one that seems to be in an inertial state."[2]

All of this was reflected on the television screens the first week of September. The *New York Times* described the sharply different pictures of the two candidates on television: "From a park in California, Mr. Reagan starred in a sun-washed patriotic extravaganza that showcased his casual, upbeat brand of oratory built around a set of simple, relentlessly repeated code words, such as 'future,' 'opportunity,' and 'home.'" "You ain't seen nothing yet," Mr. Reagan concluded triumphantly, on ABC and NBC, after a recital of his accomplishments. Meanwhile, correspondents with the Mondale entourage described a campaign that could not draw a crowd to what CBS called its "puny" parade in New York City. "In California, where Mr. Mondale arrived on what NBC, quoting Reagan aides, termed a 'fool's errand,' the candidate's microphone did not work."[3]

Reagan, the great communicator, came across much more naturally on television than Mondale. That advantage only increased when the momentum was moving in the president's direction. Television is very much a frontrunner's medium.

The Economy and the Deficits

Predictably, both candidates stressed the economy in their Labor Day kickoffs. Mondale, in New York, Wisconsin, and California, emphasized deficits, taxes, and fairness: "Whoever is elected, this budget must be squeezed and revenues must be restored. But the question is whether it will be done fairly." In California, Reagan assailed the Democrats as big spenders and big taxers who intend "to fund their campaign promises by raising taxes more than $1,500 on the average household." (Actually, that figure was a distortion; in the main Mondale's proposed tax increases would have affected upper-income taxpayers.)

Reagan never mentioned the deficit, to no one's surprise. Four years earlier candidate Reagan expressed outrage over Jimmy Carter's deficits of $27.7 billion in fiscal year 1979 and $59.6 billion in fiscal 1980. He vowed to bring them down sharply and produce an actual budget surplus of $500 million by fiscal 1985. Instead, deficits soared, reaching a record $195.4 billion in fiscal 1983; in the next fiscal year, instead of a small surplus as promised, the deficit exceeded $170 billion. Ronald Reagan, who had railed against budget deficits for the past two decades, was running up the largest deficits in history.

There were related failures in Reagan's economic policies. As a candidate in 1980, Reagan had promised to slash federal spending as a percentage of the gross national product, to 19.3 percent from 22.6 percent. Instead, spurred on by huge military outlays and unchecked growth in entitlement programs, election-year spending as a percentage of GNP actually *rose* to a little over 24 percent. Studies by such respected organizations as the nonpartisan Urban Institute demonstrated that while more-affluent Americans benefited handsomely from Reaganomics, poorer people suffered setbacks.

But for most Americans Reaganomics was working. Inflation had been reduced: The consumer price index rose 13.5 percent in 1980; in 1983 it climbed only 3.2 percent and in 1984 it was rising at an annual rate of just a little more than 4 percent. The Federal Reserve Board's tight monetary policies probably deserved much of the credit, but the results redounded to Ronald Reagan's advantage. Interest rates were down, though the effective rate most citizens paid for mortgages and consumer loans actually hadn't declined.

There were 105 million Americans holding jobs, or six million more than when Reagan took office. There was a wrenching recession in 1981 and 1982, but by the fall of 1984 only four states still had double-digit joblessness—Michigan, West Virginia, Alabama, and Mississippi. The trend was down even in those hard-hit areas.

One of the best guides to pocketbook politics is per-capita disposable income. This measurement, in 1972 dollars to factor out inflation, includes wages, salaries, interest income, and transfer payments such as welfare or Social Security benefits. It provides the most comprehensive guide to how the economy is affecting Americans. By the fall of 1984, per capita disposable income had climbed about 9 percent in the Reagan years. This was higher than the 6 percent increase during the Carter presidency. Moreover, under the Democrats much of the gain took place the first two years, little of it in the election year. Under Reagan, it was just the opposite—the boom was fresh in voters' minds.

Democratic criticism of Reagan for the record deficits didn't worry Republican strategists. Deficits are cutting political issues, they knew, only when seen as the cause of more tangible troubles, such as raging inflation or soaring interest rates. When times are good, few voters blame an incumbent for budget deficits that don't seem to affect them.

The Democrats—and the press—struggled to pin the president down on specifics. How would he reduce the budget deficit? Which programs would be cut? What were his defense priorities? It was a futile effort. Reagan was determined not to be pinned.

Themes, not issues, were the focal point of the Reagan campaign. In Reagan's campaign, the *New York Times* wrote, "issues are clearly secondary. His reelection effort is based on the macropolitics of mass communications. Issues take a backseat to invoking such themes as leadership and opportunity—to creating visual images, communicating shared values, and stimulating moods and feelings in the audience."[4]

Indeed, this presidential campaign seemed to be waged on two levels. On the micro-level of issues, Mondale was getting the best of it; on the more important macrolevel of leading the country, it was all Reagan. "The Mondale campaign is a campaign of issues—clearly delineated, forcefully argued, sincerely presented," according to a *Wall Street Journal* analysis.

> Whether the topic is the government's huge budget deficits, taxes, Medicare, or civil rights, the candidate speaks forthrightly and in detail. But running through his rhetoric is a class-struggle undercurrent, echoes of the political language wielded so successfully by the Democrats in the early decades of the New Deal era . . . in concentrating on his class-struggle motif, Mr. Mondale ceded to his opponent what seems to be the

year's most powerful issue—economic growth. Mr. Reagan's campaign, unlike Mr. Mondale's, is largely devoid of issues and specifics. Its hallmark is symbols, images and anthems. But the president is pounding away on the growth theme, glorying in the credibility he enjoys on the economic issue as a result of the current economic expansion.[5]

But Reagan was not going to rest only on his economic record or his themes. The Republican strategists were delighted when Mondale acknowledged— indeed trumpeted—his intention to increase taxes. Reagan had acquiesced in three tax increases over the past three years, but his huge tax cuts in 1981 had established his bona fides as a tax cutter, GOP planners believed.

In his San Francisco acceptance speech Mondale forthrightly declared: "Let's tell the truth. Mr. Reagan will raise taxes, and so will I. He won't tell you. I just did." To vow to boost taxes is a rare bit of political candor considered political suicide by political experts.

But top Mondale strategists felt they had little choice if they wanted to make Reagan's huge budget deficit a cornerstone of their campaign. There were three strong arguments for emphasizing the deficit. First, Mr. Mondale and his economic advisers genuinely believed that huge and continuing deficits were a prescription for economic disaster that eventually would threaten to crowd out private borrowers, drive up interest rates, and send the economy into a tailspin. Second, deficits were one of the few economic issues where Reagan demonstrably had failed to keep his promises.

Finally, the Mondale camp thought it was important to talk seriously about deficit reduction as an antidote to the perception of Mondale as a big-spending liberal beholden to special interests. That was a reputation that only grew during the primary season. Mondale made numerous promises to various interests during his long presidential campaign; one careful analysis found that he had pledged at least $45 billion of new spending schemes to fit into a $9 billion budget allocation.[6] The Mondale camp vigorously denied these actually were promises.

Some Mondale advisers recommended he adopt a one-year freeze on most spending programs, accompanied by a modest tax boost proposal, as the centerpiece of his commitment to cut the projected Reagan deficit by two-thirds by the end of the next presidential term. But others, principally top campaign official James A. Johnson, felt that while the deficit-reduction plan was essential, Mondale would lose the enthusiasm of important constituencies if he proposed to trim popular social programs. Moreover, as a matter of policy, a spending freeze was impractical. So the big tax boost route was adopted.

But Mondale's intention to boldly promise to increase taxes in his San Francisco speech was only known to a small group of insiders, and the political planning to sell it was minimal. The specific details of the Mondale plan were not offered until two months later. For instance, in September Mondale promised that the tax increases would be earmarked for deficit reduction, not go for any new spending schemes. But this was only after Republicans for eight weeks had hammered away at the theme that Mondale wanted to raise taxes so he could hatch new spending schemes for his special interests.

The actual Mondale plan, while vague in some respects, was one of the most carefully considered and detailed budget blueprints ever offered during a presidential campaign. Under this budget, the deficit, according to Congressional Budget Office figures, would be reduced from the projected Reagan $263 billion shortfall in fiscal 1989 to an $86 billion deficit. This would involve $85 billion of tax increases, mainly on wealthy individuals and businesses through measures such as a 15 percent minimum tax on corporations, a 10 percent surcharge on couples with incomes over $100,000, and capping the third year of the Reagan individual tax cuts.

On the spending side, he proposed $54 billion of cuts by 1989, about half of which would come from slowing down the rate of growth in military spending. Most of the rest would come from containing the health costs and unspecified savings in agriculture and other domestic areas. The Democratic nominee pledged, however, to restore $30 billion of Reagan cuts in education, jobs, and other domestic programs. Finally, by 1989, he envisioned a $51 billion savings from lower interest payments and $17 billion in additional revenues due to higher economic growth, producing the total net deficit reduction of $177 billion.

Still, Mondale never generated any enthusiasm or even respect for his detailed program. For one, his long-time Great Society liberal image gave him serious credibility problems as budget balancer. "Fritz Mondale embracing a balanced budget," one Washington joke went, "is like Orson Welles endorsing designer jeans."

Moreover, Mondale's budget was attacked from the left and the right. An article in the *New Republic* complained: "The trouble is that the Democrats have let the deficit issue become the only economic issue. There is little worthwhile or imaginative in the entire program; plenty of egalitarian rhetoric—and nothing to rouse the Democratic constituency but austerity. One might think Mondale were running for Director of the Office of Management and Budget."[7] Neither did the Mondale plan find sympathy with the business or financial communities, despite their fears of huge deficits ahead. "The financial markets will not find credible any deficit-cutting program that emphasizes tax increases and ducks the spending cut issue," a *Business Week* column intoned.[8]

If the Mondale camp thought the economic issue might not be a winner, they held slightly higher hopes for foreign policy. They believed the American people still feared that Reagan's hard-line approach might lead to an actual conflict. Thus Mondale missed few opportunities to suggest that all the covert

U.S. activity in Central America risked an armed confrontation in Nicaragua or elsewhere. He also blasted Reagan on the Middle East, but rather than differing much with each other, the candidates vied mainly over who could take the most pro-Israel position.

Mondale thought he could seize the high ground by attacking the Reagan defense plans as extravagant; the defense budget during Reagan's four years rose 81 percent, a record peacetime increase. Mondale advocated a smaller annual growth of 3 to 4 percent after inflation. He attacked Reagan's proposed space satellite weapons system—the so-called Star Wars—as a dangerous escalation of the arms race and assailed the MX missile as a costly and ineffective expenditure.

Arms control, or the Reagan administration's lack of success here, was the major thrust of Mondale's foreign policy assaults. Reagan, he noted, was the first American president since Herbert Hoover not to meet with his Soviet counterpart. Polls showed the public genuinely wanted an arms control pact, and Mondale's support for a mutually verifiable U.S.-Soviet freeze on the testing and deployment of nuclear weapons—while viewed skeptically even by some top Democratic defense experts—won wide acceptance from the public.

None of this fazed the Reaganites. On September 23 Soviet Foreign Minister Andrei Gromyko and Reagan met for two hours; while the substance of the talks was limited, the political symbolism sharply undercut Mondale's position. (Gromyko met with Mondale, too, a few days earlier, but the Reagan session received most of the attention.) On the defense issue the White House was convinced the notion that America was strong and respected again counted more with the public than any fears of excess.

Secondary issues surfaced from time to time. Mondale, with the active support of most environmentalists, sought to capitalize on the Reagan administration's lax policies on toxic waste. Reagan, seeking positive programs and themes, talked about creating tax incentives for enterprise zones to solve chronic unemployment and tuition tax credits for private and parochial school education.

One issue that both sides hit was the Supreme Court. Five justices were seventy-five years or older, and actuarial tables suggested the next president would make several appointments. Some Mondale advisers felt the argument that a reelected Reagan would bow to extreme right-wing pressure with any court appointments would rally the Democratic faithful and scare moderates and independents. Reagan, seventy-three years old himself, had to tread a bit carefully here, but promises of a more conservative court still had an energizing appeal to some constituencies. Further, Reagan lost few chances to brag about his one appointment to the court—Sandra Day O'Connor, the first woman justice and a staunch conservative.

By mid-September, however, the most raging issue was a surprise: religion and politics. The catalyst was a Reagan speech to religious leaders at the Dallas convention, where he said religion and politics "are necessarily related," even suggesting they are "inseparable." He charged that those who claim that religion and politics aren't linked are "intolerant of religion."

This set off a firestorm of charges and countercharges, producing plenty of piety. Generically, the question was religion's role in politics, but the issue scattered all over the place: school prayer, the role of Catholic bishops in the political process, the influence of the religious right, the political use of black churches, and issues mainly affecting Jewish voters.

To be sure, this hardly was a new topic in American political life. Almost two hundred years ago fundamentalists charged that if Thomas Jefferson, a deist, were elected president, America would become another Sodom and Gomorrah. Worries over undue influence by the pope dominated elections in 1884, 1928, and 1960. Religious figures, ranging from Father Charles Coughlin, the right-wing Roman Catholic radio celebrity of the 1930s, to Martin Luther King, Jr., the celebrated civil rights leader of the 1960s, have played an enormously important role in American political life. Religion never has been completely removed from this country's politics nor has it been officially entwined.

More often than not, political figures try to use religious issues to their advantage. James P. Gannon, editor of the *Des Moines Register*, reported one scenario: "The story was headlined 'Church & State' and it analyzed the Republican President's reelection strategy of aiming a special appeal at urban Catholic blue-collar voters, especially in the Northeast. Abortion, tuition tax credits, patriotism, 'old-fashioned morality' and anti-communism were the issues and themes of the President's emerging 'Catholic strategy'. . . ."

The analysis continued quoting a high presidential aide: "If the President is to have any kind of a majority, it has to be composed of northern Catholics and southern Protestants." Gannon then revealed he was not writing about 1984, but about 1972 and the strategy of Richard M. Nixon. Gannon called it "unholy manipulation" and "quadriennial pandering for political gain"—an apt description in 1984, as well as 1972.[9]

Clearly, the religious right has emerged as a more potent political force in recent years, and its link to Ronald Reagan was real. Jerry Falwell, head of the Moral Majority, even claimed the president was "God's instrument in rebuilding America." Reagan didn't dissent. He in turn claimed that after the attempt on his life in 1981, he had decided "whatever time I've got left, it now belongs to someone else." That someone else, he explained, was the Lord.

Reagan appealed to the fundamentalists with his advocacy of constitutional amendments to restore school prayer and prohibit abortions. Also, he gave these right-wing preachers access to the White House and even a few token appointments. The fundamentalists, in return, were enlisting white Southerners in the Reagan and Republican cause.

But the Mondale strategists believed that Reagan might well alienate some of his more moderate supporters, especially young urban professionals, with this religious talk. In a radio address, the Democratic nominee blasted Reagan for not respecting "the wall our founders placed between government and religion." He also warned that "government must not be permitted to dictate the religious life of our people." Mondale gave another speech on the topic to the B'nai Brith assembly a few weeks later, but he wouldn't wage an all-out assault.

One reason was that some Southern Democrats were warning that if Mondale totally alienated all the white fundamentalists, he could write off the entire South. Reagan, too, was eager to drop the issue. Republican strategists figured the fundamentalists had gotten their red meat and worried that the issue was starting to chip away Reagan support in other areas, especially with Jewish voters who get very nervous about upsurges in fundamentalist Christianity.

Both sides were guilty of more than a little hypocrisy. Mondale railed against Reagan's links to the Christian right but never criticized the use of black churches in the civil rights struggles or in Jesse Jackson's presidential campaign. Reagan talked piously of representing family values, yet he had never found time even to see his year-and-a-half-old granddaughter.

More significant politically was the role of the Catholic church. Like most religious leaders, the members of the Roman Catholic hierarchy aren't homogeneous in their political views; some of the most vocal opponents of nuclear weapons and most articulate voices for the poor and helpless have been Catholic priests.

But in 1984 the dominant issue was the church's strong opposition to abortion and the willingness of some bishops to make this a political litmus test. In June, New York's archbishop John O'Connor bluntly declared: "I don't see how a Catholic in good conscience can vote for a candidate who explicitly supports abortion." Later, O'Connor would expressly criticize Democratic vice-presidential candidate Geraldine Ferraro. In Scranton, Pennsylvania, the Catholic bishop (a close associate of Bishop O'Connor) went to the extraordinary step of holding a press conference after Ferraro campaigned there to criticize her abortion views. (Ferraro, the mother of three children, said she personally opposed abortion but also opposed efforts by the government to limit a woman's right to choose to have an abortion.)

Other Catholic bishops surfaced in the campaign. In Buffalo and Philadelphia the heads of the Catholic diocese appeared on the platform with Reagan.

Mondale and Ferraro weren't sure how to respond. The most serious rejoinder was made by New York governor Mario Cuomo, who first criticized

Bishop O'Connor for telling Catholic parishioners who to vote for. Then, on September 12, the Democratic governor—one of the country's best-known Catholic politicians—gave a major speech at Notre Dame University. Catholics, he declared, should not seek to impose their views on controversial moral issues like abortion on which there is no public consensus, and he warned that Catholic politicians "know that the price of seeking to force our beliefs on others is that they might someday force theirs on us." (For all his eloquence on the issue, even some sympathizers spotted some inconsistencies in his moral logic.)

The impact on the Catholic voters was elusive. In heavily Catholic Waterbury, Connecticut, for example, ambivalent attitudes surfaced. Many Catholic voters criticized church leaders for their active involvement in politics. But some of these same Catholics planned to ignore their Democratic roots and vote for Ronald Reagan, not because of abortion, but because of the improving economy.[10]

A mid-September Roper poll found that overall only 12 percent of the public said the religious debate had pushed them more toward one candidate, and it was equally divided. The knowledgeable political analyst Kevin Phillips concluded that Reagan would be helped in the fundamentalist South and would receive slightly enhanced support from Catholics, but he would be slightly hurt in higher-education precincts in the Northeast, upper Midwest and Pacific Coast, and would be hurt somewhat more among Jewish voters.[11]

But when an issue plays a major role in a short campaign for a couple of weeks and neither candidate benefits from it, the frontrunner has gained ground. And as the campaign headed into the final six weeks, Reagan and his big lead had barely been scratched.

The Last Six Weeks

Certainly Reagan had problems, some of his own creation. In mid-September, before a big Italian-American dinner, where he shared the platform with Mondale and Ferraro, the president seemed to pull off a coup, citing an Italian immigrant family who struggled to educate their children and managed to put one son through medical school. That son, the president said, became a prominent surgeon who saved the life of a president of the United States. "I know this story," Reagan said with an actor's timing, "because I was the patient."

But the surgeon, Dr. Joseph M. Giordano, who operated on Reagan after the 1981 assassination attempt, answered the president in a *Los Angeles Times* column several days later. "The government social programs enacted over the last 50 years—and so frequently criticized by this president and his administration—have played a vital role in making this success possible," Giordano wrote. "Although my father bore the brunt of expense, I received two, low-interest government loans to help finance part of my medical school education." He went on to praise the importance of the "generous federal funding" for biomedical research, noting: "In contrast to the President, who feels that government programs make people so dependent that they lose initiative, I feel that these programs have enabled people with little resources to reach their full potential." [12]

On September 20, another terrorist raid on the U.S. embassy in Beirut killed dozens more Americans. The president offhandedly suggested that the delays in improving security at that embassy were analogous to foot-dragging in remodeling a kitchen. One of the few sharp criticisms came from conservative, *New York Times* columnist William Safire, who demanded that if Reagan "does not have the means or the guts to defend our embassy, he should have the good grace to close it down." [13]

On October 1 the president's Secretary of Labor, Raymond Donovan, was indicted by Bronx County (New York) district attorney Mario Merola, a Democrat. The timing was transparently political, but Donovan was the first sitting cabinet member to be indicted in this century.

All three of these episodes had the potential to be real embarassments; with Reagan's charmed presence and the media's short attention span, however, they all vanished quickly.

And Reagan kept scoring public relations coups. As the Democrats portrayed him as insensitive and indifferent to the poor and minorities, the president and Mrs. Reagan dropped in for dinner at the home of a seven-year-old black youngster in Washington. He was Rudolph Lee Himes, and the president had been corresponding with him since visiting the boy's school in March. The coverage was pervasive and overwhelmingly positive; the *Rocky Mountain News*, for instance, ran a picture of a friendly Reagan with his hands on the youngster's shoulder next to a story headlined "Guess Who Came To Dinner: Reagan."

Strategies and Resources

The mid-September polls in every state pointed to a Reagan landslide; the president had leads of anywhere from ten to forty points. Even in supposedly Democratic strongholds, the Reagan edge was decisive. In Maryland, according to a *Baltimore Sun* survey, Reagan led 49–39 percent, and in West Virginia, the *Charleston Daily Mail* poll put the President ahead 58–40 percent. In Massachusetts, polls showed Reagan with a ten-point advantage, and Mondale was behind even in his home state of Minnesota.

At this stage the Reaganites didn't think they could retain leads in all those states, but they firmly believed that their electoral base was secure. They were confident of sweeping most of the South and the West, and, with that base secure, they figured they could concentrate their efforts in the Northeast and industrial Midwest, areas where conservative Republicans traditionally have more problems.

The Republicans certainly had resources to concentrate. The Republican National Committee had a $13 million program to target 650 counties across the country as special targets of opportunity; another $10 million was earmarked for voter registration efforts in twenty-eight states.

In addition to their base, the Reagan strategists thought they had virtually insurmountable leads in most of the border states, over half the New England states, and some medium-sized states such as New Jersey and Indiana. Overall, they saw at least 287 sure electoral votes, or 17 more than needed.

The Mondale camp faced a very different picture. It was tough to fashion a scenario to get 270 electoral votes for the Democratic nominee. Even a sweep of most of the Northeast, the industrial Midwest and the traditionally Democratic-leaning border states would have left Mondale around 50 electoral votes shy of 270. Accordingly, the Democrats decided they would make major efforts, early on, in selected Southern states, such as Alabama, Mississippi, Tennessee, and possibly Texas, and in the West, including Oregon, Washington, and the biggest prize of all, California, Ronald Reagan's home state, which had 47 electoral votes.

This may have been a strategy of necessity for the Mondale-Ferraro ticket to have any chance of winning. Yet it was a huge gamble to spend the candidate's time and the campaign's resources and energies in states that most politicians felt they had little chance to carry. Even some top Mondale strategists unsuccessfully argued that it's elemental in politics to nail down your base first, and that initially the former vice-president should be focusing on the Northeast and industrial Midwest. Then—if it was feasible—he could reach out to other areas later on. But campaign chief Jim Johnson and others argued it was desirable to make early runs into the other regions to see if Mondale's prospects might improve.

An article of faith among Mondale strategists was that huge numbers of new voters, many minorities or women, would turn out in 1984 to reject the Reagan administration and that these voters could be mustered in some of the Southern and Western states, too. But reliance on newly enfranchised voters to win an election is a hallmark of losing campaigns.

A look at two battleground states in late September underscores the situation. One is Texas—no Democrat has ever been elected president without carrying the Lone Star state. The other is Ohio—no Republican has been elected president in this century without carrying Ohio.

Texas has voted Democratic in four of the past six presidential elections. With the active support of a popular Democratic governor (Mark White) and a popular U.S. senator (Lloyd Bentsen), Democrats originally eyed this prize of twenty-nine electoral votes. By late September that seemed dubious. An ABC News/*Washington Post* poll showed Reagan leading Mondale in Texas by 60 percent to 31 percent, or almost a two-to-one margin. The Reagan advantage was pervasive in "yellow dog" Democratic east Texas, in Hispanic areas of the Valley, in south Texas, in the major cities as well as in rural areas. Democratic hopes to register 500,000 new voters were falling short; amazingly, some Hispanic politicians estimated that up to one-third of the new voters in their communities were planning to vote for Reagan. By late September few Texas Democrats thought Mondale had any chance to carry their state.

The Ohio situation was unique. An early September memorandum from top Reagan political operative Roger Stone to campaign chairman Edward Rollins underscored this fact. A Bob Teeter survey made it "very clear that the recovery has had substantially less impact in Ohio than elsewhere," Stone wrote, noting: (a) only 46 percent of Ohioans believed that the country "is moving in the right direction," which was "substantially less" than the national average; (b) only 44 percent indicated they were better off than a year before; and (c) Walter Mondale was seen as better able to foster economic prosperity for Ohio.

Thus, in Ohio, instead of using the national commercials—which stressed the booming recovery—Stone suggested emphasizing taxes. He noted that Democratic governor Richard Celeste had recently enacted a $3 million tax increase and that his popularity had plummeted. "Spots which tie Mondale to Governor Celeste and highlight the Mondale-Reagan differences on tax increases could be very effective," said Stone. "By November, we hope voters won't know the difference between Mondale and Celeste."

Yet even in Ohio there already were disquieting signs for the Democrats. In a working-class suburban Cleveland district, for example, incumbent Democratic Representative Edward Feighan's polls showed him ahead 53 percent to 32 percent; the same polls showed Mondale trailing Reagan 51 percent to 23 percent in the district. "You can't believe some of this stuff," lamented Cuyahoga County commissioner Timothy F. Hagan. Black humor abounded in Democratic circles. "We got a shot," cracked Tony Garofoli, a top Cleveland Democrat. "We're on the ballot, aren't we?"[14]

By now, according to Bob Teeter, it was clear that side issues and attacks weren't important to this election. "This is a referendum on Ronald Reagan; most people think they know him pretty well and like what they know." With these firm perceptions, the GOP pollster said Mondale "never can convince people he can handle the deficit better than Ronald Reagan. He (Mondale) has no credibility on that issue. I honestly can't figure out why they picked that one." Teeter actually thought Mondale was the perfect candidate to run against. "Basically, he's only the alternative of those that don't like Reagan. He brings almost nothing to the ticket. He's like a generic Democrat."

Teeter, at this point, thought it premature to talk about a party victory, not just a personal one, though he spotted emerging signs of a Republican surge on the congressional, state, and local levels. Did he have any fears? "Well," he said in late September, "I suppose the age issue, but it would take something dramatic to worry people about that."

Reagan was running a shrewd campaign. It was similar to the 1983 Margaret Thatcher reelection campaign in Britain, suggested *Washington Post* political columnist David Broder. Like Thatcher, Broder wrote, Reagan defined the issue as "the future versus the past," talked much about values but little about specific plans, and seized every imaginable symbol of national pride.[15] This approach was designed to produce a personal victory, rather than a philosophical one or a party mandate.

Peter Hart, who never had been enthusiastic about Mondale's emphasis on the deficit issue, still felt that his candidate hadn't yet lost the opportunity to present a clearer vision of the future. "If it starts to get closer, it'll get closer everywhere," he insisted.

But when Mondale did get bold or aggressive, he soon pulled back. After assailing Reagan's lack of knowledge about arms control issues (reliable reports suggested that the president once believed it was possible to recall nuclear missiles once they were fired), news accounts suggested he'd called the president incompetent. Mondale took offense. "I'm talking about his management style," he declared. "I did not talk about competence at all." Mondale, one line went, was "daring to be cautious." "Reagan does not fear someone who does not go for his opponent's throat—and acts, in the face of overwhelming evidence to the contrary, as if he had something to lose if he did," fumed liberal columnist Mary McGrory.[16]

Mondale gave a widely acclaimed speech on September 25 at The George Washington University, where he sought to lay out the themes of his candidacy. "I would rather lose a race about decency than win one about self-interest," he said. Also, he forcefully charged that the Reagan administration practiced showmanship instead of leadership—"all happy talk and no straight talk; all blue skies and no blueprint; all television and no vision." It was a good speech and the MacNeil/Lehrer Newshour on public television aired more than ten minutes of it. The commercial television stations, however gave only the customary quick snippets.

The ever-optimistic Mondale campaign chairman James Johnson nevertheless saw bright spots as October arrived. "We think we have got our difficulties behind us," he insisted, adding, "There is a very widespread feeling that Reagan is out of touch with the average American family." Johnson felt the Mondale task in the closing five weeks was "to convince people this is an important election. These two men have fundamentally different views of the country and what needs to be done."

The First Presidential Debate

Johnson and others also insisted they had the necessary opening: the two debates that were to take place between Mondale and Reagan on October 7 and October 21 and one between vice-presidential candidates George Bush and Geraldine Ferraro on October 11.

Reagan agreed to the debates despite the warnings of aides that, as an incumbent with a large lead, he had everything to lose. But the president didn't want to give Mondale the debate issue. Also, Reagan had great confidence in his debating skills; in two decades of politics he'd never lost a debate.

Both sides agreed the League of Women Voters would conduct the debates, despite a general feeling that others could have done it better. But the Mondale camp believed the league's readiness and eagerness assured debates would be held. The Reagan camp felt that, unlike news organizations, the league could be bullied into the most advantageous format. The Mondale people originally sought six debates almost up to election eve, but the Reagan forces, by merely agreeing to any debate, held the chips. They wanted the debates completed soon enough that if Reagan made a gaffe the campaign would have time to recover. The result was two presidential debates, the last one more than two weeks before the election, and a stilted format of journalists (approved by the candidates) asking questions with no direct exchange between the participants. The Mondale side won one concession: The debates would be ninety minutes long, rather than only an hour; some Democratic aides thought the lengthier sessions might affect the seventy-three-year-old president.

Preparations for the debates were intense. Mondale spent about half of the fifteen days proceeding the first debate in Louisville preparing for it. He brought in his old law-school professor, Michael Sovern, now the president of Columbia University, to play Reagan in mock debates. Like Reagan, Mondale felt he had a good track record in previous debates, but the stakes were much higher this time.

The mock debates on both sides were sometimes rigorous to the point of humor. One time Sovern blasted Mondale for supporting every spending scheme over the past two decades and charged if all these had been adopted, the budget deficit would approach $1 trillion. Afterward, a frustrated Mondale asked how Sovern had arrived at those devastating numbers. Sovern replied he'd made them up. Similarly, according to *Newsweek* magazine, budget director David Stockman, who played Mondale in the GOP's mock debates, so brutalized the president once that Reagan later told him: "You better send me some flowers because you've been nasty to me."[17]

Some outside advisers, principally pollster Patrick Caddell, who had fought with Vice-President Mondale when he was Carter's pollster and in the 1984 primaries when he advised Gary Hart, felt that Mondale's desperate position necessitated an unconventional strategy. Specifically, he argued that Mondale couldn't simply outpoint Reagan on the facts with the sort of aggressive assault he mounted against John Glenn and Gary Hart in the primaries. Instead, while outpointing Reagan on substance, he also must display an appealing, polite manner and leave the stage seeming both more attractive and stronger.

The other side, though, felt personality was an exclusive Reagan franchise. Their only concern was that Reagan not make an embarrassing factual mistake —devotion to facts never had been his speciality—or appear unfamiliar with important subjects. They crammed him full of facts, figures, arguments, and counterarguments. There was an irony here: The macropolitician, Reagan, was readying for a microdebate, while the micropolitician, Mondale, was focusing on the broader picture. The strategies of both were tempered by the stilted format that minimized any real give-and-take of the sort network anchors Dan Rather and Tom Brokaw encouraged in the primaries. For the first debate, only three journalists could be found who weren't blackballed by one of the campaigns and were willing to abide by this abysmal process.

From the opening moment that Sunday night, Reagan didn't seem like Reagan. The first question asked him to detail his plans to balance the budget in a second term. Reagan was hesitant, even a little rambling. Mondale wasn't a lot better, but he raised the specter of Reagan cutting Social Security benefits. Reagan took the bait and insisted he never would cut benefits for Social Security recipients. Mondale insisted that's what Reagan had promised four years earlier and had then reversed himself after the election.

The substance of the exchange was insignificant. But Mondale had drawn Reagan into a debate over whether he would cut Social Security benefits or not, and that was an argument that only could work to Mondale's advantage.

There were some sharp moments. Reagan assailed Mondale as a big spender and big taxer. Mondale stressed the huge deficits—to the discomfort of some of his advisers—and blasted the Reagan tax policies as helping the rich, even suggesting that vice-president Bush in one year probably paid a smaller percentage of his earnings in taxes than did his chauffeur or janitor. Both sides scored points on the abortion issue and affirmed strong religious beliefs, but insisted they believed in separation of church and state.

Reagan tossed out a few memorable lines. "Our problem has not been that anybody in our country is overtaxed; it's that the government is overfed." But he was never sharp, crisp, or consistently coherent.

Mondale, on the other hand, was effectively jabbing away. About two-thirds of the way through he scored his big punch. After Mondale charged that the president planned to increase taxes for middle-class working citizens, the question was addressed to the president. "You know I wasn't going to say this at all, but I can't help it," Reagan replied. "There you go again."

The audience laughed, remembering that Reagan had used that exact line so effectively four years before in his debate against Carter. This time, however, Mondale was prepared. A few minutes later, Mondale turned to face Reagan on the stage (both men were standing behind lecterns that were about fifteen feet apart) and replied: "Now, Mr. President, you said, 'There you go again.' Right? Remember the last time you said that?" Reagan looked confused and just mumbled, "Um-hmm."

Mondale then went for the kill: "You said it when President Carter said that you were going to cut Medicare. And you said, 'Oh, no, there you go again, Mr. President.' And what did you do right after the election? You went out and tried to cut $20 billion out of Medicare. And so, when you say, 'There you go again,' people remember this, you know."

Reagan gave a faltering response. For the first time in memory, he had been wounded in a debate. But Mondale wasn't just the attacker. When asked near the end what was the "most outrageous thing" that Reagan had said during the debate, Mondale brushed aside the question. "I'm going to give the president some credit. I think the president has done some things to raise the sense of spirit, morale, good feeling in the country." The task now, he said, is to start dealing with America's future. When Reagan was asked the same question, he came back to his old nemesis, Social Security, to insist once again he wouldn't cut benefits.

The Reagan forces expected the president to recoup with his planned closing statement. Reagan started strongly, saying that indeed people could say they were better off than when he took office. But he soon delved into a bewildering set of figures and economic analyses and seemed to lose the thread of his speech. At one point he even bragged about being "well on our way to a 600-ship Navy. We have 543 at present." It was a bad performance. Mondale's closing statement was memorable mainly in that it was more cogent than Reagan's, though he did end on a more future-oriented and uplifting tone.

Before the closing statements were even finished, both sides began what they euphemistically call their "spin control"—or propaganda effort to claim that their man won. Few political organizations are as adroit at "spin control" as the Reagan team. This time, however, the task was Herculean as eighty million Americans had watched Reagan's plainly disappointing performance.

The initial polls gave only a slight edge to Mondale, but as more analysis surfaced and more surveys came out, the advantage became more decided. Nowhere was this more evident than the reception and mood of the candidates themselves the next day. Reagan was in North Carolina, campaigning for Senator Jesse Helms, and the coverage was his most downbeat of the campaign. Mondale went to New York, where the Democratic response was euphoric; Mayor Koch, who couldn't find time to be seen with Mondale a month ago in the Labor Day parade, looked like his Siamese twin now. The crowds were as ecstatic and positive as the politicians.

If Monday was bad for the Reaganites, Tuesday morning was shattering. The headline of the lead story in the *Wall Street Journal*, the nation's largest-circulation newspaper, read: "New Question in Race: Is Oldest U.S. President Now Showing His Age?" [18] The article observed that while until then the seventy-three-year-old president's age hadn't been an issue, Reagan's "rambling responses and occasional apparent confusion" Sunday night might change that. A previously pro-Reagan management expert acknowledged that he'd be concerned to have Reagan, based on his debate performance, as president of a corporation, much less the country. And in layman's terms, Dr. Lawrence Klein, a professor of medicine at Johns Hopkins and Georgetown universities, explained that Mr. Reagan was going from a "young-old" person to the "old-old" bracket. Republicans ventured that the issue would be short-lived, but Democrats, for the first time, were willing to talk openly about it.

The piece was followed up by many papers the next day; the age issue had become legitimate discussion. But for the White House the most worrisome follow-ups were presented by the three networks, all of which did an age piece on Tuesday night. All of them were devastatingly negative, one showing a close-up of Mr. Reagan's hands with age spots evident, another showing the president in a disjointed response.

The White House itself tried to minimize the issue, distributing the president's medical report, and aides went on at great length about Reagan's vitality and alertness. This effort wasn't helped, however, by the president's own physician, Dr. Daniel Ruge, acknowledging to reporters that Reagan had "tired during the debate."

Much of this overshadowed the fact that both candidates made numerous substantive errors during the debate. Both misrepresented the Social Security and Medicare proposals Reagan had made during his first term. Mondale charged that "real interest rates" had doubled under Reagan, which was not the case, and Reagan claimed the rate of increase in poverty had slowed during his administration, when, in fact, it had accelerated.

Still, second-guessing and recrimination raged. Some Republicans pointed the finger at an overconfident Reagan team; Senator Paul Laxalt, Reagan's closest political confidant, charged that White House chief of staff James Baker and top White House aide Richard Darman had "brutalized" and "smothered" Reagan with "extraneous material" before the debate. Even Nancy Reagan reportedly was furious at the debate preparations.

At the same time the carefully contrived and closed GOP political strategy was coming under new attack. David Broder criticized the "political protection and insulation in which Reagan has been wrapped—often to his seeming disadvantage—by a succession of political aides and advisers . . . whatever it is they know about Reagan, it is certainly something they don't want us to find out."[19]

Reagan himself offered several excuses, including the preposterous suggestion that it was all because Mondale wore more makeup. But everytime they made such a point for the next several days, the age issue would resurface. James Reston, the distinguished seventy-four-year-old *New York Times* columnist suggested that a central question about Reagan is "that at his age neither he nor anybody else can be sure about the next four years."[20]

The impact the debates had on television coverage was the most dramatic. In some cases, noted one analysis, network television coverage found that "the very media skills for which Reagan was praised a few weeks ago, this past week were depicted as 'devices' employed by the president on the defensive, and the Mondale mannerisms a week earlier depicted as whining last week were seen as witty and adept."[21] Another analysis noted by the end of the week of the debate, "The three tv networks not only had mentioned the previously unmentioned age issue, they also aired at least seven times a snippet of the president saying in his closing debate remarks: 'The system is still where it was in regard to the uh, the uh, the uh, the uh, progressivity, as we said.' "[22]

Nevertheless, the gains in the public polls seemed modest. The Mondale camp insisted that was misleading. "Already we see unprecedented movement in our internals," Mondale campaign manager Robert Beckel told reporters at a breakfast four mornings after the debate. He said the Reagan lead had been cut to fifteen points now, the direction was all on one side, and "next week we expect to break through to single digits."

For the Democrats there were encouraging signs. By that next weekend Louis Harris reported the Reagan lead had dropped to ten points. A few days later the ABC News/ *Washington Post* survey showed Mondale cutting the lead to twelve points after the debate from eighteen points beforehand.

Still, according to most polls, any movement wasn't very sustained or significant. Mondale's private polls showed strong gains in his positive ratings and similar declines in his negatives, but, the next week, these hadn't translated into significant gains in the match-up against Reagan. By a week after the debate, William Schneider, one of the country's leading public-opinion analysts, wrote: "The Democrats' much-acclaimed momentum doesn't seem to be showing much of a payoff. The polls indicate that President Reagan's lead has narrowed only slightly, if at all, even though most voters agreed that Mondale won the debate."[23]

The Vice-Presidential Debate

The immediate concern after the first debate was the vice-presidential debate four nights later. The Democrats saw this as a rare opportunity to seize the momentum. Mondale had done unexpectedly well in the first debate, and George Bush would have a tough time debating the first woman vice-presidential candidate. If he laid back, Geraldine Ferraro could step into the void; if he attacked her too aggressively, it might redound to her advantage. Privately, some Republicans worried about the performance of the vice-president, who had a reputation for choking in debates.

At the start of the session—in Philadelphia, with the same limiting ground rules as in the presidential debates—Bush came out charging. (Analyst Kevin Phillips later suggested he looked like a "boy scout with a hormone imbalance.") Bush vigorously, almost slavishly, defended the Reagan record. Ferraro was almost subdued, trying to show she could be sober and thoughtful.

Her sex was an omnipresent factor. Once she was asked if she could handle being commander in chief without having been in the military. She replied, "Are you saying that I would have to have fought in a war to love peace? It's just as valid saying you would have to be black to despise racism." (Bush had been heralding his military background; this tactic, of course, overlooked the fact that the commander in chief, Ronald Reagan, had never seen a moment of combat.)

Bush clearly was in charge of his facts, and his erratic behavior settled down as the debate progressed. Generally, he was neither too passive nor too aggressive. Ferraro, on the other hand, had a maddening habit of continuing to look down at notes she was scribbling, a stylistic fault that distracted viewers.

The Democratic vice-presidential candidate had one shining moment. On a foreign policy exchange, Bush said, "Let me help you with the difference, Ms. Ferraro, between Iran and the Embassy in Lebanon. . . ." She shot back: "I almost resent, Vice-President Bush, your patronizing attitude that you have to teach me about foreign policy." There was sustained applause in the auditorium, and television producers knew they had a usable clip.

Polls immediately after the debate indicated that Bush got the better of the exchange, though Ferraro didn't hurt herself. But Democratic hopes of capitalizing on the momentum of the first presidential debate disappeared.

In many ways the Bush campaign was the most puzzling of 1984. The vice-president is an experienced, energetic, intelligent man, according to those who know him well. But during the year he made a number of misstatements and exaggerations. He often campaigned as a shrill sycophant of Ronald Reagan, once even suggesting that he'd be willing to "bet" that Soviet Foreign Minister Andrei Gromyko, after his session with the president, went back to the

Soviet Union exclaiming how much in charge Ronald Reagan was. The Bush family also tossed in uncustomary off-color rhetoric. Mrs. Bush once seemed to suggest that Geraldine Ferraro was a bitch, and after their debate the vice-president bragged to some dock workers that he had "kicked a little ass." These slips may have been intentional efforts to show the patrician second family as down-to-earth, real people.

The press corps following Bush became contemptuous of the vice-president during the campaign, considering him weak and wimpish. His political aides, however, insisted that his complete loyalty to The Reagan Revolution had endeared him to some skeptical conservatives and bolstered his standing for the 1988 Republican nomination; a few right-wingers, such as activist Paul Weyrich, concurred.

But few thought George Bush was much of a factor one way or the other in the 1984 contest. The same couldn't be said for his Democratic counterpart. Ferraro, for better or worse, loomed large in this campaign.

Few candidates have received the press shelling she got in September and early October. The *Philadelphia Inquirer*, the *Wall Street Journal* editorial page, *New York* magazine, and *Newsday* all ran stories raising questions about her family's ties to organized crime figures; most of the allegations dated back several decades and didn't directly involve her public career. But the toughest salvo was on October 18 when the *New York Post* reported that her father had been indicted for a minor gambling charge forty years earlier in Newburgh, New York, only months before his death.

The *New York Post* was decidedly anti-Ferraro; in October alone the paper, published by Australian Rupert Murdoch, ran ten negative front-page headlines about the Queens congresswoman. But this story was different. She was only eight years old when that incident occurred and never knew about it before the *Post* dragged it up less than three weeks before the election. On the campaign plane from Seattle, to Rapid City that morning, her staff told Ferraro about the story; the candidate, who likes to think of herself as an iron lady, cried.

Despite those very real problems, Geraldine Ferraro was a pretty good candidate. She gave an effective stump speech, was especially quick ad-libbing, and was a very fast, if not especially deep, student of issues. She drew enthusiastic crowds, often predominantly female. This raised Democratic hopes that the "Ferraro factor"—a nomination that would energize millions of silent voters, mainly women—might be real.

Most party professionals were skeptical. Even Dotty Lynch, a prominent Democratic pollster working for the ticket, acknowledged in late September: "It's good that Ferraro can get big crowds, attract attention, and inspire enthusiasm. Converting that into votes is the most important thing, and I'm not sure that's happened yet."[24] Interviews with voters suggested that while Ferraro appealed strongly to certain voters, there were offsetting drawbacks for many others.

She scored better among women than men, but that was a phenomenon apparent for most Democrats over the past four years. Most surveys indicated that the real "gender gap" in the campaign was the Democrats' sorry showing with male voters.

The August-September Gallup Report revealed that while the public's willingness to accept women candidates was growing, deep disparities persisted. "Assuming that both were equally qualified for the job, do you think a male president or a female president of the United States would do a better job of handling foreign policy?" the Gallup organization asked. The public, by a massive 58 percent to 8 percent, said male (with 26 percent saying no difference and 8 percent expressing no opinion). On handling relations with the Soviet Union, the outcome was about as lopsided, 57 percent to 11 percent; and on Central America it was 56 percent to 9 percent. On domestic matters, it wasn't much better: men won 40 percent to 18 percent on handling unemployment and 41 percent to 17 percent on handling economic conditions. Only on a "quality of life" issue did women squeak out a 32 percent to 30 percent edge.

There were encouraging signs in this survey for women politicians. More people thought the country would be better off than thought it would be worse off if more women held political office. And 76 percent said they would vote for a qualified woman for president, up from 54 percent fifteen years earlier, and from only 31 percent in 1937. Progress, to be sure, but women candidates still had a way to go.

But the contest was essentially between the presidential candidates, not between the vice-presidential ones. And, by ten days after the October 7 debate, Reagan was in command again.

No doubt there were pockets of concern. The farm belt hadn't experienced the robust recovery of elsewhere and Reagan strategists still considered places like Iowa among their toughest states. And there were some continuing embarrassing revelations about the Reagan Administration's mishandling of the situation in Beirut. Foremost was a *Washington Post* story that reported that the United States had "specific, reliable intelligence warnings that explosives had been shipped into Lebanon and were targeted against American embassy personnel."[25]

But none of this took hold, as Walter Mondale, after a week in the sun, was heading into turbulent political waters again. There were reports that he had decided to play down the deficit issue and instead dwell on broader domestic and foreign policy shortcomings of the Reagan administration. The problem, however, was that it was very late in the game to switch strategy.

The Second Presidential Debate

However, the Mondale camp hoped they had one last chip, the final debate. Such importance was attached to this October 21 showdown that the Democratic nominee even skipped the traditional Al Smith dinner, hosted by the Catholic archdiocese of New York, to bone up for the debate five days later. (The bishop and host was John O'Connor, who had so blistered Mondale's running mate. Thus, some Mondale insiders weren't disappointed at missing this event, even though President Reagan was there.)

According to Peter Hart's polling, Mondale peaked, trailing 52 percent to 42 percent, five days before the second debate, and then the gap started to widen. The Mondale team believed that this debate, on foreign policy, either would reassure people about Reagan's competence or reinforce the doubts planted during the first debate. Thus, Mondale wanted to make the point forcefully that Reagan really wasn't in charge. Reagan's preparation was more relaxed this time. But he was carefully prepared in case anyone raised the question of his age.

On debate night the contrast to television viewers was striking: Reagan looked sharper, younger, more fit than he did in Louisville; Mondale looked tired and frazzled, with very visible bags under his eyes. It was the television lighting, and it hurt the challenger.

The president was more relaxed. He got off a couple of crisp one-liners, once noting that a Mondale commercial showed the candidate on the deck of the *Nimitz* watching F-14s take off. "If he (Mondale) had had his way when the *Nimitz* was being planned, he would have been deep in the water out there, because there wouldn't have been any *Nimitz* to stand on." He parried questions about U.S.–Soviet relations well.

Reagan also stumbled and made some mistakes. Early on, he erroneously spoke of a CIA operation in Nicaragua and moments later had to correct himself. He also denied that he ever had said submarine missiles could be recalled after they had been fired, though the evidence indicated that was exactly what he said.

Mondale, despite his physical appearance, was sharp at times. He continually stressed the "Who's in charge" theme with effectiveness. When Reagan said he didn't know precisely how his proposed satellite technology would work, Mondale shot back: "That's what a president is supposed to know." And the challenger excoriated the Reagan policies on Lebanon, arms control, and Central America, more often than not getting the better of the exchange.

But if voters were waiting to be reassured or to have their doubts reinforced about Reagan's competence, the question of his age loomed large in that calculation. About halfway through the debate, the president got the opportunity he was waiting for. Henry Trewhitt, the respected diplomatic correspondent for the *Baltimore Sun*, said he wanted to "raise an issue that has been lurking out there for two to three weeks. . . . You already are the oldest President in history, and some of your staff say that you were tired after your most recent encounter with Mr. Mondale. I recall, yet, that President Kennedy, who had to go for days on end with very little sleep during the Cuban Missile Crisis. . . . is there any doubt in your mind that you would be able to function in such circumstances?"

It was the softball Reagan wanted. "I will not make age an issue of this campaign," the president solemnly said. "I am not going to exploit, for political purposes, my opponent's youth and inexperience."

The audience burst into laughter and applause. Mondale looked nonplussed. Reagan had just hit the ball out of the park, and any remote chance Mondale had to win, either the debate or the election, had just vanished.

In an extraordinary irony, Reagan's age and lack of durability may have surfaced more in his closing statement of this debate than at any other time. Within a minute of starting his closing remarks, it became apparent the president's thought processes were jumbled; he seemed to have no idea where he was heading. He started talking about driving down the California coast one day, noticing the beauty about him, as he considered writing a letter for a time capsule. None of it made much sense. This polished actor—more trained to talk for a specific length than any politician in history—was rambling on at the end and unable to finish his remarks on time.

It didn't matter. The marvelous age quip filled the television screens for the next day or two, dominating the memories of many viewers and overwhelming other matters.

The Reaganites were ecstatic afterward and the Mondale camp despondent. The polls immediately showed why, with clear majorities saying Reagan was a winner. The GOP surveys showed the president opening up a lead of more than twenty points by the next night. By that same Monday night Peter Hart showed Mondale trailing by twenty points, too, though there was some confusion as the other Democratic pollster, Pat Caddell, actually showed the gap narrowing a little to twelve points. By Tuesday night, however, everyone agreed Reagan was opening up a sizable lead.

In all, the debates probably changed very little. Many of the more thoughtful observers, however, strongly argued that future debates should be basically between the candidates, with a more limited role for journalists in the process.[26] Probably the only way to do that would be to have the debates run by the networks, which are far abler to stage a substantive and interesting encounter; with no incumbent running, 1988 will be a prime opportunity to reshape the debates.

The Stretch Drive

With the debates over, and only two weeks to go before the election, practically no one doubted Ronald Reagan was headed for a big victory—except Walter F. Mondale. But on October 24 the Mondale campaign chairman James Johnson flew to meet the candidate in Milwaukee to show him the post-debate polls and tell him that Reagan had an insurmountable lead. Another aide then leaked that story to the *Boston Globe*,[27] which further dismayed the Democratic camp.

Along with the size and scope of the expected Reagan win, the politicians started to wonder whether this would be one of those periodic realigning elections, one that would usher in Republican domination of American politics for the next generation.

One encouraging sign here for Republicans was the youth vote. In recent elections younger voters had tended to be more liberal and more pro-Democrat than the rest of the population, starting with the Vietnam War and continuing through Watergate. But, in 1984, polls showed Ronald Reagan with a huge advantage among voters between eighteen and twenty-nine years of age, an even larger lead than he had among other age groups.

There were numerous explanations for this phenomenon. On NBC's "Meet the Press" in late October, pollster George Gallup noted the president held his huge lead chiefly among younger male voters and that a key factor was the economic issue. On the same program pollster William Schneider concurred: "For them [young voters] the Great Depression wasn't in the 1930s; it was in the 1970s. That's when they entered the labor force, and it was a dire prospect for these people. President Reagan is the first President to turn things around economically and they appreciate it."

Similarly, Harvard psychiatrist Robert Coles noted that most of these young voters were removed from the social protests of the 1960s and 1970s: "We're now an entire generation removed from the civil rights movement, and the Vietnam War has been over for a decade."

But there was another factor. Few of these younger voters remembered any presidents except Reagan and Jimmy Carter, and Walter Mondale was linked to the very unpopular Carter. And, as pollster Schneider noted, Reagan appealed to the antiestablishment prejudices of youth, as Walter Mondale, to them, "looks like the ancien régime."

Whatever the reason, Republicans saw an opportunity to seize the allegiance of younger voters for years to come.

The Democrats' hopes of pulling an upset by expanding the electorate through registration of millions of new voters also was going awry. A late October survey by the *Washington Post* suggested that the Republicans, with an $11 million investment in voter registration, "at least matched Democratic gains and may have exceeded them."[28] It wasn't that the Democrats were doing that poorly; black registration, for example, was up 18 percent in states such as Louisiana and Florida. But Republican registration was up 56 percent in Louisiana and more than 26 percent in Florida. The pattern was similar in other Southern states.

A survey by the nonpartisan Committee for the Study of the American Electorate offered more pessimism for Democrats. Over the long range, this study concluded, the Democrats were losing ground, dropping from 43.8 percent of the eligible voters registered in 1972 to 35.2 percent in 1984. Republicans were at only 23 percent, so most of the gains occurred among independents.

By now the Reagan camp saw a real possibility for a fifty-state sweep. With the election only a week away, they thought Mondale had a chance in only about six states: Minnesota, Massachusetts, West Virginia, Maryland, Rhode Island, and Hawaii. And they felt the president actually enjoyed a small edge in all those states except Minnesota.

Reagan pollster Richard Wirthlin could barely maintain his innate Mormon caution in discussing the pending election. Reagan, his polls indicated, was winning more than 25 percent of the Democratic vote and doing slightly better among blue-collar workers than his good 1980 showing. The Mondale camp, he believed, "made a strategic mistake in making leadership the issue. Those charges backfired. On leadership, people prefer Reagan."

The chief concern of Republicans at this time was how many Republicans would Reagan bring in with him. To an extent, the Reagan camp calculated that would depend on the size of his victory. If Reagan won by fifteen to twenty points, they reasoned, he would bring in twenty-five to thirty new House Republicans and perhaps enable the GOP to hold their current edge in the Senate. A smaller margin of ten points would produce a less impressive GOP showing.

This was of more than academic interest to Republicans and to Reagan. The White House needed to pick up two dozen House seats to capture the "philosophical majority" that the president enjoyed in 1981 and 1982. And if the Democrats picked up two or three Senate seats in 1984, the GOP would retain a majority, but its control of the Senate would be endangered since in 1986 many more GOP Senators were going to be up for reelection. If the Senate became Democratic, the final two years of Reagan's presidency could be disastrous.

The picture didn't look much different to the Mondale camp. They never fashioned a credible strategy to win 270 electoral votes. As October came to a close, it was tough to find 70 electoral votes, much less 270. Some once-promising states now were lost irretrievably, with the slippage especially pronounced in the South. Less than a year earlier Alabama was considered an excellent state for Mondale. In December 1983 a Peter Hart survey showed that 53 percent of the white voters in that state were Democrats and only 24 percent were Republicans. With most blacks safely in the Democratic column, the Democrats ranked Alabama as perhaps their best state in the South. Ten months later, however, Hart surveyed Alabama and found that only 29 percent of the white voters identified themselves as Democrats versus 41 percent who said they were Republicans. This dramatic turnaround of forty-one points among white voters reflected both disenchantment with the Democrats and the successful GOP registration drive. As the campaign closed, no Mondale strategist thought any Southern state was winnable.

Curiously, one state that continued to attract the Democrats' attention was Reagan's home state of California, where the president had appeared on the ballot eight times and won eight times. But a mid-summer Hart poll showed Mondale trailing by only eight points and Democrats like California's liberal social attitudes and diverse views on economic and foreign policy issues. Moreover, as Hart advised, if California was uphill with the Democratic nominee usually trailing by about ten points, it was easy compared to Texas, where the Hart surveys never showed Mondale trailing by less than thirty points. The Reaganites never did take the Mondale challenge in California very seriously, though the president's wife, Nancy, pressured them into pumping extra resources into California at the end of the campaign. In February the usually reliable California poll, conducted by Mervin Field, showed Reagan ahead of Mondale 56 percent to 39 percent; eight months later, right before the election, the same poll showed the President ahead 55 percent to 39 percent.

But if one state served as a microcosm for the struggle, it was Ohio. With unemployment still hovering around 10 percent, Mondale talked the old Democratic line of jobs and more jobs. Polls, however, continued to show Reagan with a clear lead. But, as earlier, Roger Stone and other Reagan strategists still believed Ohio was their most vulnerable industrial state. Former President Nixon—who won Ohio all five times he appeared on a national ticket—privately advised the Reagan campaign to throw extra resources into Ohio. That advice was heeded.

Reagan made several October stops in Ohio, including a whistle-stop train tour that replicated much of the route that Harry Truman took in a 1948 tour. (Reagan's penchant for usurping Democratic heroes—Franklin Roosevelt, John F. Kennedy, and Harry Truman—infuriated Democrats, but they were powerless to stop it.) The polls indicated the Reagan efforts were paying off in Ohio. A Teeter survey of eight hundred voters on October 7–8, during the first debate, not only showed the president with a comfortable lead, but now indicated that most Ohioans were more optimistic about the direction the country was heading.

Stone was convinced that a key to the good situation in Ohio was the emphasis on taxes and linking Mondale to Governor Celeste. "We really are running against Dick Celeste," the young political operative gloated. And Stone still felt the issue that could motivate many voters was taxes.

A postcard was sent to all Ohio voters with pictures of Walter Mondale and Governor Celeste on the front side by side. Underneath was the caption: "If You Liked Dick Celeste's Tax Increase, You'll Love Walter Mondale's." On the back, the campaign charged that Mondale "wants to add an additional $1,890 in new tax burden on each Ohio household. Mondale's plan would cost Ohioans $8.0 billion in new taxes." The figures were made out of whole cloth, but the impact wasn't.

Days before the election, every Cuyahoga County voter received a "Dear Friend" letter from Ronald Reagan, asking them "to carefully consider your choice this election day" and to think about "the central issue of this campaign: TAXES." In a postscript, the letter summarized the case the Reaganites were making: "The choice is clear. Shall we increase taxes and slow economic recovery and cost Ohio jobs, or shall we pursue policies of economic growth and opportunity? The choice is yours."

Ironically, despite the bleak outlook, Mondale never was better on the stump than in the ten days preceding the election. He was talking about fairness, economic opportunity, civil rights and civil liberties, arms control and peace. It was a liberal litany and Mondale was comfortable. The two times that this innately cautious politician came alive on the stump in 1984 were the first two weeks of March and the final two weeks of the campaign. Both times Mondale seemed a sure loser—first for the nomination and then for the general election —so he was able to shed the careful, calculating cautiousness of trying to appeal to disparate elements and say what he really believed. This no longer was a strategy to win the election or even to capture certain states. Instead, the plan was to go out in style in the hopes that this would minimize the damage to other Democratic candidates that might result from a Reagan landslide.

Mondale scored some points, too. The campaign discovered a letter private citizen Ronald Reagan had written to then-vice-president Richard Nixon during the 1960 presidential campaign in which Reagan blasted John F. Kennedy: "Under the touseled boyish haircut is still old Karl Marx—first launched a century ago," Reagan wrote. "There is nothing new in the idea of a government being Big Brother to us all. Hitler called his 'State Socialism' and way before him it was 'benevolent monarchy.'" This was from the man who now missed few opportunities to associate himself with John F. Kennedy.

Mondale was attracting terrific crowds in the final weeks. In recession-ravaged Youngstown, Ohio, the crowd was positively ecstatic. (The rally was led by the Democratic candidate for county prosecutor, an encouraging sign for Mondale as the Mahoning Valley local Democrats care a lot more about who's the local prosecutor than who's congressman, governor, or even president.) A few days later, in New York City's garment district, six blocks of wall-to-wall people turned out to cheer the Democratic nominee and his running mate. These crowds gave some Democrats hope for an upset. That was misplaced. Basically, crowds in a general election are a function of organizational advance work and many of these people were being turned out by labor. Still, the crowds were a boost for the candidate.

Mondale's final advertising heavily stressed arms control and the dangers of war. This was the one issue that polls showed consistently worried people about Reagan. There were other commercials on fairness and leadership, but the arms control message dominated.

But the Reagan ad team—consisting of outside advertising executives and directed by pollster Bob Teeter—had more than a match for the Mondale arms control commercials: the "bear" ad. The simple ad showed a big bear prowling angrily in the forest as the announcer intoned: "There is a bear in the woods. For some people, the bear is easy to see. Others don't see it at all. Some people say the bear is tame. Others say it is vicious and dangerous. Since no one can really be sure who's right, isn't it smart to be as strong as the bear—if there is a bear?" As the ad closed, the viewer saw a man with a rifle on his shoulder and as the bear stepped back a written message said: "President Reagan. Prepared for Peace."

Research showed this to be one of the most effective ads in recent elections, portraying Reagan not as a bellicose president but as someone who wants to be strong just in case the Russian bear decides to test us.

Even at the end of the campaign, the carefully orchestrated Reagan campaign dominated the television coverage. The networks aired all the visuals the Reagan media managers devised, disregarding any sense of news judgment, but reasoning that television had to show what the president was doing, whether it was news or not. Privately, the Reagan strategists bragged about their ability to dominate, indeed, dictate, television network coverage.

Reagan did project a very uplifting portrait. One Ohio scene was described by the *Wall Street Journal*'s James Perry:

The late afternoon sun, slanting through the trees, spotlighted the President of the U.S., standing on the observation platform of a beautiful old U.S. No. 1, the Pullman car used in earlier whistle-stop campaigns by Franklin Roosevelt and Harry Truman. . . .[29]

Behind the train was the Ottawa railroad station, all in soft red brick. The band was outfitted in blue and white. The school buses were yellow, the fire engines red. The whole picture-book town gleamed.

When the speaking was over, everybody was asked to join in the singing of "God Bless America." Mr. Reagan sang along. So, not more than 20 feet away, did one of the high school cheerleaders. Her costume was gold; the braces on her teeth were silver. Tears streamed down her face as she watched Ronald Reagan.

It was the prettiest political rally this reporter has ever seen.

When it came to substance, the president wasn't as impressive. He continued to insist he would trim the deficit without raising taxes, but never explained how; at the same time the most prominent congressional Republican tax writer, retiring New York Congressman Barber Conable, was acknowledging that Reagan almost surely would have to raise taxes in a second term. In appealing to a Jewish audience on Long Island, the president suggested he sent marines to Lebanon to stop any holocaust.

None of this mattered to voters, however, and the president, in the closing days, dreamed of a fifty-state sweep and carrying in thirty to forty House members with him. He traveled to states like Massachusetts and West Virginia, for himself and to help Senate and House candidates. Two days before the election he made a last-minute unscheduled stop in Rochester, Minnesota, to campaign for himself and Republican congressional candidate Keith Spicer in Fritz Mondale's home state.

But the nature of Reagan's campaign—vague platitudes with no specifics, very much unlike the blueprint laid out in 1980—assured, in the words of columnist Mark Shields, that this election would be "a landslide without a mandate. . . . While most of the press criticism has fixed on the shortcomings of the Mondale organization, the 1984 Reagan effort may well turn out to be a campaign masterpiece and a political disaster." [30]

Conclusion

At the end, pollsters Teeter and Hart stressed how little the election had changed the political landscape. "This election has been about Ronald Reagan, a referendum on Reagan," said Teeter on election eve. "When we look back to see what has happened this year, the answer is basically nothing. This is an important election about major issues . . . voters understand the fundamental differences between Reagan and Mondale. But it's not a very complex election. Actually, it's quite simple." Hart didn't much disagree: "Reagan became a safe choice," the Democratic polltaker said. "People were comfortable with him."

As the results came in on election day, there were few surprises. Reagan won a massive personal victory, sweeping every state except Minnesota. He was the first president to win back to back landslides since Dwight Eisenhower. Yet, it seemed a uniquely personal victory. The Democrats actually gained two Senate seats and lost only fourteen House seats to maintain a more than seventy-vote edge in the House. Most of the candidates that Reagan campaigned for at the end, including Minnesota GOP candidate Keith Spicer, lost.

There is little doubt that Mondale ran less than an ideal campaign. The competence of his organization, once reputed to be the finest in memory, was exaggerated; at the end of the campaign some top aides barely were on speaking terms with each other. The candidacy suffered from some bad miscalculations; foremost was the refusal to understand, or even accept, the damage Mondale suffered from perceptions that he was an old-fashioned politician beholden to special interests. And these problems were compounded by the emergence of an irrational dislike and distrust of much of the press; the campaign spoke of "punishing" reporters who were out of favor.

And Reagan had a lot of luck. The surge of patriotism emanating from the Olympics clearly helped the incumbent; though, if the Russians hadn't boycotted the Olympics, it's likely the United States wouldn't have dominated the games and the euphoria over the victories would have been more muted. Earlier, Reagan benefited from the decline of the international oil cartel (OPEC), or at least the end of the spiraling oil price increases, though his policies had little to do with this.

But it's equally apparent that no Democrat would have beaten Reagan, and the incumbent had more than luck. He might misspeak at press conferences, but most people felt he was a strong leader, whether it was in standing up to the Soviets abroad or breaking the air traffic controllers' strike at home. The Reagan economic record, while it fell short of its promise, was decidedly better than that of his recent predecessors. Most of all, even millions of Americans who were skeptical of some of his policies grew to feel good about this president; they were, as Peter Hart suggested, comfortable with Reagan.

One of the best explanations for the Reagan personal landslide was offered by political analyst Alan Baron. "In 1984," he wrote, "the American people found themselves in the position of a diabetic, confronted with a giant piece of chocolate cake. 'Enjoy,' said Ronald Reagan. 'You feel fine now, the cure is on the way.' 'Put that fork down right now,' warned Walter Mondale. 'At this very moment, children are starving in Ethiopia.'

"Americans," Baron concluded, "did not need to believe Reagan would find the cure to know that Mondale wasn't going to get the cake to the children."[31]

Where's the Beef?
Media and Media Elites in 1984

MICHAEL J. ROBINSON

————In presidential politics, mass media come in four varieties. The first is *news*, what political consultants insist on calling the free media. News is the "reality" medium. Second closest to reality is *presidential debate*, formal, on-camera performances by candidates in a format the public now accepts as real debate. Third is *political advertising*, what the advertisers themselves label the paid media. Last is *entertainment*, a form of mass communication made relevant to the presidency before Gerald Ford walked woodenly through a scene in "Dynasty," even before Richard Nixon made a cameo appearance on "Laugh-In."

Most of the public and some of the critics combine the four types, making it difficult to appreciate the relative influence of each. But serious discussion of "the media" or "the media elite" requires us to divide the media into their principal parts. For one thing, the media come from different places. Free media people work mostly out of Washington; paid media people out of New York. Debate performances may originate anywhere, of course, even, as in 1980, from Cleveland. Entertainment reaches us mainly through Los Angeles.

Media elites do not just live in separate places; they play different parts. Each has a healthy disregard for what the other media forms are doing. News people love to write stories about the frivolous existence of the entertainment people who live in Los Angeles; people who work in entertainment regard news and political advertising as a little boring; and the press hates the very term paid media people have invented to describe their work—"free media," instead of news.

Yet, despite these differences, most of the media had something in common in 1984. Most of them had only a limited effect on the campaign. In fact, two of the more controversial hybrids—docudrama and advertising—had practically no effect, despite unprecedented speculation about the effect they were to have. Even the press had a bad year—not because it proved itself irresponsible so much as because it proved itself slightly irrelevant. And in several instances the mass media produced effects *opposite* to those expected.

Obviously at times the media did make a difference. Consider, for example, what happened to Gary Hart's campaign after the New Hampshire primary. After the media event that is New Hampshire, Hart was, for a time, capturing three million supporters a day, most of whom did not know why he had become their man. In the light of Hart, it makes about as much sense to argue that the media are impotent as to argue that Ronald Reagan is a devoted grandfather.

Still, when we consider all the things the mass media did *not* change in this election, the preponderance of evidence supports those who see the media more as factors than as forces in presidential politics. Nineteen eighty-four did more than undermine the theories of George Orwell. It also undermined the theories of those who insist that the media or the media elite determine winners and losers in presidential campaigns. But, before reaching general conclusions about the power of the mass media, we need to look at each separate medium to determine which mattered, when it mattered, and why. I am going to start by looking at entertainment and advertising, the "fictional" media.

Entertainment Media: Not Since Kohoutek Failed to Come

Until now, few elections have given social scientists an opportunity to test the political effects of the entertainment media. Until now we have amused ourselves by speculating about Pat Paulsen's first campaign or Doonesbury's effect on John Anderson. In 1984, however, we got our chance—two chances in fact. Both came in late 1983, after the entire presidential field had announced, or all but announced. Both came out of Hollywood: first, *The Right Stuff*, a should-have-been-major motion picture; and then "The Day After," a made-for-prime-time special event on ABC. *The Right Stuff* was released in October; "The Day After" reached us in November. In keeping with the calendar I ought to discuss first the movie and then the broadcast. But in order to move from the melodramatic to the "docudramatic"—from the fictional to the fictionalized—I have reversed the chronological order.

Pure Entertainment: "The Day After" and Its Lack of Fallout

ABC's "The Day After" was fiction, pure and simple—a story about life in Middle America just before and just after the outbreak of nuclear war. But with the trade journals predicting an audience of 100 million (the show turned out to be the eleventh highest rated in television history), it was obvious "The Day After" would lead to enormous speculation about its effect on real world politics. Politicians on all sides injected themselves into "The Day After" to a degree unprecedented in prime-time entertainment.

Alan Cranston, the most vociferous nuclear-freeze candidate, planned his paid media campaign in Iowa around the scheduling of "The Day After." (The Cranston staff had very high hopes that "The Day After" would make Cranston the surprise in Iowa.) The administration dispatched secretary George Shultz to appear on ABC immediately after the broadcast; Shultz's diplomatic mission: to get the White House line on camera as soon as possible after the program. Then live, on camera, came a former secretary of state, a former secretary of defense, and policy celebrities from the right, the left, and the secular center: Henry Kissinger, Robert McNamara, William Buckley, and Carl Sagan all showed up at ABC studios for seventy-five minutes of discussion after "The Day After." This was a media event if ever one was.

With a Nielsen rating of 46 and an audience share of 62, "The Day After" might have been a twentieth-century version of *Uncle Tom's Cabin*. It might have been television's answer to "The War of the Worlds." It might have been the blossoming of Alan ("The Freeze") Cranston or the withering of Ronald ("Nuclear Cowboy") Reagan. In fact, it was none of these. "The Day After" made money, even made cinematic history; but it did not help the freeze movement, or have *any* of the anticipated political consequences some had hoped for and others had feared.

Most of what we know about "The Day After" comes from a specially conducted *Washington Post* poll, from one high-powered statistical study done at the University of Kentucky, and, above all, from a survey-based field experiment conducted nationwide by a team of social scientists headed by William C. Adams.[1] From Adams we learn, for example, that "The Day After" was not Orson Welles's "The War of the Worlds"; it was not even "The Thornbirds," ABC's 1983 fictional rendition of an Australian priest gone first to Rome and then to sin. As to audience reaction, "The Day After" actually elicited a third fewer calls to ABC than had "The Thornbirds."

Nor did the program produce any measured increase in mail to fifty congressional and senatorial offices. Ground Zero and the Lawyers Alliance for Nuclear Arms Control reported no increase in interest after the broadcast. As for anticipated psychological effects, Adams concludes "psychologists and psychiatrists appear to have spent far more time talking to television station reporters [about the broadcast] than to disturbed patients."[2]

"The Day After" produced as little change in opinion as it produced panic. The evidence—whether from Adams or from Feldman and Sigelman, or from the *Washington Post*—shows that the effect on opinion was minimal. Opinions about defense spending, about the freeze movement, and about the likelihood of nuclear war showed no significant shift as a consequence of the broadcast.

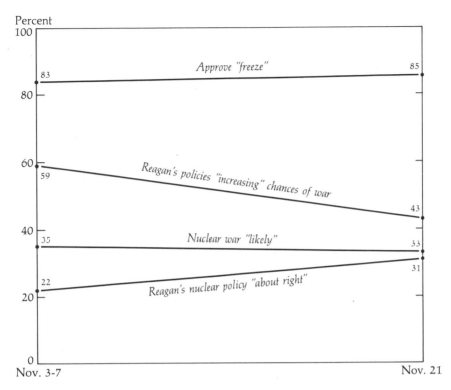

Figure 6.1 Public opinion before and after "The Day After"
Source: See note 1 on p. 353 of this volume.

Adams found that 16 percent of his pretest group thought we were not spending enough on defense; in the post-test group it was 17 percent.[3] Feldman and Sigelman found 31 percent of their respondents wanted to increase the defense budget before the show; after the show the figure was still 31 percent.[4] Adams found the percentage supporting unilateral disarmament went down a point after the program.

What about attitudes toward the likelihood of nuclear war? The *Washington Post* poll showed a 2 percent decline in public predictions of the possibility of nuclear war.[5] As for the likelihood of surviving such a war, again the evidence indicates no effect. The truth is that the public showed a little perversity on the issue of survival. After the show people became slightly more optimistic about surviving a nuclear holocaust.

Speaking of the perversity of opinion, all three studies indicate that seeing "The Day After" produced a significant increase in support for Reagan and for his policies. Figure 6.1 contains findings from the *Washington Post* poll. On most questions there was very little change one way or the other, but the two "Reagan" items shifted in his favor.

For some unexplained reason, pollster Barry Sussman of the *Post* interpreted these data as showing increasing support for the freeze but not for Reagan, a conclusion that might itself merit a story. The real story, however, is not Sussman's interpretation or the apparent rally-round-the-flag effect, which profited the president. The real story is that no single dose of political fiction will change public values or beliefs in any appreciable way on something as fundamental as nuclear war. If the American people have learned anything, they have learned how to handle political fiction on television. Despite fear in the White House and hope at Ground Zero, "The Day After" meant nothing in presidential politics. George Shultz might just as well have gone to bed.

Docudrama: The Right Stuff Fails Glenn

Docudrama did not start with "Eleanor and Franklin" or "Behind Closed Doors." Plutarch wrote more docudrama than anyone yet identified with commercial television or motion pictures. *The Right Stuff* was different, however. Never before had docudrama been so timely, coming before the major characters had died or left office or finished their careers.

The Right Stuff, based on Tom Wolfe's best-seller of the same name, chronicled the life and times of the first seven American astronauts, John Glenn among them. Glenn was a secondary hero in both the book and the movie, but he *was* a hero. And at the time of the movie's release Glenn was second in the polls among candidates for the Democratic presidential nomination.

The movie and its potential effect became the focus of major media attention. On October 3, *Time* and *Newsweek* both put *The Right Stuff* on the cover. *Newsweek* asked in bold print what turned out to be the year's dumbest rhetorical question, "Can a movie help make a president?" The answer was emphatically no. Although Adams's quasi-experimental research found that viewing *The Right Stuff* caused people to like and respect John Glenn more than they had before, in the real world the movie did nothing at all for Glenn, or for its commercial backers.[6]

The Gallup Poll presents us with two sets of data about Glenn, both of which seem to refute the notion that movies make the man in presidential politics. The first set provides answers from the traditional "trial heat" question, the hypothetical race between Reagan, the incumbent, and, in this instance, Glenn. The second set of responses deals with the rank-and-file support for Glenn's nomination. Figure 6.2 makes everything reasonably clear: Hardly a shred of evidence suggests *The Right Stuff* helped Glenn. Between July and November the lines on Glenn's graph roll about as gently as the topography of his native Ohio. In fact, the slope of one line—the trial heat item—rolls away

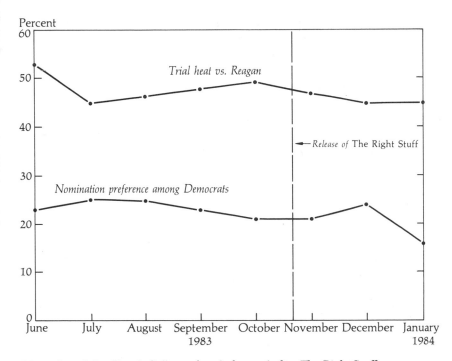

Percent

Trial heat vs. Reagan

Release of The Right Stuff

Nomination preference among Democrats

June July August September October November December January
1983 1984

Figure 6.2 John Glenn's Gallup ratings before and after *The Right Stuff*
Source: See note 6 on p. 353 of this volume.

from the notion that *The Right Stuff* helped the Glenn campaign. Combining the two sets of data shows no increase whatsoever in Glenn's public support in the two months after the movie's release.

What makes Glenn's case more intriguing is that the networks gave him considerable and favorable news attention tied directly to *The Right Stuff.* The average number of pieces about Glenn appearing on the evening news quadrupled between August and October. During October the networks gave him six times as much coverage as Gary Hart, five times as much as Jesse Jackson, and three times as much as George McGovern, much of it having to do with the movie.[7]

In retrospect, some journalists argue the film hurt Glenn, presenting him as a straitlaced astronaut, not as a savvy politician. But that interpretation does not work well either: Adams and his colleagues found that the movie probably helped Glenn's image as a politician about as much as anything.[8] *The Right Stuff* did not fail Glenn because he came across as NASA's answer to Mister Rogers. It failed him for three other reasons. First, because it failed at the box office (only about 1 percent of the electorate saw the film in its first four months, the crucial months of the early campaign). Second, because those most likely to go to the movies—the young—are least likely to go to the primary polls. Third, because people do not vote on the basis of docudrama much more readily than on the basis of prime-time science fiction.

Glenn's people admit that they figured *The Right Stuff* would help with their organizational problems or at least diminish them. Glenn's people, like Cranston's people, were thinking wishfully or not much at all. Neither "The Day After" nor *The Right Stuff* produced an effect in any way commensurate with the media hype accompanying either. Not since the Kohoutek comet failed to come has anything proved as unworthy of its predictions as the power of docudrama or political fiction in the 1984 campaign.

Paid Media: Throwing It Away

For academics and pundits the paid media are a big issue in presidential politics. Two major studies of the history of presidential advertising came out in 1984.[9] All the major newspapers had someone assigned to cover the paid media. Bill Moyers and Phil Donahue both felt the need to do special broadcasts about the power of commercials in presidential politics. CBS and NBC announced to their audiences that they would monitor the machinations of the paid media people during the year, a public service of sorts.

For the most part paid media and paid media people are controversial because they are expensive, because they traffic in misrepresentation, and because they are presumed to have an effect. As for the cost, there is no question that the absolute dollar totals are high. The Reagan-Bush people spent $740,000 on election eve to buy three half-hour slices of network prime time for their final political appeal, and that was a bargain-basement rate, given the cost of thirty-second spots. Although the relative cost of our campaigns is not nearly so high as most critics argue, there is no point in denying that candidates spend increasing amounts of money and time putting together a paid media campaign.[10]

Misrepresentation is another problem. In 1984 we had the usual spate of spot ads that misrepresented reality or managed to avoid it totally. Hart used a lighted fuse to imply that Walter Mondale was planning war in Central America. Mondale used a red phone spinning in the ether to imply Hart was not mature enough to answer the hot line. Reagan and Bush used one spot called "morning again," implying the Republican party was responsible for more than the recovery—conveying the notion that it had helped to bring marriage back into style.[11] In 1984, however, the big issue over paid media was neither content nor cost. The real issue was—and is—impact. The debate about the paid media always rests on the assumption that they "work." But the hard evidence from 1984 says no. Just as in the 1980 campaign,[12] the money spent on paid media had virtually no measurable effect on voting.

"Hart-Breaking Lessons" about Paid Media: The Drunken Sailor Syndrome

The Mondale-Reagan campaign is a poor test of the effects of the paid media. Few dramatic shifts occurred in public preferences during the fall, and none of them correlated very well with advertising effort. Besides, from September on, both campaigns had about the same amount of media money to spend. Given those facts, one would be left to argue about the relative quality of the various ads, an impressionistic enterprise if ever there was one.

The first six months of 1984, however, offered a classic confrontation in paid media campaigning: Hart versus Mondale in the Democratic primaries. In a pair of strategies that make the life of a social scientist almost worth living, Mondale spent much of his money in the beginning of the year, before the early primaries and caucuses; Hart spent his money later. What is more, the fortunes of Hart and Mondale changed almost constantly, suggesting something was going on in their campaigns. The contest between Hart and Mondale over time and across the several states provides, in other words, a lovely little test of the power of money and of the paid media in presidential politics.

Figures of the Federal Election Commission (FEC) for Hart and Mondale may not be exact, but they cannot be that far off. If FEC data tell us anything, they tell us paid media buy votes about as efficiently as the Pentagon buys spare parts and toilet seats. Hart and Mondale made major paid media efforts in eighteen states (by a major effort in a state I mean that either Hart or Mondale spent at least $100,000 to win delegates). We have figures on total expenditures in each of these states for both candidates and, of course, voting statistics for both candidates in each of the states as well. With qualification— Mondale, for example, spent more through his national office than state offices, while Hart did the opposite—we know, primary by primary, Hart's and Mondale's percentages of the "two-person" vote and their percentages of the "two-person" campaign expenditures.

Figure 6.3 plots Hart's percentage of the two-person expenditures against his percentage of the two-person vote. The pattern in the data points is a bit clouded but still visible. The higher the percentage of expenditure, the lower the share of the vote. In these eighteen major paid media states, the correlation between dollars and votes is −.31 for Hart.

One can reach the same conclusion without the benefit of correlation coefficients. Of the eleven big-media states (California, Florida, Georgia, Illinois, Michigan, New Jersey, New York, Ohio, Pennsylvania, Texas, and Wisconsin)

Percentage of vote

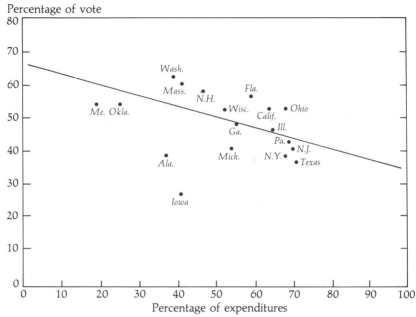

Figure 6.3   Hart's percentage of "two-person" expenditures vs. Hart's percentage of "two-person" vote.
Source: Calculated by the author.

where Hart outspent Mondale, Hart won four, lost seven. Of the five states (Ohio, New Jersey, New York, Pennsylvania, and Texas) where Hart outspent Mondale two to one or more, Hart lost four (all but Ohio).

Mondale, similarly, lost five of the seven states (Alabama, Iowa, Maine, Massachusetts, New Hampshire, Oklahoma, and Washington) where he spent more than Hart. Of the two states where he outspent Hart two to one (Maine and Oklahoma), he lost both. All told, the big spender lost in twelve of the eighteen big-media states.

What makes these figures a little alarming is that they tend to imply that spending really does hurt—heavily financed paid media efforts lose votes. I do not think that is true. Voters have never before shown any clear tendency to punish candidates for spending heavily. But I also reject the typical explanation for the negative relation between money and electoral support: that it simply reflects the tendency of those who are behind to spend more to catch up.

The truth is that candidates do not necessarily spend more where they expect to do badly: Mondale spent $236 in Colorado; Hart spent about $4,000 in West Virginia. What really happens is that candidates have a two-step strategy. First, whether ahead or behind, as a rule they spend where they feel they need to spend. Just as often in presidential politics, however, they spend when they have it to spend. That is the best explanation for the negative correlation between Hart's expenditures and his vote. Hart had little money to spend when he was winning; he had plenty of money to spend as he lost. Spending and winning are unrelated; it is the "drunken sailor" syndrome in presidential politics, spending what you have, regardless.

In a few states Hart or Mondale may have bought a victory: Hart in Ohio, Mondale in Alabama. Those obviously are exceptions. For every Ohio there is a New Jersey, a state in which Hart outspent Mondale two-and-a-half to one and outspent Jackson eight hundred to one. Mondale got about 45 percent of the vote in New Jersey, Hart about 30 percent, and Jackson more than 20 percent.[13]

Why do paid media campaigns fail so badly? One answer involves policy. By law, federally funded candidates face limits on campaign expenditures, nationally and in each state. But that can't explain places like New Jersey where limits existed but Hart did worse than Mondale and only slightly better than Jackson, despite the galactic difference in spending. The better answer is that the free media, debate performances, and "reality" all have a greater impact. Paid media are, except for entertainment, the weakest in the family of media, disdained as mere commercials by both the public and the critics.

New Jersey proves the theory. Hart should have won there: New Jersey is a Yuppie state; Hart was doing well in the polls; he was outspending Mondale seven to three. Then free media and free media mistakes caught up with Hart. He made the very worst sort of verbal mistake anybody can make concerning public opinion in self-conscious New Jersey: He told a New Jersey joke. Hart told a California audience his wife had the good luck, campaigning out there; he had the bad luck, campaigning back in New Jersey. After that, all the media consultants in Princeton and Trenton couldn't put Hart's campaign back together again, regardless of how much they had to spend.

That a New Jersey joke can move a primary electorate may not be good news for democratic theory. But the New Jersey joke fiasco proves how much more powerful free media—and free media mistakes—are than paid media. The local press in New Jersey converted Hart's attempt at humor into the second worst blunder of his campaign.

The worst was in Illinois, and it too shows how little paid media mean when compared with free media. Hart should also have won in Illinois—in the polls he was winning in Illinois by ten points with just a week to go. With momentum, money, and a paid campaign just under twice as large as Mondale's, he had everything going for him. In one of the campaign's great ironies, however, Hart messed up his free media campaign by messing up with the paid media. During the last weekend before the Illinois primary, Hart publicly (and emotionally) attacked Mondale for an ad the Mondale campaign had neither run nor planned. Then later that day, after publicly (but grudgingly) apologizing to Mondale for his mistake, Hart failed to withdraw a television ad of his own that slurred Chicago City Councilman Edward ("Fast Eddie") Vrdolyak.

Hart's behavior in each instance gave the free media and Mondale an opportunity both had wanted—a "real" blunder from Hart. At the very moment the press was asking, Who *is* Gary Hart? and the Mondale "red phone" ads were questioning Hart's maturity and experience, Hart answered them all by demeaning a local hero and vilifying Mondale for something he had never done. Hart's $600,000 worth of paid campaign fell apart in four days. He lost Illinois by five points, losing seventeen points over that last weekend.[14]

Hart's vicissitudes might force anybody to ask why candidates bother to have a paid media campaign. It costs. It does not usually work. It causes problems with the free media. But candidates want very much to be president, and presidential candidates come from political offices where paid media do work. And they all live in fear that somebody else's paid media might do the trick. Candidates know too that if they fail to assemble slick media campaigns, the free media dismiss their candidacies as frivolous. Ironic as it may be, candidates need paid media campaigns for the sake of proving themselves to the press. Finally, candidates have to spend their money on something, and they know they cannot buy reporters. So paid media and paid media consultants we will always have with us.

The 1984 campaign seems to offer four general lessons about paid media. First, paid media do not buy presidential nominations. When Hart had his biggest paid media efforts, he suffered his worst defeats, and so did Mondale. Nobody has ever won a presidential nomination or an election because he had more or better ads.

Second, paid media are no higher than third in impact—after free media and after debates. Something as trivial as Hart's New Jersey joke will, in a free media system such as ours, totally overwhelm the "limited" paid media allowed to each candidate under federal law. Besides, the public simply does not believe in paid ads as it believes in debates or in free media. The good news is money does not talk in presidential politics; the bad news is nonsense often does.

Third, presidential paid media work only when they reinforce the impressions left by facts, free media, or debate. Mondale's "red phone" ads against Hart worked when they reinforced Hart's real world behavior and free media impressions. If candidates are smart enough—or lucky enough—to plan a paid campaign that winds up meshing with the other media messages going out to voters, candidates can profit from their ads. Because Mondale was lucky enough to be running negative ads about Hart's immaturity, ads in Illinois that meshed perfectly with bad news about Hart in the press, the ads worked.

Mondale's campaign director, Robert Beckel, looked back over the campaign and made that very observation. "This has been the most inconsistent year for paid media ever in presidential politics. The key thing was free TV. . . . The ads that worked for [Mondale and Hart] were the ones that were in synch with the free media."[15] All told, 1984 should teach presidential candidates one last important lesson about the real power of paid media: Paid media are exponentially more likely to make consultants successful than to make candidates successful.

Free Media: Who Cares What Sam Donaldson Thinks?

"Free media" is a misnomer. Only for candidates are the free media really free. *We* pay for free media. As George Gerbner puts it, we pay when we wash, not when we watch.

The "free media" label presents a second problem. The words convey the notion that the free media are divorced from reality. In fact, they are as close to reality as most of us ever get. One sometimes hears a campaign manager, a press secretary, or a candidate say that he or she is having trouble with the free media, as if losing a primary, facing an indictment, or presiding over a recession is only a public relations problem.

We know better. We know, for example, the unemployment rate was the best single predictor of Reagan's public approval score throughout his first term.[16] Nobody can talk seriously about the free media without acknowledging that "fact" and "reality" are part of their message. Talking seriously about the power of the free media requires that we somehow exclude real events and real indicators from our calculations. I suggest the impact of the free media has to do with three things that go beyond or around reality: "news spin," "news agenda," and free media "performance."

News spin is the simplest of the three and the most controversial. It consists of analysis and innuendo, the interpretation journalists add to the hard news or recitation of fact. When Chris Wallace wrapped up ten months of Reagan's campaigning by concluding that this was a campaign "long on glitz, short on substance," Wallace was, whether right or wrong, doing a little news spinning.

News agenda is less obvious, having more to do with topic than with interpretation. In March 1984, the three evening news programs presented forty-three items concerning the personal and political problems of Edwin Meese. Ursula Meese, his wife, also made the evening news ten times in March, all pieces concerning her possible violations of political ethics. Justified as all that coverage may have been, "Meesegate" was very much part of the 1984 news agenda. Like "Billygate" in 1980, Meesegate reflected the news topics the media and Senator Howard Metzenbaum—not the government and certainly not Meese—wanted addressed.

During campaigns news people have extra latitude to decide what deserves coverage. Network news people, for example, decided during the general campaign that Geraldine Ferraro's imbroglio with the Catholic hierarchy was worth eleven complete stories, four more than the networks devoted to Ferraro's positions on the issues—all the issues. Nobody can say that Ferraro's fight with Archbishop O'Connor was not newsworthy, but anybody can see the emphasis on it reflects both reality and the notion of news agenda in a presidential campaign. Ferraro versus O'Connor was "mediality," a news story that had as much to do with the practices of the commercial press as with "truth" or reality.[17]

Last comes free media performance, a concept that has much less to do with the behavior of newspeople than it does with the behavior of newsmakers. The idea concerns the candidate's day-by-day (and special day) performance in the free media. The day after his landslide defeat, Mondale invoked free media performance on television to explain his loss to Reagan. He gladly admitted he was not good on or with television and that his free media performances had been less than memorable.

Reagan provided us with several memorable free media performances throughout the campaign. Take, for example, his performance just two days after his unexpectedly lackluster performance in the first debate. With all the bad news and reporters swarming around him, Reagan was asked by ABC's Sam Donaldson: "What about all these new Mondale charges?" Reagan's reply? "I think he should pay them." What makes Reagan's quip important is that Donaldson and ABC decided it just had to be used. Reagan had turned a negative news story into a successful free media performance, one likely to neutralize the negative spin Donaldson tried to put into his actual copy.

So much for definitions. What about the power of news spin, news agenda, and free media performance in 1984? News spin meant very little for many of the major candidates; news agenda meant more, but still nothing to mail home video about; free media performance may have meant as much as spin and agenda combined. In fact, 1984 is a great follow-up to the 1980 elections. Nineteen eighty was a good year for disproving the theory that the press is biased in favor of liberals: Edward Kennedy and Jimmy Carter both received worse press than Reagan in that campaign.[18] Nineteen eighty-four contradicts another theory about the free media: that they determine public preferences in presidential politics.[19] They do not, at least not often and not very much. Looking back on "free media power" in 1984, we might, for one last time (I hope), return to Clara Peller's now legendary query: "Where's the beef?"

News Spin: Three Cases of Noneffects

The Mondale prediction   News spin can be applied to anything—the condition of the horse race, the quality of the candidate, even the issues. As a rule it has mainly to do with candidates' chances, if only because the free media almost always prefer to interpret the horse race.

In the early part of the campaign the most frequently occurring spin (interpretation) concerned the invincibility of Mondale. The Mondale people themselves assiduously cultivated the notion of "Mondale, Inc.," the not-to-be-denied nomination campaign. The free media believed their own story but did not persuade the public.

The prediction started well before 1984 and, as spin, probably reached its zenith when *Newsweek* ran a cover story entitled "Can Anyone Beat Fritz?" on January 9. The subtitle of that story answered its own question: "Mondale's machine is simply the biggest and best in the history of U.S. politics."[20] That story was only the most hysterical of a steady stream of elite media pieces about Mondale's inevitability.

After the Iowa caucuses what had been spin seemed to become reality. Mondale captured 49 percent of the vote in Iowa, and all the networks covered him as if he had won his nomination, something virtually every political scientist in Washington also believed on the weekend after the Iowa vote.[21] I confess to having been part of the pack myself, having told a CBS late-night audience after the Iowa caucuses that Mondale's nomination was not to be seriously questioned any longer.

The Mondale prediction was about as close to a national media consensus as one might ever expect. It lasted at least three months; it carried the imprimatur of virtually every columnist and correspondent covering the campaign; it was based in fact. It even induced Ernest Hollings's former campaign manager to write a nasty piece about how news-people had rendered Mondale inevitable before the race was begun.[22] Yet the Mondale prediction failed completely to move those who voted in New Hampshire just a week after Iowa.

According to the ABC News/ *Washington Post* poll, the day after the Iowa caucuses Mondale led Hart in New Hampshire by almost two to one. The New Hampshire electorate, however, having seen and read the national news, which was overwhelmingly favorable in its spin concerning Mondale's chances, moved away from Mondale. On the night before the New Hampshire primary, the CBS national poll and the CBS news spin both put Mondale far out in front for the nomination—an unprecedented lead for a nonincumbent front-runner nationwide, according to CBS. On election day, Hart beat Mondale in New Hampshire by a ratio of three to two.

The Jackson paradox   Jesse Jackson rode the free media roller coaster more than any candidate since Edward Kennedy. Like Kennedy, Jackson enjoyed enormous free media attention when he toyed with the press about whether he would run. His good press spin, unlike Kennedy's, continued well beyond his formal announcement. In a candidate profile appearing on December 9, 1983, Dan Rather said Jackson is "one of the most spellbinding orators of our time," "his appeal . . . goes across racial lines to the young and those who he says are stuck at the bottom." Rather concluded, "You listen to Jesse Jackson and you hear the echoes, the echoes of his tutor Martin Luther King. . . . Jesse Jackson can lay legitimate claim to the King legacy."

It was not just spin: It was the size of Jackson's press. In November there would be more network news coverage of Jackson than of Mondale, more of Jackson than of Askew, Hart, Hollings, Cranston, and McGovern combined.

In January Jackson staged one of the greatest free media coups in history when he rescued Navy Lieutenant Robert Goodman from his Syrian captivity. This was more than mediality; this was reality: a black clergyman-politician rescuing a black prisoner of war in the name of peace and brotherhood. Goodman was even a resident of New Hampshire at the time. The free media responded as everyone knew they would.

In January the network news programs featured Jackson thirty-seven times, and in twenty-three of those instances either the news or the spin was favorable. Reviewing those pieces, I found 62 percent of the January evening news coverage of Jackson was good press or good news. For six crucial weeks between the Syria trip and the Iowa caucuses, Jackson received evening news attention that was more extensive and more favorable than any third-place candidate had ever received.

But in late February "Hymiegate" broke in the *Washington Post* and throughout the national press. In March and April Jackson's partner in the free media was no longer the adorable Lieutenant Goodman, it was the deplorable Louis Farrakhan. Farrakhan was only one of Jackson's free media problems in March, April, and May. Investigations concerning Jackson's organization PUSH (People United to Save Humanity) and his contacts with Castro and the Sandinistas turned what had been genuinely positive free media coverage into something very different. On network news the good press or good news stories about Jackson fell from 62 percent in January to 24 percent in February, 17 percent in March, and 16 percent in April.[23]

The free media, however, did not reflect Jackson's political fortunes during those months. In an apparent paradox of press power, Jackson seemed to do better in the campaign as his press got worse. His press fell apart in late February. In February he won less than 4 percent of the Democratic caucus and primary vote. In March he won over 15 percent; in April, 18 percent; in May, 21 percent. Jackson's best press preceded his worst showing at the polls; his worst press preceded his best electoral performance.

Farrakhan and Hymiegate were two of the greatest medialities of 1984. After all, neither Jackson's freindship with the fiery Farrakhan nor his semi-public use of ethnic slurs was new. Both became news only after Jackson had become a serious candidate. Jackson actually made some sense when he expressed surprise about the way old news had become big news. Yet none of this seemed to hurt him at the polls. Nor for that matter did the Goodman coverage seem to help with real voters. What mattered was not so much the spin or even the news agenda. What mattered was fact. Because Jackson was demonstrating he really could win votes, he won more, despite the free media.

To be fair, Jackson's increasing success lends itself to alternate interpretations: a smaller field ensured a larger percentage; the racial composition of a state determined the size of the Jackson vote and nothing else mattered; and so on. But the Jackson paradox is one of several cases in which the free media spin was associated with an effect opposite to the one it should have produced. Like the Mondale prediction, the Jackson paradox suggests some people really do decide which way the media are going and then, for whatever motive, move the other way.

The case of the general campaign To this point, evidence about the effects of news spin has been mostly impressionistic. During the general campaign, however, the Media Analysis Project at George Washington University collected data about network news systematically, and spin was one of its most basic concerns. But changing the methods from impressionistic to systematic did not change the conclusion: News spin counted for little in most of the campaign, especially in the general campaign.

Let us start with the aggregate numbers. Nobody disputes that Reagan and Bush won the election, but our measure of "candidate" spin shows that they lost the battle for network news and lost it badly.[24] The Republican ticket had a combined spin score of −35; the Democrats had a combined score of +2. Nothing conveys more about the inability of the free media to move an electorate than these statistics, which reveal how badly the Republican ticket lost the war for news spin. The spin scores of the individual presidential and vice-presidential candidates during the general campaign were as follows:

Bush	−40
Reagan	−33
Mondale	+ 1
Ferraro	+ 4

Throughout the general campaign the networks treated Reagan negatively and Bush even worse. The spin on Bush was that he was a buffoon, a cheerleader, or a jerk—maybe all three. All three networks treated Bush badly, but NBC's John Seveson seemed to set the pace—and the theme—with a piece he presented as early as September 16.

On the campaign Bush has tried to ignore Ferraro. He says his message is upbeat but spends much of his time beating up on Walter Mondale. [Quotation]

Republicans loved it when Bush accused Mondale of being soft on communism in Central America. [Statement by Bush on Mondale's notion that the Sandinistas are "merely liberals"]

Mondale has never called the Sandinistas "merely liberals," and Bush shrugs when he's asked if he's being the tough guy in this campaign. [Quotation]

Bush wasn't tough, he was defensive when he was forced to admit that, unlike the president, he favors abortions in some instances. He said it's the president's position that counts—then he got angry. . . .

It's the local press Bush caters to, like in Savannah, Georgia. He gave a five-minute speech, posed on a tractor, did local interviews, then left town.

Bush was the only candidate about whom not a single favorable thing was said during the general campaign by a network commentator or reporter—something implied by his spin score of −40.

Reagan, with a −33, did not do much better. The line on Reagan was not quite so pointed as that on Bush, but it was unflattering. News spin painted Reagan as unavailable, uninvolved, uninformed, unengaged, and, above all, unrelenting in his manipulation of the media. All the networks reached an implicit consensus about Reagan: He was winning but, given his politics and his behavior, probably did not deserve to be.

The networks focused much more intensely on Reagan's Machiavellian campaign than on his policy failures. On September 13 ABC's Sam Donaldson interpreted the essence of the Reagan campaign. "The essence of the Ronald Reagan campaign is a never-ending string of spectacular picture stories created for television and designed to place the president in the midst of wildly cheering, patriotic Americans. . . . God, patriotism, and Ronald Reagan, that's the essence this campaign is trying hard to project."

On October 4 CBS's Leslie Stahl presented a five-minute feature about Reagan's exploitation of television. "The orchestration of television coverage absorbs the White House," said Stahl. Reagan "tries to counter the memory of an unpopular issue with a carefully chosen package [of video] that actually contradicted the president's policy."

In November NBC televised an election eve piece that symbolized the entire Reagan campaign as the networks presented it. Chris Wallace referred to unnamed sources who considered Reagan "cynical, manipulative." Wallace went on his own to label Reagan's efforts "highly staged and low risk." "Protecting a big lead," concluded Wallace, "the president offered pomp and platitudes but never told us what he was going to do the next four years."

Libel and fairness are not the issues here. Donaldson, Stahl, and Wallace made none of this up. Quite clearly, however, all this was news spin, not hard news, and all of it was bad press for Reagan by any meaningful definition of the term.[25]

As for the Democrats, the picture was different but anything but rosy. On evening news, especially in early September, both Mondale and Ferraro were treated as losers. In late September, however, as it became increasingly clear that the Democrats did not have a chance, the networks let up a bit. On September 26 John Chancellor described Ferraro as "a poised and self-assured candidate," "a well-organized" campaigner, and an "effective speaker." In the most remarkable hyperbole of the network campaign, Chancellor concluded that "you don't hear the phrase weaker sex very often these days. . . . Ferraro may have buried that old phrase forever."

If one excludes references to their standing in the polls, the Democrats reached election day with more positive spin than negative, an unprecedented accomplishment on network news. Where Reagan was to be criticized for "packaging" his message, Mondale and Ferraro got credit for coordinating theirs. During the last week before the election, press spin for Ferraro was so positive as to be almost an embarrassment. Of course, in the end none of it carried many votes or any states.[26]

The Relationship between News Spin and Public Opinion

Aggregate statistics about spin make it abundantly obvious that one can lose the war over network innuendo and still do very well at the polls. The week-by-week measures concerning news spin suggest some truths about press and public opinion that are much more surprising than that.

Using week-by-week "favorability" measures for each candidate and correlating them with each candidate's week-by-week press score, I stumbled across a set of coefficients that contradict almost all the major interpretations of press and public opinion in presidential politics.[27] The average correlation coefficient between spin and favorability for all four candidates turns out to be +.04. In essence, across the field week by week there was no significant statistical relation between press spin about candidate quality and public opinion.

For the individual candidates, the results are even more curious:

Ferraro	−.33
Mondale	−.07
Bush	.18
Reagan	.32

Bush's candidacy produced a correlation of .18, suggesting that at least a tiny part of his public image did depend on his weekly press score. For Bush's vice-presidential opponent, however, the correlation was negative, at least implying that when Ferraro's press got better, her public image got worse, once again an apparent case of the perversity of public opinion. For Mondale, too, the sign of the correlation is negative but the size of the coefficient so puny that Mondale, like Bush, is probably a case of no effect.

Only Reagan seems to have lost support as a function of his negative press coverage. His "favorability index," as measured by Patrick Caddell, is positively correlated with his spin scores. As one went down, so did the other; as one went up, the other did too. In fact, on every press variable we constructed, Reagan's case was the same—a positive correlation between press score and favorability.[28]

What should one make of these numbers? To be fair, the relation between network evening news coverage and public response does vary considerably from measure to measure and from pollster to pollster. The strong negative correlation between Ferraro's press and her public opinion, for example, washes away when one shifts from Caddell's thermometer to Richard Wirthlin's measure. These correlations should not be considered conclusive.

Nevertheless, the correlations suggest a surprising series of conclusions:

Network spin is hardly a major force in presidential preference during a general campaign. Only Reagan seems to have paid for bad press; and since Reagan's thermometer scores shifted only a few points during the general campaign, even these correlations become problematic.[29]

Network spin may sometimes produce an effect on opinion opposite to what simple logic would predict. Ferraro's press suggests that. Still, I doubt the negative correlation between press spin and thermometer measures tells us for certain that Ferraro did worse because her press got better.

Instead, the Ferraro correlations suggest a delicious irony in network power: During a presidential election the public may influence the news media more than the news media influence the public. In short, having seen a distance of twenty points between Mondale-Ferraro and Reagan-Bush in the public polls, the networks let up on criticizing the Democrats, particularly Ferraro. The same sort of thing happened in 1980 with Kennedy and Carter. The networks covered Kennedy more negatively when he was popular, Carter more negatively when he had the lead.[30] In 1984, Mondale and Ferraro received a much less negative press as the polls showed the increasing hopelessness of their campaign. Reporters decided there was no point in being tough. The polls moved the journalism, not the other way around.

As for Reagan's press coverage in the general campaign, the evidence here offers some irony too. Reagan was the only candidate in the general election who seemed to lose real support as a function of his network news spin. Given that apparent fact, it makes no sense at all to regard Reagan as uniquely impervious to criticism or to the press. When his press was dreadful, he did slip at least a little in the polls.

Does it make any sense to believe network news spin never carries much weight in presidential politics? Probably not. It goes beyond reason to argue news spin in 1980 had no real effect on Carter and his campaign. So, in the light of Carter's disastrous reelection bid and of Reagan's history with the press in 1984, we need to reconsider the conditions under which press spin does matter more than just a little. What 1984 seems to imply is that negative spin works mainly in a bad news environment, the kind of environment Carter found in 1980; and that *bad news spin counts for almost nothing in a good news environment*, the kind Reagan enjoyed in 1984. Bad press just does not have sufficient power to carry voters when those voters feel real life conditions are good or improving.

News Agendas: Ed Meese and Other Nonissues

It is an article of faith in media research that the press does not tell us what to think but does tell us what to think about.[31] If the "first" hostage crisis had elicited forty minutes of network news in 1980 instead of 4,000, we might well have been thinking about different issues in that election as we went to vote.[32] But there was no apparent hostage crisis in 1984, and what the free media chose to emphasize did not seem to influence very much what the public was thinking or thinking about: News agenda seemed almost as inconsequential as news spin.

We can start with Meesegate, the compendium of events and allegations about Edwin Meese, his wife, and his friends. In March, Meesegate accounted for more than fifty news stories on network evening news; eight times it was the lead story. Meesegate was a big part of the free media agenda throughout the spring.

In April the Media Analysis Project surveyed about 400 people nationwide, asking, "Who is Ed Meese?" Of course, there were the usual absurdities: Meese was identified as a vicious killer, the new secretary of state, and so on. Half the respondents had no idea whatever who Meese was. Only 36 percent linked him to any of his problems.[33] Despite the intense coverage of Meesegate, the news agenda had not much penetrated the public's ken, let alone the public's concern.

The same sort of thing happened in the general election campaign—a news agenda hardly correlated with the people's agenda. At the Media Analysis Project, Maura Clancey and I classified, by topic, every campaign and presidency story on network evening news (see table 6.1). The topics that received

Table 6.1 News agenda in Autumn vs. most
important problems on election eve, 1984

Rank	Top news stories in Autumn	Rank	Most important problems on election eve
1	The debates	1	Unemployment
2	U.S.-Soviet Relations	2	The economy
3	Reagan's remarks about Beirut as a kitchen	3	Arms control
4	Reagan's age	4	Deficits
5	Taxes	5	Taxes
6	The Beirut bombing	6	Poverty
7	Reagan's inaccessibility	7	Foreign affairs
8	The CIA manual	8	The threat of war
9	Bush's "shame" remarks	9	Size of government
10	Ferraro's fight with her church	10	The elderly
11	Reagan's fundamentalist ties	11	The environment
12	Deficits	12	U.S.-Soviet relations

Sources: "Top news stories" are taken from the AEI-George Washington University Media Monitoring Study, 1984; "most important problems" data provided to the author by Cambridge Survey Research, National Phone Survey, November 5, 1984.

much network news attention were of two kinds: (1) the consensus agenda (topics everybody in government and the media agree really are the agenda, such as taxes and U.S.–Soviet relations); and (2) the media's agenda (the debates, or Reagan's age, or White House inaccessibility, or the CIA-backed assassination manual, or Ferraro's fight with her church's hierarchy).

The people's agenda is what people told Caddell on election eve about the issues that would influence their vote—the typical list of most important problems. Obviously, one cannot compute correlation coefficients for two lists with separate categories. It is astounding, however, how little the esoteric agenda of network news has to do with the meat-and-potatoes agenda of the public at large. If the consensus agenda is removed from the press campaign agenda, the lists are almost unrelated. With debates included, about 40 percent of the presidential news on network television was about campaign issues. Yet the public seemed totally unconcerned with any of those press issues. If it were not for the debates, the network agenda and the people's agenda would be practically unrelated.[34]

As for the rest of the news agenda, it failed miserably to become the people's agenda or to influence public perceptions of candidates. At least seven of the top dozen issues on the network news implied that Reagan and Bush were indecent, incompetent, or incapable. None of that penetrated the public's list of concerns. In fact, Reagan and Bush were the overwhelming winners on the leadership issue, even though the news agenda implied they should have lost it hands down. Network news gave five times as much attention to Republican leadership "problems" as to Democratic leadership problems during the general campaign.

Although Reagan-baiters can dismiss all this as the uniqueness of the Teflon Presidency, what failed to happen in 1984 often fails to happen. Media agendas frequently fail to carry much weight with voters. In 1972 the campaign issue coverage was concentrated on Watergate. Voters did not care about that campaign issue either, not until much later. Would anybody be willing to argue that Nixon enjoyed a Teflon coating? And how is it that George Bush did so wretchedly, as leader, on evening news and so terrifically in the polls?

The news media did not set the issue agenda in 1984. Without a hostage crisis or its equivalent free media rarely do.[35] In most elections and under most circumstances, candidates and officials tell the free media what to talk about, and the free media usually do just that—talk about the candidate agenda or the official agenda. In fact, the public often ignores both agendas—the leadership and the media agenda—and votes on the basis of perennial and fundamental concerns, like peace and the economy.

The real effect of the news agenda in presidential politics has far more to do with press secretaries and scheduling than with voters or public opinion. Back in 1980 nobody voted on the basis of Billygate either; but Billy Carter, as a mediality, forced Jimmy Carter and his staff to pay attention to Billy, not to their agenda. The same thing occurred in 1984, especially for Ferraro and her press secretaries in August and September. It is politicians who seem to care about the news agenda, however, not publics: The free media have much more influence over candidates' strategies than over public concerns.

My own heretical opinion is that the news agenda in 1984 followed the path professional journalism ought to take—digging, carping, investigating Ferraro's finances, Bush's manners, Reagan's vitality. That is journalism—the journalists' agenda. But that does not mean the public listens much; unless the news is cataclysmic or catastrophic, the public just does not care or bother much about the journalists' agenda. In 1984 the free media often failed in telling the public what to think and did about as badly in telling the public what to think about.

Early Returns and West Coast Voters

Before looking at those few cases in which the free media did exercise influence over public opinion, I am going to look at one more newly discredited theory about the power of the free media in presidential elections—the notion that early calls somehow disfranchise the West or the would-be late voter. The right and the left do not agree on much about the free media, but both insist that the early predictions concerning landslide victories depress turnout in the West and in the late-voting states. Critics contend early predictions do more than affect turnout in presidential voting—they also, allegedly, intrude on local elections and may even determine who wins or loses state or congressional elections.[36] I will not review the entire controversy or the voluminous literature that exit polls and early predictions have engendered, but one crucial fact emerges from 1984: Early network calls had no measurable effect on registered voters.

Once again, William Adams provides the relevant research. In the largest election-day survey ever conducted among nonvoting, registered citizens, Adams found that fewer than 3 percent of that small subpopulation believed television predictions had played any part in their decision to stay home.[37] He also found this minuscule number of nonvoters who blamed television predictions for their decision "resembled the electorate at large." Sixty-one percent would have voted for Reagan, a fact that very much calls into question the idea that television-induced nonvoters play an indirect part in a bandwagon or an underdog effect.

In the end Adams concludes television predictions in 1984 discouraged one-third of 1 percent of the registered electorate, and he all but disowns the idea that these minuscule numbers could influence even the most local of elections. We are left with one final instance in which the free media failed to live up to their reputation as powerful or even consequential.

Free Media Power: Two-and-a-Half Cases

The free media are not by any means totally impotent. We have already seen that free media coverage of Hart's press blunders in Illinois and New Jersey more than neutralized his enormous media campaign. Coverage of both sets of blunders constitutes a classic case in "mediality." Both had a big impact, and both imply serious candidates ought not to be quoted saying something stupid, especially on videotape. To understand the real power of the free media, however, we need something besides Illinois and New Jersey. We need Iowa and New Hampshire.

Iowa and New Hampshire again: press power by "convention"   As before, the free media and the candidates converted the Iowa caucuses and the New Hampshire primary into medialities of the first order. The Iowa caucuses alone attracted more than 1,000 reporters—one for every 100 caucus voters.[38] Reporters meant copy as they always do. According to my calculations, on evening news alone the commercial networks presented at least 120 stories about

Iowa and New Hampshire in January and February. In this first case study, however, the issue is not total attention. It is the attention paid to Hart after his distant second-place showing in Iowa and, then again, after his honest-to-goodness victory in New Hampshire.

The national media did not go wild over Hart after Iowa, especially if spin is taken into account. Bruce Morton at CBS spoke as most national reporters were speaking when he said of Hart's vote in Iowa, "When you've lost three to one, you've lost."

The news agenda in this case tells a different story, however. Thanks again to Adams, we have some very useful information about the news agenda before and after the caucuses. According to Adams, Hart's "relative share of coverage the week before and after Iowa was ten times what it had been the week before on NBC, and five times what it had been on CBS."[39] Both the news and the news agenda out of Iowa had an effect on voters in New Hampshire. In this case the size of the news hole really did matter.

David Moore, a professor at the University of New Hampshire, sifted through every other conceivable explanation for the 150 percent increase in Hart's support in his state in the week after Iowa. In the end Moore concluded that the free media were responsible: "The story out of Iowa was not so much that Hart had lost . . . but rather that Hart was now the viable alternative to Mondale."[40]

I believe that Moore overstates at least a bit the power of the national press. It is more the local press (the Boston press) that shifted its agenda dramatically toward Hart, and it was not just media spin or agenda. On the basis of fact, New Hampshire voters could have made the very reasonable inference after the Iowa caucuses that Hart really was the alternative to Mondale. Nonetheless, the Iowa story is at least akin to press power, because the free media made some freewheeling decisions that really mattered and made those decisions knowing they might well matter.

The national press had to make immediate choices after Iowa, and one of them was to focus more on Hart and less on McGovern, even though McGovern was also a big (real) surprise. Although McGovern came within 1,400 caucus votes (1 percent) of Hart, his share of the network news hole went down after Iowa.[41] This is not an unjustifiable decision, but it was an editorial decision that had enormous consequences for Hart, for McGovern, and, of course, for Mondale.

The notion of free media consequence is an important one in drawing distinctions about media power. It helps us understand what happened after New Hampshire. The *Television News Abstract and Index* indicates that Hart's very real victory in New Hampshire had a very real effect on any number of things, not the least of which was his share of the news hole. In February Hart appears 50 times in the network news index; in March he appears 107 times.

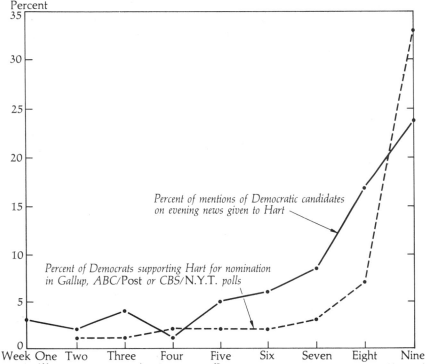

Percent

Figure 6.4   Hart's share of news hole and Hart's share of Democratic nomination preferences.
Source: Calculated by the author from data collected by the George Washington University Media Analysis Project.

For those who insist exposure alone determines political future (something I very much doubt), the relation between Hart's news attention and Hart's meteoric rise is one never to be forgotten. For about ten days after New Hampshire, news spin and news agenda helped to cause the greatest shift in polling history from one candidate to another in any contest for a major party presidential nomination. On February 25, 7 percent of the Democrats preferred Hart for the nomination; on March 2, 34 percent; on March 6, 38 percent — millions and millions of Democrats moving to a candidate they knew only from his victory in New Hampshire.

How can anybody reconcile figure 6.4 with a theory of minimal press power? It is not easy, but consider that Hart *did* win in New Hampshire and that Democrats *were* looking for an alternative. Everybody "knows" winning in New Hampshire is both an enormous psychological advantage and a free media bonanza.

This is free media power based on journalism's "tradition," not on the values or preferences of the media elite. The tradition? Emphasize anybody who wins in New Hampshire, especially if he wins unexpectedly. Every campaign manager, journalist, and pundit knows this convention in journalism before the game starts. Front-runners bank on it. Challengers borrow on it. This is, in the last analysis, the power of press "convention" as much as anything else.

Super Tuesday and double standards: real press power   Hart was, as Martin Schram aptly described him, "the live-at-five, film-at-11" candidate.[42] As such, he was extraordinarily vulnerable to free media spin. Hart's press and Hart's fortunes had begun to change dramatically by "super Tuesday"—March 13, when primaries were held in ten states.

The night before super Tuesday Jack Smith of ABC did a very tough piece about Hart, going through what was to become the press litany about him: suspicious ties to Patrick Caddell; cynical imitation of John Kennedy; marital problems; and, of course, changes in name, signature, religion, and age. Smith labeled Hart "calculated."

That same night—super Tuesday eve—Bruce Morton led the CBS "Evening News" with this: "For the first time, tough questions are being asked about Gary Hart—not just where he stands on issues, but whether he remembers where he stands." Morton used two cases to demonstrate Hart's embarrassing contradictions on the issues. In the twenty-four hours before super Tuesday, Hart's coverage in the national free media changed perhaps as fully in a day's news cycle as anyone's since Gerald Ford pardoned Richard Nixon on a Sunday morning in September ten years earlier. By the end of super Tuesday, Hart had lost his electoral magic.

It makes little sense to argue the free media had done everything in one night or that free media were the only cause of Hart's decline. Voters could have generated in themselves the idea that things were moving a bit too fast after New Hampshire. The change in free media in the last day or two before super Tuesday does seem to have played a part in slowing Hart down: Adams' computations indicate that people who decided their vote right after the New Hampshire primary preferred Hart to Mondale by ratios as great as ten to one. Those who decided just before super Tuesday, however, preferred Hart by less than two to one.[43]

Nor did the free media let up after the balloting. While the votes were still being counted, NBC's Roger Mudd made some network history by asking Hart some of the toughest questions of this or any modern campaign. Mudd asked Hart, "Why do you imitate John Kennedy so much?" and then, "Why do you think, senator, so many politicians are phony today?" Jack Germond recalls that on the morning after super Tuesday he had to argue alone on network morning news that it had not been a defeat for Hart—that Hart had had a tremendous victory in Florida and in the West as well.

Three conclusions stand out about Hart, the free media, and super Tuesday. First, what was going on was mediality. Hart had changed his name and religion decades before, his hair years before. This was not news coverage; it was analysis and spin. Second, the dramatic shift in news spin came just before public euphoria about Hart started to subside. The media spin changed some minds. Third, if power is best defined as effect plus premeditation, what the free media did with and to Hart during the middle of March was press power, pure and palpable—much more so than in the week after the Iowa vote.

The press knew what it was doing. It was getting the bad news out about the year's media-based "phenomenon" just in time for the big vote on super Tuesday and beyond. Hart's assistant press secretary, Dawn Alexander, pointed out that Mudd's first interview of the year with Hart in Iowa had been "extremely cordial," that Mudd's approach was "100 degrees different" then. In fact, Mudd probably spoke for his colleagues when he analyzed his own behavior in this, his second most famous candidate interview: "I wanted a good, strong interview, and I think that's what television doesn't have enough of. People have a better idea of who Gary Hart is and how he reacts to pressure. . . . Maybe [the viewers] don't think that much of *me*, but they know more about Hart."[44]

The Mudd interview did not harm Mudd, nor did it destroy Hart. But that interview was the bridge between all the negative spin about Hart just before super Tuesday and all the "Hart may not be the one after all" coverage that came right after it. On both sides of that bridge were a press mission and a free media capacity to warn Americans about Hart's born-in-New Hampshire candidacy.

News spin about Hart in mid-March probably carried more weight than news spin carried at any other time in 1984. Hart was new; he was mysterious; he was media made. He was a political phenomenon as great as any that ever was. Those are the conditions during which the press decides to spin heavily, and those are the conditions in which spin can work wonders or, as in Hart's case, horrors. But to argue that the free media exerted real influence—power—is not necessarily to disparage them. Press power in these circumstances seems justifiable, so long as the press does this sort of thing to candidates of all political colorations and hairstyles.

The odyssey of Hart after New Hampshire proves that press people believe they have the right to change the standards once anybody starts to ride the New Hampshire bandwagon. The press does this deliberately and, for the most part, unashamedly. Their decision to resurrect and to emphasize the dark-side information about Hart, information known years before, was both premeditated and effective—in a word, powerful.

I believe the press is right—they should employ double standards with candidates like Hart or Carter, candidates who are media-based darlings or who run far ahead of the pack. Whatever the moral case for double standards, however, the fact remains: Double standards for the frontrunner and for those who unexpectedly win in New Hampshire constitute the single greatest power of the press in presidential politics, perhaps the only power worthy of the word.

Half a case: media spin at the Democratic National Convention　For one brief moment in 1984 Mondale and Ferraro were not losers. It is easy to forget that during the week of July 21 the *Newsweek* (Gallup) poll had the Democrats ahead of Reagan and Bush by two percentage points. Harris had the Democrats just two points behind.

These results may have been due to bad sampling or the predictable result of polling the day after a national convention. But a more "substantive" interpretation involves network news coverage. News coverage out of San Francisco had started badly for the Democrats, the press focusing heavily on the firing of Bert Lance and the short-lived resuscitation of Charles Manatt. By the end of the convention, however, the networks had shifted their attention away from Lance and Manatt and toward the twin themes of unity in the party and the uniqueness of the ticket. The networks probably missed some of the real story, as Adams documents in his content analysis of network coverage at both conventions: The ticket was unique, but the Democrats were less than unified.[45] Still, a positive news spin came out of San Francisco; once Mario Cuomo gave his keynote address, the networks saw sweetness and light for the remainder of the convention.

The message—part free media, part candidate performance—seemed to be a powerful one, producing big changes in voters' perceptions of Mondale and of Reagan. Every evening during the convention the Mondale people did their own polling of 250 to 300 independents and Democrats. According to their surveys, the message from San Francisco was extremely effective.

The night before the convention, half the respondents considered the Democrats too liberal; after the convention, the figure was one-third. Before the convention the majority of Democrats and independents evaluated Reagan favorably; by the end of the convention, three-fourths said that they held less favorable views. When asked who would be more likely to stand up for working people and average Americans, the first wave of respondents chose Mondale by only a little. After the convention, respondents chose Mondale by about five to one.[46] Adding these in-house surveys to the results of the post-convention national polls suggests that the message had a real effect on public opinion.

Why not consider this a full-fledged case of free media influence? After all, the network spin on Cuomo's keynote address was nearly hysterical, and the last-hour coverage of Jennifer Halliday was gushing.[47] Why just half a case? First, this was not simply spin; it was fact. The Democrats did have a unique ticket and did present a rhetoric as powerful as the Democrats have mastered in decades. As keynoter, Cuomo was real in San Francisco. More important, all this opinion shifting was probably less network spin and agenda than Democratic party orchestration of its message. Electoral movement toward Mondale and Ferraro had at least as much to do with the power of a free media performance by political elites as with the political interpretations of the media elite. In the end San Francisco is but half a case of free media power and half a case of effective, Democratic free media performance.

Free Media Performance: The Great Communicator versus the Media Elite

If Mondale's people in San Francisco could use the free media so effectively, what might we have expected throughout 1984 from the Great Communicator and his party? Just about what we got. There is no simple way to study the power of the ten-second sound bite, the candidate's smile, or the one-liner;[48] but it is impossible to believe Reagan failed to win votes when he said his side wants every day to be the Fourth of July while the other guys want every day to be the Fifteenth of April.

Free media performance took on new importance in 1984 because Reagan was so good at it. Two vivid cases come to mind. First was the free media performance of Reagan in his June speech at Pointe du Hoc, the precipice overlooking Omaha beach. With tears in his eyes and a cadence as compelling as Walt Whitman's, Reagan looked at both the cameras and the veterans and delivered to the Western Hemisphere one of the most moving speeches in the history of presidential television. Throughout his trip to Normandy Reagan was superb.

Did his performance there have any impact? The Gallup poll shows that between the anniversary of D Day on June 6 and June 22, Reagan's lead over Mondale more than doubled—jumping from 9 percent to 19 percent. Obviously this figure reflects not just the performance at Pointe du Hoc but all of Reagan's televised nation hopping in June. Still, northern France had not seen such a successful Yank since Patton.

But Americans had seen something very much like it seven months earlier when Reagan, with another free media performance, in one day moved more national opinion on a serious issue than free media spin has ever done in a year. On Sunday, October 23, the Marine compound in Beirut was destroyed, and more than 250 Americans died. On that Tuesday Reagan ordered the invasion of Grenada. On Thursday he made his prime-time appeal for his policies in Lebanon and the Caribbean. In perhaps his greatest free media performance, Reagan totally disarmed his critics and neutralized the bad news and the bad press swirling around him and his policies.

An ABC News/ *Washington Post* poll taken the day before the speech showed that 41 percent approved of his handling of the Lebanese situation. The day after the speech 52 percent approved. Before the speech 52 percent approved of his decision to invade Grenada. After the speech that figure jumped to 65 percent. The day before the speech, 44 percent approved of his overall foreign policy. After the speech 57 percent approved. Most remarkable, among those who actually watched the speech, support for Reagan's policy toward Lebanon and his decision about Grenada jumped thirty points overnight on both issues.[49]

This sort of thing has happened before — with John Kennedy's speech after the Bay of Pigs and with Nixon's prime-time appeal after the Cambodian invasion — but it had been a while, and during that time we had forgotten how important a speech or a free media performance can be. The recent emphasis has been on the network correspondents' capacity to mold opinion not the president's. But whether it is Ferraro's picture-perfect smile or Reagan's letter-perfect speeches, free media performances count. Performance is obviously not everything, but free media performance is something. Once again, the power of free media performance — whether based on substance, or speeches, or on smiles — wreaks havoc with theories concerning the media elite. In 1984, in terms of power, the media "elite" were as likely to be members of the administration as members of the press.

Summing Up on the Free Media

Liberals look back at 1984 and convince themselves that only the free media performance mattered. Conservatives since the 1960s have tended to believe that news agenda and news spin determine public opinion. Who is right?

The relative strength of spin, agenda, and performance shifts with each election. In 1984 free media performance probably did carry more weight than during most elections, suggesting the liberals may have had one small victory this time out — analyzing more correctly the meaning of free media in this campaign. Nonetheless, the 1984 campaign implies the following *general* "truths" about the free media, some of which will sit well with neither liberals nor conservatives: bad press is not necessarily fatal, or even debilitating, to strong candidates. News agendas are very much overrated as a force in public opinion; the public influences the news about as often as news influences the public; free media performance does not overwhelm the power of the press but can, for an incumbent, help quite a bit.

Let us avoid free media determinism, however. Five years ago it was fashionable to believe the free media made reelection impossible. Now it is believed that colorful visuals, one-liners, and great speeches make reelection inevitable. Neither thesis holds up. In 1984 it seems free media performance did move

Table 6.2   Television debates, 1984

Location	Date
Dartmouth, New Hampshire	January 15
Ames, Iowa	January 21
Boston (*Boston Globe*)	January 31
Boston (Women's Forum)	February 3
Des Moines, Iowa	February 11
Manchester, New Hampshire (St. Anselm's College)	February 23
Atlanta	March 11
Illinois	March 18
New York	March 28
Pittsburgh	April 5
Texas	May 2
Burbank, California	June 3
Louisville	October 7
Philadelphia	October 11
Kansas City	October 21

people more than free media spin or agenda moved them, but that does not mean that Reagan carried three of five voters merely because he looked good on television. What it does mean is that the media elite are far less important than their newly popular sobriquet implies.

Presidential Debates: The Ultimate in Free Media Performance

Televised debates could easily be classified as just another kind of free media performance. Debates are so big and so important, however, they deserve a category all their own. In 1984 televised debates proved far more consequential than anything the paid media were doing and at least as consequential as the free media.

The New World of Televised Debate

Despite their legendary reputation, the Kennedy-Nixon debates now seem almost quaint, given the size and shape of debates in the last three presidential elections. In 1976 televised debates moved into the primaries for the first time. We had three televised debates among Democratic candidates for the nomination in that campaign.[50] In 1980 we had twice as many primary debates, and for the first time we had direct, no-holds-barred personal exchange among contestants. Nineteen eighty-four offered no major changes in format but did establish a very new precedent—an incumbent president with a big lead agreeing to debate his challenger. We also had another leap in the number of debates—fifteen nationally televised performances, twelve among the Democrats and three between the major party nominees (see table 6.2). That was about double the number of debates in 1980.[51]

Given newly established precedents and the sizable increase in the number of debates, we have probably entered a new era of presidential debating, one that requires a brand-new set of theories and notions. But, because my mission involves the relative importance of the different forms of presidential media, I restrict myself to those conclusions that do either of two things: run counter to the recent conventional wisdom about debate or tell us something about the importance of debate as compared with that of the other media, especially the free media.

1. Challengers and underdogs have the advantage but only in the fall, not during the primaries.   In their first debates Kennedy beat Nixon, Ford beat Carter, Reagan beat Carter, and Mondale beat Reagan. With that much history supporting them, most pundits naturally believe that either the challenger or the underdog has an inherent advantage—the biggest advantage, of course, going to an underdog challenger. Challengers allegedly have that advantage because they get to stand next to a sitting president, increasing their credibility and their visibility. Underdogs (like Ford) allegedly have it because expectations about them are so low.

Reasoning and evidence support these conclusions but with one major qualification. Almost none of them apply to the primaries and caucuses, when candidates debate for nomination, not for election. In 1984 we saw how little advantage the challengers and underdogs had in Iowa and in New Hampshire. In both instances Mondale did very well.[52] In fact, as front-runner Mondale "won" virtually every debate he entered. The advantage for challengers simply does not exist if several candidates are debating. The viewers, with dozens of cues coming from reporters or the candidates, fall back on their predispositions, and each thinks his or her horse has probably won. Mondale's staff chuckled among themselves after the Dartmouth debate in New Hampshire: The press reported that Democrats rated Mondale's performance best but then neglected to say that his lead going in was so large he would almost certainly win in a field of eight unless, of course, he stumbled badly.[53]

David Moore makes an interesting case: He concludes because the free media have just moments to review videotaped performances during the news, the frontrunner in a many-person debate has another advantage—his footage will get used. Indeed, those who watched the first New Hampshire debate were mightily impressed with Jackson, but those who saw the news accounts thought Mondale had won.[54] Either way, the advantage in primary debate, particularly in a crowded field, lies with the frontrunner and the overdog.

Table 6.3 Mondale's advantage over Reagan in polls on who won first debate, October 1984 (percentage points)

Time of poll	Mondale advantage
During debate (ABC)	−3
One hour after debate (ABC)	1
One day after debate (ABC)	37
Two days after debate (CBS)	49

Sources: Polls conducted by networks, as shown in the table.

Only front-running incumbents need to worry much about the challenger's advantage.

2. Following debate, the free media have tremendous power to influence perceptions of victory but little power to influence preferences in voting. Ever since 1976 and Ford's insistence that there was no Soviet domination in Eastern Europe, everybody understands the free media play a major role in determining perceptions of who won. Until the free media followed up on that gaffe, nobody much knew or cared: Ford was considered the winner of that debate until the press turned his stumble into one of history's most legendary medialities.[55]

The power of the free media in televised debates works like this: Correspondents watch the debates like the rest of us, but then, unlike the rest of us, they comment and produce instant analysis on camera, pointing to and magnifying gaffes, great slogans, and dramatic moments. That spin influences the next round of polling, which influences spin, which influences polling.

It does not always work that way. Most television spin after the Ferraro-Bush debate seemed to hold that it was a tie. Still, the public generally held to its original notion that Bush had won. But in 1984 the typical pattern held perfectly in the first Mondale-Reagan debate. The national media turned original public opinion around almost completely on the question of who had won and did so in forty-eight hours (see table 6.3). The initial public response was that Reagan had won; with the passage of time and news media spin, his early victory turned into something approaching a historic defeat. The first ABC poll —conducted during the last few minutes of the debate—had Reagan ahead, by three points. It seemed one more instance in which selective perception had aided the frontrunner.

Then came the network interpretation. Sam Donaldson's remarks were vintage, Donaldson even acknowledging that his interpretation was made on his own:

Mr. Reagan's aides were not particularly pleased by this debate tonight....
That's not what they said, but you can tell from their reactions. ... It was
something they didn't like to see. The "champ" was still there, they believed, but, as I say, the legs of the champ were a little bit wobbly tonight.

An hour after the debate—and after the spinning had reached consensus—
the next ABC poll showed Mondale ahead by one point. The next day the ABC
poll had Mondale ahead by thirty-seven. The CBS News/*New York Times* poll
conducted on Tuesday showed an advantage for Mondale of forty-nine points
—a fifty-two point shift in two days, the kind of change in opinion usually
associated with presidential appeals in desperate international circumstances,
not with free media spin.

Was this earthquake in opinion so important? We do know the networks
were committed to emphasizing Reagan's failure. Our content analysis shows
that Reagan got thirteen times as much network spin for losing his first debate
as for winning the second.[56] There is little question the public changed its mind
about the winner and the loser in direct response to what the free media were
offering. Still, the truth is most of this change in opinion was on the most
superficial sort of issue—who debated better, who debated worse. The free
media had, in fact, persuaded the public to believe something it had not originally believed—that Reagan had lost the debate—but that "fact" changed
only a meager percentage of presidential vote preferences. In a fairly brief time
virtually all the polls showed the electoral gap between Reagan and Mondale
back to "normal."[57] Adam Clymer, looking at the results on both dimensions
—Who won? and How will you vote?—practically dismissed the first debate
as a cause of real opinion change.[58]

Free media people can claim Reagan really did lose the first debate, just
as Donaldson claimed. Fair enough. On the other hand, free media critics
have since pointed to the lopsided emphasis on Reagan's poor showing to
support their claim that the media are both biased and powerful. But bias and
power are different things. Whatever the motives for news coverage of the
first Reagan-Mondale debate, the power of the networks to move opinion,
even in this case, was much less than it seemed. The networks "achieved"
something far less formidable—a shift in opinions concerning performance in
debate—than the shift in policy opinion after Reagan's Grenada-Lebanon address. NBC's own polls show that although majorities had opinions about who
won and who lost in each debate, a phenomenally high 94 percent said the
debates had not changed their mind about whom they supported in the presidential election.[59] Apparently they were *not* lying.

3. Debates mean more than news spin or news agenda but do not matter
much absolutely.   Debates move perceptions, even if they fail to move many

votes. After her debate with Bush, the best data available indicate that within twenty-four hours Ferraro climbed an impressive four points on Wirthlin's 100-point thermometer.[60] Within forty-eight hours after his first debate with Reagan, Mondale had jumped five points, again more movement for Mondale in a two-day period than occurred at any other time during the general campaign.[61] My own surveys among students indicate almost one-fifth of them felt the first debate would make them take another look at Mondale as a possible preference. The fact is, given the size of the debate news hole and the size of the audience, it would be absurd to dismiss debate performance as anything but important. Debate performance and free media spin concerning debate are probably the most important factors in presidential politics, except for reality and honest-to-goodness conditions. Still, that does not mean debates are magic. People win the presidency without winning their debates; only a close race will allow debates to appear determinative. And, in the last analysis, nominees and candidates do far more to determine who wins and loses than the newspeople who cover the debates; the power rests mostly with the politicians who do the performing. In 1984 the public was, at the outset, wrong; Sam Donaldson was right. Reagan, not the media elite, lost the first debate.

Conclusions

I begin with the good news.

1. *The terrible things the media might have done in 1984 they did not do.* John Glenn might have gained a nomination through docudrama. He did not. Nuclear policy might have been influenced by prime-time melodrama. It was not. Geraldine Ferraro might be ending her political career on the basis of unproven and irresponsible allegations in the tabloids. She is not, at least not yet.

2. All those things that did not happen imply a second conclusion: *media power in national politics is, in the 1980s, overstated.* During the 1950s social scientists understated the power of the mass media, but in the past two decades the pendulum has swung too far in the other direction. It is time to moderate our theories about the power of the media, whichever variety.

3. Perhaps most gratifying, in 1984 *the factualized media totally overwhelmed the fictionalized.* That is always true in presidential politics. The closer to reality any medium is, the more likely it is to have a political impact. The classical Athenian assertion is that he who writes the songs controls the politics. The modern-day adaptation of that theory is that he who handles the commercials does the controlling. Not so. He who writes the songs and the commercials makes money, not opinion. News does far more than advertising, advertising more than docudrama, docudrama more than melodrama.

Although debates make the pattern a little less certain, in 1984 the "reality" media made some difference. The rest did not.

4. Powerful as they may have seemed by comparison, the *free media did not determine much of what finally happened in 1984.* The press agenda did not become the public's agenda. More often than not the news spin provided by the free media failed to influence political preferences, especially in the general campaign.

The one true exception is Gary Hart. The national press played a fairly inadvertent role in making Hart, but it played a very conscious role in bringing him down. This is the one real power that free media elites possess in presidential politics: adopting tougher standards for front-runners and emerging challengers. This "power" is a given, something every serious candidate expects and understands. It is, as well, a power that a free press will be able to justify so long as the double standards are based on the candidate's standing in the race, not his or her standing on the issues.

5. *The free media usually do more early, when the field is larger and newer.* In the beginning a news agenda about surprise victories could help candidate Hart. In the end, news agendas about a manipulative incumbent meant nothing to nominee Mondale. The explanation is obvious, but the fact remains: free media spin and free media agenda mean much more at the outset, when voters are still mostly uncommitted and comparatively impressionable.

6. *Negative spin sticks in a bad news environment, then slides off when the news is good.* The national press feels compelled to criticize incumbents, especially front-running incumbents. But even if a Teflon-coated Reagan had not been president, it is highly unlikely that the kinds of things the news media do to disparage a front-running incumbent would have mattered much—not so long as voters believed the country was moving in the right direction. Nobody cares if Reagan—or another incumbent—is inaccessible, unspecific, manipulative, or less than involved. In essence, then, incumbents—Reagan or otherwise—do not need good press; they just need good news.

7. *The left and the right are both wrong about the free media in this campaign.* Despite right-wing complaints that the liberal press attacks conservative candidates for partisan reasons, the free media behaved responsibly—if superficially—in 1984. There was no issue bias on the evening news. There was no egregious error in the campaign news reporting. There was no wild-eyed journalism in print or broadcasting. The most obstreperous performance on network news came when Roger Mudd asked Hart a few rude questions about his Kennedy impersonation. That is hardly grounds for vocal complaint by anybody but Hart and certainly not by conservatives. Conservative critics also miss the mark in believing that news spin and news agenda matter very much. They usually do not.

The left is also wrong about 1984. The free media followed after Reagan on all kinds of campaign issues and even a few substantive issues—on Lebanon, for example, and on his fundamentalist ties. The free media did its job—going after a front-running incumbent within the limits that responsible media accept. In 1983, with unemployment at almost 11 percent, that kind of free media coverage pushed Reagan to the lowest approval score ever endured by an incumbent after twenty-four months in office. The left must understand that the free media nipped constantly at Reagan in 1984; without inflation, recession, Watergate, or a war, nipping was all they could do without becoming partisan themselves.

8. *The "media elite" are less than they seem.* Given that the free media elite usually vote Democratic and the modernday nation usually votes Republican in presidential elections, the whole concept of a media elite seems shaky. But the real problem with the theory of a media elite is that it fails to recognize how unimperially—and how unliberally—the press behaves in covering campaign politics. In the fall the media elite broadcast—and rebroadcast—almost all of Reagan's best one-liners. In the summer they sounded like another George Bush as they did cheerleading for the U.S. Olympic team.

The same ABC that gave us Donaldson's criticism of Reagan gave us Jim McKay's adulation of Mary Lou Retton. It is altogether conceivable that in the long run ABC's Roone Arledge, who directs news and sports, did more for Reagan by promoting the Olympics than he did *to* Reagan by unleashing Donaldson. But, like most of the media elite, Arledge and ABC accepted their fate and ran the Olympic videotapes, over and over again.[62]

Arledge's case is not unique. After the Olympics, the big news story was the "new patriotism." All the free media did feature after feature about it. Would anybody expect that sort of thing to help the Democrats or Mondale? No, but the story was more or less true, more or less new, and tailor-made for mass audiences in an Olympic victory year. So the story kept on coming. The media elite are, then, more likely to be consequential than powerful—doing as much by accident, by inertia, by popular demand, or by convention as by design.

The media elite *can* leave home without an American Express card. They do get recognized in shops and restaurants. But neither recognition nor big salaries translate directly into political power. Their power is less than that. The real power they possess in selecting presidents has mostly trickled down to them, down through a crazy-quilt system of nominations concocted by the states, the national parties, and the candidates—not by the media elite. So it is still mainly the political leadership that sets the terms of press power in presidential elections. Let's brace ourselves to face these final truths about political power in modern America. Nineteen eighty-four it was; but the Reagan administration was hardly acting like "Big Brother," and the press was not acting much like a "media elite."

The November 6 Vote for President:
What Did It Mean?

WILLIAM SCHNEIDER

There is no mandate out there. —Thomas P. (Tip) O'Neill, speaker of the House, November 8, 1984

The Republicans won the election and the Democrats are winning the interpretation. — David R. Gergen, former White House communications director, November 12, 1984

————After an interminable presidential campaign with its share of twists, turns, and surprises, the November 6, 1984, election was something of an anticlimax. Of course Ronald Reagan was reelected. Everyone knew he would be.

Consider the evidence:

Reagan's job approval ratings had been running about 50 percent in the Gallup Poll since November 1983. Historical experience suggests that a party can expect to retain control of the White House if the incumbent's job rating is 50 percent or higher.[1]

According to *Public Opinion* magazine, Reagan and Walter Mondale were matched against each other 101 times in publicly released trial heats taken between the beginning of 1984 and election day. One hundred of these polls showed Reagan ahead.[2] (Mondale was ahead only once, by two points, in a Gallup Poll taken for *Newsweek* on the day after the Democratic national convention.)

Between January and November Reagan's "favorable" ratings averaged 56 percent, according to polls taken by CBS News and the *New York Times*. His ratings reached a peak of 61 percent favorable just before the election in November. Mondale's "favorable" ratings averaged 35 percent. His high point, 42 percent, came in January.

Even if presidents do not always win second terms, parties usually do. In this century, with one exception, every party elected to the White House has held on to the presidency for at least a second term; the exception was the Democrats in 1980. Thus Herbert Hoover, a one-term president, was the third of three Republican presidents in succession. Lyndon Johnson participated in two consecutive terms of Democratic rule, just as Gerald Ford finished out a two-term Republican administration. That the Republicans won a second term in 1984 was therefore, not surprising.

In dealing with the 1984 election as a political event, we enter the elusive realm of "expectations." Reagan was expected to win by the press, the public, and anyone who knows anything about American politics. The issue is: Did he do as well as expected? A widely publicized state-by-state survey taken a month before the election by ABC News and the *Washington Post* showed Reagan ahead everywhere but in the District of Columbia. The real suspense on election night was waiting to see whether he would win an unprecedented fifty-state sweep. He very nearly did.

On the one hand, Reagan's reelection margin was breathtaking. He carried forty-nine states—all but Mondale's home state of Minnesota, which he lost by fewer than 4,000 votes, and the District of Columbia. He won 98 percent of the electoral votes (525 electoral votes for Reagan, 13 for Mondale). His share of the total popular vote went up eight percentage points over 1980, to 59 percent. His margin over his Democratic opponent doubled, from 8.4 million votes in 1980 to 16.9 million in 1984. In 1980 it could be argued that Reagan carried New York, Massachusetts, and Michigan because John Anderson took votes away from the Democrats. In 1984 Reagan won those states convincingly in a straight fight.

On the other hand, Reagan was not just competing with the Democratic ticket; he was also competing with the expectation of a historic landslide. In this admittedly unfair competition (see appendix C), the results were impressive, though not quite record breaking. Four previous presidential candidates, all in this century, have won a larger share of the popular vote; two Republicans (Warren G. Harding in 1920 and Richard M. Nixon in 1972) and two Democrats (Franklin D. Roosevelt in 1936 and Lyndon B. Johnson in 1964) were elected with more than 60 percent of the vote. The Democratic share of the vote in 1984, 40.6 percent, was just half a percentage point lower than it had been in 1980.

Certainly the greatest disappointment for the Republicans was the weakness of Reagan's coattails. In 1980 the impression of a historic mandate was produced in part by the Republican takeover of the Senate through a net Republican gain of twelve Senate seats. In 1984, despite Reagan's improved margin, the Republicans suffered a net loss of two Senate seats. In the House of Representatives the Republicans gained thirty-four seats in 1980 but only fourteen in 1984. They picked up four governorships in 1980 but just one in 1984. They won control of both houses of the state legislatures in fifteen states in 1980 and in only eleven states in 1984. As Kevin Phillips has pointed out, never before has a Republican president taken office with his party controlling so few House seats, governorships, and state legislatures.[3]

The weakness of the president's coattails tended to reinforce the impression that 1984 was a personal victory for an extraordinarily popular president but meant little for partisanship or political philosophy. Even though the election was a more sizable victory for Reagan, it did not have the same dramatic impact as the 1980 election.

This chapter takes issue with the view that not much happened in 1984—that it was little more than a personal victory for Ronald Reagan. Even if the 1984 election was simply a rerun of 1980, which in some respects it was, that is not insignificant—it confirmed and consolidated the previous result. Both were elections in which the paramount factor was neither ideology nor personality but the performance of the incumbent administration. In 1980 the public's judgment of that performance was overwhelmingly negative, and people voted for change. In 1984 the public's assessment of the incumbent administration was strongly positive, and the electorate voted for continuity. There was no sense of upheaval, as there had been four years earlier.

If we consider the 1980 and 1984 elections together, however, it becomes clear that something fundamental has changed in American politics. The Democratic party has lost its national governing majority. The party had already lost most of its social-issue conservatives during the 1968–72 election cycle. In the 1980–84 cycle the party lost its economic credibility, the one thing that had held it together for fifty years.

Democrats have managed to do well in state and local elections for several reasons: the inertial force of incumbency, the lack of ideological focus in most local elections, and their own political resourcefulness. That is, they have done well in spite of, not because of, the direction their party has taken. In those elections Democrats look more like the past, not the future, of their party.

Moreover, Reagan's successful performance as president relieved the fears many voters expressed about his foreign policy tendencies and social policy inclinations in 1980. Although his rhetoric remained hard-line, his actions as president were moderate and cautious. One result has been a partisan shift; more Americans identify themselves with the Republican party than at any time in the past thirty-five years. An ideological shift has also occurred, not in the sense that people's policy preferences have shifted to the right, but in the sense that more Americans express confidence that the conservative approach—less government—may be the best way to solve the nation's problems. In short, after two decades of failure and frustration, conservatism has been tried and has been found to work.

Is this the long-awaited realignment? Not quite. The Republicans cannot yet claim to be the nation's new majority party. They remain hostage to Reagan's popularity and, to a considerable extent, to the performance of the economy. But the precondition for realignment has been met. The old majority coalition and the economic confidence that sustained it have been demolished.

The Election Results

The Census Bureau estimated that there were nearly 174 million Americans of voting age on November 1, 1984.[4] According to the Federal Election Commission, 92,652,793 Americans cast presidential ballots on November 6, 1984. The resulting turnout figure, 53.3 percent, may be slightly understated. Census Bureau projections of the voting-age population are not an entirely reliable measure of the eligible electorate since they include aliens and other persons not qualified to vote.

The figure of 53.3 percent is slightly lower than the 54.0 percent reported for 1980 on the basis of comparable data.[5] The census has released later, presumably more accurate, estimates of the 1980 electorate that put the presidential turnout that year at 52.6 percent. If that is so, turnout appears to have risen slightly in 1984.

Although the increase seems to have been small, it constitutes the first rise in voter participation in a presidential election since 1960, when turnout reached a high of 62.8 percent. A small increase in turnout was also reported for the 1982 mid-term election. That figure also reversed a long-term decline; turnout in mid-term elections had been falling since 1962.

Yet another piece of evidence confirms the impression of higher turnout in 1984. In 1984, as for previous elections, the Census Bureau conducted interviews in about 50,000 households during the two weeks following election day. Among those surveyed, 59.9 percent were reported, either by themselves or by some other family member, as having cast a ballot in the 1984 election. As usual, the reported vote overstated the actual vote. The relevant point, however, is that the 1984 figure was slightly higher than the reported vote in 1980.

The census survey found that women, blacks, and voters sixty-five or older showed the highest increases in voting. In fact, 1984 was the first time more women reported voting than men.[6] These turnout patterns suggest that Reagan's presidency has reversed the trend of declining interest and participation by voters, particularly among groups that feel adversely affected by the president's policies. Although in 1984 the candidacies of Jesse Jackson and Geraldine Ferraro may have stimulated interest in voting among blacks and women, Reagan appears to have been the key factor. The rise in turnout was already evident in 1982, most notably among blacks and blue-collar voters in economically distressed areas.[7]

Percentage for Mondale, 1984

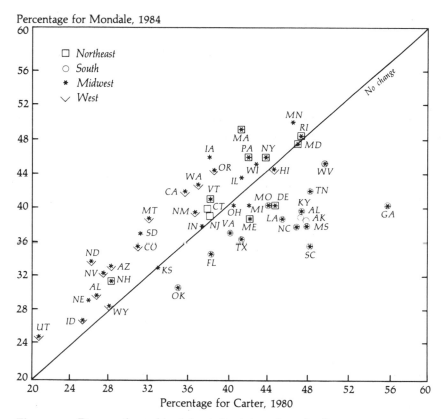

Figure 7.1 Democratic presidential vote by state, 1980 and 1984

To Democrats the prospect of a higher turnout in 1984 seemed promising. Party operatives had calculated that, if they could stimulate a turnout of over 100 million voters, the Democrats stood a good chance of winning the election. Although the turnout does appear to have gone up a bit and the Democrats may have benefited from the increase, the final participation figure was over seven million votes shy of the Democrats' target.

The Republicans were apparently more successful in their election-year registration campaign. Both the CBS News/*New York Times* exit poll and the *Los Angeles Times* exit poll showed voters who registered for the first time during 1984 going 60–40 for Reagan. In fact, it is not clear that a substantial increase in voting would actually have helped the Democrats. According to postelection interviews conducted by CBS News and the *New York Times*, nonvoters showed an even stronger preference for Reagan than those who participated in the election.[8]

Table 7.1   Presidential votes by region, 1980 and 1984

| | Votes cast (in thousands) | | | | | | |
| | 1980 | | | | 1984 | | |
Region	Reagan	Carter	Anderson	Total*	Reagan	Mondale	Total*
New England	2443	2206	749	5467	3153	2437	5614
Mid-Atlantic	7517	6775	1147	15,689	9244	7679	17,011
Deep South	3385	3491	127	7106	4712	2945	7719
Outer South	7250	5711	486	13,568	9837	5730	15,612
Border	2739	2318	179	5283	3363	2101	5484
Great Lakes	8824	7221	1149	17,458	10,303	7279	17,703
Farm belt	2927	2138	449	5612	3274	2384	5705
Mountain	2636	1251	353	4341	3131	1546	4736
Pacific	6177	4368	1080	11,972	7528	5476	13,159
Total U.S.	43,899	35,481	5719	86,460	54,455	37,577	92,653

| | Percentage of votes cast and turnout | | | | | | |
| | 1980 | | | | 1984 | | |
	Reagan	Carter	Anderson	Turnout	Reagan	Mondale	Turnout
New England	44.7	40.3	13.7	60.1	56.2	43.4	59.0
Mid-Atlantic	47.9	43.2	7.3	50.7	54.3	45.1	52.9
Deep South	47.6	49.1	1.8	49.5	61.0	38.2	47.9
Outer South	53.4	42.1	3.6	49.5	63.0	36.7	48.4
Border	51.9	43.9	3.4	55.3	61.3	38.3	53.4
Great Lakes	50.5	41.4	6.6	58.9	58.2	41.1	58.5
Farm belt	52.2	38.1	8.0	63.1	57.4	41.8	62.6
Mountain	60.7	28.8	8.1	57.3	66.1	32.6	53.1
Pacific	51.6	36.5	9.0	53.0	57.2	41.6	52.0
Total U.S.	50.8	41.0	6.6	52.6	58.8	40.6	53.3

Source: See Appendix A.
*Includes votes for minor parties and write-ins.

Altogether, about 6.2 million more votes were cast for president in 1984 than in 1980. The Republican vote went up by about 10.6 million, but the Democratic vote also increased, by about two million. The virtual collapse of third-party voting provided additional support for both major parties. In 1980, 7.2 percent of the presidential vote went to non–major party candidates, prin-

Change, 1980–84

Republican	Democratic	Total vote*
+ 710	+ 231	+ 147
+ 1726	+ 904	+1322
+ 1327	− 546	+ 613
+ 2588	+ 19	+2044
+ 624	− 218	+ 201
+ 1479	+ 58	+ 245
+ 346	+ 245	+ 93
+ 496	+ 295	+ 396
+ 1350	+1090	+1187
+10,556	+2096	+6193

Change, 1980–84

Republican	Democratic	Turnout	Swing to GOP
+11.5	+ 3.1	− 1.1	4.2
+ 6.4	+ 2.0	+ 2.2	2.2
+13.4	−10.9	− 1.6	12.1
+ 9.6	− 5.4	− 1.1	7.5
+ 9.4	− 5.6	− 1.9	7.5
+ 7.7	− 0.3	− 0.4	4.0
+ 5.2	+ 3.7	− 0.5	0.9
+ 5.4	+ 3.8	− 4.2	0.8
+ 5.6	+ 5.1	− 1.0	0.2
+ 8.0	− 0.4	+ 0.7	4.2

cipally Independent John Anderson, who got 5.7 million votes (6.6 percent of the total). In 1984 the third-party vote shrank to 0.6 percent of the total. Even the Libertarian party, which won almost a million votes in 1980 (1.1 percent), was down to less than a quarter of a million in 1984 (0.2 percent). In 1980 third-party voting was a sign that many voters who felt Carter did not deserve reelection were not quite ready to support Reagan as the alternative. By 1984 Reagan had managed to reassure many of those who had been fearful of him and to drive his critics into the Democratic camp. The protest vote disappeared.

Reagan's share of the vote went up in every state. (See appendix A for detailed state-by-state results.) The increases ranged from 0.4 percent in the District of Columbia where two-thirds of the voters are black, to 19.2 percent in Carter's home state of Georgia. The largest gains for the Republicans were in the South and in states where third-party voting had been especially high four years earlier (New England, Alaska, and Hawaii).

The trend in the Democratic vote was less uniform. Figure 7.1 plots every state's 1980 and 1984 Democratic presidential votes. States falling on the diagonal had the same Democratic percentage both years. (In Indiana, for example, the Democrats won 37.7 percent of the vote in both elections.) In the twenty-eight states above the diagonal, the Democrats' share of the vote went up, and in the twenty-two below the diagonal it went down. Fifteen of the states where the Democratic vote went down were in the South. The Democratic improvement was most marked in the District of Columbia, Massachusetts, the West Coast, and certain Midwestern states with troubled farm economies (Iowa, North Dakota).

Thus the fact that the Democratic share of the national vote hardly changed from 1980 to 1984 obscures more than it reveals. In some areas the Democrats gained votes, and in others they lost votes. The two countertrends canceled each other.

Table 7.1 breaks down the 1980 and 1984 presidential votes by region. In New England, for instance, where turnout increased by 147,000 votes, the Republican vote went up by over 700,000 and the Democratic vote by over 200,000. Most of the new votes came from the almost 750,000 votes cast by New Englanders for John Anderson in 1980. In the South, however, where there had been very few Anderson votes in 1980, turnout shot up by over 2.5 million. Reagan gained almost four million votes, while the Democratic vote was sharply down.

The one region of the country where Democratic and Republican gains were about equal was the Pacific (California, Oregon, Washington, Alaska, and Hawaii). Turnout in these states went up by just over one million votes in 1984. Anderson's Pacific total was just over one million. The Republicans gained a little over one million votes, and the Democrats gained a little over one million votes.

The percentage results substantiate the divergence between the South and the rest of the country. They show a sharp Democratic decline in the South and Democratic gains toward the two coasts. Reagan made above average gains not only in the South, but also in New England. Why New England?

Table 7.2 How 1980 voters voted in 1984

1984 vote	1980 Vote			
	Reagan	Carter	Anderson	Didn't vote
Reagan	80%	25%	27%	22%
Mondale	6	61	66	18
Didn't vote	14	14	7	60
Total	100%	100%	100%	100%
(*N*)	(692)	(530)	(76)	(451)

Source: CBS News/*New York Times* poll, November 8–14, 1984.

New England is the homeland of liberal Republicans, who voted for Anderson in large numbers in 1980. In 1984 many of them may have felt sufficiently reassured about Reagan to return to the party fold. (Connecticut and New Hampshire, for instance, saw major Republican gains in their state legislatures.)

"Swing" is a useful concept for summarizing the changes from 1980 to 1984. The swing to the Republicans is calculated as half the difference between the Republican and the Democratic changes. Thus the national swing, with a Republican gain of 8.0 points and a Democratic loss of 0.4 points, was 4.2 points toward the Republicans. As table 7.1 shows, every region of the country swung Republican, but the swing was the greatest in the South—almost twice the national swing in the outer South and Border states and almost three times the national swing in the deep South. The South was the part of the country where Carter had done best in 1980. Whatever residual favorite-son sentiment Southern voters felt toward Carter obviously did not carry over to his vice-president. By contrast, in those regions where Carter did poorly in 1980—the farm belt, the Mountain States, and the Pacific Coast—there was not much further swing to the Republicans in 1984.

CBS News and the *New York Times* conducted a survey immediately after the election to assess the behavior of both voters and nonvoters. Table 7.2 shows the flow of the vote from 1980 to 1984.

First of all, there appears to have been no difference in turnout between former Carter voters and former Reagan voters. Exactly the same percentage of each group reported not voting in 1984. That is quite different from the situation in 1980, when differential abstention produced major losses for the Democrats. In 1980, those who had supported Carter in 1976 were four times as likely to abstain as those who had supported Gerald Ford.[9] Many of these Democratic abstainers may have come back to the polls in 1984 to vote for Mondale—or against Reagan. Among people who did not vote in 1980 (including both abstainers and those too young to have voted), about 40 percent cast ballots in 1984; they favored Reagan, but by a relatively narrow margin.

Reagan held on to 80 percent of his original supporters. Only about one in seventeen switched to Mondale. Reagan's gains came mostly from former Carter voters, among whom one in four switched to Reagan. Among Southern whites, the Democratic defection rate was even higher; 40 percent of former Carter voters in this constituency switched to Reagan in 1984.

Mondale was clearly helped by John Anderson's decision not to run as an Independent, along with his endorsement of the Democratic ticket. Former Anderson supporters not only turned out to vote in large numbers but followed their leader's advice and went five to two for Mondale. When turnout is taken into account, former Anderson voters were more likely to support the Democratic ticket than former Carter voters. Of course, many were liberal Democrats and Independents to begin with; they voted Independent in 1980 to punish the Democratic party for failing to nominate a real liberal. Apparently Mondale was much more to their liking than Carter.

In sum, the Democrats suffered major losses among former Carter supporters, particularly Southern whites. These losses were compensated for by significant gains from former Anderson voters and former abstainers. The Democrats appear to have lost some old conservative allies and gained some new liberal friends, ending up ideologically more coherent, perhaps, but no better off than they were in 1980—indeed, worse off, considering the gains made by the Republican ticket.

The recovery appears to have sealed the Democrats' fate in the election. As the economic situation began to improve in 1983, Reagan's job approval ratings started to climb. The president was given a further boost by the foreign policy crises in Lebanon and Grenada at the end of October 1983. This pushed him over the critical 50 percent mark in the Gallup Poll, where he remained through the ensuing election year.

Reagan led Mondale in 100 of 101 trial heats taken during 1984. In January 1984 the margin was still fairly close, averaging seven points. Reagan's lead grew, however, during the primary season; in polls taken between February and August, the president was typically running ten to sixteen points ahead of Mondale. The final, decisive phase came during the fall general election campaign, when the Republican ticket held a lead of seventeen to twenty-one points over the Democratic ticket, culminating in an eighteen-point margin on November 6.

Mondale's successful performance in the first debate between the presidential candidates on October 7 raised his favorable rating, but it did not significantly diminish Reagan's rating or his lead in the trial heats. The final preelection polls varied considerably (from a ten-point lead for Reagan in the Roper poll to a twenty-five-point lead in the *USA Today* poll), but, when averaged, they predicted a seventeen-point margin—almost exactly the actual margin.

The primary campaign certainly exacted a heavy toll on Mondale. His 42–28 percent favorable rating in January reversed to 40–30 percent unfavorable shortly after the New Hampshire primary, according to the CBS News/*New York Times* poll. Mondale's "unfavorables" dropped slightly during the late primaries, but he never fully recovered. During the fall campaign his favorable ratings went up, particularly after the first debate, but so did his unfavorable ratings. He ended up with a 48–37 percent negative rating. Reagan, by comparison, maintained a two-to-one favorable rating throughout the year.

Could any Democrat have beaten Reagan? Among the three final Democratic contenders, the Reverend Jesse Jackson ran much more poorly against Reagan in the trial heats, and Senator Gary Hart usually did somewhat better. In fact, in several polls taken during the primary season, Hart had a significant lead over the incumbent. When the *Los Angeles Times* asked voters on election day how they would have voted if the choice had been between Reagan and Hart, Reagan still won, though by a slightly smaller margin (fourteen points). Perhaps the most revealing piece of information was that almost half the voters said they had made up their minds how they were going to vote before the campaign even started in February; these voters went two to one for Reagan. In other words, the outcome was never really in doubt.

Why didn't Reagan sweep more Republicans into office? The key factor seems to have been incumbency. Incumbents have a large and growing advantage in American politics because of their dominance of the media, fund raising, communication with constituents, and campaign technology. Americans regularly reelect over 90 percent of those members of Congress who decide to run for reelection. And most do.

Republicans actually did quite well in open seats, where no incumbent was on the ballot. Open House seats were split 50–50 before the election and ended up going two to one Republican. But they accounted for only 27 of 435 contests. True, the Democrats gained one seat (Tennessee) in the four open Senate races. But in the seven open races for governor, Republican control went from three to six.

As Norman Ornstein has pointed out, congressional incumbents usually do well when a president is reelected. The mood of the country is to vote for continuity, not change, even if that means reelecting incumbents from the party opposed to the president. Moreover, Ornstein adds, Republicans had difficulty in recruiting good congressional candidates in 1984, while Democratic incumbents were exceptionally skillful in building "political niches to withstand strong adverse tides."[10]

Republican candidates captured about 47 percent of the national vote for the House of Representatives. Democrats nevertheless retained a three-to-two lead in House seats. In part, that disproportion is built into the electoral system. In any single-member district system, the party that wins the most votes usually wins an even larger share of the seats (theoretically, a party could win 100 percent of the seats with 51 percent of the vote in every district). However, it is also true that after the 1980 census, state legislatures that were mostly controlled by Democrats redrew congressional district boundaries. These were typically redrawn so as to protect incumbents of both parties by giving them districts with safe electoral majorities. Redistricting therefore tended to insulate House elections from national political swings.

According to Kevin Phillips, the Republicans also suffer because of turnout patterns:

> Republicans disproportionately represent the more affluent part of the population, where 60–70% of persons old enough to vote do so, while Democrats represent the less electorally motivated poor. GOP Congressmen win suburban districts by 200,000 to 60,000, while Democrats in similarly safe minority districts win by 50,000 to 15,000.[11]

In other words, more votes are wasted in Republican seats than in Democratic seats. Phillips estimates that to capture the House of Representatives, even if all districts were neutrally drawn, the Republicans would need 52 or 53 percent of the national congressional vote.

It was the power of incumbency more than anything else that saved the Democratic party from ruin in 1984. State and local Democratic incumbents ran well in spite of, not because of, their party label. If the government had passed a decree prohibiting incumbents from running for reelection, the Republican party would probably have gained control of both houses of Congress and a substantial number of state legislatures and governorships.

The Issues

The Republicans would probably have held on to the White House as well. Far too much has been made of the personality factor in the 1984 election. As demonstrated by the ratings cited above, Americans like Reagan, and he is an effective television performer. But Mondale's complaint that he lost the election because he could not communicate effectively on television is entirely unconvincing. One can hardly imagine less effective television performers, or less congenial personalities, than Lyndon Johnson, Richard Nixon, and Jimmy Carter. Reagan's personal ratings were high even in 1982, but if he had run for reelection under the conditions prevailing that year, the polls indicate that he would have lost decisively, his charm and amiability notwithstanding.

The 1984 election was won by the incumbent for the same reason that the 1980 election was lost by the incumbent—performance. In September 1980

Carter's job approval rating was 55–37 percent negative in the Gallup Poll. In September 1984 Reagan's job approval rating was 57–36 percent positive—about twenty points higher.

In judging performance, the voters acknowledged that President Reagan had done the two things he was elected to do. He had curbed inflation, and he had restored the nation's sense of military security. As it happens, many people disagreed with the way he did those things. Inflation was reduced at the cost of a severe recession. The military buildup was achieved at the cost of significantly higher international tension. Still, after four failed presidencies in a row, the electorate was grateful to have a president do what he was elected to do. As Reagan is fond of saying, "You don't quarrel with success."

Three times during the campaign—in February, April, and October—the *Los Angeles Times* poll asked the public to judge which candidate, Reagan or Mondale, would do a better job of handling various issues (in October, people were asked to compare the Reagan-Bush and Mondale-Ferraro tickets). After each category—the economy, foreign affairs, social issues, and personal characteristics—respondents were asked which specific issue they considered most important. The results are displayed in table 7.3.

What is striking is that there were few changes over the course of the campaign. Each candidate's strengths and weaknesses remained much the same throughout.

Chief among Reagan's strengths was the economy, and chief among his economic strengths was inflation. Having brought the hyperinflation of the late 1970s to a halt, Reagan maintained a large and growing advantage over his opponent on this issue. Another of the president's accomplishments was the tax cut, and on taxes too he held a sizable lead—one that increased noticeably after the Democratic National Convention, where Mondale committed himself to raising taxes (and warned that Reagan would do the same). Taxes were not rated by the voters as one of their more important economic concerns, however.

The two economic issues that most concerned the electorate were those on which the president was theoretically most vulnerable—unemployment and the federal budget deficit. In the early part of the year the two candidates were rated about equal on handling unemployment. But, as the recovery proceeded and the memory of the 1982 recession faded, Reagan's advantage on the unemployment issue increased to ten points. Thus did the recovery rob the Democrats of one of their most powerful issues.

Whenever voters have been asked to name Reagan's major failure as president, they have unhesitatingly pointed to the federal budget deficit. The Democrats naturally tried to exploit the deficit as a campaign issue. They failed. However alarmed the voters may have felt over a $200 billion deficit, the Democrats had little credibility as a party that could bring government spend-

Table 7.3   Ratings of candidates on issues, 1984

Issue	Importance of issue	Prefer Mondale	Prefer Reagan	Advantage
The economy				
Handling inflation				
February	(13)	19	44	R 25
April	(12)	20	46	R 26
October	(14)	19	50	R 31
Handling taxes				
February	(3)	30	44	R 14
April	(4)	21	34	R 13
October	(7)	23	43	R 20
Making America more competitive in international trade				
February	(2)	29	41	R 12
April	(3)	26	44	R 18
October	(5)	27	46	R 19
Handling the federal budget deficit				
February	(21)	19	35	R 16
April	(25)	22	36	R 14
October	(24)	23	37	R 14
Handling unemployment				
February	(30)	39	41	R 2
April	(38)	39	38	M 1
October	(30)	37	47	R 10
Helping the poor and the disadvantaged				
February	(13)	52	14	M 38
April	(9)	50	16	M 34
October	(11)	51	22	M 29
Foreign affairs				
Keeping America secure militarily				
February	(7)	15	54	R 39
April	(19)	15	53	R 38
October	(24)	15	56	R 41

Table 7.3 (*continued*)

Issue	Importance of issue	Prefer Mondale	Prefer Reagan	Advantage
Keeping peace in the world				
February	(16)	32	38	R 6
April	(40)	31	40	R 9
October	(34)	29	46	R 17
Handling the situation in the Middle East[a]				
February	(38)	30	38	R 8
April	(8)	27	40	R 13
October	(7)	26	40	R 14
Handling the situation in Central America				
February	(11)	19	27	R 8
April	(9)	21	25	R 4
October	(5)	21	33	R 12
Handling the control of nuclear weapons				
February	(12)	24	26	R 2
April	(17)	23	28	R 5
October	(25)	31	34	R 3
Social issues				
Handling crime				
February	(45)	18	37	R 19
April	(43)	11	26	R 15
October	(37)	12	29	R 17
Handling prayers in public schools				
February	(10)	21	46	R 25
April	(7)	23	46	R 23
October	(7)	27	42	R 15
Handling the abortion issue				
February	(10)	18	25	R 7
April	(8)	17	22	R 5
October	(10)	25	26	R 1

Table 7.3   (*continued*)

Issue	Importance of issue	Prefer Mondale	Prefer Reagan	Advantage
Protecting the environment				
February	(17)	41	27	M 14
April	(15)	38	22	M 16
October	(16)	40	23	M 17
Protecting the civil rights of blacks and other minorities				
February	(13)	32	13	M 19
April	(18)	34	16	M 18
October	(19)	40	15	M 25
Personal characteristics				
Has stronger qualities of leadership				
February	(20)	22	60	R 38
April	(21)	23	62	R 39
October	(36)	24	63	R 39
Has more ability to get things done				
February	(21)	22	53	R 31
April	(23)	23	53	R 30
October	(20)	27	51	R 24
Is more trustworthy[b]				
February	(31)	19	26	R 7
April	(31)	20	30	R 10
October	(17)	21	32	R 11
Has more concern for people like yourself				
February	(14)	34	23	M 11
April	(12)	34	22	M 12
October	(16)	36	34	M 2
Has more new ideas				
February	(5)	28	23	M 5
April	(3)	27	22	M 5
October	(4)	32	23	M 9

Table 7.3   *(continued)*

Importance of issue areas	
Percentage of respondents selecting:	
The economy	
February	56
April	59
October	58
Foreign affairs	
February	21
April	19
October	19
Social issues	
February	10
April	10
October	10
Personal characteristics	
February	7
April	6
October	6

Source: Los Angeles Times polls.

[a]In February, "handling the situation in Lebanon."

[b]In October, "has more integrity."

Questions:

"Regardless of which candidate for president you happen to prefer right now—Walter Mondale, the Democrat, or Ronald Reagan, the Republican—which one do you think [would do the best job of] . . . ?"

[October only] "Regardless of which candidates for president and vice-president you happen to prefer right now—Walter Mondale and Geraldine Ferraro, the Democrats, or Ronald Reagan and George Bush, the Republicans—which ticket do you think [would do the best job of] . . . ?"

[After each group of comparisons] "Which one of all those problems [or characteristics] just mentioned do you consider the most important right now? [List repeated]"

[After all comparisons] "Of all the problems we talked about, which different kinds of issues do you consider the most important right now—those having to do with the economy, or foreign affairs, or social issues, or the personal characteristics of the different candidates for president [and vice-president]?"

ing under control. The table reveals that, while confidence in Reagan was low on the deficit issue, confidence in his Democratic opponent was always lower.

Mondale had a strong lead on one economic issue—helping the poor and the disadvantaged. This is the famous "fairness" issue that had worked so well for the Democrats in 1982—the belief, still prevalent, that "Reaganomics" helps the rich at the expense of the poor. The figures show, however, that only about one voter in ten considered it a major issue. The fairness issue had obviously lost salience. In 1982, when the economy was bad, to most voters fairness meant "us." In 1984, when the economy looked good, fairness undoubtedly meant "them."

Foreign policy was supposed to be another area of weakness for Reagan. The president's foreign policy ratings had been relatively low throughout his administration. Within a year of his taking office, a grassroots movement demanding a mutual, verifiable nuclear freeze arose in various parts of the country. Despite several major speeches aimed at rallying public support, Americans remained profoundly skeptical of the president's policies in Central America and the Middle East. Most disturbing was the fact that Reagan could not claim credit for a single arms control agreement.

The table reveals that Reagan bested Mondale on every foreign policy issue tested during the campaign. These included military security, on which the president's record elicited a solid vote of confidence, and keeping peace in the world, which had been a persistent cause of public concern since Reagan took office. The two issues on which Reagan might have been thought vulnerable, Central America and the Middle East, tended to diminish in importance over the year, particularly after American troops were withdrawn from Lebanon. On these and other foreign policy issues, the president's advantage improved during the campaign.

Early in the year Reagan held only a narrow lead on the peace issue, which in the end was the dominant foreign policy concern; by the fall, however, he was the clear favorite for "keeping peace in the world." Only on "control of nuclear weapons" did his lead remain precarious. Here, as with the deficit, the Democrats were unable to exploit the incumbent's vulnerability, and for the same reason: The voters showed little recognition of the Democrats' superior ability to handle the problem.

The Gallup Poll substantiates the finding that the president's perceived ability to manage foreign policy improved during the campaign. In January Mondale was nine points ahead of Reagan as the candidate more likely to keep the United States out of war. In June they were tied. In September and October Reagan was seven points ahead. It was not simply a function of Mondale's weakness. Another Gallup question asked whether Reagan's defense policies had brought the United States closer to war or peace. Between the summer of 1983 and the summer of 1984, more people said "war" (43–47 percent) than "peace" (26–28 percent). By the fall of 1984, however, the two figures were almost equal.

Why did the voters gain confidence in Reagan's foreign policy? The campaign focused attention on the administration's record. True, the Reagan administration had no foreign policy triumph comparable to Carter's Camp

David peace treaty. But it also had no foreign policy disaster comparable to Iran.

The Democrats ran television advertisements suggesting that Reagan might start a nuclear war. Many voters had been worried about that in 1980, but not in 1984. For one thing, Reagan had been president for almost four years, and we were still here. To an electorate that had initially been apprehensive about Reagan's foreign policy tendencies, his record in office—for instance, his cautious response in September 1983 to the Soviet downing of the Korean plane—was immensely reassuring.

Many Democrats thought they could use the administration's failure in Lebanon as an issue in the campaign. After all, we lost a great many more American lives in Lebanon than in Iran. But Iran is still seen as a national humiliation and a disgrace. Lebanon is not. Why? Because when it became clear that our peacekeeping mission in Lebanon was not working, Reagan had the good sense to cut our losses and get out. That, to many Americans, is leadership—exactly the kind of leadership we did not get in Vietnam.

During the Vietnam trauma, polltakers regularly asked Americans if they preferred a "hawkish" or a "dovish" policy in Southeast Asia. The answer, over and over again, was, "We should either win or get out." What did Reagan do as president? In Grenada we won. And in Lebanon we got out. So much for the Vietnam syndrome.

As one election analysis put it, "[President Reagan] loves to display American military muscle, yet prefers to do so without there being any American victims. He supports peace from a position of American strength but is against this strength resulting in the threat of a nuclear war." That description by *Izvestia* was intended to convey the impression that Reagan's policy is inconsistent and contradictory. In fact, it turns out to be exactly the kind of foreign policy the American public wants.

Social issues were also supposed to cause serious problems for the Republican ticket. These issues are often deeply divisive, and Reagan has taken forthright positions on many of them. On some important social issues, including a constitutional amendment to prohibit abortions, the Equal Rights Amendment for women, and the priority of environmental protection, polls show that most Americans disagree with the administration's positions.

Reagan himself introduced social issues into the campaign in a way that seemed likely to give him trouble. At an ecumenical prayer breakfast during the Republican National Convention in Dallas, he said, "The truth is, politics and morality are inseparable. And as morality's foundation is religion, religion and politics are necessarily related." The notion that religion and politics do not mix and a belief in the principle of separation of church and state are deeply embedded in American political culture. A poll taken by NBC News and the Associated Press in 1981 asked, "Do you think religious convictions should be a basis for political action?" The answer, four to one, was no. By 66–26 percent, those polled by the *Los Angeles Times* in 1983 agreed "we must maintain the separation of church and state." In the *Los Angeles Times* exit poll, opinions of the Reverend Jerry Falwell, the leader of the Moral Majority and an influential figure in the Reagan administration, were found to be three-to-one unfavorable.

Both Democrats and Republicans profess to be defending religious pluralism. Both believe they are protecting people's personal liberties against efforts by culturally aggressive groups to impose their values on the rest of society. To Reagan and many Republicans the cultural aggressors are liberals who promote antireligious ("secular humanist") values. To Mondale and many Democrats the enemy is the religious right, which is attempting to Christianize American society and impose its fundamentalist values on other Americans.

As table 7.3 shows, Mondale held a significant advantage on some social issues (environmental protection, civil rights) while Reagan enjoyed more confidence on others (school prayer). Interestingly, although the public opposes the kind of antiabortion amendment the president has endorsed, neither candidate had a significant advantage on the abortion issue. In polls taken since 1972 by the National Opinion Research Center at the University of Chicago, resounding majorities have accepted a woman's right to obtain a legal abortion if her own health is in danger, if there is a strong chance of a serious defect in the baby, or if the woman became pregnant as a result of rape. But most Americans oppose the right to an abortion if the family cannot afford another child, if the woman does not want any more children, if the woman does not want to marry the father, or if the woman wants an abortion "for any reason." The public opposes an absolute prohibition of abortions, which is the position of many Right-to-Life activists, but it does not endorse abortion as a form of birth control, which is the position of some prochoice activists.

The social issue considered by far the most important—crime—received the least attention in the campaign. While Reagan had the advantage over Mondale on the crime issue, neither candidate received a strong vote of confidence. Crime is the most important social problem facing most Americans, but it is not one for which either party appears to have a convincing solution.

Reagan took a calculated risk on the social issue. He bet the same thing would happen in 1984 that happened in 1980. In an analysis of data from that election, Arthur H. Miller and Martin P. Wattenberg found that "social issues . . . were a far more significant predictor of the vote for people with politicized fundamentalist beliefs than for those at the secular end of the scale." Although issues such as abortion and school prayer were extremely important to fundamentalists, "the remainder of the population voted on the basis of other concerns."[12] In other words, Reagan gained votes from those who agreed with his positions but did not lose votes from those opposed to them. The risk paid off again in 1984, although the president's intermingling of religion and politics did cost him the support of one influential group of voters, as will be shown below.

The one personal characteristic that overshadowed all others in importance was leadership. As in 1980, it was Reagan's issue all the way. Reagan had a smaller, though still strong, advantage on the second most-valued quality, "the ability to get things done." In 1980 strong, effective leadership was what Americans thought they were not getting under Carter and what attracted them to Reagan. Fortunately for Reagan, these were still the top-ranked presidential qualities in 1984. "Caring" about people, for example, which tended to work in Mondale's favor, was not considered as important as effectiveness.

Interestingly, Mondale, whose nomination had been threatened by a "new ideas" campaign during the Democratic primaries, was seen as having more new ideas than Reagan. He was, after all, the challenger. The important point, however, is that few voters seemed interested in new ideas when it came time to elect a president. The old ideas were working fine.

Another issue that did not work to the Democrats' advantage was the so-called sleaze factor, that is, the many scandals and conflicts of interest that had plagued members of the Reagan administration. The issue of personal integrity was critical to Carter's election in 1976. According to the table, however, little sleaze rubbed off on Reagan. He was generally rated higher than Mondale on trustworthiness, although about half the electorate saw no meaningful difference between the candidates in this regard.

Having taken respondents through this long list of issues, the *Los Angeles Times* poll asked them to make a final, summary evaluation: "Of all the problems we talked about, which kinds of issues do you consider most important right now, those having to do with the economy, or foreign affairs, or social issues, or the personal characteristics of the different candidates?" The answers, shown in table 7.3, were remarkably consistent throughout the campaign. Economic issues, mentioned by close to 60 percent, completely overshadowed all others. Of distinctly less concern were foreign affairs (about 20 percent), social issues (10 percent) and personal characteristics (about 6 percent).

Since, as the evidence indicates, social issues were of very low salience to most voters, Reagan's gamble paid off. Moreover, the argument that the election was dominated by personal factors—style, image, personality—receives little support here. The election was about performance, and economic performance was what counted most. That was why Reagan was elected in the first place—to get the economy back on track after ten years of economic crisis and decline. The voters' obsession with the economy was good news for the Republicans in 1984, but the lesson of 1982 is still pertinent. If the economy should sour, as it did that year, the Republicans will once again be in deep trouble. Their political fortunes are hostage to the nation's economy.

The 1984 Mandate

The Democrats' nomination of Carter's vice-president virtually ensured that the 1984 election would be a reenactment of 1980. A vote for Reagan would reconfirm the 1980 mandate. A vote for Mondale would say, in essence, that 1980 was a mistake and that the nation would be better off returning to the status quo ante Reagan.

Predictably, Reagan's 1980 vote and his 1984 vote were highly correlated state by state (.90). The 1980 Carter vote and the 1984 Mondale vote were only slightly less highly correlated (.80). The principal difference between the two elections was the more liberal cast to the Democratic vote in 1984. In 1980 the Carter and Anderson votes were negatively related (−.25); the region in which Carter did best (the South) was the one in which Anderson did worst. In 1984, as table 7.2 revealed, Mondale picked up most of the Anderson vote, and the correlation between the Mondale and Anderson votes was positive (.24).

In September 1984 CBS News and the *New York Times* asked people to compare Reagan and Mondale by the same criteria they had used to compare Reagan and Carter in 1980. The results are shown in table 7.4.

In some respects Mondale was a stronger candidate than Carter. More people thought of Mondale as competent, forceful, and clear in his positions on the issues and in his vision of the country's future. Reagan, however, was notably stronger in 1984 than in 1980. His greatest advantage in both years was leadership. Although Mondale was seen as a somewhat stronger leader than Carter, Reagan's rating as a leader was considerably stronger in 1984 than in 1980. Interestingly, while Reagan's reputation for leadership went up, his reputation for forcefulness went down. That was probably good news for the president, since a tendency to rely on force was one of the things people feared about him in 1980. Reagan managed to assure people that he was strong while reassuring them that he was not reckless.

Mondale, like Carter, enjoyed an advantage on compassion "cares about people like you." The age issue, however, was less of a disadvantage for Reagan in 1984 than it had been in 1980, even though he was four years older. The percentage of voters who described Reagan as "physically up to the job of president" was noticeably higher in 1984. On intelligence, judgment under pressure, and "understanding the complicated problems a president has to deal with"—where Carter was ahead of Reagan in 1980—Reagan was ahead of Mondale in 1984. Voters once had doubts about Reagan's judgment and intellectual abilities, but his success as president had obviously been reassuring.

Issue differences were more sharply defined in 1984 than they had been four years earlier. "Clear positions on the issues" and "a vision of the country's future" were more readily attributed to Mondale than to Carter. Clarity and vision were also more widely attributed to Reagan after four years in office. There is no evidence here that the voters found the choice between Reagan and Mondale unclear or confusing: They felt that they were voting between two distinct alternatives.

Table 7.4 Ratings of presidential candidates on personal qualities and on issues, 1980 and 1984

Characteristic	1984			1980		
	Reagan	Mondale	Advan-tage[a]	Reagan	Carter	Advan-tage[a]
Personal qualities						
Question: "Do you think that [Ronald Reagan, Walter Mondale, Jimmy Carter] . . . ?"						
Is a strong leader	74	41	R 33	57	34	R 23
Is forceful	51	21	R 30	68	8	R 60
Would have good judgment under pressure	64	54	R 10	50	51	C 1
Understands the complicated problems a president has to deal with	76	67	R 9	48	68	C 20
Is highly intelligent	45	36	R 9	33	44	C 11
Has clear positions on issues	63	57	R 6	50	44	R 6
Is competent	71	65	R 6	59	50	R 9
Has a vision of the country's future	72	70	R 2	67	47	R 20
Cares about people like you	56	71	M 15	59	77	C 18
Is physically up to the job of president	73	90	M 17	59	85	C 26
Says too many things carelessly, without considering the consequences	58	33	M 25	66	42	C 24

Table 7.4   (*continued*)

Characteristic	1984			1980		
	Reagan	Mondale	Advan- tage[a]	Reagan	Carter	Advan- tage[a]
Ability to handle problems						
Question: "Regardless of which man you happen to prefer for president— [Ronald Reagan, Walter Mondale, Jimmy Carter] —which do you feel would do a better job of handling each of these problems?"						
Reducing inflation	53	32	R 21	44	29	R 15
Handling foreign relations	50	33	R 17	37	43	C 6
Improving the economy	52	36	R 16	44	30	R 14
Increasing respect for the United States overseas	48	34	R 14	42	31	R 11
Dealing with Russia	48	34	R 14	37	40	C 3
Building trust in government	41	36	R 5	37	32	R 5
Reducing unemployment	45	41	R 4	41	32	R 9
Spending taxpayers' money wisely	38	37	R 1	42	29	R 13
Keeping the United States out of war	35	47	M 12	25	50	C 25
Improving the environment and dealing with environmental issues	31	47	M 16	32	37	C 5
Improving things for minorities, including blacks and Hispanics	25	54	M 29	22	49	C 27
Helping the poor and needy	25	60	M 35	24	49	C 25
Improving women's rights	20	63	M 43	23	48	C 25

Sources: CBS News/*New York Times* poll; Gallup Poll.
[a]Percentage points.

The Gallup Poll compared the candidates on the same issues in 1984 and in 1980 (see table 7.4). With one important exception, each side's issue advantages remained the same both years. Reagan's lead on "reducing inflation" and "improving the economy" grew larger. He continued to lead his Democratic opponent on the unemployment issue, although the difference was somewhat smaller. The deficit issue also had a cost; Reagan's advantage on "spending the taxpayers' money wisely," which was fairly large in 1980, essentially disappeared in 1984.

In the case of certain issues on which Carter had been ahead in 1980, Mondale's lead was even greater in 1984; these included environmental protection and support for minorities, the poor, and especially women's rights, on which Mondale's selection of a female running mate obviously boosted his credibility. In 1984 as in 1980 the Democratic party's strength was on issues of equality, compassion, and social justice. Its problem was that these were not the dominant issues on the voters' minds either year.

The one important change from 1980 was in the area of foreign policy. Carter was ahead of Reagan on handling foreign relations and dealing with Russia, but in 1984 on both issues Reagan's lead over Mondale was substantial. Moreover, the Democrats' advantage on "keeping the United States out of war" had become much smaller; by the time the fall campaign got under way, Reagan had moved ahead on the peace issue. In 1980 the Democrats went into the campaign with a strong peace record, while voters had doubts about Reagan's commitment. Those doubts were substantially resolved by Reagan's record in office.

Thus the principal difference between 1980 and 1984 was that the advantages of incumbency shifted to Reagan. Voters felt better about his physical stamina, intellectual competence, good judgment, prudence, and dedication to peace. Even though Mondale was seen more positively than Carter, incumbency made Reagan a much stronger candidate in 1984 than he had been four years earlier.

Was there an ideological mandate in 1984? Here the data reveal a paradox. Voters seemed to be more attracted not only to Reagan but also to conservatism and the Republican party. At the same time, there is little evidence that the electorate's policy preferences shifted to the right.

A Gallup "national public opinion referendum" taken during the campaign found most voters in disagreement with Reagan's positions on relaxing pollution controls to reduce costs to industry (opposed two to one), the Equal Rights Amendment (favored two to one), increased spending for social programs (favored three to one), and an immediate, verifiable nuclear freeze (favored four to one). They supported Reagan on school prayer, taxes, and maintaining cost-of-living increases in Social Security benefits (which, under pressure from Mondale, the president endorsed).

Trend data on policy preferences indicate that public opinion since 1980 has moved away from Reagan's positions. Thus the Roper poll showed more support for government regulation in 1984 than in 1980 or 1981. In 1980, for example, 37 percent said there was not enough government regulation of "the health and safety of working conditions"; in 1984 the figure was 48 percent. Between 1981 and 1984 those holding the view that there was too much government regulation of the automobile industry dropped from 34 to 22 percent.

Negative views of the Soviet Union tended to diminish during Reagan's presidency. In 1981 one-third of the public accepted the view that the Soviets would risk a major war to achieve global domination; that proportion fell to one-fifth in 1984. In 1980, 36 percent endorsed the view that "Russia can't be trusted and we will have to rely on increased military strength to counter them in the future." That figure had fallen by half in 1984. The belief that the United States was behind the Soviet Union in nuclear strength was expressed by 43 percent in 1980 and by 27 percent in 1984. The belief that we were behind in conventional military power declined from one-half to one-third of the public over the same period.

The National Opinion Research Center regularly tests support for various kinds of government spending. In 1980 an average of 42 percent thought the government was spending too little on the environment, health, education, welfare, and urban aid. That figure went up in each year of Reagan's presidency, reaching 50 percent in 1984. Conversely, the number who felt we were spending too much on these problems steadily declined. By 1984 support for higher domestic spending was greater than at any time since 1973, when these questions were first asked.

The view that we were spending too little on defense was at 56 percent in 1980. It fell to 29 percent in 1982, 24 percent in 1983, and 17 percent in 1984, when more than twice as many people thought we were spending too much on defense. To some extent, these trends reflect the success of Reagan's policies. The administration's military buildup made the public feel more secure about our military power and reduced support for higher defense outlays. Similarly, the administration's domestic budget cuts, plus the 1982 recession, tended to raise public support for higher domestic spending.

Reagan was elected in 1980 at the low point of a sixteen-year trend of declining confidence in government. The success of his antigovernment program had the anomalous effect of turning that trend around. Thus in 1980 the view that the government wastes "a lot of the money we pay in taxes" reached a peak of 78 percent. It fell to 63 percent in a postelection survey taken in 1984 by CBS News and the *New York Times*. The view that "you can't trust the government in Washington to do right most of the time" was held by 73 percent in 1980 and 51 percent in 1984. Reagan's success as president managed to restore some of the public's declining faith in government—which may not have been exactly what he had intended to accomplish.

Surveys taken during the campaign revealed that, on many specific policy issues, the public's views differed from Reagan's. In the July ABC News/ *Washington Post* survey the public favored the Equal Rights Amendment, opposed a constitutional amendment that would outlaw abortions, favored a national health insurance program, opposed increasing military aid to El Salvador, opposed U.S. support of antigovernment guerrillas in Nicaragua, and opposed the construction of more nuclear power plants. A five-to-four majority felt that the federal government should see to it that everyone who wants to work has a job. In September majorities opposed reductions in domestic spending and favored cuts in military spending. In the CBS News/ *New York Times* poll a 75 to 22 percent majority felt that religion should be kept out of presidential campaigns.

The *New York Times* reported, "On many issues, ranging from arms control to abortion, the public is closer to the Democrats' stand than to Mr. Reagan's." The *Times* added, however, that those issues were not helping the Democrats. Many voters continued to favor Reagan even when they disagreed with him on the issues. In a *Newsweek* survey, respondents said they felt Reagan came closer than Mondale to their way of thinking on abortion, military spending, and the role of religion in politics—even though their responses to issue questions in the same poll gave direct evidence to the contrary.

Confidence in the president's performance seemed to produce the feeling that he must be right on the issues. In the CBS News/ *New York Times* survey an almost two-to-one majority said they agreed with Reagan's positions on most issues. By five to four, they said they disagreed with most of Mondale's positions.

Whatever their policy preferences, more and more Americans decided to call themselves Republicans in 1984. More and more Americans were also identifying their views as "right of center," according to the Gallup Poll. In 1976, 31 percent of the public described themselves as right of center. In 1980 the figure was 32 percent, and in 1984, 36 percent. The proportion describing themselves as left of center fell from 24 to 18 percent over the same period. Americans' ideological description of themselves in 1984 (two to one conservative) put them closer to their description of the Republican party (four to one conservative) than to their description of the Democratic party (three to one liberal).

Thus voters seemed to believe that they agreed with Reagan even if they did not. They also felt closer to the conservative philosophy and the Republican party even if their opinions were not moving in that direction. Why did they feel that way? The explanation can be found in the basic pragmatism of the American electorate. Americans believed the administration's policies were working. The public's approach to politics is pragmatic—whatever works must be right. Ideologues believe that whatever is wrong cannot possibly work, even if it does work. Thus many die-hard Republicans never admitted that the New Deal was a success, and many Democrats in 1984 refused to believe in the recovery. To pragmatic Americans, if big government policies worked during the New Deal, they were probably right, at least for that time. If Reagan's antigovernment policies worked in 1984, then they too were probably right, at least for the time being.

When a realignment occurs, ideology is usually the last thing to change, if it changes at all. There is little evidence that the electorate moved sharply to the left during the 1930s. In February 1936, at the depth of the Great Depression and only nine months before Franklin D. Roosevelt's landslide reelection, a Gallup poll found that 70 percent of the public favored cuts in government spending to reduce the national debt. Voters did not accept the New Deal philosophy until they were convinced that it worked. In 1984 the public's identification with Reagan, with conservatism, and with the Republican party appeared to be based more on the demonstrated success of administration policies than on any fundamental ideological conversion.

The 1980 and 1984 elections were similar in that both were decided on the basis of performance more than ideology. That is surprising because Reagan is one of the most ideological figures in American politics. Reagan's achievement in 1980 was to win the support (at the last minute) of many voters who did not agree with him ideologically. He did it again in 1984. But there was one important difference in 1984: The success of his policies caused many more voters to believe they agreed with him and to identify themselves with his party and his philosophy.

What, then, was the mandate of the 1984 election? The message seemed to be this: "We like the peace and prosperity the country is now enjoying. Keep it up." Probing a little deeper, though, one finds that people were worried about two problems that threatened to undermine those conditions. One was the federal budget deficit. The other was arms control. What saved the president was that the voters had more confidence in the Republicans than in the Democrats to handle both problems. The voters were really saying, "Keep it up. But try to give these two problems a little more attention. We are confident you can do it."

Social Forces

Table 7.5 gives the demographic profile of the 1980 and 1984 presidential votes. Also shown for each group is the change in support for the Republican and Democratic tickets and the swing to the Republican party, as defined earlier.

Table 7.5   Presidential vote, by group, 1980 and 1984 (in percentages)

Group	Percentage of 1984 voters	1980 vote		1984 vote		Change 1980–84[a]		Swing to GOP
		Reagan	Carter	Reagan	Mondale	Rep	Dem	
U.S. total	100	51	41	59	41	+8	0	+4
Men	47	55	36	61	37	+6	+1	+2.5
Women	53	47	45	57	42	+10	−3	+6.5
Whites	86	55	36	66	34	+11	−2	+6.5
Blacks	10	11	85	9	90	−2	+5	−3.5
Hispanics	3	33	59	33	65	0	+6	−3
Age 18–29	24	43	44	58	41	+15	−3	+9
Age 30–44	34	54	36	58	42	+4	+6	−1
Age 45–59	23	55	39	60	39	+5	0	+2.5
Age 60+	19	54	41	63	36	+9	−5	+7
0–11 years school	8	46	51	50	49	+4	−2	+3
High school graduate	30	51	43	60	39	+9	−4	+6.5
Some college	30	55	35	60	38	+5	+3	+1
College graduate	29	52	35	59	40	+7	+5	+1
White Protestant	51	63	31	73	26	+10	−5	+7.5
Catholic	26	49	42	55	44	+6	+2	+2
Jewish	3	39	45	32	66	−7	+21	−14
Born-again white Christian	15	63	33	80	20	+17	−13	+15
Union household[b]	28	41	49	45	54	+4	+5	−0.5
Nonunion household[b]	72	55	33	64	36	+9	+3	+3
Professional and managerial	30	57	32	62	37	+5	+5	0

Table 7.5   (*continued*)

Group	Percentage of 1984 voters	1980 vote		1984 vote		Change 1980–84[a]		Swing to GOP
		Reagan	Carter	Reagan	Mondale	Rep	Dem	
White-collar	13	50	41	59	40	+9	−1	+5
Blue-collar	14	47	46	53	46	+6	0	+3
Unemployed	3	39	51	31	68	−8	+17	−12.5
East	24	47	42	52	47	+5	+5	0
Midwest	28	51	40	61	38	+10	−2	+6
South	29	52	44	63	36	+11	−8	+9.5
West	18	53	34	59	40	+6	+6	0
Southern whites	25	61	35	72	28	+11	−7	+9
Republicans	35	86	9	92	7	+6	−2	+4
Independents	26	55	30	63	35	+8	+5	+1.5
Democrats	38	26	67	26	73	0	+6	−3
Liberals	17	25	60	29	70	+4	+10	−3
Moderates	44	48	42	54	46	+6	+4	+1
Conservatives	35	72	23	81	18	+9	−5	+7

Sources: CBS News/*New York Times* exit poll, November 6, 1984 (N = 8,696); and CBS News/ *New York Times* exit poll, November 4, 1980 (N = 15,201).
[a]Percentage points.
[b]From ABC News poll (N = 11,023).

Reagan made impressive gains among white voters and Southern voters generally and among Southern whites specifically. Nothing demonstrates the Democrats' dilemma so clearly as the fact that Reagan carried the white vote by almost two to one—and whites are seven-eighths of the national electorate. The cost of not having a Southerner on the Democratic ticket is clearly visible in the heavy loss of Democratic support in the South. The Southern white vote split about five to two for Reagan. In presidential politics the South, which now includes more than a quarter of the electorate, is becoming the most reliably Republican region of the country. Even Carter could not hold Southern whites in 1980.

Class differences, though still noticeable, diminished a bit in 1984. Among high-status groups (professionals and managers, the college educated), Reagan's gains were partially offset by Democratic gains. These are the groups that had given John Anderson strong support in 1980. The decision of most Anderson voters to cast their lot with the Democrats held Reagan's margin to about three to two in high-status groups. Among low-status voters, Democratic support remained stable or diminished while Reagan picked up votes. Blue-collar workers and those with less than a high school education split their votes very closely. Thus, despite the economic downturn of the past ten years, class differences in American politics have continued their long-term decline. In the 1950s professionals tended to vote about twenty points more Republican than manual workers; the difference in recent presidential elections has been about half as wide.

The union vote takes on a special importance because organized labor decided to endorse Mondale even before the campaign for the Democratic nomination began. It can be argued that the labor endorsement created problems for Mondale in the Democratic primaries, in that it enabled Hart to attack Mondale as the candidate of the "special interests." Most Americans are not antilabor, but they are opposed to unions—or business firms, or churches, or other organized interests—trying to wield political influence. Is there any evidence that the union endorsement either helped or hurt Mondale in the general election?

The table shows that the union vote remained fairly constant in 1984. In 1980 Carter led Reagan by eight points among union voters; in 1984 Mondale led Reagan by nine points. In fact, no change is really a positive outcome for the Democrats, since the rest of the electorate was swinging Republican. It appears that the labor endorsement helped union voters resist the national trend. Still, it is no great triumph for union voters to go Democratic by a bare majority. In fact, white union voters split their presidential vote just about 50–50. The ABC News exit poll asked voters whether "union endorsements of Mondale" were very important to them in deciding how to vote. Of the 6 percent who said yes, 50 percent voted for Mondale and 49 percent for Reagan. Since these voters reported giving Reagan a fourteen-point lead over Carter in 1980, it appears that the union endorsement did help the Democratic nominee, at least among the small number of voters to whom it made a difference.

Religious differences have also been declining since the 1950s. In the 1952 presidential election, the Gallup Poll showed Protestant and Catholic voters about twenty points apart. In 1960, with a Catholic at the top of the Democratic ticket, the gap widened to forty points. In 1976 and 1980 only about ten points separated Protestant and Catholic voters. This year the Gallup Poll shows no difference at all between Protestants and Catholics, while the ABC News and NBC News exit polls found about ten points between them, with Catholic voters still more Democratic.

Religion did play an important role in the 1984 election, although its effect was more limited than in 1960. The group that swung most strongly Republican in 1984 was born-again white Christians. Reagan's lead doubled in this constituency, from two to one in 1980 to four to one in 1984. Part of the explanation, of course, is the absence of Carter from the Democratic ticket. The nomination of Mondale and Ferraro did not have much appeal to fundamentalists.

Still, there was something more going on in 1984 than the absence of Carter. The group that swung most strongly Democratic between 1980 and 1984 was the Jews. Their swing was equal and opposite to that of born-again white Christians. There is some controversy over the exact division of the Jewish vote in 1984, but the evidence is strong that Reagan lost Jewish support. Moreover, his loss of support is attributable primarily to Jewish concern over his efforts to mix religion and politics.[13] It appears that, although the religion-and-politics issue was not a matter of dominant concern to most voters, it did affect two constituencies that had a special interest in it. Reagan attracted white Christian fundamentalists by his outspoken appeal to religious values at the same time that he repelled many Jewish voters who are strongly committed to a secularist and pluralistic tradition. That the two constituencies responded by moving in equal and opposite directions does not mean that the issue was a "wash" for the president, however. Born-again white Christians outnumbered Jews five to one.

Religion may also help explain Reagan's gains among older voters, who were somewhat fearful of him in 1980. For reasons that are not very mysterious, older voters tend to be more interested in religion. Moreover, Reagan's promise to leave Social Security benefits intact was undoubtedly reassuring to them. What about the issue of Reagan's age? According to the ABC News exit poll, to only 10 percent of the voters was "Reagan's age" a very important factor in their presidential choice. Those who felt that way voted six to one for Mondale, up from seven to three for Carter in 1980. The age factor, like the union endorsement, made a difference to the small number of voters to whom it was important. In that group the issue seemed to work against the president.

Only two groups swung strongly against Reagan—Jewish voters and the unemployed, each about 3 percent of the electorate. The Jews had their own quarrel with the president, and it is hardly surprising for the unemployed to turn against the incumbent. Black voters, already heavily Democratic, became a bit more so in 1984. Hispanics also appear to have moved in the Democratic direction, although the exit polls differ on how they voted. (The CBS News/ New York Times and NBC News polls show Reagan with 32–34 percent of the Hispanic vote; ABC News and the Los Angeles Times put his Hispanic support at 44–47 percent. Sentiment among Hispanic Americans is highly diverse and notoriously difficult to measure.) Both Democrats and liberals showed greater support for Mondale than for Carter, in part because of reclaimed Anderson voters. The groups that swung most strongly toward the Republicans included several overlapping categories: whites, Southerners, Southern whites, conservatives, white Protestants, and born-again white Christians.

Table 7.5 indicates that polarization by party and ideology was greater in 1984 than it had been in 1980. Conservatives and Republicans voted more heavily for Reagan while liberals and Democrats swung toward the Democratic party. What happened seems fairly clear. Many conservative voters (mostly white Southerners and born-again Christians) who had stuck with Carter in 1980 went to Reagan in 1984, while Mondale picked up Anderson liberals and some additional minority support. The Democrats' shift from Carter to Mondale, whom Carter had picked as his running mate in 1976 to pacify the liberal wing of the party, clarified the party choice.

The behavior of two groups, however, does not fit this model: women and young voters. Both tend to be relatively liberal in their inclinations, but they both swung strongly to Reagan in 1984. Thus:

There was still a gender gap in 1984, but it was smaller than in 1980—not larger, as might have been expected with a woman on the Democratic ticket.

According to the Gallup Poll, voters under thirty have been more Democratic than the rest of the country in every election since 1952 (the difference reached a peak of ten percentage points in 1972). One of the great surprises of 1984 was that age differences turned out to be very weak; young people voted in more or less the same way as everyone else. That fact must be treated as a gain for the Republicans.

The *Los Angeles Times* exit poll indicates that in 1984 as in the past women were less likely to describe themselves as conservative than men, and voters under thirty were less likely to do so than older voters. These groups' attraction to Reagan appears to have been based on something other than ideology. The most likely possibility is economic confidence. Young people and women, particularly single women, feel vulnerable as a result of the economic trends of the past ten years. Reagan is the first leader to reverse a decade-long economic decline. To young people, for example, the Great Depression did not happen in the 1930s; it happened in the 1970s, when they were entering the job market. Similarly, women—who, according to the polls, tend to be averse to risk and apprehensive about the future—were extremely sensitive to the hyperinflation of the 1970s. They could not have failed to notice Reagan's major achievement as president, which was to cut the inflation rate nearly to zero.

Mondale never had much appeal to young voters. Hart's nearly successful challenge to Mondale's nomination (Hart carried 36 percent of the nationwide

Democratic primary vote to Mondale's 38 percent) was made possible more by Mondale's glaring weakness among younger voters than for any other reason.[14] Young voters were put off by Mondale's identification with the Democratic party establishment and organized labor. They are more independent by inclination and tend to prefer the new politics — "new ideas," problem solving — to the old politics of interest-group liberalism represented by Mondale and his mentor, Hubert Humphrey. The young voters who cared little for Mondale during the spring primaries did not seem to like him any better during the fall campaign. Although they disagreed with Reagan on many social and foreign policy issues, he had done little that could be called threatening in those areas. What he had done was to turn the economy around, and that was enormously important to younger voters.

Why did the historic nomination of Representative Geraldine Ferraro not produce a bigger payoff for the Democrats? For one thing, men and women do not differ very much on women's rights issues. In the CBS News/ *New York Times* poll taken just after the naming of Ferraro, women tended to agree with men that she was selected "because of pressure from women's groups" (60 percent) rather than "because she was the best candidate" (22 percent).

The most important reason, in all likelihood, was that voters behaved in 1984 as they had behaved in the past — they voted for president, not for vice-president. Among all voters, according to the NBC News exit poll, 16 percent said Ferraro's presence on the Democratic ticket made them more likely to vote Democratic, and 26 percent said it made them less likely to do so; the rest said it made no difference. ABC News identified 11 percent of the voters to whom Mondale's choice of a woman as his running mate was a "very important" factor in their presidential choice. They voted Democratic 58 to 42 percent — a Democratic gain from 1980, when they had split their vote equally between Reagan and Carter.

In other words, Ferraro's nomination may have helped among the small number of voters to whom it was important. But for most voters it made very little difference. That is something of a victory for the women's rights movement. Although Ferraro did not live up to the exaggerated expectations of women's rights activists — she did not "deliver" the women's vote to Mondale — it is impossible to argue that her presence on the ticket was a major reason for the Democrats' loss. A breakthrough has been made: having a woman running mate has demonstrated to be neither unthinkable nor costly.

Realignment, Again

The Democrats have now lost four of the past five presidential elections. The party won only in 1976, by a narrow margin, and that victory can be attributed

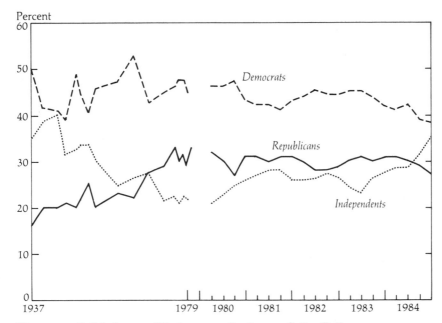

Percent

Figure 7.2 Political party affiliation, 1937–84. *Source:* Gallup Polls.

in part to the extraordinary experience of Watergate. The question inevitably rises; Is the United States experiencing a political realignment?

The question is usually taken to mean, Have the Republicans become the nation's new majority party? The answer appears to be no, or at least not yet. For a variety of reasons reviewed earlier, the Democrats have managed to hold on quite well in state and local elections. But there are ominous signs of change. The inertial force of incumbency will do the Democrats less and less good over time. And there are already indications that the partisanship of American voters is shifting decisively.

Since the late 1940s no poll has shown more self-described Republicans than Democrats in the national electorate. That is still true—but just barely. Figure 7.2 traces the numbers of Americans calling themselves Democrats, Republicans, and independents since the 1930s. Except in 1946, when the Republicans won control of both the House and the Senate, Democrats have consistently outnumbered Republicans, although only rarely (1937, 1964) has Democratic identification reached a majority. The ratio of Democrats to Republicans increased from nearly three to two in the 1950s to about five to three in the 1960s and two to one in the 1970s.

Actually, the Democratic proportion of the electorate held fairly steady during those decades while the Republican share declined. Only self-described independents were growing more numerous, their ranks increasing sharply during the late 1960s and early 1970s from about one-fifth to one-third of the national electorate. The enfranchisement of eighteen- to twenty-year-olds in 1972 accelerated this trend.

The proportion of independents leveled off at about 30 percent after 1972. In 1980 and 1981 the polls revealed rising Republican identification (from 21 to 28 percent) and declining Democratic support (from 48 to 41 percent). This shift was obviously associated with the 1980 election and the ensuing Reagan honeymoon. The trend was reversed during the 1982–83 recession and then resumed during the recovery.

Gallup figures from the last quarter of 1984 show Democrats barely out-numbering Republicans (38 to 35 percent). Gallup's finding is substantiated by the four nationwide exit polls taken on November 6, 1984.

	Democrats	Republicans
ABC News	38	32
CBS News/*New York Times*	38	35
NBC News	34	32
Los Angeles Times	34	30

The largest Republican gains occurred among young voters. The Gallup Poll found that the proportion of self-described Republicans among voters under the age of thirty had more than doubled since 1977. In the CBS News/ *New York Times* exit poll, the strongest Republican partisanship was found among eighteen- to twenty-nine-year-olds. That the Republicans gained most rapidly among young voters is not altogether surprising, since young voters have long been the most independent group in the electorate and therefore the least resistant to partisan conversion. Winning the young is likely to have a substantial payoff for the Republicans because political commitments acquired when young tend to be conserved as voters age. Young liberals usually become old liberals; young Republicans, old Republicans. It can also be safely assumed that, on the average, young voters will be around longer than older voters.

But can the Republicans hold on to these young voters? As the figure shows, the gains of 1980–81 quickly dissipated with the recession. The rebound of the Republican party appears to be linked to the perception that it can solve the nation's problems. That perception is linked mainly to the economic recovery. To a considerable extent, partisanship travels with the vote and may reflect nothing much more than the currently strong Republican performance. Thus, although the Republicans have clearly made gains in partisanship that outstrip any that occurred in 1952–56, 1968–72, or 1980–81, there is still no indication that they have become the nation's new majority party.

What has happened is half a realignment: The Democrats have lost their standing as the nation's normal majority party. The electorate is now about one-third Democratic, one-third Republican, and one-third independent. According to the Gallup Poll—except for 1964—independents have favored the Republican candidate in every presidential election since 1952. In congressional elections, independents have usually favored Democratic candidates, but not in 1984; all four exit polls showed a majority of independents voting for Republican candidates for Congress.

Realignment, though still inconclusive, has been going on for twenty years. Democrats have made substantial inroads among affluent upper-middle-class suburban voters outside the South. Many of those voters were traditional Republicans who could not accept the reactionary social conservatism of the new Republican party. They were attracted to new politics Democrats like George McGovern but not to moderates like Carter. Anderson, the liberal Republican who ran as an Independent in 1980 and then endorsed the Democratic ticket in 1984, led the way for many of them.

Anderson's independent candidacy represented one stream of realignment—liberal Republicans and independents becoming Democrats. The other important independent candidacy of the past twenty years, that of George Wallace in 1968, represents another stream of realignment: conservative Democrats and independents, mostly Southern whites, moving toward the Republican party. It is of some relevance that Wallace's share of the vote in 1968, 13.5 percent, was over twice as large as Anderson's 6.6 percent in 1980.

The first stage of the realignment occurred between 1966 and 1972, when race and foreign policy were the major issues of contention. It was during this period that the Democratic party lost most of its "social issue conservatives," primarily, but not exclusively, Southern whites. The Wallace voters in 1968 protested the commitment of the national party to civil rights; neoconservative Democrats were shocked by the nomination of McGovern in 1972 and the conversion of the party of Harry Truman to a noninterventionist foreign policy.

It was during this period that the Democratic party became consistently liberal; it endorsed a new social and foreign policy liberalism while retaining its traditional economic liberalism. The Republican party was also moving in the direction of ideological consistency, maintaining its traditional antigovernment economic conservatism while turning toward a more vigorous social and foreign policy conservatism. These trends—the legacy of the 1960s—appear to be irreversible.

As Everett Ladd has pointed out, these changes have tended to erode the class basis of American politics.[15] The Democrats, who had long had a populist economic appeal, acquired "elitist" support from educated upper-middle-

Table 7.6   Mondale vote, 1984, and Stevenson Vote, 1956 (in percentages)

Group and region	Mondale 1984	Stevenson 1956	Difference, 1956–84[a]
Group			
Blacks	90	61	+29
College-educated	39	31	+8
Professional/managerial	37	32	+5
Jews	67	62	+5
Women	42	39	+3
White-collar	40	37	+3
Union households	54	57	−3
Blue-collar	46	50	−4
Whites	34	41	−7
Catholics	44	51	−7
Men	37	45	−8
Region			
New England	43.4	37.8	+6
Middle Atlantic	45.1	39.5	+6
Farm belt	41.7	40.2	+2
Great Lakes	41.3	40.4	+1
Pacific	41.6	44.5	−3
Mountain	32.6	39.5	−7
Outer South	36.7	45.2	−9
Border	38.3	47.2	−9
Deep South	38.2	53.4	−15

Sources: Gallup Poll, 1956; CBS News/*New York Times* poll, 1984; U.S. Bureau of the Census, *Statistical Abstract of the United States: 1960* (80th Edition), Washington, D.C., 1959.
[a] Percentage points.

class liberals. To the Republicans' historically elitist economic conservatism— the party of business, the party of the rich—was joined a muscular, populist conservatism that espoused, for example, tough military policies and traditionalist religious values. In short, the two parties were becoming ideologically consistent but sociologically inconsistent.

With the nomination of a born-again white Southerner in 1976, the Democrats reclaimed many of the moderate and conservative voters they had lost in 1968 and 1972. But the larger realignment process was confirmed in 1980 and 1984. In 1980 Carter lost conservative supporters to Reagan and liberals to Anderson.[16] In 1984 Mondale reclaimed many Anderson liberals but lost many conservatives who had stuck with Carter.

Mondale's 1984 vote was noticeably similar to the votes for Humphrey in 1968 and McGovern in 1972. (Mondale, at 41 percent, did slightly worse than Humphrey's 43 percent and slightly better than McGovern's 38 percent.) All three votes had Northern liberal contours. That is not surprising. In all three years the party nominated Northern liberal Protestants for president and northern liberal Catholics as their running mates.

Compare, for instance, Mondale's 1984 vote with the vote for Adlai Stevenson in 1956. Stevenson was also a Northern liberal Protestant, although his running mate in 1956, as in 1952, was a Southerner. Stevenson won about the same proportion of the popular vote (42 percent) as Mondale. But the sources of their support were very different, as can be seen in table 7.6.

Mondale did significantly better than Stevenson among black voters, the college educated, women, Jews, and professionals. Stevenson's support was stronger among whites, men, blue-collar workers, union households, and Catholics. Mondale ran better than Stevenson in the Northeast, and Stevenson ran a good deal more strongly in the South and West.

The two streams of voters that have been leaving the Democratic party in significant numbers since the early 1960s have been white Southerners and working-class Catholic "ethnic" voters in the North. White Southerners voted between 50 and 55 percent Democratic in presidential elections from 1952 to 1964, according to polls taken by the University of Michigan. The Democratic vote among white Southerners dropped to 37 percent in 1968 and a catastrophic 18 percent in 1972. With Carter as the party nominee, the white Southern Democratic vote rose, but even Carter could not restore a Democratic majority; his fellow white Southerners gave him 48 percent in 1976 and 45 percent in 1980. It was the black vote that carried the South for Carter in 1976, and in 1980 there were not enough black voters for him to do it again. Mondale's 28 percent of the white Southern vote, which is the average of Humphrey's and McGovern's support, restores the status quo ante Carter in the South.

The Catholic Democratic vote reached a peak of 78 percent for John F. Kennedy in 1960. It remained nearly that high, 76 percent, in 1964, and Humphrey managed to retain 60 percent support from Catholics. McGovern, at 48 percent, lost the Catholic vote for the first time in recent memory. Carter regained a Catholic majority (57 percent) in 1976 and then lost it (46 percent) in 1980. With a Catholic vote of 44 percent in 1984, Mondale did worse in this constituency than any Democratic presidential candidate since 1924.

Essentially the Democratic party has lost its conservative wing, which used to be a considerable segment of the party. Its moderate support is also diminishing. (Consider how poorly John Glenn, Ernest Hollings, and Reubin Askew did in the 1984 Democratic primaries.) To some extent the party's losses have been compensated for by gains from blacks and from educated upper-middle-class liberals. (Over one quarter of the votes cast for Mondale came from blacks. In the South, blacks made up the majority of Democratic voters.) Overall, however, the losses have outweighed the gains.

The second stage of realignment, 1980–84, was more devastating for the Democrats because the party lost its credibility on economic issues. The economic issue had always held the Democratic party together, even when, as in 1968, the race issue and Vietnam were tearing it apart. Since the 1930s the Democrats have defined themselves primarily as the party that protects people against economic adversity. That is what kept white working-class voters and Southerners in the party despite their mistrust of its racial and foreign policy liberalism. The economic issue, in the form of the mid-seventies recession, played no small role in allowing the Democrats to recover in 1974 and 1976, even after the party had lost many of its racist and neoconservative supporters.

But current polls show that the Democrats' longstanding advantage as the party more likely to keep the nation prosperous has disappeared. For most of the past thirty-five years, the Democrats have been rated better for prosperity while the Republicans have usually been seen as the party of peace. In 1980 those perceptions shifted. As a result of Carter's economic failure, the voters saw no difference between the two parties on the prosperity issue. Given Carter's strong peace record and the voters' apprehensiveness about Reagan, however, the Democrats pulled seventeen points ahead on the peace issue.

In 1984 an even more decisive change took place. As a result of Reagan's reassuring record in foreign affairs, the Democratic advantage on the peace issue vanished. The Democrats went from a twelve-point lead in April 1984 as the party more likely to keep the United States out of war to a four-point lead in August. In September the Republicans pulled ahead on the peace issue, 39–38 percent. Moreover, as a result of Reagan's economic success, the Republicans established a commanding lead over the Democrats as the party more likely to keep the nation prosperous: eight points in April, twelve points in August, and seventeen points in September. In sum, Carter neutralized the prosperity issue; Reagan reversed it.

By losing the economic issue, the Democrats have become less of a populist party and more of a liberal party. In 1981—a good year for Republicans—the Gallup organization asked Americans which party they thought better served the interests of various groups. The question was repeated in 1984. The Democrats' lead as the better party for retired people dropped from forty points in 1981 to twenty points in 1984. For unemployed people, the Democrats' lead went from forty-six to twenty-six points; for small business people, from twenty to ten points; for farmers, from twenty-one to fourteen points; and for labor union members, from forty-five to thirty-four points.

For blacks the Democrats' lead held up fairly well (forty-nine points in 1981, forty-one points in 1984), as it did for women (twenty-nine points in 1981, twenty-three points in 1984). The Democrats were seen as thirty points better for skilled workers in 1981; in 1984 the Republicans were seen as two points better. The Republican advantage of six points for white-collar workers in 1981 became an advantage of thirty-six points in 1984; for business and professional people, the Republican lead went from thirty-three to fifty-three points.

Finally, which party did people feel better served the interests of "people like yourself"? In 1981 the Democrats led by sixteen points. In 1984 the Republicans led by five points.

If the Democrats cannot offer people economic security, what reason is there to stay in the party? The answer is that it offers a liberal vision that is appealing to certain elite groups and minorities. In 1968 and 1972 the Democrats conceded social populism to the Republicans. In 1980 and 1984 they conceded economic populism. That is essentially why the Democrats have lost their majority status.

Can the Republicans become the nation's new majority party? Yes, if the party continues to turn in a strong economic performance and does not make a major foreign policy mistake or get mired in a scandal. Results, not ideology, are what count for American voters. As pointed out earlier, the perceived success of the New Deal caused a majority of Americans to become Democrats; there was no sudden shift to the left in the public's policy preferences. Thus, although Americans' policy attitudes have drifted to the left since 1981, the administration's economic success has brought about a surge in Republican identification.

The bad news for Republicans is that they remain hostage to events. After all, Ford and Carter had to pay a heavy political price for economic reversals that, to a considerable degree, were not their fault (soaring oil prices were a major factor). The good news for Republicans is that the many divisions in the party over deficits, taxes, and the role of religion in politics do not mean a great deal to the voters unless they threaten the party's ability to perform. The New Deal Democratic coalition included Southern racists, blacks, and Northern liberals, all of whom managed to stick together for thirty years, mostly by avoiding the subject of civil rights. A majority party does not have to be unified. It only has to be effective.

Democrats now face the same kind of choice Republicans faced during the 1940s and 1950s. To the extent that Republican policies succeed, Democrats will be driven in the "me too" direction; that is, they will be impelled to develop a "realistic" liberalism that tries to reach an accommodation with Reaganism. If Reagan has created a new antigovernment consensus in the country, Democrats must learn to live with it and stop defending the burden of big government. That, more or less, is the message of neoliberalism, and it is of some significance that Hart, the bearer of the message of "new ideas," did best among 1984 primary voters who expressed confidence in the economic recovery. Economic reversals like the 1982 recession make the arguments of "I told you so" Democrats sound more plausible—that the Democratic party has nothing to apologize for, nothing to explain, and it is only a matter of time before the country realizes that Reaganism is wrong.

That kind of argument will sound good if there is another major recession before 1988. But Democrats should learn a lesson from the old guard Republicans who never accepted the New Deal. They said the excessive growth of government would bring about massive inflation. It did—fifty years later. They had to wait an awfully long time to say, "I told you so."

How will we know if a realignment has occurred? During the 1930s and 1940s Republicans liked to believe that Roosevelt's majorities were personal and would vanish once he left the political scene. What happened after four straight Roosevelt victories? Truman won, and the Republicans finally had to face the fact that something fundamental had changed. If the Republicans can win without Reagan on the ticket in 1988, we will know that the same thing has happened in our time.

The Elections for Congress

NORMAN J. ORNSTEIN

————For the Republican party, the 1980 election was a landmark for a generation. In that election, a presidential victory for Ronald Reagan was accompanied by a dramatic Republican surge in Congress. Republicans gained their first majority in the U.S. Senate in a quarter century, and moved as close to a majority in the House of Representatives as they had been in more than twenty years. Although the strong across-the-board performance of 1980 was followed by disappointment in 1982, Republicans looked toward 1984— another presidential year—with renewed high hopes. Their expectation was that a smashing reelection victory by Ronald Reagan would reverberate down the ticket and bring Republicans even closer to their goal of majority status.

These high hopes went unrealized with a disappointing GOP gain of only fourteen (or fifteen)[1] seats in the House and a net loss of two seats in the Senate. On the one hand, Republican disappointment probably reflected an undue preelection optimism. Recent history did not favor the possibility of substantial Republican congressional gains: In both 1956 and 1972, Republican presidential reelection landslides were accompanied by disappointment at the Congressional level. In 1956, when Dwight Eisenhower won 57.5 percent of the popular vote and 457 electoral votes, the Republicans gained no seats in the Senate and actually lost two in the House. In 1972, when Richard Nixon got 60.7 percent of the popular vote and 520 electoral votes, carrying 49 states as did Ronald Reagan, the Republicans gained a mere dozen seats in the House and lost two in the Senate, results astonishingly close to the party's fortunes in 1984. So 1984 fit comfortably within the confines of Republican political history.

But at another level, Republican disappointment was understandably sharp and bitter. In both 1956 and 1972, Republican presidents ran independent campaigns, carefully avoiding close connections with contests at other levels.

This was particularly true in 1972, when Richard Nixon set up an independent apparatus and explicitly ran away from the Republican party and Republican congressional candidates.

In 1984, however, Ronald Reagan and the Republican party ran a comprehensive party effort, both coordinating activities to a considerable degree and running an expensive and massive party-based campaign to win seats in the Congress. In the final weeks of the 1984 campaign, President Reagan and Vice-President George Bush geared their campaign schedules largely (though not exclusively) to state and congressional districts where Senate and House contests were close.[2] And the national Republican party spent over $10 million, including $6 million in the final two weeks, for a television advertising blitz designed to win votes for Republicans running for Congress.

In the election aftermath, many Republicans, including House Minority Leader Robert Michel of Illinois, criticized the Reagan effort bitterly (Michel even went so far as to call Reagan a "son of a buck"). While Reagan undoubtedly could have done more (Michel was especially incensed about a last-minute campaign visit to Minnesota, where there were no evident close House races), his efforts outdid those of any other contemporary president. The frustration of Republicans reflected less a concern about complacency on Reagan's part, or self-centeredness, than a frustration that the effort they all invested paid so few dividends. Republican results at the congressional level in 1984, after all, were no better than Nixon's party-detached reelection efforts in 1972.

Why did the Republicans do no better, given their party and presidential efforts? And what do the 1984 results portend for the next Congress and for the future of congressional election results? In this chapter we will address those questions.

The Parties' Efforts in 1984

In the aftermath of 1982 both political parties had reason to be cautious. Republicans had seen their optimistic hopes of a new, realigning trend in American politics dashed. At the same time Republicans knew that after two Senate elections where they faced more potentially vulnerable Democrats with fewer Republican seats in jeopardy, 1984 would reverse that trend, bringing nineteen Republican seats up compared to only fourteen Democrats.

The Democrats, however, had few reasons to be particularly ebullient. The Republicans had shown in the previous two contests an awesome ability to raise dramatic amounts of money for House and Senate contests through direct mail and other sophisticated fundraising techniques. Despite their best efforts, the Democrats were not likely to come much closer at the national level than they had in the past, leaving a substantial financial edge at the national level to the Republicans. While the Democrats had managed in previous congressional elections to raise enough money through individual candidates to bring about parity or something more, the centralized element of Republican fund raising gave them an advantage in allocating money to particularly needy, close races; thus the Republicans, partly through their edge in centralized resources, were able in 1980 and 1982 to win the lion's share of close contests. In 1980 and 1982, seventeen Republican senators won with 52 percent of the vote or less, compared to only four Democrats. If that pattern continued in 1984, the Democrats would not be likely to turn their potential edge in vulnerable seats into a Democratic majority, or even a Democratic Senate gain.

Both parties were also concerned about the impact of national forces. In 1980, to a degree greater than either party would have imagined, national forces had contributed to the dramatic shifts in the election, especially in the Senate. In 1982 Republican efforts to create a national trend through $9 million in national advertising were unsuccessful. As 1984 approached, the Democrats were nervous that national presidential tides might work against them, undoing their best efforts to hold and win seats district by district. The Republicans were also concerned about the possibility that a national tide in the direction of President Reagan would not translate down to other political levels—they were well aware that the 1972 Nixon landslide had not worked to the advantage of Republican House or Senate campaigns.

In the House, Republicans began the campaign season well organized, well-financed, and with a well developed strategy to aim for major gains in November 1984. The strategy started, as most party efforts usually do, with the freshmen. In July 1983 National Republican Congressional Committee chairman Guy Vander Jagt (R-Mich.) noted: "I think the old axiom still holds that the most vulnerable time for congressmen is in the first election, and if you miss them on the first election, it gets more difficult to beat them on the second time around or the third or the fourth."[3]

In several elections in the 1970s Republican targeting of Democratic freshmen had failed, as the newcomers experienced the phenomenon known as "sophomore surge." But because many of the Democratic freshmen elected in 1982 had beaten Republican freshmen first elected in 1980, GOP strategists saw some signs of weakness among freshmen congressmen and also had high hopes that the Republican losers would come back again for rematches in 1984. Republicans also believed that some of those 1982 losses had come about because of redistricting implemented in 1982, and that their candidates in 1984 could expand their name recognition and political bases to erase that disadvantage.

The Republicans also went back to an old strategy that had failed in the past: targeting Democrats first elected in the Watergate year of 1974. In 1976, the National Republican Congressional Committee (NRCC), under Vander Jagt, had concentrated its resources almost entirely on ousting the seventy-five Democratic members of that Watergate class. The result was dismal failure, as only two were defeated. But the Republicans continued to believe that many of these Democrats had escaped defeat in essentially Republican districts through luck. Thirty-three sought reelection in 1984, and many were targeted yet again. Finally, the Republicans picked individual seats of more senior Democrats who might be in trouble because of their high visibility as liberals in conservative districts, or because they had lost touch with their districts, or because redistricting had prevented a strong GOP campaign two years earlier.

The Democrats, for their part, began the campaign trying to raise enough money to overcome the overwhelming GOP advantage and to protect their major asset—strong and solid incumbents. The Democrats, as a result, could not devote resources to a wide range of GOP districts, including many which were long shots at best; there were few Republican incumbents the Democrats could effectively target at the national level. The Democrats turned their resources to shoring up their vulnerable candidates (there was a striking amount of concurrence between the two parties as to which candidates were vulnerable) and to targeting potential open-seat battles where, with incumbent advantages removed, chance of a party turnover is generally greater.

For the Senate, the attention of both parties focused on the seats where the chances seemed strongest for a potential party turnover. There were more potentially vulnerable seats, clearly, among the nineteen Republicans than among the fourteen Democrats. As the campaign process began, the Republicans were particularly worried about the seats held by Senators Charles Percy of Illinois, Gordon Humphrey of New Hampshire, Thad Cochran of Mississippi, Roger Jepsen of Iowa, and Jesse Helms of North Carolina. The GOP's nervousness increased in 1983 when popular Senate majority leader Howard Baker of Tennessee and powerful Armed Services Committee chairman John Tower of Texas announced their retirements; these two seats, considered certain for the GOP in the case of Baker and probable in the case of Tower, immediately became potential Democratic gains. There were several other Republican seats, in Maine, Colorado, New Mexico, and South Carolina, that were strong potential turnovers if the Democrats managed to recruit their strongest potential challengers.

The Republicans began the campaign year with very few Democratic seats they could see as certain close battles. The Republicans were hopeful that challenges could be mounted against Senator Claiborne Pell in Rhode Island and against Max Baucus in Montana, Carl Levin in Michigan, and David Pryor in Arkansas. When Senator Jennings Randolph of West Virginia announced his retirement, Republican hopes rose at the possibility that former governor Arch Moore would run for the seat against Democratic governor John D. (Jay) Rockefeller IV. None of these seats, however, began the year in the toss-up category.

In both houses, the parties geared their campaign efforts toward recruiting strong candidates to run in seats where a turnover might occur. The recruitment efforts, which had been the key to Republican successes in 1980 and were considered by many an important factor in restricting Republican losses in 1982, took an increasing share of NRCC resources. Eight full-time field coordinators went through congressional districts looking and encouraging strong congressional candidates to throw their hats into the ring.[4] House Republicans looked to encourage 1982 losers, like Bill Moshofsky of Oregon, Pat Haggerty of Texas, Larry DeNardis of Connecticut, and Kenneth McMillan of Illinois to run again.[5] In Washington in 1983, the NRCC held a number of "recap" meetings with the previous year's losers to rehash their campaigns and discuss strategy for 1984. Republicans also made major efforts to get strong and well-financed candidates for the open seats voluntary retirements would generate. For example, the announcement by Democratic representative Albert Gore, Jr., that he would run for the Senate slot vacated by Howard Baker stimulated an intense effort by the Republicans to find a strong candidate to capture his House seat.

Lacking the field operatives or other resources necessary to make a major and sustained recruiting effort, the Democratic Congressional Campaign Committee (DCCC), under Representative Tony Coelho of California, focused more on raising money and targeting it to the best districts. In prior years the money raised by the DCCC was distributed first to Democratic incumbents, with each incumbent certain to receive at least some money regardless of his or her vulnerability. In 1984 Coelho decided that the limited resources demanded a change in strategy: The money should be used more directly to protect vulnerable incumbents and to boost potentially successful Democratic challengers. At the same time, House Democrats, through Coelho, tried to raise more money through direct mail and through more explicit solicitation of business interests and business political action committees (PACs). Coelho invited business political operatives to candidate forums to meet Democratic congressional candidates, and he used the help of some conservative Southern Democrats— like Charles Wilson and Kent Hance of Texas and Beryl Anthony of Arkansas —who had contacts in the oil and gas industry.[6] The Democratic party's efforts to raise money from business had some direct success, and some additional indirect success: By reminding business PACs that Democrats were in the majority in the House and were almost certain to stay in the majority, the DCCC probably diluted some business willingness to gamble on alienating Democrats by giving PAC money to their Republican challengers.

The Senate Campaign

Senate elections usually bring two or three surprises, where states expected to have no serious contest turn out to have close battles, when strong incumbents retire or resign, or sometimes die. This was the case with the 1984 election. It began with the sudden death in the early fall of 1983 of veteran, Democratic, Senate power Henry Jackson of Washington. The Republican governor of that state, John Spellman, appointed former Republican governor Dan Evans in the interim, and Evans ran for the unexpired portion of the term in a special election in November 1983. Evans faced a primary challenge from conservative Lloyd Cooney, while the Democrats had a vigorous primary battle between Seattle mayor Charles Royer and Congressman Mike Lowry. The primary victors, Evans and Lowry, faced off in a vigorous campaign that fall, with Evans emerging the winner. Thus, Democrats, who had expected to enter the 1984 campaign needing five seats at most (only four if they captured the White House) to regain a party majority in the Senate, suddenly found the gulf one seat greater.

The unexpected events continued with the announced retirements, late in 1983, of the Republican majority leader Howard Baker and the Armed Services Committee chairman John Tower. Baker's seat, which had been rated a sure thing by the Republicans, shifted to an almost certain gain for the Democrats when popular Democratic representative Albert Gore, Jr., the son of a former occupant of the seat, announced his candidacy and was not challenged by a comparably strong Republican. In Texas, where Tower had been expected to face a strong challenge but was still rated a clear favorite, the unexpected retirement announcement threw the seat up for grabs.

Perhaps the biggest shock of all came in January 1984 when forty-two-year-old Democratic Senator Paul Tsongas of Massachusetts, a very strong favorite for reelection, indicated that he was going to retire for health reasons at the end of his term. Tsongas was considered one of the brightest leaders of the Democratic party, and his surprise announcement set off a scramble in both parties in Massachusetts for the nominations to run for his seat. Before Tsongas's withdrawal, his announced opponent had been conservative businessman Raymond Shamie, who had run a losing but respectable race in 1982 against the senior Massachusetts senator, Ted Kennedy. But with the race now altered, GOP heavyweight Elliot Richardson, who had been the elected attorney general of Massachusetts as well as a member of the cabinet, entered the Republican nomination fray. On the Democratic side, several prominent candidates joined battle, led by Lieutenant Governor John Kerry and Congressman James Shannon. Suddenly, a seat rated as a solid Democratic choice had become one of the best opportunities for a Republican takeover.

Each of these four seats indicates how important the quality of candidates can be to a Senate contest. This is particularly true when unassailable incumbents suddenly depart, but it is also true when parties seek appropriate challengers to seemingly strong incumbents. For both parties, the Senate campaign focused on major recruitment efforts to get strong candidates to run against the other party's incumbents. The story of 1984, however, was that most of those efforts were unsuccessful. As the campaign began, for example, the Republicans saw real chances to topple Democratic incumbent senators in Delaware, Montana, and Rhode Island; however, they failed to convince either popular Delaware governor Pierre du Pont, Rhode Island representative Claudine Schneider, or Montana secretary of state Jim Waltermire to run. So too was the GOP unsuccessful at convincing ex–West Virginia governor Arch Moore to run for the Senate in that state, or Tennessee governor Lamar Alexander to run against Representative Gore. The Democrats had failures of their own. Such strong potential Senate challengers as governors Richard Riley of South Carolina, Joe Brennan of Maine, Chuck Robb of Virginia, and Richard Lamm of Colorado all declined to run despite vigorous party efforts; thus GOP senators Strom Thurmond, William Cohen, John Warner, and William Armstrong were relieved of the prospect of facing well-financed, vigorous opponents with statewide recognition. The same good fortune befell senators Pete Domenici in New Mexico and Alan Simpson in Wyoming.

While seeking to recruit strong Republican governors and representatives to run against Senate Democratic incumbents, the national Republican party also sought to blunt a major Democratic strength in the electorate, one which got great public attention during the first Reagan term. The gender gap was an issue that made Senate Republicans particularly sensitive and spurred their efforts to recruit women to run for the Senate. In many cases the recruitment of women candidates came only after more prominent alternatives had failed; nevertheless, Republicans recruited women candidates to run against Democratic senator Bill Bradley in New Jersey (Montclair mayor Mary Mochary), Nebraska senator J. James Exon (University of Nebraska regent Nancy Hoch), and Rhode Island senator Claiborne Pell (Providence businesswoman Barbara Leonard, recruited after Representative Schneider declined the challenge). In addition, Republicans had the only woman incumbent senator running for reelection, Nancy Kassebaum of Kansas.

Democrats also found a number of women challengers coming forward to take on Republican incumbent senators, though in most cases they emerged as primary or convention winners only after other prominent male Democrats declined to run. In Colorado, Maine, Minnesota, New Mexico, Oregon, and

Virginia, Democrats ended up with women candidates for Republican Senate seats, some holding statewide office and others with less political experience.[7]

For many seats where the parties saw a chance of unseating an incumbent, the battle for the opposition nomination went on well into 1984. In Illinois, Charles Percy faced a stiff primary challenge from the right, from GOP congressman Tom Corcoran, while four prominent Democrats fought a vigorous and often bitter statewide battle as the March 20, 1984, primary approached. Downstate Congressman Paul Simon, a former lieutenant governor, was well respected but had not run statewide in a decade; Democratic State Senate president Phil Rock also lacked statewide recognition; Alex Seith, the 1978 Democratic challenger to Percy, ran again, well financed but without much chance of winning; and Roland Burris, the state comptroller, ran with a strong base in the black community.

Percy beat back the challenge from Corcoran by 59 percent to 36 percent, a margin that suggested potential problems in the fall. Simon won a surprisingly solid victory in the four-way Democratic race thanks to strong support downstate, but he was considered by most observers to have run a lackluster campaign and to enter the general election campaign with little momentum.[8]

In Michigan, Republicans saw an aggressive and bitter primary campaign develop for the right to challenge first-term Democratic senator Carl Levin. At an early point in the campaign, former congressman Jim Dunn appeared to be a certain winner of the Republican nomination, when Peace Corps director Loret Ruppe, wife of former congressman Phillip Ruppe, decided not to enter the race. But a number of Republican leaders convinced former astronaut Jack Lousma to enter the race. Lousma, a Michigan native who had lived in Texas for the previous twenty-five years, was bitterly attacked by Dunn as a carpetbagger and as somebody who switched issues frequently to gain political support. But the more moderate Dunn found that conservative Lousma was able to build a coalition of conservatives and moderates who felt that he had a better chance of winning, and a seemingly close contest turned into a 62 percent to 38 percent victory for Lousma. Lousma, however, was clearly hurt by the bitter charges and countercharges of a primary campaign that lasted into August.

In Minnesota the early favorite for the Democratic-Farmer-Labor (DFL) nomination to challenge freshman Republican senator Rudolph Boschwitz was Secretary of State Joan A. Growe. But several other prominent candidates, including former governor and former senator Wendell Anderson, and Representative James Oberstar from the politically potent iron range, challenged Growe for the party convention endorsement. While Growe went into the June convention as a clear favorite, it took multiple ballots for her to emerge with the convention endorsement, leaving her extremely weak. State Treasurer Robert Mattson then challenged her in the September party primary. Although Growe beat back his challenge as well, she was sapped by the interparty rivalry as the fall campaign got under way.

In other states the identity of the challenger to the incumbent was clear long before the election campaign formally began. This was particularly true in Iowa, New Hampshire, and North Carolina. In Iowa and New Hampshire popular and well-known congressmen representing substantial portions of their respective states, Tom Harkin and Norman D'Amours, announced early on that they would challenge conservative one-term Republican senators Roger Jepsen and Gordon Humphrey. In North Carolina it had been clear for at least two years that popular governor James Hunt would make the race against Republican Jesse Helms. In two other states the challenges to incumbent senators were a little bit longer in coming, but were still clear as the 1984 election year began. In Arkansas, Democratic senator David Pryor was challenged by aggressive conservative congressman Ed Bethune, who announced in January that he would leave his House seat to make the Senate challenge, and in Alabama, Democratic senator Howell Heflin was pitted against former congressman Albert Lee Smith, a conservative who had lost his seat in 1982 and decided to challenge statewide instead of seeking to regain his Birmingham congressional seat.

In Mississippi strong Democratic efforts to recruit a vigorous opponent for one-term Republican senator Thad Cochran were finally rewarded in February 1983, when former governor William Winter decided to enter the race. Winter had left the governorship in 1983, after winning passage of a landmark comprehensive public education bill, and was seen by Democrats as the strongest challenger by far to Cochran, the state's first GOP senator since Reconstruction. Democrats saw Cochran as vulnerable in part because his 1978 victory had been based on a split Democratic party encouraged by the independent candidacy of black activist Charles Evers. But Winter waivered for months before deciding to take on the Senate challenge. In December 1983 he announced that he would accept the chancellorship of the University of Mississippi (a post for which he had campaigned actively), but changed his mind and rejected the position little more than a week later. When he subsequently decided to run for the Senate, it was with a new, tarnished image of indecisiveness.[9]

While many Senate election years are enlivened by several sharp primary challenges to incumbent senators, 1984 saw only the serious conservative challenge to Republican Charles Percy in Illinois. However, there was suspense in Kentucky for many months with speculation that former governor John Y. Brown, Jr., would mount a primary challenge to Democratic senator Walter D. Huddleston. Brown's health problems caused him to withdraw from a possible challenge in the spring of 1984, and Huddleston won renomination without opposition. He entered the general election campaign with a wide lead against Jefferson County judge Mitchell McConnell who, despite his limited political experience was an aggressive and well-financed challenger.

In several states strong incumbents managed to escape without serious or well-funded challenges. Republican Whip Ted Stevens of Alaska was challenged by former state attorney general John Havelock, who had been out of public office for more than a decade and was neither well known nor aggressive. Popular Georgia Democrat Sam Nunn was endorsed by both parties, and faced only a token challenge from substitute teacher Jon Michael Hicks. Veteran Idaho Republican James McClure was challenged by real estate broker Pete Busch. Of Busch, *Congressional Quarterly* noted, "He has little money, little name recognition and an uncertain organization. About the only thing he has to look forward to in a race against McClure is the possibility that a respectable showing might set the stage for another campaign later on."[10]

In Kansas the possibility of a serious challenge to Republican Nancy Landon Kassebaum was reduced to near zero early in the campaign season when Democratic congressman Dan Glickman, after commissioning preliminary polls, decided against a challenge. Instead, Kassebaum faced investment banker James Maher, an unsuccessful candidate in the past with little backing from within his own party or across the state.

New Mexico's Pete Domenici, who won a close contest for reelection in 1978, found by 1984 that his national reputation as chairman of the Senate Budget Committee made him a heavy favorite for reelection, an advantage expanded when former governor Bruce King decided against a challenge. The Democratic primary contest gave the nomination to state representative Judy Pratt, an ideological liberal who ran strongly on a nuclear freeze platform. In Oklahoma, the Republican party found it nearly impossible to find a strong and credible challenger to popular former governor and one-term senator David L. Boren. Republicans eventually settled for a state Transportation Department employee and former unsuccessful congressional candidate, Will E. Crozier, an unknown with little party backing or financial support.

A similar phenomenon occurred in South Carolina, where Strom Thurmond, eighty-one, and the object of a stiff challenge six years earlier, escaped with a modest Democratic opponent, minister Melvin Purvis, Jr., whose major asset was his name (his father had been a famous FBI agent) but whose lack of political experience and money were compounded by controversy caused when his black primary opponent challenged the results and ran as a write-in. In Wyoming incumbent Republican Alan Simpson drew a minimal challenge from political novice Victor Ryan, a University of Wyoming chemistry professor.

In South Dakota and Virginia incumbent Republican senators Larry Pressler and John Warner drew modestly funded Democratic challengers in longtime George McGovern aide George Cunningham and former state delegate Edythe Harrison, but were faced at least with the prospect of aggressive and vigorous campaigns. The same was true in Delaware, where incumbent Democrat Joseph Biden had escaped the challenge of Governor Pete du Pont, and faced former state majority leader John Burris, and Maine where incumbent Republican William Cohen saw an aggressive challenge from state majority leader Elizabeth Mitchell after Governor Joseph Brennan decided not to run.

In Oregon veteran incumbent Republican Mark Hatfield appeared to have an easy race against a weak opponent, liberal Democratic state senator Margie Hendricksen, who tried the novel tactic of challenging Hatfield strongly from the left. Hendricksen accused Hatfield of being conservative because he supported a bilateral nuclear freeze—she supported a *unilateral* nuclear freeze. A scandal that developed in summer of 1984 briefly threatened Hatfield's position and appeared for a time to create another sudden shift that could turn a seemingly safe seat into a toss-up. Hatfield's wife had received $55,000 from Greek businessman Basil Tsakos, allegedly for real estate services. At the same time Hatfield had actively supported some of Tsakos's legislative goals. When the services provided by Hatfield's wife were questioned, investigations were launched by the FBI and the Senate. The Hatfields diffused the scandal by apologizing and donating $55,000 to charity, and the threat disappeared before the fall.[11]

One contest among the thirty-three Senate races was decided long before November 6. Louisiana has a unique electoral system with a multiparty primary that settles the election contest if a candidate gets more than 50 percent of the votes. In 1984 incumbent Democrat J. Bennett Johnston escaped a serious threat to his seat when former Republican governor David Treen decided not to run. As a result, the September 29 primary was a romp, with Johnston getting nearly 86 percent of the vote and avoiding a runoff on November 6.

As these races began to settle down and as the candidacies were more clearly developed, political observers of both parties began to develop some consensus of where the real races would be, and what would be likely to happen in the Senate. An early estimate, that did not change dramatically for some time, was offered in April 1984 by political observer Kevin Phillips. In his newsletter, *The American Political Report*, Phillips identified ten serious races, eight for Republican-held seats and two for Democratic seats. One GOP seat, the Tennessee one, he saw as "likely to change parties." Four state elections he viewed as "marginal/too close to call": three for Republican seats (in North Carolina, Texas, Iowa) and one for a Democratic seat (in Massachusetts). Five states' seats were viewed as "incumbent party somewhat favored to hold": Mississippi, New Hampshire, Illinois, Minnesota (all Republican), and Michigan (Democratic). Viewing all of these together, Phillips saw the most likely outcome as a Republican loss of two to four seats, with a slim chance (about 25 percent) of a Democratic takeover of the Senate and an even slimmer chance (7 percent) of Republicans being able to hold the Democrats to a wash, or to gain a net seat of their own.[12]

By midsummer the assessment had not changed much at all. On June 30, journalist Richard E. Cohen of the *National Journal* wrote,

> The most vulnerable Republican seats include those held by Thad Cochran of Mississippi, Jesse A. Helms of North Carolina, Gordon J. Humphrey of New Hampshire, Roger W. Jepsen of Iowa, and Charles H. Percy of Illinois and those being vacated by retiring senators Howard H. Baker, Jr., of Tennessee and John Tower of Texas. Democrats worry most about the reelection prospects of Carl Levin of Michigan and about replacing Paul E. Tsongas of Massachusetts who is retiring.[13]

As the fall campaign began, Republicans became more optimistic, an optimism fueled by the problems of Democratic vice-presidential nominee Geraldine Ferraro in August, and by the ebullience of the GOP National Convention in Dallas. On September 1, Cohen wrote,

> Republican confidence over the party's presidential prospects this fall has spread to the Senate campaign. . . . The GOP's surge of election optimism contrasts with the party's caution earlier this year when Republican strategists were saying that Senate control was "hanging in the balance." . . . "I am more optimistic now than I was a few months ago when I said we might end up with fifty-two or fifty-three seats," Senator Richard Lugar said in an assessment consistent with the findings of recent statewide public opinion polls and the views of many political observers. He said a "probable scenario" now is that the GOP will retain its fifty-five seats, although it could drop as low as fifty-two seats or climb as high as fifty-eight if everything breaks well.[14]

Cohen suggested concern among Republicans at that time about senators Jesse Helms of North Carolina, Roger Jepsen of Iowa, and Charles Percy of Illinois, and Republican optimism about unseating Democratic incumbents Carl Levin of Michigan and David Pryor of Arkansas.

These five races, along with the open-seat contest in Massachusetts, drew the most national attention during the fall campaign. In North Carolina, in the Senate race that received enormous national attention, two well-known, well-financed, and politically savvy contestants squared off in a contest called by Helen Dewar of the *Washington Post* "a southern-fried alley fight."[15] In a race that ultimately cost nearly $20 million, the campaign seesawed back and forth. An early lead for Democratic governor James B. Hunt disappeared by midsummer after a series of negative campaign commercials by incumbent Republican Jesse Helms. The Helms ads, focusing on Hunt's record and his alleged connections to Jesse Jackson, among other things, were tough and nasty. By May a Gallup poll showed Helms ahead of Hunt by fifty to forty-six, more than overcoming a near twenty-point Hunt lead from the early spring. In June, Hunt struck back with his own well-financed negative advertising campaign, with commercials that hit just as hard as Helms's. One Hunt commercial, for example, showed close-ups of dead bodies with a voice-over saying, "This is what they do—the death squads in El Salvador—men, women, and children murdered in cold blood." This was followed by pictures of El Salvadoran archconservative General Roberto D'Aubuisson ("This is the man accused of directing those death squads.") and Helms (". . . this is Roberto D'Aubuisson's best friend in Washington, maybe his only friend"). The ad ends, "Jesse Helms may be a crusader but this is not what our senator should be crusading for."[16] The Hunt ads in June appeared to turn the momentum around; an early July poll showed Hunt three to five points ahead. Through the summer and into the fall, and through several televised debates, the two candidates seesawed back and forth in their support, with each trying to go back on the offensive and attack his opponent when a lead seemed to be slipping away.

Both national parties saw the North Carolina contest as having great significance, both symbolically for the parties and in real terms for policy direction. Democrats saw Jesse Helms as the symbol of the New Right, even more than Ronald Reagan. Republicans, worried about their majority margin and also concerned about the fallout from a highly publicized loss by conservative Helms to moderate Democrat Hunt, put enormous national resources into the race. Nearly every major Senate Republican figure visited North Carolina to give his blessing to Senator Helms. Retiring majority leader Howard Baker went to the state, as did Wyoming senator Alan Simpson, who had denounced Helms the previous year on the Senate floor, saying of Helms's delaying tactics, "Seldom have I seen a more obnoxious and obdurate performance." These Senate Republicans tried to counter the Hunt charge that Helms was so extreme that he was ineffective in the Senate. In addition, Ronald Reagan and Vice-President George Bush made several visits to the state, with Reagan's most publicized one coming soon after the second televised presidential debate. Right before the election, *Congressional Quarterly* wrote,

> The Helms-Hunt clash has been the most widely publicized and the most expensive Senate campaign in the country this year, but it has also been one of the most static. Most surveys taken in recent weeks have shown a difference of no more than four percentage points between Hunt and Helms—the same sliver of daylight that separated the two candidates last May.

Over the past few months, the national media have energetically reported each twist and turn in the campaign, from Hunt's charge that Helms backs right-wing death squads in El Salvador to Helm's complaint about Hunt's use of state airplanes. But most North Carolinians have been little affected by the long and tedious course of the Senate debate. Faced with a choice between an apostle of the New Right and an activist Democratic governor, most have known from the outset how they would vote. The undecided contingent has never been very large.[17]

The campaign in Iowa was well publicized also, and nearly as hard-hitting, but with much wider fluctuation in support through the course of the campaign. By mid-summer 1984, incumbent Republican Roger Jepsen, who had been plagued by a number of embarrassing situations in Washington and in Iowa, trailed his opponent, Representative Tom Harkin, by as many as seventeen points in the Iowa polls. Jepsen's personal difficulties—including his claim of congressional immunity to avoid a traffic ticket for driving in restricted lanes on his way to work in Washington, his embarrassing reversal on the 1982 vote on AWAC planes to Saudi Arabia, and his publicized membership in 1977 in a Des Moines massage parlor/spa—had been reflected in Harkin's campaign slogan, "A Senator Iowans Can Be Proud Of." But in the fall, Jepsen fought back, running television commercials attacking Harkin for misrepresenting Jepsen's record, with the ad announcer saying, "Have you no decency, Mr. Harkin? Have you no honor at all?" By the fall campaign kickoff, Harkin had dropped ten points behind Jepsen, hurt at least in part by a backlash of sympathy toward Jepsen after the enormous publicity given his visit to the massage parlor. At that point, Harkin struck back himself with commercials attacking Jepsen's record in Washington. The *New York Times* described one late Harkin commercial: "One commercial shows Mr. Jepsen sweating profusely, while another shows a hog snorting loudly while an announcer intones, 'When two Iowa farmers drove a tractor all the way to Washington to talk to him about farm debt, Roger Jepsen fell asleep.'"[18]

Both candidates also attacked each other about their relative war records. Harkin was quoted as having said that he flew "combat air patrols" in the Vietnam War; Republican senator Barry Goldwater flew to Iowa to accuse Harkin of distortion. Harkin conceded that he had actually flown planes from Vietnam to Japan for repairs. Jepsen had claimed that he was a paratrooper in World War II, but in fact had not entered the service until 1946. He defended himself by stating that the Veteran's Administration considered the war as having been "technically ended" in 1946. With charges and countercharges, the campaign remained close into the final days, though polls late in October showed a steady, if narrow, lead for challenger Harkin.

In Illinois, Republican senator Charles Percy saw conservative Republican support slip away in the months following his primary victory over conservative Tom Corcoran, but a good deal of that support returned to Percy's camp when many Republicans began to fear the loss of their majority in the Senate. Nevertheless, a number of New Right conservatives continued to oppose Percy, hoping that a Percy defeat and a Jesse Helms victory in North Carolina would clear the way for Helms to ascend to the chairmanship of the Senate Foreign Relations Committee.[19]

Percy faced the additional problem of stiff opposition from many pro-Israel groups, including the American Israel Public Affairs Committee, which objected to Percy's record on the Middle East. In a close contest with veteran Democrat Paul Simon, Percy moved in the final weeks of the campaign to hit Simon hard, accusing him of supporting a tax increase larger than that endorsed by the Democratic presidential candidate, Walter Mondale. In an emotional and bitter televised debate Simon accused Percy of deliberately distorting his record; bitter charges and countercharges dominated the final weeks of a campaign that showed no clear favorite on election eve.

Throughout the fall, Republicans saw Michigan's Carl Levin as the most vulnerable Democratic incumbent. Indeed, Levin's own polling showed him with less than majority support at different times in the campaign. However, astronaut Jack Lousma was not able during much of the campaign to move on to the offensive and mount an aggressive challenge, despite President Reagan's strong support in the state.

Lousma's campaign focused heavily on Mondale's pledge to raise taxes. A Lousma television commercial stated, "Lousma's *against* the Mondale tax *hike*. Levin is *always* for higher taxes." Lousma pledged that he would be against any effort to raise taxes, except in a "national emergency." Levin countered with a television commercial in which he said, "The last thing we ought to do is raise your income tax." Levin distanced himself from his presidential candidate's tax pledge, and underscored that Lousma's promise would have forced him to oppose the "bipartisan" Social Security rescue package.[20] Lousma's greatest hope was that a surge in support for President Reagan in Michigan would provide coattail support for his campaign. Reagan visited Michigan right before the election to urge support for Lousma, and the campaign featured a television commercial in which the president warned voters, "Don't vote against me by voting against Jack Lousma." As the election approached, polls showed a steady but small Levin lead, leaving Democrats nervous about the potential effect of a Reagan landslide.

With fall polls showing a large Reagan lead in Arkansas (a state that Reagan had barely carried in 1982), and incumbent Democrat David Pryor conducting a low-key campaign, Republicans were very optimistic that the substantial

Pryor edge in fall polls (which showed a roughly 60 percent to 30 percent Pryor margin) would shrink dramatically in the face of a vigorous challenge from conservative GOP congressman Ed Bethune.

While Bethune ran his campaign by attacking Pryor for his liberal record, Pryor managed to distance himself from the Mondale tax package and to portray himself as a centrist concerned first about the needs of Arkansas. On the eve of the election, Bethune turned a Reagan visit on his behalf into a major advertising blitz designed to create substantial Reagan coattails. As the polls opened in Arkansas, national Republican political operatives were extremely optimistic that an upset was in the making.

Three open seats became major battlegrounds for party shifts in 1984. Tennessee's seat quickly became a virtually certain party turnover, as the wide lead enjoyed by Democrat Albert Gore, Jr., stayed wide throughout the campaign, despite the efforts of Republican Victor Ashe. The wide lead enjoyed by Democratic, West Virginia governor Jay Rockefeller narrowed considerably, however, during the campaign, despite the inexperienced and underfinanced campaign of his opponent, businessman John Raese. Although Rockefeller outspent Raese by more than ten to one (approximately $10 million to $1 million), the antipathy that many West Virginians felt towards their two-term governor was exploited skillfully by Raese. In early October, polls showed Rockefeller with an approximately 55 percent to 40 percent edge, indicating substantial vulnerability for a well-known governor facing an anonymous and underfinanced opponent. Tracking polls in late October showed the margin narrowing even more.

Outside of North Carolina, Iowa, and Illinois, the most vigorous and negative campaign in the nation was fought to fill Democrat Paul Tsongas's seat in Massachusetts. Most of the Senate campaign in Massachusetts was fought over party nominations, as the rough-and-tumble primary contest continued through the summer and into the fall. In the September primary, underdog conservative Ray Shamie upset the establishment candidate, Elliot Richardson, swamping him by a 62 percent to 38 percent margin, while Democrats resolved their bitter primary campaign with a very narrow victory for Lieutenant Governor John Kerry over Congressman James Shannon. The fall campaign, begun late, quickly turned bitter. Kerry and Shamie each took opposite ends of the political spectrum and sought to make inroads into ethnic communities. While each campaign pointed out the sharp ideological differences between the candidates, Shamie tried to emphasize his Lebanese background and his down-to-earth populist qualities as a small businessman. Kerry, a Vietnam veteran who had first come to national prominence as the leader of Vietnam Veterans Against the War, stressed his own ethnic roots and his war record. The close campaign was shaken by the disclosure in the *Boston Globe* in mid-October of memos written for the Shamie campaign that indicated a one-time connection between Shamie and the John Birch Society. Shamie admitted his brief former membership, but the connection became damaging when a Birch society spokesman attacked Kerry for treasonous activity during his protests against the Vietnam War. Indications that Shamie might have had contact with the anti-Semitic Liberty Lobby further hurt him, placing Shamie on the defensive in the final two weeks of the hard-hitting campaign.[21]

In Texas the Republicans settled quickly and easily on former Democrat-turned GOP representative, Phil Gramm. But the three-way race for the Democratic nomination to replace John Tower turned from an early, comfortable lead for former representative Robert Krueger (the 1978 challenger to Tower) into a tight three-way race. Krueger was challenged on the right by Lubbock congressman Kent Hance and on the left by state senator Lloyd Doggett. The May 5 primary saw a three-way photo finish, with the candidates separated by only 2,237 votes out of nearly 1.5 million cast. No candidate polled a majority, so the top two — Doggett and Hance — faced a runoff, one Krueger missed by only .08 percent of the vote. The bitter, ideological runoff was equally close; the liberal Doggett squeaked to victory by 1,345 votes out of almost 1 million cast.

As the election neared, political observers were in general agreement about the Senate. There were four contests that were extremely close — North Carolina, Iowa, Illinois, and Massachusetts. Several other states had races that could turn into close contests, including Texas, Mississippi, West Virginia, Michigan, and Arkansas. And a handful of other states had races that could very easily turn out to be upsets, including Kentucky and Nebraska, where strong Reagan efforts combined with late voter shifts showed potential vulnerability for Democratic incumbents Walter Huddleston and James Exon. Overall, upsets aside, the Republicans had three vulnerable incumbents with one virtually certain party loss in the open seat in Tennessee, while Democrats faced a potential turnover in the open seat in Massachusetts and a handful of incumbents who were ahead but still in danger. The outlook, barring dramatic changes at the last minute, was for a modest Democratic gain.

The House Campaign

As the House campaign got under way, both parties were cautiously optimistic. The Republicans were hopeful that a strong tide in favor of Ronald Reagan would turn the election in a direction much more favorable than conventional political wisdom would suggest. The Democrats, surveying the battleground district by district, were optimistic because they saw very few of their own seats in serious jeopardy, and a significant number of Republican seats they could target. But — with the wreckage of the 1980 campaign all around them in the form of thirty-three Republican freshmen who had beaten Democrats, many unexpectedly, in the wake of the Carter campaign—they were worried about the impact of their own presidential campaign.

For both parties the watchword was caution, because the election started without any significant grouping of seriously contested seats. For one thing, after a series of elections with a large number of open seats created by voluntary departures and retirements, 1984 shaped up as a year with a strikingly low number of open seats. Indeed, as it turned out, there were only twenty-four (plus three ultimately opened up through primary defeats of incumbent Democrats), leaving more than 94 percent of the House seats to be contested with an incumbent representative running. Both parties had had long, painful, and nearly futile experiences attempting to knock off well-placed, well-known, and well-financed incumbent politicians from the opposing side. Both parties targeted the majority of the open seats (fourteen initially held by the Democrats and thirteen by the Republicans), but each party also had its target list of incumbent congressmen it felt were vulnerable.

The Republican list, not surprisingly, included a large number of Democratic freshmen first elected in the strong Democratic year of 1982. Anticipating a better year for the GOP in 1984, and aware that many of these freshmen were in marginal districts, had not consolidated their bases, and, in many cases, were forced to do battle with the same GOP candidates they had faced two years earlier, the Republicans saw a number of opportunities in this freshman group. Indeed, one early GOP target list showed eighteen freshmen, ranging from Thomas Carper of Delaware and James Clarke of North Carolina to Bruce Morrison of Connecticut, Charles Robin Britt of North Carolina, Marcy Kaptur of Ohio, Robert Mrazek of New York, Ronald Coleman of Texas, and Gerry Sikorski of Minnesota.

In addition to the freshmen, Republicans also targeted a number of Democratic members of the class of '74, the so-called Watergate Babies. In 1976, as I noted earlier, the GOP had made a massive effort to defeat a large number of the seventy-five Democratic freshmen elected two years earlier, and had met with utter frustration, defeating only two. But throughout the three elections thereafter, the Republicans did not give up their hopes of defeating some of these Watergate-era freshmen who had won in seemingly strong Republican areas. Some, like Pennsylvania's Robert Edgar, showed remarkable staying power, eluding by the narrowest of margins major Republican challenges in 1978, 1980, and again in 1982. For 1984, Edgar showed up once again as a GOP target, joining several among the thirty-three remaining classmates who ran for reelection again in 1984, such as Les AuCoin of Oregon, Jerry Patterson of California, Jack Hightower of Texas, Stephen Neal of North Carolina, Philip Sharp of Indiana, and Bob Carr of Michigan. (The GOP had beaten Carr in 1980, only to see him retake the seat in 1982.) In addition, Republicans had a small list of other Democrats who were potentially vulnerable, through scandal (Gerry Studds of Massachusetts), redistricting (Robert Young of Missouri), losing touch with their districts (Clarence "Doc" Long of Maryland), and/or because they were controversial and prominent (Budget Committee chairman Jim Jones of Oklahoma).

Democratic targets on the Republican side were smaller in number. Democrats saw few opportunities among those few Republican freshmen elected against the tide in 1982. There were a handful, such as Herbert Bateman of Virginia, who Democrats felt had not grabbed hold of his district, but Democrats looked more toward Republicans plagued by scandal (such as Daniel Crane of Illinois and George Hansen of Idaho), or who seemed out of partisan step with their districts (like Bill Green of New York or Lyle Williams of Ohio, two moderate Republicans in strongly Democratic districts), or, in a few instances, Republicans who had faced several serious challenges in the past but had always, if narrowly, dodged the bullet (like Arlen Stangeland of Minnesota and Stan Parris of Virginia). In a couple of instances, Democrats also hoped that they would be helped by redistricting, as in the case of Denny Smith of Oregon. But Democratic chances for gains realistically centered more on open seats created by the departure of such Republican luminaries as Phil Gramm in Texas, Ed Bethune in Arkansas, and Jim Martin in North Carolina, all running for higher office.

The common assessments of the likelihood of modest changes in the 1984 House elections did not shift from the beginning of the calendar year up to the party conventions. At the Republican convention in Dallas in August, Republicans became somewhat more optimistic. With the expectation that a positive convention would boost President Reagan's image and popularity, Republican strategists like Bob Teeter and Ed Rollins turned bullish. While both noted the limited number of competitive seats, they also expected that the favorable economy, growing nationwide support for the Republican party, and the likelihood of an aggressive Reagan campaign focusing on Republican House incumbents and challengers would translate into greater GOP gains in the House. At the convention Rollins, Reagan's campaign manager, said of the president, "He will emphasize holding the Senate and adding House seats. Otherwise it would be a hollow victory." [22]

In the ebullient mood surrounding Dallas, Joe Gaylord, executive director of the National Republican Congressional Committee, emphasized as well the potential benefit of Reagan's coattails. Gaylord said that a big Reagan victory could help Republican House candidates who might end up four or five percentage points behind if they were running without the president. [23] In the weeks that followed, members of both parties reacted to the impact of the presidential campaign. In mid-September the *New York Times* headlined one article, "Democrats in Congress Eye Mondale With Anxiety For Their Campaigns," [24] while the *Washington Post* headlined another piece, "Reagan's

Fast Start Increases Optimism of Hill Republicans."[25] As a result, Republicans throughout the country tried to tie themselves to Ronald Reagan and their Democratic incumbents and challengers to Walter Mondale, while Democrats worked to keep their distance from the top of their ticket. This was particularly true in the South; one Democratic congressional campaign manager in a southern state commented in September, "Most Democratic Southerners are running their own campaigns and sticking to the conservative things they've always stood for."[26] It wasn't just in the South that Democrats worried about the impact of a faltering Mondale campaign. Freshman Democrat Bruce Morrison of New Haven, Connecticut, facing a rematch with the incumbent he had beaten two years earlier, Lawrence De Nardis, commented, "We have from day one dealt with the issue of a possible Reagan landslide. He carried my district in 1980, as Ford did in 1976, and Nixon did before that. I'd be a fool to wait for Democratic coattails to carry me in. So my strategy is to run a personally oriented campaign. It doesn't mean I'm rejecting Mondale and Ferraro, only that I'm putting my focus on my personal qualifications, my record."[27]

Democratic nervousness was eased substantially with the first presidential debate on October 7. The widespread view that Mondale won the debate cheered Democrats for two reasons. First, of course, was the possibility that the presidential tide moving toward Reagan would reverse, creating a real horserace and eliminating the possibility of massive Reagan coattails. But the second reason was more immediate and tangible. Political operatives in both parties agreed that the debate results would give the Reagan campaign substantial pause before going out and aggressively campaigning in House districts to defeat potentially vulnerable Democratic incumbents. In the days following the debate, both Representative Tony Coelho, chairman of the Democratic Congressional Campaign Committee, and Senator Richard Lugar, chairman of the Republican Senate counterpart, expressed the belief that President Reagan's personal appearances would be geared now more toward shoring up his own support than toward helping Republican candidates in specific House races.[28]

After the second debate and in the final three weeks of the campaign, as the presidential contest showed a steady and wide lead for President Reagan, the Democrats became nervous once again. However, it became clear that President Reagan's efforts on behalf of Republican incumbents and challengers was focused more on the Senate than the House; Vice-President George Bush became the Republican emissary sent to garner support for Republican challengers facing vulnerable Democratic incumbents and to a handful of beleaguered GOP incumbents. In the final week of the campaign Bush took his "coattails crusade" to fifteen congressional districts in Alabama, Mississippi, Illinois, Ohio, New York, Connecticut, Delaware, and New Jersey, campaigning against incumbent Democrats Wayne Dowdy (Mississippi), Lane Evans (Illinois), Thomas Downey (New York), Robert Mrazek (New York), Stanley Lundine (New York), Marcy Kaptur (Ohio), Bruce Morrison (Connecticut), Tom Carper (Delaware), and Joseph Minish (New Jersey). Bush also campaigned for GOP incumbents Bill Green (New York), Daniel Crane (Illinois), and William Carney (New York) and for three open-seat GOP candidates, including Joe Dioguardi, running to replace retiring Democratic representative Richard Ottinger of New York.[29]

As is always the case in congressional elections, each individual contest took on a coloration of its own. In Delaware, for example, Republican challenger Elise du Pont, the well-known wife of popular governor Pierre F. du Pont IV, ran a well-financed, aggressive campaign against freshman Democrat Tom Carper. Du Pont hoped for strong Reagan coattails in a state where polls showed fifteen to twenty point Reagan leads, and she built her campaign around efforts to tie Carper to the Democratic ticket. But, as one analyst noted late in the campaign, "she is pitted against a freshman congressman who has made all the right moves."[30] Du Pont tried to focus her attack on fiscal issues; one ad, for example, had her saying "a strong governor in Delaware had the guts to force spending cuts by ruling out higher taxes. The result has been eight straight balanced budgets and two tax *cuts*. Now Tom Carper wants to raise taxes in Washington to wipe out the tax cuts we've worked so hard to achieve in Delaware." Carper's campaign distanced itself from the Mondale pledge for a tax increase, and Carper stressed his support for a constitutional amendment to balance the budget, a line-item veto, pay-as-you-go legislation to cut the deficit, and a flat tax. Carper also stressed his background as a Navy veteran to counter charges that his opposition to the B-1 bomber and MX missile made him weak on defense." As the election approached, polls on all sides placed Carper six to ten points ahead of his challenger; du Pont continued to count on the strong Reagan tide.

In Tulsa, House Budget Committee Chairman Jim Jones, probably the top Republican target, was faced with a strong and well-financed challenge from U.S. Attorney Frank Keating, who had strong support from conservatives and campaign appearances by, among others, Vice-President George Bush and Secretary of the Treasury Donald Regan. In a district that President Reagan had carried with 64 percent of the vote in 1980, George Bush noted, "Make no mistake about it. It's Reagan, Bush, and Keating. Or Mondale, Ferraro, and Jones. You can have your pick."[32] Jones downplayed his tie to the Democratic presidential candidate, countered the charge that he was a rubber stamp for Speaker Tip O'Neill, and emphasized his hard work for the district, including the oil and gas industries. Jones portrayed himself as hardworking, independent, and a moderate conservative. Late in the campaign, Jones went on the offensive, using ads to challenge Keating's credibility. Keating had run a television commercial that cast himself as Rocky, showing him in a boxing ring saying, "As a Tulsa prosecutor, I won every case I tried. . . . This campaign is another tough fight—for our values, our future. Jim Jones has met his match."

Jones retaliated with a television spot that noted Keating's loss in two trials he had handled while serving in the U.S. Attorney's post. The Jones spot closed, "In Oklahoma, we believe a man is only as good as his word." The attacks on Keating's credibility put him on the defensive in the final days of the campaign, a posture he could not counter, particularly without a visit from Reagan. Despite Reagan's absence and the turn of the campaign, the race remained a toss-up to most observers as election eve approached.[33]

In Georgia's Fourth Congressional District the Republican challenge to class of '74 Democrat Elliot H. Levitas focused, as most southern campaigns did, on the incumbent's ties to the Democratic presidential ticket. Challenger Patrick Swindall aired late campaign television commercials comparing Levitas to Geraldine Ferraro. "Do you want a congressman who votes like a New York liberal?" asked the ads, while showing a picture of Levitas juxtaposed with an unflattering photo of Ferraro.[34]

As the campaign moved towards its conclusion, many close races turned into negative campaigns, with the candidates attacking one another. For example, in Alabama's open First Congressional District in Mobile, the battle between Democrat Frank McWright and Republican Sonny Callahan to replace retiring Republican Jack Edwards focused on charges and counter-charges between the two conservative candidates. McWright focused on a local government scandal involving a slush fund and illegal contributions, while Callahan attempted to paint McWright as a stooge of labor unions and liberal pressure groups. As *Congressional Quarterly* noted: "One Callahan flier lists such controversial topics as gay rights, gun control, higher taxes, and a reduced commitment to national defense, and then says that McWright is 'committed' to them and Callahan is not. A Callahan commercial all but accuses McWright of doctoring pictures to conceal the fact that he is bald, then announces that McWright 'has a lot to hide' besides his lack of hair."

McWright strenuously denied all those charges, and countered with a new round of commercials that went beyond the vague charge that Callahan was part of a "courthouse crowd" that condoned the illegal activities to specific mention of illegal money given to the Callahan campaign.[35] Although Callahan saw his wide lead in this Republican district dwindle substantially by election time, he still went into the campaign finale confident of his chances.

In Connecticut, in one of the several "replays" around the country, the campaign between incumbent Bruce Morrison and the man he unseated, Republican Lawrence DeNardis also developed a bitter tone. DeNardis, who had been beaten by Morrison when the economy turned down in 1982, remained furious over Morrison's original campaign, which tied him to attempts to cut

Social Security. DeNardis described Morrison as "a manipulative person, a dishonest person."[36] While in 1982, Morrison had emphasized the difficult economy, he was put on the defensive by DeNardis in 1984 as the economy surged. DeNardis's name recognition, combined with strong Reagan support and the Connecticut voting system's tilt toward straight-ticket voting gave the challenger some advantages. But Morrison's tireless efforts during his freshman term to take care of district problems and maintain high visibility kept him with a narrow lead through the waning days of the campaign.

As the national campaign moved to its conclusion, both parties expressed public optimism. Republicans, heartened by Reagan's strong showing in the second debate, began talking again about strong presidential coattails. Right after the debate, James Baker, the White House chief of staff, commented, "Two or three days down the road, we may be in a position to go into a congressional district we might otherwise not have gone into."[37]

While Republicans became more optimistic, they also saw relatively little late change in the forecasts regarding the potential district switches. As the election loomed, both parties privately saw the likelihood of a modest Republican gain, ranging from five to fifteen seats, absent any great national tide. Democrats were particularly bullish, buoyed by the failure, in their tracking polls, to see any national tide that might threaten their congressional incumbents. Republicans, slightly disappointed by the failure of President Reagan in the final days to aggressively attack Democratic incumbents in vulnerable House districts, still remained hopeful that the likely Reagan landslide would spill over to their benefit, enabling them to reach their stated goal of a twenty-six-seat gain, to recoup their losses in 1982.

The Election Results

As the election results began coming in, the Senate contests showed several surprises, with some contests that had been expected to be close turning out to be routs. For example, in Mississippi, Minnesota, New Hampshire, and Texas Republican incumbents Thad Cochran, Rudy Boschwitz, Gordon Humphrey, and open-seat GOP candidate Phil Gramm respectively won easy victories. There were also surprises on the other side, including unexpectedly tight races for Democratic incumbents in Nebraska and Kentucky, along with a surprisingly close contest in the open seat of West Virginia. In these three states Republican challengers Nancy Hoch, Mitch McConnell, and John Raese all ran vigorous and aggressive campaigns that brought them within striking distance of their Democratic opponents.

Other races expected to be tight turned out indeed to be so. Republican incumbents Charles Percy, Roger Jepsen, and Jesse Helms were all locked in difficult battles to preserve their seats. So too were Democratic incumbent Carl Levin and Democratic heir John Kerry.

The unexpected contests and potential upsets kept an air of excitement around the Senate returns on Election Tuesday, but the results, as in 1982, ultimately fit with most preelection predictions and resulted in a very small Senate freshman class of seven. Three incumbents were defeated, two Republicans and one Democrat. Charles Percy and Walter Huddleston lost their seats by the narrowest of margins to challengers Paul Simon and Mitch McConnell, while Roger Jepsen lost his seat by a somewhat larger edge to challenger Tom Harkin. The other four freshmen represented the open seats vacated by retirements. Only the election of Albert Gore, Jr., in Tennessee, resulted in a party turnover. The other three newcomers, from Massachusetts, Texas, and West Virginia, brought continuity in party control. The net shift thus was two seats to the Democrats.

The Democratic net gain of two, going counter to the presidential election tide, captured a great deal of attention on election eve and in the weeks thereafter and had a highly significant effect on the broader interpretation of the Reagan mandate. But the overall Senate results suggest other important patterns. Putting aside for the moment those incumbents who lost, the clearest theme in the 1984 Senate races was the outstanding performance of Republican incumbents. Of the fifteen running for reelection who won, eight captured 70 percent of the vote or better, four got more than 61 percent, and two won by better than 56 percent. Only one, Jesse Helms, ended up in the marginal category. Thirteen of the fifteen did better than they had in their previous election of 1978. While there were individual exceptions, caused by individual personalities and strong challengers, the basic fact was that 1984 was a good year to be a Republican incumbent.

It was also not a bad year to be a Democratic incumbent senator running for reelection. J. Bennett Johnston, after winning the open primary handily in Louisiana, was uncontested in November, while Sam Nunn, David Boren, Bill Bradley, Howell Heflin, Claiborne Pell, and Joe Biden, some of whom faced vigorous challengers, all captured between 60 and 80 percent of the votes in their states. Max Baucus and David Pryor, both considered potentially vulnerable at one stage of the campaign, each got 57 percent of the vote. Among Democratic incumbent senators running, only Carl Levin, with 53 percent, came relatively close to losing his seat. Over all, with twenty-nine incumbent senators running for reelection and three incumbent defeats, the reelection return rate of 90 percent was among the highest in modern-day Senate elections.

What about the role of money? The fundamental fact was that every incumbent senator raised more money than his or her challenger, with the sole exception of Roger Jepsen in Iowa. Right after the election Michael J. Malbin and Thomas W. Skladony offered a preliminary analysis of Senate campaign spending that indicated other key trends in money and Senate elections. First, Senate candidates raised money at an impressive rate, piling up $125 million by October 1984. They note, "That was 33 percent more than Senate candidates raised in 1982. The growth rate was higher than 1980's (17 percent) or 1982's (20 percent) but lower than 1978's rate of 68 percent, when these same seats were last contested."[38] Clearly, a handful of elections accounted for an enormous proportion of this growth—led particularly by the North Carolina race where the two candidates raised nearly $23 million between them between January 1, 1983, and October 17, 1984! In any previous election year the Texas race between Phil Gramm and Lloyd Doggett, which involved in the same time frame nearly $13 million, would have set a new record. Several other races, including Illinois, Iowa, Massachusetts, Minnesota, and Tennessee, were in the $5 to $8 million range.

One additional very expensive race, in West Virginia, made another point. Democratic governor John D. Rockefeller IV out-raised (and outspent) his little-known Republican opponent, John Raese, by eleven to one ($12,057,039 to $1,147,123). Despite that enormous financial edge, Rockefeller beat Raese by only 52 percent to 48 percent, indicating that while money is important, it isn't everything. One other factor noted by Malbin and Skladony: PAC contributions to Senate candidates increased by 31 percent, the lowest rate of growth since disclosure provisions began, and contrasted with previous Senate rate increases of 53, 77, and 37 percent.

The House Results

The Democratic loss of fourteen seats in the House of Representatives was a combination of ten net incumbent turnovers combined with a Republican gain of four among the twenty-seven open seats. Republicans were able to beat three prominent members of the Watergate class of 1974, Jerry Patterson in California, Elliot Levitas in Georgia, and Jack Hightower in Texas, along with five Democrats first elected in 1982. Three of the freshmen (Robin Britt, James Clarke, and Tom Vandergriff) were from the South. Democrats lost three seats *each* in North Carolina and Texas. Along with Levitas in Georgia, that meant that seven of the fourteen Democratic incumbents beaten were Southerners. The rest included a scattered collection of individuals targeted by Republicans for one reason or another, such as redistricting (Joe Minish in New Jersey); losing touch with the district (Clarence Long in Maryland); national controversy (Michigan's Donald Albosta, who achieved notoriety from the "debategate" scandal). Three Democrats—freshmen Jim McNulty in Arizona and James Clarke in North Carolina, along with five-term veteran Ike Andrews in North Carolina—were defeated in rematches with the same opponent each had bested two years earlier. On the other side, three Republican incumbents were defeated. Two of these lost because of scandals (George Hansen in Idaho and Daniel Crane in Illinois). The third, Lyle Williams of Ohio, had survived for six years in a predominantly Democratic Youngstown district plagued by unemployment.

The Republicans' greatest success came in the open seats. They were able to take five of the fourteen contested from departing Democrats while losing only one of their own, in Arkansas. Republicans took three districts where Democratic House members ran for the Senate, replacing Iowa's Tom Harkin with James Lightfoot, New Hampshire's Norman D'Amours with Robert Smith and Texas' Kent Hance with Larry Combest. Republicans also captured the seats of retiring Democrats Ray Kogovsek in Colorado and Richard Ottinger in New York's suburban Westchester County. Democrats countered by taking the seat of GOP Senate candidate Ed Bethune in Arkansas. Democrats fell just short in several other Republican open seats, including those of Jack Edwards in Alabama, Jim Martin in North Carolina, and Dan Marriott in Utah.

As in the Senate, the real story in the House was not in the turnovers but in the continuity. Nineteen eighty-four was a year for incumbents. Of 254 Democratic incumbents running for reelection on November 6, 240 won—a success rate of 94.4 percent. Of the 154 Republican incumbents up on election eve, 151 were victorious, a return rate of an astounding 98.1 percent! The overall incumbent success rate of 95.8 percent was among the highest in modern times. Just as significant was the *margin* of victory of the incumbents. Eighty percent of the Republican incumbents increased their percentages from the last time they had run. Even among the Democrats, 47 percent increased their margins over 1982 (which, of course, had been an excellent year for congressional Democrats). It was, in short, a very good year to be an incumbent running for reelection.

There were, of course, many reasons why 1984 was a good year for House incumbents, some of which we will get to shortly. One reason, however, was money. Most incumbents faced challengers who were underfinanced and unable to mount serious races. Incumbents managed to muster more money, in part because of their access to PACs. Malbin and Skladony found that for 1984 House races, political action committees "continued to mean more for House races than for Senate, for incumbents than for challengers and for Democrats than for Republicans." The relatively few serious challengers were, in almost every case, those who raised large amounts of money. Even losing challengers in close races (45 percent or better) raised more on average than incumbents with 60 percent or more of the two-party vote. Malbin and Skladony further note that challengers who defeated incumbents in 1984 House races spent an average of $512,000 in 1984, compared to $296,000 in 1982.[39]

Malbin and Skladony also suggest one reason for the comparative good fortune of House Democrats in this Republican landslide presidential year. They note that through October 17:

> House Democrats did a far better job channeling campaign contributions to candidates in close races than they did in 1982. House Democratic challengers who lost with 40 to 50 percent of the vote in 1982 raised an average of $182,232. At least some of these might have won with some more money. In 1984, Democratic challengers in the same 40 to 50 percent category raised an average of $293,549. No other group of candidates shows as marked a change over the past two years.[40]

Implications for Future Elections

Let us now return to the question raised at the beginning of this essay: Why did the Republicans not do better in the 1984 congressional elections, given their party and presidential efforts? Answers to that question may give us clues to the future outlook for Republican success in congressional elections and for Republican hopes of a realignment that might give them a Republican majority in both houses of Congress for the first time since 1954.

The first question to address is why, in general, successful presidential reelection efforts are not accompanied by substantial congressional gains for the president's party. An answer begins with the typical national mood and related presidential campaign focus that accompany big incumbent reelection victories. Almost inevitably, a successful presidential reelection bid is an indication of public satisfaction with the president's performance in office—that is, a general public feeling that things are all right in Washington. This general mood is, almost inevitably, reinforced by the president's campaign. Presidents who know that they have public approval of their performance in office tend to run by asking, "Haven't the last four years been just wonderful?" When a president wins a major reelection victory, he is getting the public's answer to that question: Yes.

But if the public is satisfied with the status quo in Washington, they are unlikely to be so dissatisfied with the other political actors in Washington that they will move to eliminate large numbers of them. It is for this reason that we find incumbents in Congress, who are normally quite successful, doing that much better in presidential reelection years. Over the last sixteen congressional elections, twenty-two House incumbents, on average, have been defeated; but in the three GOP presidential reelection successes, only thirteen incumbents, on average, have been defeated. Since in each of these elections Republican presidents ran at the same time as Democratic congresses, and since in each election, therefore, there were more Democratic incumbents running, the mood and the presidential campaign reinforced a Democratic advantage and tended to blunt Republican congressional gains.

To turn the issue around, presidential coattails are much easier to come by when the presidential campaign reinforces the president's party's congressional campaign. That situation existed for Republicans in 1980 when both the presidential and congressional campaign of the Republicans was "throw the rascals out." Many more rascals, including thirty House incumbents and nine Senate incumbents, were defeated at that time.

This basic element provides at least a partial explanation for why the national Republican congressional media effort in 1984 did not result in more victories. A national congressional television campaign is run in tandem with the presidential campaign. No matter how extensive, clever, or dramatic—a congressional television campaign will not be terribly effective if it does not reinforce the presidential campaign themes. The tremendous Republican media effort in 1980 did so. But while the Republican campaign in 1984 did not contradict President Reagan's campaigns or appeals, its heavy focus on the issue of tax increases was in no way consonant with his overall theme. That made it relatively easy for Democratic incumbents to evade the attack made by their opponents. Not having to face a hostile public mood, nearly every incumbent worth his salt could brush aside the charge that he was foursquare behind a big tax increase. Virtually every Democratic incumbent was more than willing to disavow his presidential candidate's pledge to increase taxes to deal with the deficit, and most did so effectively.

Detailed postmortems on congressional campaigns where Republicans had targeted Democratic incumbents for defeat, and failed, demonstrate the point well. Consider, for example, Oklahoma's First Congressional District (incumbent Jim Jones), Michigan's sixth (Bob Carr), and Minnesota's sixth (Gerry Sikorski). Each case shows the frustrations GOP challengers met attempting to tie Democratic incumbents to Carter, Mondale, or big tax increases.[41] Even in districts such as these, with well-financed and capable Republican challengers, savvy incumbents were able to make their own themes reinforce the national mood and the national campaign.

But themes, of course, also worked to the advantage of Republican incumbents. As we have noted, of the 149 GOP House incumbents running for reelection, 118 increased their reelection percentages over 1982, and only 3—or 2 percent—were defeated. But such figures, while they are wonderful news for Republicans already sitting in Congress, are not much help for a party trying to gain enough seats to challenge for a majority. Perhaps the election results, and the effectiveness of Republican congressional television commercials, would have been different if President Reagan had thrown caution to the winds and had run hard and exclusively on an anti-incumbent, throw the rascals out theme. But if Ronald Reagan had tried to convince Americans that there was something deeply rotten in Washington, he might have succeeded too well, reinforcing Walter Mondale's theme enough to damage his own position and his own reelection margin. Understandably, like his successful predecessors, Reagan was reluctant to do so. While he payed lip service to the notion of anti-incumbency, his basic theme, punctuated by American flags, Norman Rockwell–like television commercials, and marching bands, was "America Is Back." It worked — but only for the president.

It wasn't just Republican campaign commercials that made 1984's campaign a different one. As we noted above, Ronald Reagan worked hard, comparatively speaking, for the Republican ticket. He and his vice-president went to a number of congressional districts and campaigned expressly for Republican congressional candidates. They did miss some crucial ones — Reagan, for example, was conspicuously absent from Jim Jones's district in Oklahoma — but their effort was still major. And it made at least some difference.

But the limitation of that impact was underscored by the limited number of districts targeted by the Republicans for a presidential or vice-presidential visit, and the extremely small number of districts acknowledged by the Republican party as being strongly vulnerable to a Republican takeover. The basic fact was that long before the formal 1984 campaign began, most Democratic districts were rendered utterly safe by the failure of Republicans to mount a significant challenge; in other potentially vulnerable districts, they fell short by the margin of a challenge that was weaker or more poorly financed than anticipated. One basic reason was that, by all accounts, Republicans had a mediocre recruitment year. In mid-August *Washington Post* writer Michael Barone noted, "neither party, leaders of both concede, has many first-class challengers this year."[42] The point was underscored after the election by Republican campaign consultant Eddie Mahe, who noted, "We did burn up a bunch of really fine candidates in 1982," then added that 1984's candidates, in comparison, were "less qualified, less able, less everything."[43]

These qualitative judgments have been reinforced by the more systematic work of political scientist Gary C. Jacobson. Jacobson has pointed out that a very small proportion of 1984's challengers were prior officeholders compared to other recent elections, a good rough indicator of challenger quality.

Even where Republicans had solid challengers with the savvy and resources to run good campaigns, many fell far short. A good example is Delaware, where Reagan administration official Elise du Pont lagged far behind freshman Democratic congressman Tom Carper, despite name recognition, ample funds, and Reagan's impressive victory in the state. Carper's success, like that of Carr and Sikorski, reflects less the ineptitude of the challenge than the impressive abilities of Democratic House incumbents to build political niches in their own districts that can withstand strong tides in the other direction.

Generally, it takes a strong and resourceful challenger to give an incumbent a run for his or her money; but that run may not necessarily mean a challenger victory. If most incumbents encounter weak or nonexistent challengers, and the lion's share of those few who face strong opponents still prevail, the task of the minority party becomes daunting.

The results in 1984, coupled with Democratic gains in the House in 1982, suggest the possibility of a deeper Republican problem in Congress—a more chronic failure in the recruitment game. Republicans had a marvelous recruitment year in 1980, and a good one in 1982—but these may be exceptions, not part of a trend. While one can only speculate, it appears at least that Democrats in general have an easier time recruiting exceptional candidates to run for federal office. One can imagine many reasons for this. One is the relative party thrust. Republicans run against government. It is difficult to find people willing to devote a major portion of their lives and careers to come to a place they identify with evil, and to spend their lives doing things they preach against. Democrats, on the other hand, see government as doing good things, making it easier to find willing recruits of high caliber to devote their lives to it.

Another reason, very likely, is financial disclosure requirements. While the need for full financial disclosure is an impediment to many people, and has resulted in embarrassment for members of both parties, it is likely that Republicans, more of whom tend to come from business backgrounds, would find these requirements more distasteful than Democrats who, on the whole, have less complex financial backgrounds or arrangements to disclose. In a related fashion, it is likely as well that coming to Congress involves a more significant financial sacrifice for many potential Republican candidates than it does for comparable Democrats. These generalizations are overstated, of course, but they still point to the possibility of an endemic Republican problem.

That problem is reinforced by two other political factors. One is the recruitment base, or the "farm system" for candidates. For several decades, Democrats have dominated political offices below the national level. Even after the 1984 election, and its significant GOP gains in state legislatures, Democrats still control sixty-six state legislative chambers compared to only thirty-two for the Republicans, and still have a better than three-to-two edge in the number of state legislators. In other words, Democrats have many more individuals with appropriate political experience ready to run for Congress when the opportunity presents itself. Although Republicans gained 305 state legislative seats in 1984, that gain will not provide much benefit to future congressional recruitment efforts. Raymond Wolfinger has noted that nearly a third of the GOP seats gained were in Connecticut and New Hampshire, two states where Republican opportunities are quite limited.[44] And, for the reasons suggested above, in the last several elections Republicans have had a harder time than

Democrats convincing their top state legislative leaders to abandon their positions and run for congressional office.

A second factor relates to presidential elections. Ironically, it may well be that the impressive Republican success at winning the presidency has worked directly to hurt the party's efforts at winning seats in Congress. Every twentieth-century president save Teddy Roosevelt has left the White House with fewer seats in Congress than his party possessed when he arrived. The loss is considerably greater for two-term presidents than it is for one-term incumbents, reflecting the almost inexorable deep loss in the sixth year of a two-term presidency.

Many theories have been postulated for presidential party losses in mid-term congressional elections, but one aspect may well be the peculiar cycles of recruitment of congressional candidates. The out party seems to manage to come up with its best and most impressive crops of congressional candidates in those second-term, off-year elections. The growing frustration of the out party after six years of presidential exile, combined with a usual economic downturn that makes it easier for challengers to run against incumbents, means that the classes of candidates running in these sixth-year elections have been unusually strong.

We have a good indicator of this phenomenon in the freshman classes. Very clearly, the Democratic classes of 1958 and 1974 count among the most impressive arrays of politicians of any in the last forty years; the same can be said for the comparable Republican class of 1966. The Democratic House class of 1958 included such luminaries as Chester Bowles, John Brademas, Robert Giaimo, Ken Hechler, Dan Inouye, and Dan Rostenkowski. The Democratic class of 1974, the "Watergate Babies," included, among others, Max Baucus, Bill Brodhead, Bob Carr, Chris Dodd, Tom Downey, Tom Harkin, Norm Mineta, Paul Simon, Steve Solarz, Paul Tsongas, Henry Waxman, and Tim Wirth. The GOP class of 1966 included Pete Biester, George Bush, Marvin Esch, Gilbert Gude, Margaret Heckler, Paul McCloskey, Tom Railsback, Don Riegle, William Roth, Bill Steiger, Charles W. Whalen, and Charles Wiggins. No other congressional classes came close.

With another sixth-year election looming for 1986, Republicans have to brace for the likelihood of another sterling Democratic recruitment year, with few GOP stars willing to challenge for opposing congressional seats. With only one such election, 1966, working for the Republicans in recent decades, the possibility exists that Republicans may find their congressional aspirations consistently foiled in future years despite—or maybe because of—their stunning presidential successes.

There are still some signs to make GOP hearts beat with hungry anticipation. The recent survey evidence of increasing GOP partisan identification in the electorate may be enduring, and may begin to seep down to the congressional level, creating problems for previously secure Democratic incumbents and turning some Democratic seats over to the Republicans when incumbents retire or run for other office. It may also be that such changes in the partisan balance will encourage ambitious Republicans to run for Congress, creating a better class of challengers for Democratic seats. And, finally, it may be that the whole base of Republican recruitment in future years will change, as the new generation of conservative intellectuals nurtured by public policy centers like the Hoover Institution and the Heritage Foundation and the new generation of conservative grassroots activists bid for congressional seats, employing the more positive rhetoric of the conservative opportunity society. But without these changes, Republicans may find their frustration compounded as it becomes increasingly difficult to mount a serious challenge to recapture the majority in the House of Representatives that has eluded them now for thirty consecutive years.

Dealignment, Realignment, and Mandates in the 1984 Election

RAYMOND E. WOLFINGER

―――――Someone who waits five months to write about the meaning of an election is badly handicapped. On the one hand, his chances for originality are slim, because almost every conceivable interpretation already has been offered. The usual alternative to originality is rigorous analysis of evidence, but, at the present writing, no data about voting patterns in 1984 are available, except for a few simple tabulations from media campaign surveys and exit polls. I cannot test the numerous speculations about the outcome in November 1984 to see which ones hold water and which are without merit.

Fortunately, almost all interpretations of the 1984 election have intellectual ancestors in commentaries offered about past events. Much of what has been said about the present can be evaluated by seeing whether the similar comments about the past are valid. Observers who report that the 1984 election continued the process of dealignment that has marked several recent elections can be judged by analyzing the past case for dealignment. The past also provides a useful background for thinking about alleged new departures in 1984. President Reagan's appeal to young voters, for example, is much more meaningful if it is unprecedented for a Republican candidate to do so well with people under thirty. Thus this chapter looks at 1984 largely through the perspectives of the past.

Dealignment?

The timelessness of many interpretations of the 1984 results is illustrated by the familiar theme that the two political parties are becoming increasingly irrelevant to ordinary Americans' thinking about politics. "But, instead of a realignment, many analysts believe that what the [1984] election produced was a continuation of the trend toward 'dealignment'—the erosion of voter allegiance to either party."[1] "Dealignment" can also mean not the defection of individual partisans but a decline in the number of people who identify themselves with a party in the first place. These are two variations on the larger theme that the parties are losing their meaning for the public.

The idea that most Americans have an enduring identification with the Democratic or the Republican party was perhaps the most important single result of the national sample surveys that, beginning in 1952, powerfully shaped scholars' and journalists' views of voters and elections.[2] For a generation political scientists believed that partisan affiliations governed voting decisions and perceptions of political news. "Because of its apparent ability to simplify and make sense of distant, complicated, and often arcane events,"[3] party identification was "the central thread connecting the citizen and the political process."[4]

In this sense partisanship is a matter of self-identification, ascertained by asking survey respondents, "Generally speaking, do you usually think of yourself as a Republican, a Democrat, an Independent, or what?"[5] In the 1950s scarcely a fifth of adult American citizens chose to call themselves Independents, but by the late 1960s an increase in this proportion became apparent. At first gradual, this trend intensified during the 1970s. In 1974 and again in 1978, fully 38 percent called themselves Independents. The proportion fell slightly in the most recent elections, to 36 percent in 1980 and 31 percent in 1982, but the importance that political observers attach to the long-term trend has apparently not declined. As one widely cited book put it, "Perhaps the most dramatic political change in the American public over the past two decades has been the decline of partisanship."[6]

This putative trend and its far-reaching implications for the political system have become articles of faith to many observers, including scholars who specialize in the study of parties and elections. Consider these examples:

> Independents have increased markedly in number to the point where they now rank in some polls as equal to or slightly behind the Democrats and well ahead of the Republicans. The day is not far off when independent will clearly be the identification preferred by most Americans. . . . From an electorate in which 75 percent of its members loyally associated themselves with the major parties to one (in future elections) in which the majority may well claim to be independents is a major transition that, in itself, has changed, and will continue to change, the practice of American politics. . . . Independents operate under no such constraints. By definition, their vote (and, for that matter, whether they choose to vote at all) is not anchored by party ties. . . . It is an unstable vote (and turnout) that is basically unpredictable over time, and introduces into elections an increased volatility that today's fluid politics do not need. . . . The inde-

pendent vote is up for grabs. It has no allegiances. Its volatility and malleability does [*sic*] little to ease the concerns of those who value stability and order in American politics.[7]

The fact that a very large proportion of the electorate has been cut loose from relatively stable party ties and has been left free to float necessarily compounds the fragility of the mandate a modern president enjoys. . . . By now it is wholly evident that the dealignment interpretation of contemporary American electoral politics is correct.[8]

The central assumption in these and many other discussions of dealignment is that respondents who call themselves Independents are "simply and tautologically unconstrained by partisanship."[9] It is easier to accept this characterization of Independents as a large, uncommitted bloc if one does not know that the Michigan National Election Study (NES) has always followed up its initial question about party identification with one of two probes. If the respondent has called himself a Democrat or a Republican, the interviewer responds: "Would you call yourself a strong Democrat (Republican) or a not very strong Democrat (Republican)?" If the respondent's initial answer has been "Independent," the interviewer asks: "Do you think of yourself as closer to the Republican or Democratic party?" Thus probed, only 35 to 39 percent of respondents who initially label themselves Independent fail to admit that they lean toward one or the other party.

These "Pure Independents" have nothing in common with the Independents who lean toward a party. Respondents who say they are closer to the Democratic party are, in every important respect, similar to those who initially identify themselves as Democrats. The same is true of "Independent Republicans," those respondents who initially claim to be Independent and then admit that they are closer to the Republican party.[10] The most striking example of this generalization is that leaners vote like those outright partisans who say they are "not very strong" Democrats or Republicans. In all the presidential elections from 1952 through 1980, 66 percent of the Independent Democrats and 63 percent of the "not very strong" Democrats voted for the Democratic presidential candidate.[11] The mean vote for the Democratic candidate among Independent and Weak Republicans was 12 and 14 percent, respectively.

Some scholars and commercial survey researchers accept the basic point that most people who claim to be Independents are no such thing, but others do not.[12] Some nonacademic pollsters use the NES follow-up question, which at least permits correct analysis of the leaners; but others, including the Gallup organization, do not usually use this probe and thus inescapably exaggerate "dealignment."

None of this should obscure the rise in the proportion of Pure Independents in the population. But this increase has been paralleled by a decline in their turnout rate. They are therefore no larger a proportion of voters now than they were during the 1950s. In the 1956 presidential election, 9 percent of the voters were Pure Independents, the same proportion as in 1980. In the intervening contests, the proportion of all voters who were Pure Independents varied from 5 percent in 1964 to 11 percent in 1976. The same is true of voters in House elections, where the range is from 5 percent in 1958 and 1964 to 9 percent in 1956, 1976, and 1978. (It was 6 percent in 1982.)

One implication of these findings is that the Republican party's prospects have been underestimated; they were never as bad as suggested by the Gallup Poll's quarterly announcements that Republicans constituted only 21 or 22 percent of the population. One reason is simply that the Gallup Polls usually exclude leaning Independents. Counting leaners would boost the Republican share to about a third—still a minority, to be sure, but not so submerged a minority. The other reason is the higher turnout of Republicans and the lower turnout of Pure Independents. The political payoff of party identification is at the polling place, not in conversations with interviewers. More important in judging a party's strength is its share of all voters. In 1980 some 40 percent of voters were Republicans, 52 percent were Democrats, and 9 percent were Independents. This distribution still makes the Republicans the minority party, but the dimensions of a Republican candidate's task are not nearly as heroic as is suggested by the distribution of party identification among the entire population in 1980: 54 percent Democratic, 34 percent Republican, and 13 percent Independent. Trailing by a twelve-point margin is better than trailing by a twenty-point margin.

A second major implication is that the number of people whose votes can be swayed during a campaign has been exaggerated. The number of genuine Independents has been overestimated by a factor of three, and their electoral importance has been inflated by failure to recognize their low turnout. The degree of electoral volatility has likewise been exaggerated. There is still a good deal of validity in the observation about the 1950s by Nie and his associates that "political parties to which citizens have continuing commitments provide an important degree of stability to the political process."[13]

What about the other kind of "dealignment": people who profess identification with one party and then vote for the other party's candidate? Is it true that party loyalty is dying? The answers are different for presidential and congressional elections and also for Democrats and Republicans. In 1956 about 15 percent of voters identified themselves with one party but voted for the other party's presidential candidate. This proportion of presidential defectors held fairly steady until the 1968 and 1972 elections, when it rose to 23 and 25 percent. It fell to 15 percent in 1976 and then rose again to 23 percent in 1980. In 1984 the sharp increase in the number of voters identifying themselves as Republicans (discussed in the next section) may mean a better fit between

Table 9.1 Party loyalty in presidential elections, 1964–84

	Percent of party identifiers voting for their party's presidential candidate:					
	1964	1968	1972	1976	1980	1984
Democrats	89	68	58	79	67	73
Republicans	73	87	91	85	85	92

Sources: For 1964–80, the National Election Studies of the University of Michigan Center for Political Studies; for 1984, the CBS News/*New York Times* poll, reported in the *New York Times,* November 8, 1984.
Note: Except in 1984 Independents who say they lean toward a party are included in that party's identifiers. If these partisan Independents were excluded, party loyalty would appear a bit lower in most of these presidential elections.

party identification and candidate choice. Such a decline in defection would be the opposite of dealignment.

The three years with high defection rates—1968, 1972, and 1980—all saw Democratic candidates who proved unappealing to portions of their own party. Most of the defectors were Democrats who found Richard Nixon, George Wallace, Ronald Reagan, or John Anderson more attractive than Hubert Humphrey, George McGovern, or Jimmy Carter. The Republicans won in each of those years by attracting millions of Democratic voters and by not losing many of their own. This pattern suggests that what we have seen in the past half-dozen presidential races is not a general decline in party loyalty but rather intermittent defection by Democrats. The Republican party does not usually seem to have much of a problem with defection in presidential contests. These points are confirmed by table 9.1, which shows the proportions of Democrats and Republicans who voted for their party's presidential candidate from 1964 through 1984. (Here and elsewhere in this chapter each party's identifiers include the "leaners.")

House elections are quite a different story. There has been a trend toward greater defection, and Republicans are more likely to defect (see table 9.2). In 1958 just 11 percent of the voters in House elections were partisans of one party who voted for the other party's candidate; over twenty years, this proportion doubled. This trend resulted entirely from a sharp rise in the proportion of voters who defected to incumbents; defections to challengers remained stable.[14] Because most incumbents are Democrats, most defectors will be Republicans. The reasons for the increased power of incumbents cannot be estab-

Table 9.2   Party loyalty in House elections, 1964–82

	Percent of party identifiers voting for their party's House candidate							
	1964	1968	1970	1972	1976	1978	1980	1982
Democrats	88	77	82	84	82	76	76	83
Republicans	76	84	84	78	76	69	73	78

Source: The National Election Studies of the University of Michigan Center for Political Studies.
Note: Independents who said they leaned toward a party were included in that party's identifiers.
If these partisan Independents were excluded, party loyalty would appear slightly higher in most
House elections.

lished with any certainty, because the NES did not ask adequate questions
about congressional elections before 1978. The best-informed guess is that the
dramatic expansion of members' perquisites—staff, franked mail, travel, media subsidies, and the like—provided them with many more resources to make
favorable impressions on their constituents.[15]

Two conclusions at least can be drawn from tables 9.1 and 9.2: (1) Party-
line voting is far from dead in either presidential or congressional elections;
and (2) there is no evidence that either Republicans or Democrats are inherently more likely to vote for the other party's candidate. The strength of each
party's claims on its identifiers' loyalty is a function more of its candidates than
of the nature of those identifiers.

Realignment?

"Dealignment" means that party identification is less common or less influential in voters' decisions; "realignment" means that one or more groups that
once identified predominantly with one party have become partisans of the
other party. Observers who wish to invest election outcomes with meaning
are often tempted to see realignment when all that has happened is a temporary deviation from long-standing party loyalties in voting for presidential
candidates. Many commentators were unable to resist the temptation to dis-
cern a realignment in 1952, when Dwight Eisenhower ended the twenty-year
Democratic monopoly of the White House. History soon revealed, however,
that Eisenhower's triumph was an adverse judgment on the Truman administration and an endorsement of his own apparent personal qualities, not a sign
of an enduring shift in party identification. The Democrats regained control of
Congress in 1954 and kept it for a generation; and Republican identification
among the public did not significantly increase.

Republican victories in 1968, 1972, and 1980 were followed by the same claim that realignment was imminent, that the New Deal coalition had once again broken up. (Democratic victories are greeted with the judgment that the Republican party is on the verge of fading away like the Whigs and can save itself only by giving up its presumed concentration on country club members in favor of appealing to a wider range of American society.) The predictability of this interpretation does not mean that it is always wrong to the same extent. Sometimes election results do provide evidence that such a shift has begun or is continuing. It does appear that the 1984 election was another milestone in the continuing trend of Southern whites away from their formerly lopsided Democratic allegiance.

Moreover, a really astonishing development occurred in 1984: the disappearance of the substantial advantage in partisan identification usually enjoyed by the Democrats. From 1968 through 1980 the ratio of Democrats to Republicans in postelection surveys was generally about three to two, which amounted to a gap of about 20 percentage points. The *New York Times* and CBS News conducted surveys every month or two during 1984. This time series shows the party identification gap narrowing gradually during the first three quarters and, rather suddenly in October, shrinking almost to nothing. From October through January 1985 it was never larger than sampling error. An immediate postelection survey found that Republicans actually outnumbered Democrats (with leaners included), 47 to 44 percent. Other surveys produced similar findings, sometimes with the Democrats still ahead by a whisker, sometimes with Republicans more numerous. "Realignment" was a headline word in many newspapers and magazines.

A glance at the record will help us interpret this trend. Some past landslides were marked by concurrent movement in party identification toward the winning party, but others were not.[16] The elections of 1956 and 1964 are in the first category; 1972 is in the second. In 1956, when the Democratic presidential candidate received 42 percent of the vote, the Democratic advantage in party identification fell to 13 percentage points from 23 points in 1952. When Lyndon Johnson took 61 percent of the vote in 1964, the gap swelled to a 31-percentage-point advantage for the Democrats, a 15-point gain from 1960. On the other hand, Richard Nixon's landslide in 1972 was accompanied by a mere 4 percent drop in the Democrats' advantage, from 22 points in 1968 to 18 in 1972. Although past elections have varied in the extent to which the presidential outcome is accompanied by a parallel shift in party identification, nothing resembling the magnitude of the movement in 1984 has been observed previously. At the very least, party identification has become more volatile. Increased identification with the Republican party did not appear to be associated with a concomitant shift in ideological identification or attitudes on issues, nor a perceived turn to the left by the Democratic party. Instead, the

Republican trend seemed based on a growing conviction that the Republicans were better caretakers of the economy and managers of the government.[17]

A similar convergence in party identification was reported shortly after the 1980 election, in the spring of 1981, by one or two pollsters. It faded from sight by the summer.[18] The Republican surge in 1984 may be equally short-lived. The CBS News/*New York Times* Poll was showing an eight-point Democratic advantage by February 1985, and the ABC News/*Washington Post* Poll, which had the Republicans ahead by one point in January, reported a ten-point Democratic lead by March.[19]

After past Republican landslides, claims about realignment were refuted by voting patterns below the presidential level, which suggested that the Republican party's capture of the White House reflected personal appeal by its presidential candidate rather than a thoroughgoing shift in partisan affiliation. In 1972, for example, Richard Nixon's margin over George McGovern (23 percentage points) was accompanied by a gain of just 12 House seats and a loss of two Senate seats. The similarity of this outcome to 1984 led to some immediate claims that Reagan's victory had no greater significance than Nixon's.

A rebuttal was not long-delayed. Merely counting Democratic and Republican House seats is misleading because Democratic gerrymandering after the 1980 census produced in many states a highly imperfect relationship between votes and seats. Perhaps the worst case was in California, where the Democrats emerged from the election with 27 of the 45 House seats, despite an even split in the aggregate popular vote. Nationwide, Republican House candidates won 49.3 percent of the votes cast in contested races, a fraction of a percentage point less than the Democratic share.[20]

What is more, the advantages of incumbency also insulated congressional races from current partisan tides:[21] "It was incumbency that saved the Democratic party from ruin. If the government had passed a decree prohibiting incumbents from running for reelection, the Republican party would probably have gained control of both Houses of Congress and a substantial number of statehouses."[22] The principal evidence for this assertion is that Republicans took two-thirds of the U.S. House seats not contested by an incumbent in 1984 and picked up over 300 state legislative seats as well. It is also true that 13 Democratic and only three Republican incumbents were unseated.

The rejoinder to this line of argument is convincing, however. Although the Democrats did lose 305 seats in state legislatures, they nevertheless won 58 percent of all seats that were filled in 1984.[23] Moreover, nearly a third of the 305 lost seats were in Connecticut and New Hampshire. The party lever on Connecticut voting machines, combined with the difficulty of splitting one's ticket, provides mechanical coattails that make legislative candidates in that state unusually vulnerable to the appeal of the top of the ticket. The lower house in New Hampshire, with 400 members, is one of the largest legislative

Table 9.3 Differences between selected groups' vote for the Democratic presidential candidate and his nationwide vote, 1964–84 (percentage points)

	1964	1968	1972	1976	1980	1984
Blacks	+39	+54	+48	+44	+52	+49
Jews	+28	+41	+31	+20	+7	+25
Catholics	+18	+13	+1	+7	0	+3
Blue-collar families[a]	+17	+4	0	+11	+5	+5
Union families	+22	+5	+5	+13	+9	+12
Southern whites	−3	−17	−18	−3	−6	−13
Northern white Protestants[b]	−4	−16	−12	−13	−13	−15
Nationwide vote (percent)	61	43	38	50	41	41

Sources: For 1964–80, the National Election Studies of the University of Michigan Center for Political Studies; for 1984, the CBS News/*New York Times* poll, reported in the *New York Times*, November 8, 1984.

[a]Classified by occupation of head of household.

[b]For 1984, all white Protestants, irrespective of region.

bodies in the world. The fifty-eight seat gain by the Republicans in 1984 reflects the decisions of fewer than 100,000 voters. In congressional elections, open-seat outcomes and incumbent success rates in 1984 surely favor the Republicans, but not by very much. Just twenty-seven seats were open in 1984. Republicans lost only one of the fourteen seats they had held, while the Democrats lost five of thirteen. This record does not provide very many straws in the wind.

In 1980, when Reagan won just 51 percent of the total vote, all these measures were much more favorable to the Republicans. They took ten open seats away from the Democrats in 1980 and unseated twenty-eight Democratic incumbents while losing just three incumbents and a single open seat. Since incumbent advantages were surely no more lavish in 1984 than four years earlier, the 1980 outcome demonstrates that incumbency alone does not provide much protection to a party on the short end of a strong partisan tide.

So much for what might be called realignment in general. What about particular segments of the population whose voting choices were the subject of so much speculation during the campaign? According to many commentators, the durable New Deal coalition died once again in 1984. Here is a representative example, which appeared under the headline "Longtime Democratic Coalition in Splinters":

> Tuesday's presidential election returns show that the half-century old Democratic coalition in which Franklin D. Roosevelt united Northern liberals, Southern whites, blue-collar workers, organized labor, blacks and Jews has lost the glue that long held its disparate parts together. . . .
>
> Having in fact accomplished most of that [New Deal] agenda, the party has failed to come up with a new set of themes and goals to match the changing times. . . .[24]

In fact, most of the groups mentioned in this passage gave a larger share of their votes to Mondale than did the national electorate. Mondale carried very few groups (according to the ABC News exit poll, "Reagan won every category of white males except Jews"), but he still did better among most of the traditional backers of the Democratic party than among other groups in the society. Mondale received 41 percent of the vote nationwide. He got 90 percent of the black votes, and more than three-fifths of the votes of Jews and self-defined liberals.[25] In winning a majority of the union vote, he ran about 12 percentage points better among union voters than he did among the whole population of voters.

Mondale did better among liberals, Jews, and union families than Carter did in 1980. For that matter, he equaled Carter's 1976 vote from union families, although he fell a bit short of Carter's appeal to liberals and Jews in 1976.

A broader perspective on the New Deal coalition can be gained by looking beyond the immediate past to the six elections from 1964 through 1984. Arrayed in table 9.3 are the differences between Democratic presidential candidates' total vote and the vote each received from a half-dozen groups: blacks, Jews, Catholics, families headed by a blue-collar worker, families with a union member, and white Southerners. For purposes of comparison with the last group, I have also included Northern white Protestants. Several conclusions are apparent from this table:

Jews (except in 1980) and blacks have been reliable Democratic voters.

There is some validity to the cliché about the New Deal coalition: when the national Democratic ticket does well, Catholics and working-class families vote substantially more Democratic than other Americans. When the Democrats do badly, Catholics and blue-collar families are usually not far away from the national vote.

Although Southern whites are indeed disaffected from the Democratic party, they have not been notably different from their Northern counterparts, except in response to Carter's candidacies.

Union members and their families are consistently more Democratic than all blue-collar workers. All the talk about the erosion of union leaders' authority and credibility clearly needs to be qualified. To be sure, a firm conclusion on the relation between union membership and vote choice requires more sophisticated analysis, but table 9.3 should give some pause to hasty valedictories to union political influence.

The same might be said about the 1984 election and the New Deal coalition. Nineteen eighty-four was not the worst year for the appeal of Democratic presidential candidates to Jews, Catholics, blue-collar families, union families, and Southern whites. Every one of these groups was further away from the Democratic ticket in some year before 1984.

The South Is Different

The one group that does seem to be in the process of realignment is white Southerners. In three of the past four elections the South has been more Republican than the country as a whole. The exception, of course, was in 1976, Jimmy Carter's winning year.[26] In 1984 Reagan's margin of victory in every Southern state was bigger than his national margin. The Southern appeal of Republican presidential candidates has been recognized for some time. Less acknowledged—and less understood—is the depth of the Republican swing in the South. Ten of the region's 22 Senate seats are held by Republicans, as are 42 of the 116 Southern House seats, a gain of seven in 1984. (This works out to 36 percent. Whether this is a lot or a little is something of an open question. To put the figure in perspective, Republicans hold 44 percent of all Northern House seats.)

Until 1980, Republicans gained Southern House seats almost entirely in districts where the incumbent was not running for reelection.[27] This pattern was broken in 1980, when six Democratic incumbents lost; 1982 brought Republican losses in the South, as elsewhere, but in 1984 seven Southern Democratic representatives were turned out of office.

In 1984 the Republicans also gained four or more state legislative seats in six Southern states. Most of this success was in Texas and North Carolina, where very conservative Republican candidates for the U.S. Senate won hotly contested, lavishly funded races against liberal Democratic opponents. The political mobilization and ideological polarization in these two contests doubtless were important considerations in the gain of three House seats and 25 state legislative seats in North Carolina, and four House and 17 legislative seats in Texas. In the months after the election, the Republicans added to their state and local strength by the defection of Democratic officeholders, a process that has been a thin but steady source of reinforcement at least since Senator

Strom Thurmond changed parties in South Carolina in 1964. Perhaps the most impressive recent switch was by seven Louisiana state legislators in the first ten weeks of 1985.

No one should jump from the indisputable fact that Southern Democratic representatives are more conservative than other Democrats to the mistaken conclusion that replacing a Southern Democrat with a Republican has no effect on the outcome of legislative struggles. In 1982 Southern Democratic representatives had a mean AFL-CIO approval score of 50; Southern Republicans scored 9.3. This means that the Democrats voted for the position favored by labor half the time; the Republicans, less than one out of ten times. Another ideological measure is *Congressional Quarterly*'s Conservative Coalition Support Score, which measures each member's agreement with the position favored by a majority of Southern Democrats and Republicans voting together, when such an alliance is evident in House (or Senate) roll calls. In 1984 the mean Conservative Coalition Support Score for Southern Democrats was 63.1; for Southern Republicans, 86.3.[28] In short, Southern Republicans are considerably more conservative than Southern Democrats; the realignment of the South has implications on Capitol Hill. (Of course, the Republican trend in the South also reduces the South's power in the congressional Democratic parties.)

The South's move toward the Republican party clearly goes far beyond presidential voting, although it is most pronounced there and in Senate elections. The Southern proclivity for uncontested elections obscures accurate observation of Republican strength. In 1984, when sixty-five House elections in the country as a whole were uncontested by one or the other major party, forty-seven of those seats were in the South; there was no Democratic candidate in ten of them, and no Republican challenger in thirty-seven.

The Republican trend in the South is often called a consequence of the civil rights movement and the identification of the Democratic party with demands for racial equality. This explanation is surely an oversimplification and most likely without substantial merit. The clearest way to show why this is so is to describe those Southerners who support Republican candidates.[29] The following discussion is limited to whites because blacks (17 percent of all Southern votes in 1980) are clearly not contributing to the Republican trend. By the same token, the trend is not for the most part a matter of Southern whites voting for selected Republican candidates while continuing to think of themselves as Democrats. That was the pattern thirty years ago, when most of Eisenhower's supporters were defecting Democrats. But by 1980 only a quarter of Reagan's Southern votes came from Democrats; 13 percent of his supporters were Independents, and the rest were people who identified themselves as Republicans. The South is one part of the country where party loyalty, far from declining, is actually on the rise.

The obvious implication is that more and more Southerners are identifying themselves with the Republican party. Indeed, the regional gap in party identification between white voters in 1980 was just seven percentage points: Republicans constituted 45 percent of white Northern voters and 38 percent of white Southern voters. In 1984 NBC exit polls found only 5 percent more Democrats than Republicans among all Southern voters, whites and blacks combined.[30] Two quite distinct groups contribute to this development: Northern migrants and a new generation of Southerners. In 1980 some 23 percent of Southern voters were whites who grew up in the North (hereinafter "migrants"), and 60 percent were whites who grew up in the South (hereinafter "natives").

Compared with other Southerners, the migrants are younger, better educated, richer, more active politically, and more liberal on racial issues. They are also far more Republican than native Southerners. For that matter, they are more Republican than almost any other substantial demographic group in the country. Fully 44 percent of them (voters and nonvoters alike) were Republicans in 1980. The migrants are responsible for nearly half the total increase in Republican voting strength in the South since the 1950s and constitute nearly a third of all white Southern Republicans. They include various social groups; by far the most important is made up of people moving south to participate in the region's economic growth. This boom is expected to continue; economic projections forecast above-average economic growth in the South. The migrants will be an increasingly important—and Republican—component of the Southern electorate.

The other source of Southern Republicanism is natives who reached voting age in 1964 or later. By 1980 this younger cohort (people aged eighteen to forty) equaled in number the older generation of native white Southerners. Only 22 percent of the older group were Republicans, and 34 percent of the younger generation. Where else are young people so much more Republican than their elders?

One reason for doubting that racial resentment fuels the Southern realignment is now evident: the most Democratic whites (the older generation) are the most racially conservative. The other reason is that no analyst of survey data on Southern voters has been able to discover evidence linking racial issues and the realignment.

What of the future? The Republicans can hardly fail to continue their gains. Their support comes from the migrants and the new generation of natives, the one likely to increase further, the other inevitably becoming more active and important. The Democrats, on the other hand, depend on blacks and the older generation of native whites. The potential for substantial increases in voting strength in this political odd couple is much weaker. The older natives, of course, will become a progressively smaller part of the Southern population. Continued political mobilization and reduction of the educational disparity between the races might close the gap between white and black turnout rates. As far back as 1972, however, the racial disparity in the South (and also in the North) was explainable by differences in education and age.[31] Moreover, blacks are so outnumbered in the South that percentage increases in their voting participation are balanced by much smaller gains in white turnout rates. For example, preliminary data from the Current Population Survey indicate a turnout increase from 1980 to 1984 of 6.3 percent for Southern blacks, compared to 1.6 percent for Southern whites, but the increase for whites represents more voters.[32] In short, time is not on the side of the Democrats in the South.

These predictions of a bright future for Southern Republicans depend mostly on inexorable actuarial considerations and partly on demographic probabilities. Racial polarization may give a further boost to Republican prospects. For now, it is sufficient to observe that there were plenty of reasons other than race relations to expect a cool reception in the South for the Mondale-Ferraro ticket in 1984.

The Youth Counterrevolution

One of the big news stories about the 1984 election was the putative new-found Republicanism of young voters. Numerous preelection polls showed extraordinary pro-Reagan majorities among Americans under thirty. Columnists who (to be charitable) knew nothing about the rock-throwing, meeting-disrupting reality of campus life fifteen years ago, found this a sorry contrast to the mythical idealism of young people in the hallowed 1960s. Pundits were not reticent, of course, about offering reasons why young voters would prefer Reagan to Mondale. One was that they were selfish, abjuring the altruism that led some of us to vote Democratic. The conservative variation on this theme is that the quotas and preferences embraced by some elements in the Democratic party have left young white males the only group in the country without an endorsed grievance, but with the responsibility of paying for everyone else's benefits and the assurance that any claims made on their behalf will be considered mere selfishness. A kindlier explanation is that Reagan's talk about Americans standing tall gave young idealists hope they could not find in Mondale's dour ruminations about deficits and tax increases.

Then there was the social scientists' story. People just attaining political consciousness are more susceptible to contemporary trends because they have not developed the habits and affiliations—party identification—that keep more mature voters from being swept away by the passions of the moment. I used this argument to explain misguided youth and soothe Democratic friends worried about the future until I actually looked at some data while writing this

Table 9.4 Vote for Democratic presidential candidate by age group, 1964–84

Age	1964	1968	1972	1976	1980	1984
18–29	72%	38%	47%	51%	34%	41%
30–44	69	47	34	48	37	42
45–59	70	37	31	52	37	39
60+	59	40	29	50	47	36

Sources: For 1964–80, the National Election Studies of the University of Michigan Center for Political Studies; for 1984, the CBS News/*New York Times* poll, reported in the *New York Times*, November 8, 1984.

chapter. I discovered that, *among voters*, people under thirty are not much more likely than any other group to be Independents.

Election-day exit polls showed that the expectations of a youthful swing to Reagan were somewhat exaggerated. Indeed, it appeared that, up to the age of sixty, there were no age differences at all. According to the CBS News/*New York Times* Poll, Mondale got 41 percent of the under-thirty vote, 42 percent from people aged thirty to forty-four, and 39 percent from those forty-five to fifty-nine. Among those sixty and over, his share fell to 36 percent. Some observers found even this development noteworthy:

> The strong support young voters gave President Reagan in his reelection victory turns 20th century political tradition on its ear. It alone is enough to make people wonder about a political realignment in the United States. . . . The young as a group have for generations been more Democratic and liberal than their elders.[33]
>
> Winning the young is likely to have a substantial payoff for the GOP because political commitments acquired when young tend to be conserved as voters age. . . .[34]

Since young voters presumably always had been much more Democratic in the past, the challenge now was to explain why they had fallen from the liberal vanguard and were just like everyone else. Moreover, the thought that as the twig was bent, so the tree would grow gave youthful voting choices exceptional significance.

The flaw in all this is fundamental: more often than not in past elections, young people have not voted all that differently from other age groups. The evidence is in table 9.4, which shows no particular pattern in most elections.[35] The two notable exceptions are 1968, when young voters were pretty much like everyone else except the thirty-to-forty-four group, who were substantially more supportive of Hubert Humphrey; and 1972, the only time when young voters lived up to their image as strongly pro-Democratic.

Another point is evident: The youth vote in one election does not predict much about the next election. If anything, young people seem to alternate being disproportionately more and disproportionately less favorable to the Democratic candidate. Whatever else young voters are, they are not harbingers of future outcomes.

Looking for a Mandate

My dictionary defines a mandate as "an instruction as to policy given by voters to elected officials." "Mandate" was one of the favorite nouns on the election night television coverage, and little doubt was displayed that the voters had given one to President Reagan. In the weeks after the election, quite a lively debate developed about what message, if any, the voters had sent to Washington. On one side were those like the conservative columnist James J. Kilpatrick: "It was not a mandate. . . . It is useless to search for deep meaning in the president's landslide reelection. There isn't any deep meaning there. . . . The only significant issue was summed up in Reagan's rhetorical question: Are you better off than you were four years ago? Most of the people said yes."[36]

Some of Kilpatrick's fellow conservatives disagreed with him, and they were not alone. Samuel L. Popkin, a political scientist and Democratic polling consultant, argued that Kilpatrick was wrong, essentially because there were sharp divisions between Mondale and Reagan voters on an assortment of perceptions and predictions.[37] The president himself also discerned a substantive endorsement in the election returns:

> Reagan and his top advisers avoided using the word "mandate" in their postelection analyses, but it was obvious that the president felt he had won a major vote of confidence for his policies and was prepared to use his wide popularity to, as he often has described it, "make them [lawmakers] feel the heat if they won't see the light.
>
> I feel the people of this country made it very plain that they approved what we've been doing," Reagan asserted.[38]

The president's interpretation was that the voters wanted him to keep doing what he was doing. There is no doubt that most Americans felt that the country was enjoying peace, prosperity, and stable price levels, and attributed those blessings to Reagan. This is not the same as saying that they approved of either the various administration programs and policies that may (or may not) have produced peace and prosperity or any new departures that Reagan promised during the campaign.

We care about mandates because in legislative and intraparty struggles politicians use election outcomes as evidence that their policies should be adopted. A plausible claim that the people are on one's side — that a particular proposal will win votes — is advantageous. Election returns are almost always useless as measures of public opinion on particular measures. Evidence of what the people think about abortion, school prayer, or the mortgage interest deduction is supplied by polls. The winning candidate may have a popular majority for his platform as well as his person; but if so, it has no necessary connection to the reasons for his victory. It is probably true, for example, that most Americans reject busing, racial quotas, protecting jobs in obsolete industries, comparable worth, and "blaming America first." Yet Mondale's association with these and other unpopular ideas had little to do with his loss.

Mandates are inherently implausible. For one thing, many people vote for their party's candidate almost reflexively; a cataclysm would be necessary for some faithful Democrats and Republicans to cross party lines. Others base their votes on the candidates' apparent personal qualities. A survey that revealed opposition to Reagan's position on aid to the Nicaraguan *contras*, arms control negotiations with the Soviet Union, responsibility for the American dead in Lebanon, the "star wars" missile defense, and the Reverend Jerry Falwell asked whether respondents had more confidence in Reagan's or Mondale's ability to deal with "a difficult international crisis"; 52 percent expressed more confidence in Reagan, just 32 percent in Mondale.[39]

People who believe in mandates usually say that those who voted for a candidate did so because they favored the policies he advocated. The search for the mandate becomes a textual analysis of the winner's campaign utterances. The problem here, of course, is that candidates say a great many things, as well as running on platforms that are devoted to programmatic commitments. Not all these promises can be important. As Chairman Mao might have said, "Many issues, one vote."

An alternative approach to mandate hunting is a big-picture look at each campaign. Sometimes such a look does not reveal many specific policy commitments. Almost everyone agrees that Reagan ran a John Wayne–Andy Hardy campaign in 1984. America was standing tall again, back in a world of steady prices and happy neighbors, free of worry about poverty, big city blight, bigotry, deficits, Japanese imports, and other problems Democrats insist on talking about. The principal island of specificity in this sea of generalities was taxes: Mondale said he would raise them, and Reagan would do so only "over my dead body." Almost everyone recognized this difference, and most preferred Reagan's position. One could say that Reagan has a mandate not to raise taxes. This may not, however, be much of a deterrent to the administration's plans. Most voters also expected that the president would request a tax increase.[40]

Even when candidates take what appear to be unmistakably clear and op-posed positions on major issues, however, the voters may still have trouble perceiving those differences. In 1976 Carter repeatedly attacked Ford for high unemployment and promised to follow the familiar Democratic policy that the government would guarantee everyone a job. Ford put his faith in free enter-prise. Yet only 44 percent of the public associated Carter with a belief that the government should see to jobs for everyone, and 21 percent attributed this position to Ford. Four years earlier McGovern failed even to secure recogni-tion of his fundamental commitment to putting a quick end to the war in Vietnam. Less than two-thirds of the people who favored withdrawal from Vietnam believed that McGovern agreed with them. On other issues as well, many who shared McGovern's position did not think he was on their side. Nixon seldom had this trouble. He won the votes of almost half the people with the most liberal views on social problems, those who backed protest and the counterculture and were hostile to the military and symbols of "law and order."[41]

Candidates with weak personal appeal, like McGovern and Mondale, have trouble getting their basic policy stands across even to people who agree with them. When asked by various polls whether their opinion of Mondale was favorable or unfavorable, most respondents said it was unfavorable. This re-sponse, I believe, explains why Mondale lost so many votes from what would appear to be his strongest constituencies. The ABC News/*Washington Post* Poll found that Reagan got the votes of 26 percent of the liberals, 21 percent of the self-described feminists, and fully 41 percent of the "strong environmen-talists."[42] Mondale consistently had less appeal to self-described conservatives than Reagan had to liberals. In the poll cited above, only 18 percent of conser-vatives chose Mondale. In the *Los Angeles Times* Poll, 18 percent of the con-servatives voted for Mondale and 32 percent of liberals voted for Reagan.[43] The corresponding figures in the CBS News/*New York Times* Poll were 18 and 29 percent.[44] With all the talk about Yuppies, it may be noteworthy that Mondale got 38 percent of the votes of people who called themselves "young professionals."[45]

In contrast to Reagan's bland and largely issueless 1984 performance, his campaign in 1980 featured several specific promises, all of which he kept, increasing defense spending while cutting taxes and domestic programs. He could not have achieved these major successes in 1981 without the cooperation of the Democratic House of Representatives. In dealing with the House, Rea-gan was aided by a widespread Democratic conviction that the 1980 results really were a mandate, that the voters had expressed their discontent not just with an unpopular Democratic president but with the basic thrust of Demo-cratic policy since the New Deal. This interpretation could not be based on Reagan's bare 51 percent majority of the popular vote. The message of the

1980 election came loudest and clearest from the astonishing Senate results. In taking control of the Senate for the first time since 1954, the Republicans won twelve of the twenty-four Democratic seats contested while holding every one of their own. What really impressed the political community was the defeat of nine incumbent Democratic senators. This, more than anything else, is what made the 1980 election look like a verdict not just on Jimmy Carter but on two generations of New Deal, Fair Deal, New Frontier, and Great Society programs. The liberal columnist Anthony Lewis summarized the prevailing view: "The Senate results make the point even more compelling than Ronald Reagan's electoral vote landslide. What happened in the 1980 election reflected a profound and general turn to conservatism in this country."[46]

Was this the right way to look at what had happened? One indisputable consequence of the 1980 election was the huge gain in Republican seats that made the Senate safe for Reagan's legislative program. But more reflective analysis of the results showed that they offered very little comfort to people who saw a mandate for conservative policies in the defeat of the Democratic incumbents.

> A look beneath the surface of this tremendous GOP sweep of the Senate in 1980 suggests that the election trend, while broad, was shallow. Many individual races were extremely close. . . . Indeed, if one could shift barely 50,000 votes—less than one-hundredth of 1 percent of all votes cast— one could move *seven* Senate seats from the GOP to the Democrats and change the election into a typical one. With a Democratic loss of only five seats, the party would have retained firm control of the Senate, fifty-four to forty-six, and the analysis of 1980 would have focused almost exclusively on the personal defeat of Jimmy Carter.[47]

The same point can be made by looking at the aggregate nationwide vote for all Senate candidates. Combining all votes cast in Senate elections in 1980 does not lead to the view that the Senate voting constituted such a rejection of the Democratic party, because Democratic candidates won fully 52.5 percent of all the votes. This puts the matter in quite a different light than if one looks just at seats.

How does this help us understand policy preferences in 1984? The usual interpretation is that, by gaining two Senate seats, the Democrats provided evidence that Reagan's victory was personal, not a sign of ideological endorsement. The conclusion is correct, but the evidence is shaky. In contrast to the 1980 Democratic majority in Senate votes, 1984 saw a slight Republican advantage. Republican candidates won 50.6 percent of the total votes cast in Senate elections.

Claims about mandates are generated primarily not by evidence, but by political fashion. Perhaps chastened by their excessive interpretations of the

1980 results, politicians and journalists alike refrained from making much of a somewhat better set of facts than those that led to so much mistaken interpretation four years earlier. In contrast to their down-the-line loyalty to the president in 1981, congressional Republicans were conspicuously detached in the first months of the 99th Congress: "The Republicans [in the House's freshman class] especially appear to sense that they are walking a thin line between supporting their triumphant President and voting for a highly unpopular budget. . . . They do not feel beholden to any particular group or person, including Reagan, nor are they committed to a specific ideological program."[48]

In short, people who want to know who will run the government should look at election results. Those who want to learn about public opinion should consult a good pollster.

Realignment at the Top,
Dealignment at the Bottom

JAMES Q. WILSON

————It was a perfectly ordinary election. During the preconvention phase, there were intense debates over social issues and some agitation concerning scandals in the administration. Nevertheless, the conservative Republican incumbent easily won renomination and the Democratic party selected a challenger who, though somewhat colorless, did not alienate any major factions in his party. But even had the Democrats nominated a magnetic personality, there was little they could have done to unseat a popular president who was in office when the country was more or less at peace, the economy was reasonably strong, and the people were seeking a reaffirmation of traditional values. The incumbent won in a landslide.

I refer, of course, to the reelection of Calvin Coolidge in 1924.

Nobody ever puts the 1924 election on a list of critical, or even interesting, contests. The compilation by Arthur M. Schlesinger, Jr., of sixteen important elections between 1789 and 1964 does not mention 1924. Nor does it mention 1900, 1904, 1948, or 1956.[1] Yet each of these five contests (plus that in 1964, which Schlesinger does include) are, collectively, among the more important we have had in this century, for the following reason—they were all normal elections that reveal how the electoral system is supposed to work. In each case, an incumbent president sought reelection at a time when the country was reasonably prosperous and more or less at peace (by 1964, of course, the fighting had begun in Vietnam, but most people were not aware of that). In each case, the election was a retrospective referendum on the record of the incumbent. In each case the incumbent won. Never in this century has an incumbent lost an election held during peace and prosperity.

Nineteen eighty-four was also an ordinary election. It is difficult to see how any Democrat could have defeated Ronald Reagan, or even won many more states than did Walter Mondale. What makes it appear extraordinary are two facts: First, it has been a long time—twenty years—since we had an incumbent running in an ordinary (i.e., prosperity at home, peace abroad) election. Second, commentators, using such terms as "realignment" acquired from professional political scientists, urgently sought some deeper meaning in the results.

The supporters of President Reagan speak of a mandate. The winners always say that. The Democrats deny there was a mandate; the losers always say that. But to the voters, the biggest single issue was the state of the economy. In the CBS News/ *New York Times* poll, ten times as many voters mentioned the economy as mentioned Central America and five times as many voters referred to the economy as cited abortion. Arms control and the fear of war was mentioned by about a quarter of the voters, a group almost exactly balanced by the quarter who thought having a strong defense was an important issue.[2] Reagan voters were three times as likely to say the economy was an important question as were Mondale voters. During the three years preceding the election, President Reagan's approval rating in the Gallup Poll tracked almost precisely changes in the unemployment rate—for every 1 percent increase in unemployment, Reagan's popularity declined by six points.[3] In their effort to explain the landslide vote by reference to his personal qualities or his ideology, most commentators forgot that less than two years earlier, his approval rating was as low—35 percent—as had been that of Richard Nixon during Watergate or Carter during his last year in office. The reason was simple—the recession had reached its lowest point, with the unemployment rate at a postwar high. Only during the campaign itself did the economic and popularity trends move somewhat independently of one another, with the president continuing to gain in popularity even as the level of employment flattened out.

No doubt the president's amiable, sincere style adds to the support he gets from some voters, but in all probability his tendency to speak hastily and inaccurately about current policy issues alienates other voters. The net effect of his popularity, over and above the condition of the country during his first term in office, is hard to assess, but, as Walter C. Adams has recently shown, Reagan's personal popularity has not been as consistently great as was Dwight Eisenhower's and was not much higher in 1984 than was Richard Nixon's in 1972.[4] If the economy turns sour again, we can confidently expect that the "Great Communicator" will have as much trouble communicating as he did in January 1983 when his approval rating dropped through the floor.

Some will object that if a good economy and the absence of a foreign crisis were so important in returning Reagan to office, why didn't the Republicans also do well in Congress? The answer is that they did, but the advantages of incumbency and the way House seats are apportioned conceal that fact. In the aggregate, Republican House candidates won almost exactly the same number of votes as did the Democrats, a remarkable feat considering that the great majority of Democrats running were incumbents. (In those few races where there was no incumbent running, the Republicans did much better than the Democrats.) But for various reasons—including Democratic control of most state legislatures, where House district lines are drawn—the Democratic House vote is more highly leveraged than the Republican, so that the Democrats win seats considerably in excess of their proportion of the total congressional vote.

William Schneider has neatly summarized the last two presidential elections this way: "What people were voting for in 1980 was not conservatism but change. What people were voting for this year was neither conservatism nor change but continuity."[5]

There are many patterns in the 1984 vote that ought to worry the Democrats, but there is as yet no evidence that these patterns constitute a realignment of the electorate in a fashion that will make the Republicans the majority party. The Democrats made no inroads on the youth vote; saw the gender gap that had once given them a majority of female voters narrow to the point of irrelevance (at least for the moment); lost in every occupational grouping (except the unemployed), including teachers, blue-collar workers, government employees, and full-time students; lost a third of the voters who had supported Gary Hart in the Democratic primaries; lost three-quarters of the votes of white Southerners; and lost the competition to register new voters and get them to vote Democratic. In almost all these categories, the Democrats fared worse in 1984 than they had in 1980.

None of this means that the voters have permanently deserted the Democratic party or acquired an ideological affinity for Republican policies and candidates. For there to be a mass realignment of voters, there must either be some seismic event, akin to the Civil War, that stamps an enduring partisan identity on voters, or there must be a conversion to a new view of politics, akin to that which followed the advent of the New Deal. No seismic event has occurred and there is little sign of programmatic conversion.

Voters are somewhat more likely today than ten years ago to call themselves conservatives and somewhat less likely to call themselves liberals, but beneath these ambiguous labels one encounters a profound constancy in policy preferences. For many years, voters have given essentially unchanged answers on most key domestic policy questions. They want a balanced budget, but they also want more money spent on protecting the environment, improving the educational system, and lowering the crime rate. They want a solvent and dependable Social Security System, and they are counting on Medicare to be there when they need it. They favor capital punishment, support tough laws against drunk driving, oppose the legalization of marijuana, strongly oppose school busing, support the Equal Rights Amendment, want people to get a police permit before they can buy a gun, and don't object to a woman having an abortion if she has a good reason.[6]

Only on foreign and military matters is public opinion volatile. How much people think should be spent on defense varies with the extent to which other nations seem to be pushing us around and with the tenor of the public debate on the matter. The public does not want to see the U.S. military embroiled abroad but, up to certain limits, will support the president should he decide to get us involved.

Not only are opinions on most domestic issues quite stable, there are only a few voting blocs that either party can take for granted. The Democrats can count on black voters (and, to a lesser extent, Jewish ones), but neither party can reliably count on much else. White Southerners of both sexes overwhelmingly backed Reagan in 1984, but white Southern women supported Jimmy Carter in 1980, and Southern whites helped Carter defeat Ford in 1976. During the last four elections, Catholics and blue-collar workers have split their votes about evenly between the two parties. There has been some increase in the proportion of the voters who say they identify with the Republican party, but this change has hardly made a dent in the large proportion who say they identify with neither.

So far, there is little reason to describe what is happening to the average voter as a realignment; if anything, the process involves a more or less continuous *de*alignment. But this fact is not good news for either Republicans who hope to stay in power or Democrats who hope to return to power. If the rank-and-file voters have experienced no realignment, the party activists have.

The central change that has occurred in American party politics in the last twenty years has been the realignment of party elites. Scholars and reporters looking for signs of a mass realignment may have failed to grasp the extent to which the changed circumstances of the parties have made a mass realignment less likely and an elite realignment more so. By a mass realignment I mean a sharp, enduring change in the coalitions supporting each party. By an elite realignment I mean a change in the identity and views of those persons who play important roles in the selection of the candidates, the writing of the platforms, the definition of the rules, and in conducting the affairs of each party.

Over the last two decades, the elites most influential in the Republican party have moved more or less steadily to the right and those most influential in the Democratic party have moved more or less steadily to the left. The facts are, I think, well known to political scientists and to the party activists themselves, but we have not attended to the possibility that this elite realignment may not only be a substitute for a mass realignment—the former may have made the latter unlikely.

The Goldwater candidacy in 1964 was the beginning of the transformation of the Republican party, the McGovern candidacy in 1972 was the beginning of a similar change in the Democratic party. Though the changes were neither smooth nor continuous (Nixon and Carter, for a while, brought their respective parties back closer to the center), it has continued. The signal events occurred in 1976 and 1980. In 1976, an incumbent Republican president was challenged for renomination by a conservative rival, Ronald Reagan; in 1980, an incumbent Democratic president was challenged by a liberal rival, Edward M. Kennedy. The challenges were made possible by the ability of activists, drawn to their parties by ideological enthusiasm and sustained in their endeavors by issue movements, to mobilize like-minded voters to participate in direct primary elections and grassroot caucuses.

Since 1972 the delegates to the national nominating conventions, especially those selected in the primaries, have been ideologically more extreme than the voters who identify with each party. Jeane Kirkpatrick first provided systematic evidence of this tendency in her study of the delegates to the 1972 Democratic and Republican conventions. The cleavage between the views of delegates and those of the party identifiers was, at that time, greatest in the Democratic party—so great, indeed, that, in her words, "the Democratic elite and rank-and-file were found on opposite sides" of such issues as crime, welfare, the military, school busing, and the police.[7] Ironically, the views of rank-and-file Democrats were better represented by delegates to the *Republican* convention that year than they were by delegates to the Democratic convention.

This cleavage was in marked contrast to what had been true in 1956, when Herbert McClosky found that there was a "substantial consensus" between Democratic convention delegates and the Democratic rank-and-file. Then, the cleavage was in the Republican party, where delegates and rank-and-file differed sharply.[8] Subsequent studies have made clear that Kirkpatrick's 1972 findings were not a fluke occasioned by the McGovern candidacy. In 1980, the CBS News/*New York Times* poll found that twice as many Democratic delegates as Democratic identifiers described themselves as being liberals, and a third more Republican delegates than Republican rank and file called themselves conservatives.[9] The cleavage was even wider in 1984, according to a *Los Angeles Times* survey. The proportion of Democratic delegates describing themselves as liberals was four times greater than that proportion among Democratic voters; the percentage of Republican delegates calling themselves conservatives was 50 percent greater than that percentage among Republican voters.[10]

The widened gap between Democratic and Republican elites is not confined to the nominating conventions. In Congress, as William Schneider has shown (see table 10.1), the Democrats are consistently left-liberal and the Republicans are consistently right-conservative across almost all issue areas, as revealed by the ratings of the Americans for Democratic Action, Americans for Constitutional Action, and similar ratings.[11] Though I know of no recent

Table 10.1   Members of Congress voting on liberal side of issues, by party, 1983

Kind of issue	House		Senate	
	Democratic (%)	Republican (%)	Democratic (%)	Republican (%)
Economic	85	8	93	7
Social	75	27	91	18
Foreign and military	82	9	85	7

Source: The Baron Report, May 7, 1984. Percentages computed by William Schneider.

comparison of congressional and public views on policy issues, it seems clear that Democratic representatives are much more likely to support school busing, affirmative action, and civil liberties than are Democratic voters, and Republican representatives are much more likely to support school prayer and oppose abortion than are Republican voters. In Congress, the party label has come to be more closely associated with ideological position than was the case when there were many more conservative Southern Democrats and liberal Eastern Republicans than there are today. Among the voting public, Democrats and Republicans differ, but to a far lesser degree.

From time to time, the extent to which the party elites are deeply and systematically opposed is papered over by particular circumstances. The 1984 conventions provided the outward signs of wide—indeed, nearly unanimous—support for the two presidential nominees. A popular Republican incumbent was renominated, but the ease of that convention victory reflected, I think, not only his popularity, but also the fact that his administration left no effective opening for an attack from the right and there is little realistic chance in today's Republican party for an attack from the left. A not-so-popular Democratic candidate won nomination after a strenuous primary campaign in which it seemed, for a while, that he might be vulnerable to a challenge from Gary Hart and the younger, nonideological Democrats he claimed to represent. But at the San Francisco convention, Mondale's actions indicated where *he* thought concessions had to be made, and they were not generally in the direction of the Hart (or the Ernest Hollings) forces. Mondale was able to lead a "unified" party largely by having made concessions to its left wing.

The largest concession was to the forces supporting Jesse Jackson. Allegedly in recognition of the fact that Jackson has supposedly "revitalized the Democratic party and broadened its base," a "Fairness Commission" was created to revise the party rules so as to assure the "full participation" of "Blacks, Hispanics, Asian/Pacifics, Native Americans, women, persons of all sexual preferences and other members of the Rainbow Coalition." In particular, the commission was instructed to "examine the question"—that is, presumably, to take steps toward instituting "assured percentages of various disadvantaged groups in the composition of state delegations by racial, ethnic, and other categories." These "assured percentages" would be similar to the "allocations" (i.e., quotas) now made on the basis of gender.[12] (Elsewhere in the report, the Rules Committee clarified what it meant by "disadvantaged groups." They include lesbians and gay men, persons over 65 years of age, persons with a high school education or less, the physically handicapped, persons with low and moderate incomes, and others.)

Another concession was the decision by the Rules Committee to "reduce the number of unpledged party and elected official delegates to not more than 5 percent of the total delegates." Officeholders with an interest in finding a winning candidate, rather than in simply serving as the bound representatives of particular candidates, were to be kept to a minimum.[13]

At the convention, two traditional mainstays of the Democratic party— Southerners and organized labor—received virtually no recognition. During the subsequent search for a vice-presidential candidate, Mondale gave further evidence of whom he believed required concessions: Of the seven candidates interviewed, three were women, two were blacks, one was Hispanic, and one was a white male senator. Only two of the seven were in Congress. By contrast, in 1976 Jimmy Carter, in choosing a running mate, gave serious consideration to six senators and one representative, all white males.

My colleague, Samuel Huntington, has called the creation of the Fairness Commission and the vice-presidential selection process examples of the growing tendency of the Democratic party to organize itself on the basis of the principle of "categorical representation."[14] Though all parties seek to incorporate representatives of the politically important components of their popular coalitions, the Democratic party, beginning with the McGovern–Fraser Commission report, has done more than incorporate such persons—it has gone a long way toward redefining the legitimacy of party participation so as to imply that participants who do not meet a specific demographic test are not legitimate representatives. The traditional basis of party representation had been the ability to win office by election or win power by controlling political resources. These bases have been downgraded and made subject to numerical constraints; demographic (or categorical) bases have been upgraded by numerical allocations. As a consequence, the Democratic party in the next four years—unless the Fairness Commission is somehow derailed or its purposes altered—will present to the voters in 1988 a face (and possibly a candidate) shaped by the issue preferences of persons active in those social movements identified with feminists, racial minorities, and the gay community.

There are, of course, still rival claimants to Democratic party leadership. As Morton K. Kondracke has noted, the "sub-parties" within the Democratic party include the Mondale-Kennedy-Cuomo group of liberals, the Hart wing (with which several Western governors are associated) that questions traditional liberal doctrine on domestic affairs, the Sam Nunn–Ernest Hollings group of conservative Southern Democrats, and the Jesse Jackson sub-party that has embraced what is essentially Third World radicalism.[15] Having lost so badly, one might expect the party activists to note how many electoral votes they need to get in the South and West if they are to win and, thus, to decide what candidate can attract support in these regions as well as in the Northeast. But if the creation of the Fairness Commission, the restriction on unpledged elected officials, and the selection of a woman vice-presidential candidate are reliable clues to the direction the party will in fact move, then the elite realignment that has been going on since 1972 will continue in the direction the Jackson wing has pointed. (Though perhaps the realignment won't be as extensive as the Jackson wing would like.)

Paul Kirk, the new chairman of the Democratic National Committee (who was elected after this chapter was largely written), gives every indication of being worried about what the Fairness Commission might do unless carefully restrained. He has tried to put on it people who will not use it to advance the interests of the various party caucuses and he has pressed it to act quickly on specific issues without completely revamping (again) the presidential nominating rules. But whether he can succeed in restraining the forces that increasingly constitute the guiding spirit of the party's elite remains to be seen. Already he has felt obliged to reaffirm his commitment to those affirmative-action rules that assure that various constituencies will be represented in party affairs in accordance with their numbers in the population.

The strains in the Republican party, though less evident today because for eight years it has had a winner, are even older than those in the Democratic party. Recall that McClosky discovered a cleavage between the Republican elites and the Republican rank-and-file in 1956 even though the party then held the White House. The victory of Dwight Eisenhower over Robert Taft may have been the last hurrah of the liberal eastern Republican establishment. The Taft supporters were overpowered by a national hero, but it was only a temporary setback. By the early 1960s conservative activists were determined to find a truly conservative nominee. That they managed to nominate Goldwater was a measure of their commitment and influence, because the candidate himself did not, until almost the last minute, really seek the presidency. In 1961 and 1962 when F. Clifton White and his associates were trying, behind the scenes, to deliver the Republican nomination to a Goldwater, one of their biggest problems was that Goldwater himself seemed unresponsive to their solicitations.[16] Goldwater's crushing defeat in the 1964 election paved the way for a more centrist candidate, Nixon, but by 1968 the next conservative candidate, Reagan, had already been identified and a twelve-year struggle for his nomination had begun. Only the resignation of President Nixon and the elevation to the presidency of an appointed vice-president, Gerald Ford, prevented Reagan from winning the nomination four years earlier than he did.

The Dallas convention in 1984 was, of course, wholly Reagan's to command. But it was quite evident from the platform deliberations that the battle over the party's future had begun. But unlike 1956 or 1960, it was not a fight between the liberal and conservative wings of the party, but rather a fight between two different strains of conservatism. One, represented by Jack Kemp, was a self-styled populist conservatism that combined a commitment to those tax cuts justified by supply-side economics with a strong position on those social issues advocated by the New Right. The other was what might be called business conservatism that wished to see the deficit reduced and investment encouraged but had little interest in, and much quiet aversion to, the school prayer and anti-abortion planks. The Kemp forces were clearly the more powerful of the two, dominating the platform deliberations.

Unlike the Democrats, the Republicans are not much given to changing party rules or revamping delegate selection procedures. They tend to operate each convention under rules very much like those in effect four years earlier, rules that give considerable freedom to the state parties to determine the character of their own delegations. But those rules give a substantial advantage to smaller, staunchly Republican states. For example, in 1984 Wyoming and Vermont each received one delegate for every 26,000 residents, while Pennsylvania and Ohio received one for every 121,000 residents. This means that the Republican convention tends to be dominated by delegates from states where conservative, New Right activists are influential and to underrepresent those states where liberal Republicans are influential. An effort by some liberal Republicans to create 1,076 new delegates to the 1988 convention, apportioned among the states on the basis of voter turnout (and thus to be given in large measure to the most populous states where liberal Republicans are strongest), was resoundingly defeated.[17]

The mechanisms by which ideological or issue-movement elites have been able to move the nominating conventions of each party further toward the Democratic left and the Republican right are generally well understood. The rise of direct primary elections and participatory caucuses has increased the influence of issue-oriented party identifiers at the expense of victory-oriented elected officials. Though all political observers recognize the great importance today of primary elections, we sometimes forget just how great the change in the nomination process has been. Recall how the world once worked by answering these questions: What do Robert Taft, Harold Stassen, Estes Kefauver, and Eugene McCarthy have in common? (Each won more primaries than their rivals, yet each was denied his party's nomination.) What do Adlai Stevenson and Hubert Humphrey have in common? (Each won his party's nomination without either being an incumbent president or winning a single primary.)

Primary elections are not the whole story. In 1964 conservatives won the Republican nomination for Goldwater, not by dominating the primary elections, but by enlisting the support of party activists meeting in precinct caucuses and county and state conventions. The caucus strategy of the Goldwater backers was a precursor of the same strategy of the McGovern supporters in 1972. Moreover, campaign finance laws have placed a premium on the ability of presidential candidates to attract large numbers of small donations, and this, in turn, has placed a premium on the development of a distinctive persona or ideology that large numbers of small donors will find so compelling as to lead them to write checks for $50 or $100 to candidate Smith rather than to (or in addition to) the Sierra Club, the National Rifle Association, the nuclear-freeze campaign, or the right-to-life movement.

More interesting than the mechanism by which polarized elites have come to exercise such influence in the presidential nomination process is the question of why political elites have become so polarized. Persons with a powerful interest in some issue or ideology—abolitionists and slaveholders, feminists and their rivals, free-traders and the backers of high tariffs—have always made claims on the political parties, and from time to time have helped win the nomination for a favored candidate. Today, such advocates are inside the party, planning its future, not outside demanding its change. Activity in an issue movement is now a major avenue of political recruitment. At the 1984 Democratic convention 60 percent of Walter Mondale's delegates came from three organizations—the AFL-CIO, the National Education Association, and National Organization of Women.[18] Congresswoman Barbara Milkuski described party leaders thus: "The issue movements are now our farm clubs."[19]

More effort has been devoted to studying the sources of mass realignments than elite realignments. In general, one party or the other comes to be supported by a new popular coalition as a result of either a seismic event or a programmatic conversion. The Civil War was a seismic event, fixing the partisanship of almost all the South as Democratic and that of much of the North as Republican for generations thereafter. The Great Depression was also a seismic event, but it was not the Depression itself that produced for the Democrats enduring party loyalties, but the programs of the New Deal that followed that event. I conjecture that a seismic event has an immediate effect on partisanship when it divides people over what *goals* the government should pursue (slavery or union, abortion or right-to-life). The Depression, though a traumatic experience, did not lead some people to favor depressions while others opposed them; rather, it led to a new administration coming to power (initially committed, it must be remembered, to programs—such as cutting federal expenditures—not too different from those of the administration it replaced). To deal with the Depression, this new administration then devised, often by trial and error, policies that attracted widespread popular support. Here, an electoral realignment occurred over the *means* used to deal with a common crisis.

Presumably, elite realignments occur in much the same way, the difference being that elite opinion is both more volatile than mass opinion and more sensitive to a wider range of issues. In contrast to the relative constancy of mass opinion regarding the economy, civil rights, or the quality of neighborhood life, elite opinion has embraced, within the last thirty years, a view of economic policy that has encompassed: a commitment first to economic regulation and later to selective deregulation; a belief in both the virtues of a balanced budget and those of Keynesian deficit finance; and an acceptance first of the claims of monetarists and then of those of supply-siders. With respect to civil rights, key elites first defined it as equality of opportunity (a "fair chance") and then as equality of result ("affirmative action"). And as far as social issues go, the transformation of opinion is startlingly clear with respect to one of them, street crime: To liberals, it was first a non-problem, then it became a real problem but one that could be solved by rehabilitation, and then one that required strengthening the criminal justice system (meanwhile, conservative elites were going through their own transformation, first claiming that crime was rising because the courts were handcuffing the police so they couldn't make any arrests, then arguing that the courts were being too lenient with the large numbers of persons the police were in fact arresting).

Foreign policy is a more complex matter, for on it both mass and elite opinion tend to be volatile, driven by events and circumstances. The public at large prefers to keep American troops at home, but is willing to support the president after they are committed; elite opinion tends to be divided between persons who favor using force and who have high hopes about the good that can thereby be achieved and those adamantly opposed to its use and skeptical that anything but evil will result from its employment. At one time, Democratic elites embraced the first view and Republican elites the second; now, the positions are very nearly reversed. But whereas public opinion rarely draws any clear and firm lessons from past military experiences, elite opinion draws such lessons in abundance (and often in error).

The differences between mass and elite opinion are probably the result, more than anything else, of the distribution of higher education. Apart from race, schooling seems to be the single variable most powerfully correlated with differences in policy preferences, the presence or absence of "constraint" (or ideology) in the makeup of those preferences, and the level of political participation.[20] This correlation may have always existed, or it may be the result of changes in recent decades in the content of higher education. In any event, what is distinctive about the present time is that persons with college and postgraduate degrees are far more numerous than ever before and far more deeply involved in party activity.

At the 1984 Democratic convention nearly *half* the delegates had a postgraduate degree (only 7 percent of Democratic voters had one). The gap was somewhat smaller at the Republican convention; there, 29 percent of the delegates had a postgraduate degree (10 percent of Republican voters had one).[21] Obviously, higher education alone cannot explain the polarization of party elites. After all, far more college graduates voted for Reagan than for Mondale, yet persons with a college degree made up a larger proportion of delegates to the Democratic than to the Republican convention. But whatever these other explanatory factors are, they probably work in conjunction with—or to amplify the effect of—higher education.

The greater the polarization of party elites,- the greater the likelihood of mass dealignment. When the activists control each party and select candidates that are ideologically acceptable to them, they are likely to select candidates that the average voter will find unappealing. In the aftermath of the sweeping Reagan victory of 1984, we may forget that during the 1972 and 1980 campaigns, people were regularly talking about casting a "clothespin vote" (i.e., putting a clothespin on your nose and choosing the lesser of two evils). In 1980 neither Carter nor Reagan was especially popular; in 1972 neither Nixon nor McGovern generated widespread enthusiasm. In 1984 very few people felt it necessary to wear a clothespin; the economy seemed to be in good shape and the president was free to emphasize traditional values in his campaign appearances and television advertisements, values that (when neither war nor recession intrudes on the voters' minds) will usually strike a deep and resonant chord. The 1976 election was, of course, not a contest between candidates representative of the activist wing of each party, but recall how they won the nomination: Jimmy Carter was able to win key early primaries by portraying himself as an "outsider" at a time when people were fed up with scandals in Washington, and Gerald Ford was elevated to the presidency after having been appointed vice-president by a president who was deliberately courting centrist Republican opinion in Congress in order to stave off impeachment.

Today, activists in both parties are preparing themselves for 1988. Since no one can predict the vagaries of the early primaries (Will Gary Hart repeat his New Hampshire victory? Will Jesse Jackson again split the liberal vote?), it would be a mistake to assume that in 1988, or in any given election, the realigned party elites will produce candidates who will prove so far from the preferences of the modal voter as to lead him or her to reach once again for the clothespin and tell the pollsters of his or her weakened partisanship. But the structure of the situation tends, in my view, to precisely that result over the long run.

In avoiding the risk of further mass dealignment, the Democrats face a more severe problem than the Republicans. The political arithmetic is against them. In the last seven presidential elections the Republicans have established an electoral base in four regions by winning states in those regions in at least five of the seven contests. These regions are:

South, 78 electoral votes: Alabama (9), Florida (21), Louisiana (10), Mississippi (7), South Carolina (8), Tennessee (11), Virginia (12)
Center, 21 electoral votes: Indiana (12), Kentucky (9)
New England, 11 electoral votes: Maine (4), New Hampshire (4), Vermont (3)
West, 138 electoral votes: Alaska (3), Arizona (7), California (47), Colorado (8), Idaho (4), Iowa (8), Kansas (7), Montana (4), Nebraska (5), Nevada (4), New Mexico (5), North Dakota (3), Oklahoma (8), Oregon (7), South Dakota (3), Utah (5), Washington (10)

Together, these four GOP regions supply the party with a reasonably firm base of 248 electoral votes. To win the additional 22 votes required to capture the presidency, the Republicans need only extend their base in one of these regions. The most obvious opportunity is in the South, where Arkansas (6), Georgia (12), North Carolina (13), and Texas (29) are available. Texas has been a decisive state for the Democrats; they have never won a presidential election in this century without carrying it. Yet the Republicans could concede Texas and still win the presidency, simply by picking up the rest of the Southern states. Even if they were to lose, say, Georgia, they could win by substituting a victory in Missouri. The belief that elections must be decided in the industrial Northeast is no longer true. The Republicans can concede most industrial states, as well as Hawaii, Minnesota, and Wisconsin and still win.

Given this electoral arithmetic, it is not enough for the Democrats to recapture their industrial base. They must take the fight to the Republicans in regions—the South and the West—where the Republicans have a historical advantage. The principal liability of the dominant Democratic party elites is that their kind of candidate does very poorly in the South and West. Humphrey, McGovern, and Mondale could not carry those areas; there is not much likelihood that Edward Kennedy could either. In the last twenty years, only Lyndon Johnson and Jimmy Carter, both Southerners and both roundly mistrusted by the liberal party activists, have done well in these areas. The major asset of the dominant Republican party elites is that their favored candidates, by exploiting a distrust of the federal government and reaffirming traditional values, are likely to have a strong appeal in these areas.

Though the Republicans have an advantage, they do not have an insuperable one. An economic downturn while the Republicans hold the White House would hurt badly. Even among born-again Christians in the South, there is a strong desire to see the federal government accept responsibility for economic growth and for maintaining the essentials of the welfare state.[22] The great majority of the voters believe the federal government should have a balanced budget, and a similar majority is opposed to achieving that balance by cuts in entitlement programs.

There is a tendency among those who write about politics to think that "new ideas" are the key to a party's future. That is rarely the case. Ideas are important in politics, but they tend to be elite ideas that influence, between elections, elite actions. Popular ideas change very slowly, are rooted in personal experience, and assign an important place to candidate character. The future of a party is determined by events (especially economic ones) and by the ability of a party's candidate to embody the core values on which the daily lives of most people are based. Gary Hart's "new ideas" won him few votes— indeed, few of his primary supporters could describe a single one of these ideas. Gary Hart's perceived position as a more moderate, less constrained alternative to Mondale won him a lot of votes. Jack Kemp's "new ideas" will probably not win him many votes, either. His success as a candidate—the success of almost anyone as a candidate—will depend on his ability to present himself as a person who is an economic and foreign policy moderate with few encumbering ties to "the mess in Washington," has a capacity for leadership, and is sensitive to traditional values.

Given the unpredictable nature of the early primaries and caucuses, it is not easy for a candidate who can win in November to win in March. It is especially difficult if the candidate with the right mix of qualities from the point of view of the general electorate starts so late or lacks the necessary national attention. To avoid ending up as just another also-ran in the primaries and caucuses, a candidate may have to pick a fight, two or three years before the nominating process begins, over the future of the party, so as to make it clear that he or she stands for a certain vision of what the party represents, a vision different from that of his or her principal rivals.

This may be especially necessary for the Democratic candidates, given the adverse political arithmetic they face. The Democratic candidate who can win in November, 1988 (when no incumbent will be running) will be the one who can crack the Republican political base in the South and the West. Acquiring a reputation as someone who can crack that base will not be achieved by simply traveling about, giving vague speeches. He or she will have to pick a fight with the liberal activists in the Democratic party elite, and with the social movements that supply those activists, so as to make it clear to the voters that he or she shares the latters' concerns—economic prosperity, fiscal prudence, protection of the environment, help for the deserving poor, financial security for the elderly, military strength, openness to arms control negotiations, and support for traditional values. Finding the particular phrases and issues with which to make vivid this stance is no easy matter; winning the nomination after picking a fight on these grounds would be even harder.

Appendices

Appendix A

Presidential election popular votes by state and region, 1980 and 1984

Region and state	1980 (percent)				
	Reagan	Carter	Anderson	Other	Turnout
Nation	50.8	41.0	6.6	1.6	52.6
Total vote	43,899,248	35,481,435	5,719,437	1,395,558	86,459,678
New England					
Connecticut	48.2	38.5	12.2	1.1	60.6
Maine	45.6	42.3	10.2	2.0	66.1
Massachusetts	41.8	41.7	15.2	1.3	58.8
New Hampshire	57.7	28.4	12.9	0.9	58.8
Rhode Island	37.2	47.7	14.4	0.7	60.5
Vermont	44.4	38.4	14.9	1.3	59.8
Total vote	2,443,081	2,205,666	748,946	69,498	5,467,191
Percent	44.7	40.3	13.7	1.3	60.1
Middle Atlantic					
Delaware	47.2	44.9	6.9	1.0	55.9
District of Columbia	13.4	74.9	9.3	2.4	35.4
Maryland	44.2	47.1	7.8	0.9	50.7
New Jersey	52.0	38.6	7.9	1.6	55.3
New York	46.7	44.0	7.5	1.8	48.0
Pennsylvania	49.6	42.5	6.4	1.5	52.6
Total vote	7,517,431	6,775,422	1,147,310	249,089	15,689,252
Percent	47.9	43.2	7.3	1.6	50.7

	1984 (percent)			Change, 1980–84 (percentage points)		
Reagan	Mondale	Other	Turnout	Republican	Democratic	Turnout
58.8	40.6	0.6	53.3	8.0	−0.4	0.7
54,455,074	37,577,137	620,582	92,652,793	—	—	—
60.7	38.8	0.4	61.0	12.5	0.3	0.4
60.8	38.8	0.4	65.2	15.2	−3.5	−0.9
51.2	48.4	0.4	57.9	9.4	6.7	−0.9
68.7	30.9	0.4	53.9	11.0	2.5	−4.9
51.8	47.9	0.3	56.0	14.6	0.2	−4.5
57.9	40.8	1.3	60.0	13.5	2.4	0.2
3,153,308	2,436,901	23,358	5,613,567	—	—	—
56.2	43.4	0.4	59.0	11.5	3.1	−1.1
59.8	39.9	0.3	55.7	12.6	−5.0	−0.2
13.7	85.4	0.9	43.8	0.3	10.5	8.4
52.5	47.0	0.5	51.4	8.3	−0.1	0.7
60.1	39.2	0.7	56.9	8.1	0.6	1.6
53.8	45.8	0.4	51.1	7.1	1.8	3.1
53.3	46.0	0.7	53.9	3.7	3.5	1.3
9,243,833	7,679,062	88,413	17,011,308	—	—	—
54.3	45.1	0.6	52.9	6.4	1.9	2.2

Presidential election popular votes by state and region, 1980 and 1984 (*Continued*)

Region and state	1980 (percent)				
	Reagan	Carter	Anderson	Other	Turnout
Deep South					
Alabama	48.8	47.4	1.2	2.6	49.9
Arkansas	48.1	47.5	2.7	1.7	53.5
Georgia	41.0	55.8	2.3	1.0	44.1
Louisiana	51.2	45.7	1.7	1.3	55.8
Mississippi	49.4	48.1	1.3	1.1	54.2
South Carolina	49.5	48.2	1.6	0.7	43.1
Total vote	3,384,743	3,491,458	127,253	102,109	7,105,563
Percent	47.6	49.1	1.8	1.4	49.5
Outer South					
Florida	55.5	38.5	5.1	0.8	54.2
North Carolina	49.3	47.2	2.8	0.6	45.8
Tennessee	48.7	48.4	2.2	0.6	50.8
Texas	55.3	41.4	2.5	0.8	47.7
Virginia	53.0	40.3	5.1	1.6	48.8
Total vote	7,250,044	5,711,482	485,514	121,004	13,568,044
Percent	53.4	42.1	3.6	0.9	49.5
Border					
Kentucky	49.0	47.7	2.4	0.9	51.4
Missouri	51.2	44.3	3.7	0.8	58.8
Oklahoma	60.5	35.0	3.3	1.2	54.4
West Virginia	45.3	49.8	4.3	0.6	54.5
Total vote	2,739,231	2,318,087	179,022	46,534	5,282,874
Percent	51.9	43.9	3.4	0.9	55.3
Great Lakes					
Illinois	49.6	41.7	7.3	1.3	58.9
Indiana	56.0	37.7	5.0	1.4	58.1
Michigan	49.0	42.5	7.0	1.5	59.7
Ohio	51.5	40.9	5.9	1.6	55.5
Wisconsin	47.9	43.2	7.1	1.9	66.2
Total vote	8,824,365	7,221,140	1,148,745	264,098	17,458,348
Percent	50.5	41.4	6.6	1.5	58.9

1984 (percent)				Change, 1980–84 (percentage points)		
Reagan	Mondale	Other	Turnout	Republican	Democratic	Turnout
60.5	38.3	1.2	52.2	12.4	−9.2	−1.3
60.5	38.3	1.2	52.2	12.4	−9.2	−1.3
60.2	39.8	—	42.2	19.2	−16.0	−1.9
60.8	38.2	1.0	54.2	9.6	−7.5	−1.6
61.9	37.4	0.6	52.0	12.5	−10.7	−2.2
63.6	35.6	0.9	40.6	14.1	−12.6	−2.5
4,711,560	2,945,410	61,724	7,718,694	—	—	—
61.0	38.2	0.8	47.9	13.4	−10.9	−1.6
65.3	34.7	—	49.0	9.8	−3.8	−5.2
61.9	37.9	0.2	47.7	12.6	−9.3	1.9
57.8	41.6	0.6	49.3	9.1	−6.8	−1.5
63.6	36.1	0.3	47.0	8.3	−5.3	−0.7
62.3	37.1	0.6	51.1	9.3	−3.2	2.3
9,837,459	5,730,343	43,720	15,611,522	—	—	—
63.0	36.7	0.2	48.4	9.6	−5.4	−1.1
60.0	39.4	0.6	50.7	11.0	−8.3	−0.7
60.0	40.0	—	57.7	8.8	−4.3	−1.1
68.6	30.7	0.7	51.2	8.1	−4.3	−3.2
55.1	44.6	0.3	51.3	9.8	−5.2	−3.2
3,362,903	2,101,327	19,316	5,483,546	—	—	—
61.3	38.3	0.4	53.4	9.4	−5.6	−1.9
56.2	43.3	0.5	57.3	6.6	1.6	−1.6
61.7	37.7	0.6	56.3	5.7	—	−1.8
59.2	40.2	0.6	58.2	10.2	−2.3	−1.5
58.9	40.1	1.0	59.1	7.4	−0.8	2.5
54.2	45.0	0.8	63.4	6.3	1.8	−2.8
10,303,048	7,278,798	121,277	17,703,123	—	—	—
58.2	41.1	0.7	58.5	7.7	−0.3	−0.4

Presidential election popular votes by state and region, 1980 and 1984 (*Continued*)

Region and state	1980 (percent)				
	Reagan	Carter	Anderson	Other	Turnout
Farm Belt					
Iowa	51.3	38.6	8.8	1.3	62.6
Kansas	57.9	33.3	7.0	1.9	55.9
Minnesota	42.7	46.6	8.6	2.1	69.4
Nebraska	65.6	26.0	7.0	1.4	56.2
North Dakota	64.2	26.3	7.8	1.6	64.3
South Dakota	60.5	31.7	6.5	1.3	67.1
Total vote	2,927,358	2,138,463	448,786	97,410	5,612,017
Percent	52.2	38.1	8.0	1.8	63.1
Mountain					
Arizona	60.6	28.2	8.8	2.3	49.8
Colorado	55.1	31.1	11.0	2.9	58.3
Idaho	66.5	25.2	6.2	2.1	69.5
Montana	56.8	32.4	8.0	2.7	64.7
Nevada	63.6	27.4	7.2	1.8	47.0
New Mexico	55.0	36.8	6.5	1.8	53.1
Utah	72.8	20.6	5.0	1.7	67.9
Wyoming	62.6	28.0	6.8	2.6	54.2
Total vote	2,635,648	1,251,261	353,390	100,273	4,340,572
Percent	60.7	28.8	8.1	2.3	57.3
Pacific					
Alaska	54.6	26.6	7.1	11.7	60.0
California	52.7	35.9	8.6	2.8	50.9
Hawaii	42.9	44.8	10.6	1.8	46.5
Oregon	48.3	38.7	9.5	3.5	62.7
Washington	49.7	37.3	10.6	2.4	59.6
Total vote	6,177,347	4,368,456	1,080,471	345,543	11,971,817
Percent	51.6	36.5	9.0	2.9	53.0

Source: Official state returns, *Congressional Quarterly Weekly Report* (April 13, 1985): 687–95. Regional aggregates and percentages calculated by William Schneider.

1984 (percent)				Change, 1980–84 (percentage points)		
Reagan	Mondale	Other	Turnout	Republican	Democratic	Turnout
53.3	45.9	0.8	62.3	2.0	7.3	−0.3
66.3	32.6	1.1	57.0	8.4	−0.7	1.1
49.5	49.7	0.8	68.5	6.8	3.1	−0.9
70.6	28.8	0.6	56.1	5.0	2.8	−0.1
64.8	33.8	1.4	62.9	0.6	7.5	−1.4
63.0	36.5	0.5	63.8	2.5	4.8	−3.3
3,273,644	2,383,541	47,988	5,705,173	—	—	—
57.4	41.8	0.8	62.6	5.2	3.7	−0.5
66.4	32.5	1.1	46.6	5.8	4.3	−3.2
63.4	35.1	1.5	54.8	8.3	4.0	−3.5
72.4	26.4	1.2	60.4	5.9	1.2	−9.1
60.5	38.2	1.3	65.0	3.7	5.8	0.3
65.8	32.0	2.2	41.6	2.2	4.6	−5.4
59.7	39.2	1.1	51.6	4.7	2.4	−1.5
74.5	24.7	0.8	60.5	1.7	4.1	−7.4
70.5	28.2	1.3	51.8	7.9	0.2	−2.4
3,131,423	1,546,244	58,792	4,736,459	—	—	—
66.1	32.6	1.3	53.1	5.4	3.8	−4.2
66.7	29.9	3.4	60.2	12.1	3.3	0.2
57.5	41.3	1.2	50.0	4.8	5.4	−0.9
55.1	43.8	1.1	44.5	12.2	−1.0	−2.0
55.9	43.7	0.4	62.5	7.6	5.0	−0.2
55.8	42.9	1.3	58.8	6.1	5.6	−0.8
7,527,806	5,475,511	155,994	13,159,311	—	—	—
57.2	41.6	1.2	52.0	5.6	5.1	−1.0

Appendix B

Electoral votes for president by state and region, 1980 and 1984

Region and state	1980 Republican	1980 Democratic	1984 Republican	1984 Democratic	Change, 1980–84 Democratic to Republican	Change, 1980–84 Stayed Republican	Change, 1980–84 Stayed Democratic
Nation	489	49	525	13	36	489	13
New England							
Conn.	8	—	8	—	—	8	—
Maine	4	—	4	—	—	4	—
Mass.	14	—	13	—	—	13	—
N.H.	4	—	4	—	—	4	—
R.I.	—	4	4	—	4	—	—
Vt.	3	—	3	—	—	3	—
Total	33	4	36	0	4	32	0
Middle Atlantic							
Del.	3	—	3	—	—	3	—
D.C.	—	3	—	3	—	—	3
Md.	—	10	10	—	10	—	—
N.J.	17	—	16	—	—	16	—
N.Y.	41	—	36	—	—	36	—
Pa.	27	—	25	—	—	25	—
Total	88	13	90	3	10	80	3
Deep South							
Ala.	9	—	9	—	—	9	—
Ark.	6	—	6	—	—	6	—
Ga.	—	12	12	—	12	—	—
La.	10	—	10	—	—	10	—
Miss.	7	—	7	—	—	7	—
S.C.	8	—	8	—	—	8	—
Total	40	12	52	0	12	40	0
Outer South							
Fla.	17	—	21	—	—	21	—
N.C.	13	—	13	—	—	13	—
Tenn.	10	—	11	—	—	11	—
Tex.	26	—	29	—	—	29	—
Va.	12	—	12	—	—	12	—
Total	78	0	86	0	0	86	0

Region and state	1980		1984		Change, 1980–84		
	Republican	Democratic	Republican	Democratic	Democratic to Republican	Stayed Republican	Stayed Democratic
Border							
Ky.	9	—	9	—	—	9	—
Mo.	12	—	11	—	—	11	—
Okla.	8	—	8	—	—	8	—
W.Va.	—	6	6	—	6	—	—
Total	29	6	34	0	6	28	0
Great Lakes							
Ill.	26	—	24	—	—	24	—
Ind.	13	—	12	—	—	12	—
Mich.	21	—	20	—	—	20	—
Ohio	25	—	23	—	—	23	—
Wis.	11	—	11	—	—	11	—
Total	96	0	90	0	0	90	0
Farm Belt							
Iowa	8	—	8	—	—	8	—
Kans.	7	—	7	—	—	7	—
Minn.	—	10	—	10	—	—	10
Neb.	5	—	5	—	—	5	—
N. Dak.	3	—	3	—	—	3	—
S. Dak.	4	—	3	—	—	3	—
Total	27	10	26	10	0	26	10
Mountain							
Ariz.	6	—	7	—	—	7	—
Colo.	7	—	8	—	—	8	—
Idaho	4	—	4	—	—	4	—
Mont.	4	—	4	—	—	4	—
Nev.	3	—	4	—	—	4	—
N. Mex.	4	—	5	—	—	5	—
Utah	4	—	5	—	—	5	—
Wyo.	3	—	3	—	—	3	—
Total	35	0	40	0	0	40	0

| | 1980 | | 1984 | | Change, 1980–84 | | |
Region and state	Repub-lican	Demo-cratic	Repub-lican	Demo-cratic	Demo-cratic to Repub-lican	Stayed Repub-lican	Stayed Demo-cratic
Pacific							
Alaska	3	—	3	—	—	3	—
Calif.	45	—	47	—·	—	47	—
Hawaii	—	4	4	—	4	—	—
Oreg.	6	—	7	—	—	7	—
Wash.	9	—	10	—	—	10	—
Total	63	4	71	0	4	67	0

Source: Same as for Appendix A.

Appendix C

Presidential "landslide" elections, 1868–1984

Measured by the winner's share of all popular votes cast

1. 1964: Lyndon B. Johnson, 61.05
2. 1936: Franklin D. Roosevelt, 60.79
3. 1972: Richard M. Nixon, 60.69
4. 1920: Warren G. Harding, 60.30
5. 1984: Ronald W. Reagan, 58.77

Measured by difference between winner's and loser's shares of all popular votes

1. 1920: Warren G. Harding 60.30, James M. Cox, 34.17, difference 26.13
2. 1924: Calvin Coolidge 54.06, John W. Davis, 28.84, difference 25.22
3. 1936: Franklin D. Roosevelt 60.79, Alfred M. Landon, 36.54, difference 24.25
4. 1972: Richard M. Nixon 60.69, George McGovern 37.53, difference 23.16
5. 1964: Lyndon B. Johnson 61.05, Barry M. Goldwater 38.47, difference 22.58
6. 1904: Theodore Roosevelt 56.41, Alton B. Parker 37.60, difference 18.81
7. 1984: Ronald W. Reagan 58.77, Walter F. Mondale 40.56, difference 18.21

Measured by states carried and percent of electoral votes

1. 1936: Franklin D. Roosevelt carried 46 of 48 states and 98.5 percent of electoral votes
2. 1984: Ronald W. Reagan carried 49 of 51 states and 97.6 percent of electoral votes
3. 1972: Richard M. Nixon carried 49 of 51 states and 96.6 percent of electoral votes

Sources: The figures for 1868–1972 are taken from Congressional Quarterly, *Guide to U.S. Elections* (Washington, D.C.: Congressional Quarterly, 1975), p. 273–99. The figures for 1976 and 1980 are taken from Richard M. Scammon, ed., *America Votes* (Washington, D.C.: Congressional Quarterly, 1982), 17, 19. The figures for 1984 are taken from appendix A and appendix B of this volume.

Appendix D

Table D.1 Presidential primary election results and turnout by state, 1984

Primary and date	Aggregate turnout	Democrats				
		Askew[a] (%)	Cranston[b] (%)	Glenn[c] (%)	Hart (%)	Hollings[d] (%)
New Hampshire (2/28)	101,131	1.0	2.1	11.9	37.3	3.6
Vermont (3/6)	74,059	0.6	—	—	70.0	—
Alabama (3/13)	428,283	0.4	0.3	20.8	20.7	1.1
Florida (3/13)	1,182,190	2.2	0.2	10.8	39.2	0.3
Georgia (3/13)	684,541	0.3	0.1	17.9	27.3	0.6
Massachusetts (3/13)	630,962	0.2	0.1	7.2	39.0	0.2
Rhode Island (3/13)	44,511	0.2	0.6	5.1	45.0	0.2
Puerto Rico (3/18)	143,039	—	—	—	0.6	—
Illinois (3/20)	1,659,425	0.1	0.2	1.2	35.3	—
Connecticut (3/27)	220,842	2.8	0.1	0.4	52.7	1.0
New York (4/3)	1,387,950	0.2	0.5	1.1	27.4	—
Wisconsin (4/3)	635,768	0.1	0.5	1.0	44.4	0.3
Pennsylvania (4/10)	1,656,294	0.3	1.4	1.4	33.4	0.2
Dist. of Columbia (5/1)	102,731	—	—	—	7.1	—

Jackson (%)	McGovern[e] (%)	Mondale (%)	Other (%)	Republicans			Total turnout both parties[f] (%)
				Aggregate turnout	Reagan (%)	Other (%)	
5.3	5.2	27.8	5.8	75,570	86.1	13.9	24.5
7.8	—	20.0	1.6	33,643	98.7	1.3	27.5
19.6	—	34.6	2.5	—	—	—	g
12.2	1.5	33.4	0.2	344,150	100	—	17.9
21.0	1.6	30.5	0.7	50,793	100	—	17.5
5.0	21.4	25.5	1.4	65,937	89.5	10.5	15.8
8.7	4.8	34.4	1.0	2,235	90.7	9.3	6.4
—	—	99.1	0.3	—	—	—	g
21.0	1.5	40.4	0.3	595,078	99.9	0.1	26.8
11.9	1.1	29.1	0.9	—	—	—	g
25.7	0.3	44.8	—	—	—	—	g
9.8	1.6	41.1	1.2	294,813	95.2	4.8	26.7
16.0	0.8	44.8	1.7	621,206	99.3	0.7	25.3
67.3	—	25.6	—	5,692	100	—	22.5

Table D.1   *(continued)*

Primary and date	Aggregate turnout	Askew[a] (%)	Cranston[b] (%)	Glenn[c] (%)	Hart (%)	Hollings[d] (%)
			Democrats			
Tennessee (5/1)	322,063	—	—	1.3	29.1	—
Louisiana (5/5)	318,810	—	—	—	25.0	—
Texas (5/5)	—	—	—	—	—	—
Indiana (5/8)	716,955	—	—	2.2	41.8	—
Maryland (5/8)	506,886	—	0.3	1.2	24.3	0.3
North Carolina (5/8)	960,857	0.3	0.1	1.8	30.2	0.9
Ohio (5/8)	1,447,236	—	0.3	—	42.1	—
Nebraska (5/15)	148,855	—	0.1	—	58.3	0.1
Oregon (5/15)	397,892	—	—	2.7	58.8	—
Idaho (5/22)	54,722	—	—	—	58.0	—
California[h] (6/5)	2,869,155	—	—	2.2	38.4	—
Montana (6/5)	28,385	—	—	—	—	—
New Jersey (6/5)	676,561	—	—	—	29.7	—
New Mexico (6/5)	187,403	—	—	—	46.8	—
South Dakota (6/5)	52,561	—	—	—	50.7	—
West Virginia (6/5)	369,245	—	—	—	37.3	—

Jackson (%)	McGovern[e] (%)	Mondale (%)	Other (%)	Republicans Aggregate turnout	Reagan (%)	Other (%)	Total turnout both parties[f] (%)
25.3	1.2	41.0	2.1	82,921	90.9	9.1	11.6
42.9	1.0	22.3	8.8	16,687	90.0	10.0	10.7
—	—	—	—	319,839	96.5	3.5	g
13.7	—	40.9	1.4	428,559	100	—	28.9
25.6	1.1	42.5	4.7	73,663	100	—	17.8
25.4	1.1	35.6	4.6	—	—	—	g
16.4	0.6	40.3	0.3	658,169	100	—	26.8
9.1	1.1	26.7	4.6	146,648	99.0	1.0	25.4
9.3	—	27.7	1.5	238,594	100	—	32.5
5.7	—	30.0	6.3	105,687	92.2	7.8	23.6
20.8	1.7	35.4	1.5	1,874,897	100	—	24.9
—	—	—	100	71,810	92.5	7.5	16.9
23.6	—	45.2	1.5	240,054	100	—	16.2
11.8	2.7	36.1	2.6	42,994	94.9	5.1	23.1
5.2	—	39.0	5.1	—	—	—	g
6.7	—	53.8	2.2	136,996	91.8	8.2	35.3

Table D.1   *(continued)*

Primary and date	Democrats					
	Aggregate turnout	Askew[a] (%)	Cranston[b] (%)	Glenn[c] (%)	Hart (%)	Hollings[d] (%)
North Dakota (6/12)	33,555	—	—	—	85.2	—
Totals	18,071,252	0.3	0.3	3.2	36.0	0.2

Source: Elections Research Center.

[a] Askew withdrew on March 1.

[b] Cranston withdrew on February 29.

[c] Glenn withdrew on March 16.

[d] Hollings withdrew on March 1.

[e] McGovern withdrew on March 14.

[f] Calculated by dividing the total number of votes cast in both parties' primaries by the estimated voting-age population in each state.

[g] Not calculated because only one party held a primary.

[h] California Democrats had no direct presidential preference vote; Democratic voters voted for from 4 to 10 delegates each, with the average number voted for being 6. The figures in the table represent the percentages of the votes cast for delegates pledged to each candidate, and the (admittedly arbitrary) turnout figure is the total number of votes for all delegates divided by 6.

| Jackson (%) | McGovern[e] (%) | Mondale (%) | Other (%) | Republicans | | | Total turnout both parties[f] (%) |
				Aggregate turnout	Reagan (%)	Other (%)	
—	—	2.8	12.0	44,109	100	—	15.8
18.6	1.7	37.8	1.9	6,570,744	98.7	1.3	—

Table D.2 Primary results and turnout by region, system and phase, 1984

| | Democrats | | | | | |
	Aggregate turnout	Askew (%)	Cranston (%)	Glenn (%)	Hart (%)	Hollings (%)
By region						
East	5,771,172	0.3	0.6	1.8	32.5	0.2
South	3,896,744	0.8	0.1	9.3	30.9	0.5
Midwest	4,694,355	0.2	0.1	0.9	40.8	0.1
West	3,565,942	—	—	2.1	41.1	—
By system						
Closed	10,789,954	0.4	0.3	3.3	35.1	0.2
Open	7,138,259	0.1	0.2	3.2	37.6	0.2
First (2/28–3/13)	3,145,677	1.0	0.2	12.7	34.8	0.5
Second (3/20–5/8)	9,935,817	0.2	0.1	1.1	34.5	0.3
Third (5/15–6/12)	4,846,719	0	a	1.5	40.2	a

Source: The Elections Research Center.

[a]Less than 0.1 percent

Jackson (%)	McGovern (%)	Mondale (%)	Other (%)	Republicans		
				Aggregate turnout	Reagan (%)	Other (%)
18.6	2.9	41.6	1.5	1,254,996	97.3	2.7
21.4	1.2	33.3	2.5	814,390	98.1	1.9
16.3	1.0	39.8	0.8	2,167,376	99.3	0.7
18.7	1.5	34.2	2.4	2,333,982	98.5	1.5
20.0	1.0	37.8	1.9	3,821,366	99.2	0.8
16.6	2.8	37.9	1.4	2,749,378	98.0	2.0
13.4	5.4	30.9	1.1	572,328	96.8	3.2
20.7	0.9	40.6	1.6	3,096,627	98.7	1.3
17.9	1.2	36.8	2.4	2,901,789	99.0	1.0

Appendix E

State systems for choosing national convention delegates, 1968–84

State, district, or territory	1968	1972	1976	1980	1984
Alabama	DP	DP	OP	OP	CPI
Alaska	CC	CC	CC	CC	CC
Arizona	(D)CO (R)CC	CC	CC	CC	CC
Arkansas	CO	CC	OP	(D)OP (R)CC	CC
California	CP	CP	CP	CP	CP
Colorado	CC	CC	CC	CC	CC
Connecticut	CC	CC	CC	CP	(D)CP (R)CC
Delaware	CC	CC	CC	CC	CC
District of Columbia	CP	CP	CP	CP	CP
Florida	CP	CP	CP	CP	CP
Georgia	(D)CO (R)CC	CC	OP	OP	CPI
Hawaii	CC	CC	CC	CC	CC
Idaho	CC	CC	OP	(D)CC (R)OP	D ;CPI
Illinois	DP,CC	CP	OP	OP	DP
Indiana	OP	OP	OP	OP	CPI
Iowa	CC	CC	CC	CC	CC
Kansas	CC	CC	CC	CPI	CC
Kentucky	CC	CC	CP	CP	CC
Louisiana	CO	CC	CC	CP	CP
Maine	CC	CC	CC	CC	CC
Maryland	(D)CO (R)CC	CP	CP	CP	DP
Massachusetts	CPI	CPI	CPI	CPI	CPI
Michigan	CC	OP	OP	(D)CC (R)OP	CC

State systems for choosing national convention delegates (*Continued*)

State, district, or territory	1968	1972	1976	1980	1984
Minnesota	CC	CC	CC	CC	CC
Mississippi	CC	CC	CC	(D)CC (R)DP	CC
Missouri	(D)CC,CO (R)CC	CC	CC	CC	CC
Montana	CC	CC	OP	OP	DP
Nebraska	OP	OP	OP	OP	CP
Nevada	CC	CC	CP	CP	CC
New Hampshire	CPI	CPI	CPI	CPI	CPI
New Jersey	CPI	CPI	CPI	CPI	DP
New Mexico	CC	CP	CC	CP	CP
New York	DP,CO	DP,CO	DP	(D)CP (R)DP	DP
North Carolina	CC	CP	CP	CP	CP
North Dakota	CC	CC	CC	CC	DP
Ohio	OP	OP	OP	OP	CPI
Oklahoma	CC	CC	CC	CC	CC
Oregon	CP	CP	CP	CP	CP
Pennsylvania	CP,CO	CP	CP	CP	DP
Rhode Island	(D)CO (R)CC	CPI	CPI	CPI	CPI
South Carolina	CC	CC	CC	(D)CC (R)OP	CC
South Dakota	CP	CP	CP	CP	CP
Tennessee	CC	OP	OP	OP	CPI
Texas	CC	CC	OP	CP	(D)CC (R)OP
Utah	CC	CC	CC	CC	CC
Vermont	CC	CC	X	X	X
Virginia	CC	CC	CC	CC	CC
Washington	(D)CC,CO (R)CC	CC CP	CC CP	CC CP	CC
West Virginia	CP	CP	CP	CP	CP

State systems for choosing national convention delegates (*Continued*)

State, district, or territory	1968	1972	1976	1980	1984
Wisconsin	OP	OP	OP	OP	(D)X (R)OP
Wyoming	CC	CC	CC	CC	CC
(Puerto Rico)	(D)C	CC	CC	OP	(D)CPI (R)CC

Sources: The information for 1968–1980 is taken from *The American Elections of 1980*, ed. Austin Ranney (Washington, D.C.: American Enterprise Institute, 1981), Appendix D, pp. 366–368. The information for 1984 is taken from releases issued by the Democratic National Committee and the Republican National Committee.

Notes: CC = Delegates chosen by state and local caucuses and conventions. CO = delegates chosen by state party committee. CP = delegates chosen or bound by presidential preference primaries open only to voters preregistered as members of the particular parties. CPI = delegates chosen or bound by presidential preference primaries open only to voters preregistered as members of the particular parties or as independents. D = Democrats. DP = delegates chosen directly by voters in primaries; no binding presidential preference poll. OP = delegates chosen or bound by presidential preference primaries open to all registered voters without regard to party preregistration. R = Republicans. X = Have nonbinding presidential preference primaries, but delegates are chosen by party caucuses and conventions.

Appendix F

Status of presidential primaries, 1968–84

Party and coverage	1968	1972	1976	1980	1984
Democratic party					
Number of states using a primary for selecting or binding national convention delegates	17	23	29[a]	31[a]	30[a]
Number of votes cast by delegates chosen or bound by primaries	983	1,862	2,183	2,489	2,091
Percentage of all votes cast by delegates chosen or bound by primaries	37.5	60.5	72.6	74.7	53.2
Republican party					
Number of states using a primary for selecting or binding national convention delegates	16	22	28[a]	35[a]	25[b]
Number of votes cast by delegates chosen or bound by primaries	458	710	1,533	1,482	1,369
Percentage of all votes cast by delegates chosen or bound by primaries	34.3	52.7	67.9	74.3	61.3

Source: The figures for 1968, 1972, 1976, and 1980 come from Austin Ranney, ed., *The American Elections of 1980* (Washington, D.C.: American Enterprise Institute, 1981), appendix E, 369. The figures for 1984 were compiled by Austin Ranney from materials distributed by the Democratic National Committee and the Republican National Committee.

[a] Does not include Vermont and Wisconsin, which held nonbinding presidential-preference polls but chose all delegates of both parties by caucuses and conventions.

[b] Does not include Vermont.

Appendix G

Table G.1 Senate outcomes by state and region, 1984

	Party lineup before election		Number of incumbents retired		Number of incumbents lost in primaries		Number of incumbents lost in election		Party lineup after election		Net gain	
	D	R	D	R	D	R	D	R	D	R	D	R
Nation	45	55	2	2	0	0	1	2	47	53	3	1
New England												
Conn.	1	1	0	0	0	0	0	0	1	1	0	0
Maine	1	1	0	0	0	0	0	0	1	1	0	0
Mass.	2	0	1	0	0	0	0	0	2	0	0	0
N.H.	0	2	0	0	0	0	0	0	0	2	0	0
R.I.	1	1	0	0	0	0	0	0	1	1	0	0
Vt.	1	1	0	0	0	0	0	0	1	1	0	0
Total	6	6	1	0	0	0	0	0	6	6	0	0
Mid-Atlantic												
Del.	1	1	0	0	0	0	0	0	1	1	0	0
Md.	1	1	0	0	0	0	0	0	1	1	0	0
N.J.	2	0	0	0	0	0	0	0	2	0	0	0
N.Y.	1	1	0	0	0	0	0	0	1	1	0	0
Pa.	0	2	0	0	0	0	0	0	0	2	0	0
Total	5	5	0	0	0	0	0	0	5	5	0	0
Great Lakes												
Ill.	1	1	0	0	0	0	0	1	2	0	1	0
Ind.	0	2	0	0	0	0	0	0	0	2	0	0
Mich.	2	0	0	0	0	0	0	0	2	0	0	0
Ohio	2	0	0	0	0	0	0	0	2	0	0	0
Wis.	1	1	0	0	0	0	0	0	1	1	0	0
Total	6	4	0	0	0	0	0	1	7	3	1	0
Farm Belt												
Iowa	0	2	0	0	0	0	0	1	1	1	1	0
Kans.	0	2	0	0	0	0	0	0	0	2	0	0
Minn.	0	2	0	0	0	0	0	0	0	2	0	0
Nebr.	2	0	0	0	0	0	0	0	2	0	0	0
N. Dak.	1	1	0	0	0	0	0	0	1	1	0	0
S. Dak.	0	2	0	0	0	0	0	0	0	2	0	0
Total	3	9	0	0	0	0	0	1	4	8	1	0

Table G.1 (*continued*)

	Party lineup before election		Number of incumbents retired		Number of incumbents lost in primaries		Number of incumbents lost in election		Party lineup after election		Net gain	
	D	R	D	R	D	R	D	R	D	R	D	R
Deep South												
Ala.	1	1	0	0	0	0	0	0	1	1	0	0
Ark.	2	0	0	0	0	0	0	0	2	0	0	0
Ga.	1	1	0	0	0	0	0	0	1	1	0	0
La.	2	0	0	0	0	0	0	0	2	0	0	0
Miss.	1	1	0	0	0	0	0	0	1	1	0	0
S.C.	1	1	0	0	0	0	0	0	1	1	0	0
Total	8	4	0	0	0	0	0	0	8	4	0	0
Outer South												
Fla.	1	1	0	0	0	0	0	0	1	1	0	0
N.C.	0	2	0	0	0	0	0	0	0	2	0	0
Tenn.	1	1	0	1	0	0	0	0	2	0	1	0
Tex.	1	1	0	1	0	0	0	0	1	1	0	0
Va.	0	2	0	0	0	0	0	0	0	2	0	0
Total	3	7	0	2	0	0	0	0	4	6	1	0
Border												
Ky.	2	0	0	0	0	0	1	0	1	1	0	1
Mo.	1	1	0	0	0	0	0	0	1	1	0	0
Okla.	1	1	0	0	0	0	0	0	1	1	0	0
W. Va.	2	0	1	0	0	0	0	0	2	0	0	0
Total	6	2	1	0	0	0	1	0	5	3	0	1
Mountain												
Ariz.	1	1	0	0	0	0	0	0	1	1	0	0
Colo.	1	1	0	0	0	0	0	0	1	1	0	0
Idaho	0	2	0	0	0	0	0	0	0	2	0	0
Mont.	2	0	0	0	0	0	0	0	2	0	0	0
Nev.	0	2	0	0	0	0	0	0	0	2	0	0
N. Mex.	1	1	0	0	0	0	0	0	1	1	0	0
Utah	0	2	0	0	0	0	0	0	0	2	0	0
Wyo.	0	2	0	0	0	0	0	0	0	2	0	0
Total	5	11	0	0	0	0	0	0	5	11	0	0
Pacific												
Alaska	0	2	0	0	0	0	0	0	0	2	0	0
Calif.	1	1	0	0	0	0	0	0	1	1	0	0
Hawaii	2	0	0	0	0	0	0	0	2	0	0	0
Oreg.	0	2	0	0	0	0	0	0	0	2	0	0
Wash.	0	2	0	0	0	0	0	0	0	2	0	0
Total	3	7	0	0	0	0	0	0	3	7	0	0

Sources: Congressional Directory, 98th Congress (Washington, D.C.: United States Government Printing Office, 1983), 213–22. *Congressional Quarterly Weekly Report*, November 10, 1984, 2907.

Table G.2 House outcome by state and region, 1984

	Party lineup before election		Number of incumbents retired		Number of incumbents lost in primaries		Number of incumbents lost in election		Party lineup after election		Net gain	
	D	R	D	R	D	R	D	R	D	R	D	R
Nation	266	167	9	13	3	0	13	3	253	182	4	19
New England												
Conn.	4	2	0	0	0	0	1	0	3	3	0	1
Maine	0	2	0	0	0	0	0	0	0	2	0	0
N.H.	1	1	1	0	0	0	0	0	0	2	0	1
Mass.	10	1	1	0	0	0	0	0	10	1	0	0
R.I.	1	1	0	0	0	0	0	0	1	1	0	0
Vt.	0	1	0	0	0	0	0	0	0	1	0	0
Total	16	8	2	0	0	0	1	0	14	10	0	2
Mid-Atlantic												
Del.	1	0	0	0	0	0	0	0	1	0	0	0
Md.	7	1	0	0	0	0	1	0	6	2	0	1
N.J.	9	4[a]	0	1	0	0	1	0	8	6	0	2
N.Y.	20	14	2	1	0	0	0	0	19	15	0	1
Pa.	13	10	0	0	1	0	0	0	13	10	0	0
Total	50	29	2	2	1	0	2	0	47	33	0	4
Great Lakes												
Ill.	12	10	1	2	0	0	0	1	13	9	1	0
Ind.	5	5	0	0	1	0	0	0	5	5	0	0
Mich.	12	6	0	1	0	0	1	0	11	7	0	1
Ohio	10	11	0	0	0	0	0	1	11	10	1	0
Wis.	5	4	0	0	0	0	0	0	5	4	0	0
Total	44	36	1	3	1	0	1	2	45	35	2	1
Farm Belt												
Iowa	3	3	1	0	0	0	0	0	2	4	0	1
Kans.	2	3	0	1	0	0	0	0	2	3	0	0
Minn.	5	3	0	0	0	0	0	0	5	3	0	0
Nebr.	0	3	0	0	0	0	0	0	5	3	0	0
N. Dak.	1	0	0	0	0	0	0	0	1	0	0	0
S. Dak.	1	0	0	0	0	0	0	0	1	0	0	0
Total	12	12	1	1	0	0	0	0	11	13	0	1
Deep South												
Ala.	5	2	0	1	1	0	0	0	5	2	0	0
Ark.	2	2	0	1	0	0	0	0	3	1	1	0
Ga.	9	1	0	0	0	0	1	0	8	2	0	1
La.	6	2	0	0	0	0	0	0	6	2	0	0
Miss.	3	2	0	0	0	0	0	0	3	2	0	0
S.C.	3	3	0	0	0	0	0	0	3	3	0	0
Total	28	12	0	2	1	0	1	0	28	12	1	1

Table G.2 (*continued*)

	Party lineup before election		Number of incumbents retired		Number of incumbents lost in primaries		Number of incumbents lost in election		Party lineup after election		Net gain	
	D	R	D	R	D	R	D	R	D	R	D	R
Outer South												
Fla.	12	7 [b]	0	0	0	0	0	0	12	7	0	0
N.C.	9	2	0	1	0	0	3	0	6	5	0	3
Tenn.	6	3	1	0	0	0	0	0	6	3	0	0
Tex.	21	6	1	2	1	0	3	0	17	10	0	4
Va.	4	6	0	1	0	0	0	0	4	6	0	0
Total	52	24	2	4	1	0	6	0	45	31	0	7
Border												
Ky.	3 [c]	3	0	0	0	0	0	0	4	3	1	0
Mo.	6	3	0	0	0	0	0	0	6	3	0	0
Okla.	5	1	0	0	0	0	0	0	5	1	0	0
W. Va.	4	0	0	0	0	0	0	0	4	0	0	0
Total	18	7	0	0	0	0	0	0	19	7	1	0
Mountain												
Ariz.	2	3	0	0	0	0	1	0	1	4	0	1
Colo.	3	3	1	0	0	0	0	0	2	4	0	1
Idaho	0	2	0	0	0	0	0	1	1	1	1	0
Mont.	1	1	0	0	0	0	0	0	1	1	0	0
Nev.	1	1	0	0	0	0	0	0	1	1	0	0
N.Mex.	1	2	0	0	0	0	0	0	1	2	0	0
Utah	0	3	0	1	0	0	0	0	0	3	0	0
Wyo.	0	1	0	1	0	0	0	0	0	1	0	0
Total	8	16	1	2	0	0	1	1	7	17	1	2
Pacific												
Alaska	0	1	0	0	0	0	0	0	0	1	0	0
Calif.	28	17	0	0	0	0	1	0	27	18	0	1
Hawaii	2	0	0	0	0	0	0	0	2	0	0	0
Oreg.	3	2	0	0	0	0	0	0	3	2	0	0
Wash.	5	3	0	1	0	0	0	0	5	3	0	0
Total	38	23	0	1	0	0	1	0	37	24	0	1

Sources: Congressional Directory, 98th Congress (Washington, D.C.: United States Government Printing Office, 1983), 213–22. *Congressional Quarterly Weekly Report*, November 10, 1984, 2900, 2909–10.

[a] District 13 seat vacant as Edwin Forsythe (R) died March 29, 1984.

[b] District 10 Congressman Andy Ireland is recorded as a Republican after leaving the Democratic party.

[c] District 7 seat vacant as Representative Carl Perkins (D) died on August 3, 1984.

Appendix H

Gubernatorial election results, 1984

State	Candidates	Party	Vote	Percent
Arkansas	Bill Clinton[a]	D	554,561	63
	Woody Freeman	R	331,987	37
Delaware	William T. Quillen	D	108,315	45
	Michael N. Castle	R	135,250	55
Indiana	W. Wayne Townsend	D	994,966	48
	Robert D. Orr[a]	R	1,097,879	52
	James A. Ridenour	L	6,745	0
Missouri	Kenneth J. Rothman	D	913,700	43
	John Ashcroft	R	1,194,506	57
Montana	Ted Schwinden[a]	D	266,578	70
	Pat M. Goodover	R	100,070	27
	Larry Dodge	L	12,322	3
New Hampshire	Chris Spirou	D	127,156	33
	John H. Sununu[a]	R	256,571	67
North Carolina	Rufus Edmisten	D	1,011,209	46
	James G. Martin	R	1,208,167	54
	H. Fritz Prochnow	L	4,611	0
North Dakota	George Sinner	D	173,922	55
	Allen I. Olsen[a]	R	140,460	45
Rhode Island	Anthony J. Salomon	D	157,814	40
	Edward DiPrete	R	237,160	60
Utah	Wayne Owens	D	275,669	44
	Norman H. Bangerter	R	351,792	56
Vermont	Madeleine M. Kurnin	D	116,938	50
	John J. Easton, Jr.	R	113,264	49
	William Wicher	L	1,904	1
	Richard Gottlieb	LU	695	0
Washington	Booth Gardner	D	1,006,993	53
	John Spellman[a]	R	889,994	47
West Virginia	Clyde M. See, Jr.	D	346,565	47
	Arch A. Moore, Jr.	R	394,937	53

Source: Elections Research Center.
Abbreviations: D = Democrat;
             L = Liberatarian;
             LU = Liberty Union;
             R = Republican.
[a]Denotes incumbent.

Appendix I

Partisan control of state legislatures, 1968–84

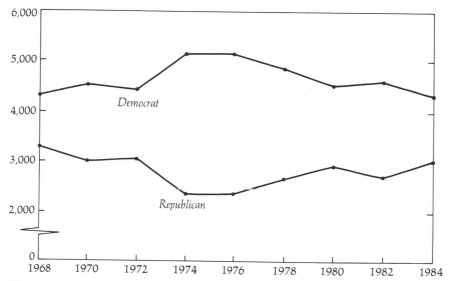

Figure I.1 Number of state legislators by party, 1968–84

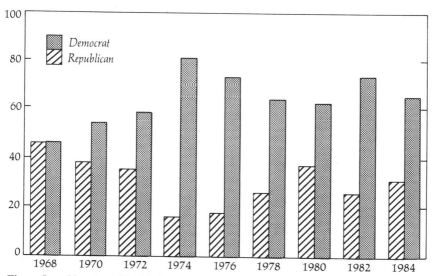

Figure I.2 Number of legislative chambers by party, 1968–84. *Sources for figures I.1 and I.2:* Data for 1968–80 are from *The American Elections of 1980*, ed. Austin Ranney (Washington, D.C.: American Enterprise Institute, 1981), p. 379. Data for 1982 and 1984 are collected by the author.

Notes

Preface

1   The first two were *The American Elections of 1980*, ed. Austin Ranney (Washington, D.C.: American Enterprise Institute, 1981); and *The American Elections of 1982*, ed. Thomas E. Mann and Norman J. Ornstein (Washington, D.C.: American Enterprise Institute, 1983).

Reagan's First Term

1   The election returns are given in detail in appendixes A and B.
2   See appendix C.
3   The congressional results are given in detail in appendix G.
4   Hugh Heclo and Rudolph G. Penner, "Fiscal and Political Strategy in the Reagan Administration," in *The Reagan Presidency: An Early Assessment*, ed. Fred I. Greenstein (Baltimore: Johns Hopkins University Press, 1983), 25.
5   William Schneider, "The November 4 Vote for President: What Did It Mean?" in *The American Elections of 1980*, ed. Austin Ranney (Washington, D.C.: American Enterprise Institute, 1981), 248.
6   Samuel H. Beer, "In Search of a New Public Philosophy," in *The New American Political System*, ed. Anthony King (Washington, D.C.: American Enterprise Institute, 1978), 5–44.
7   The most complete, accurate, and balanced history of Reagan's career I have seen is Lou Cannon, *Reagan* (New York: Putnam, Perigee Books, 1982).
8   *New York Times*, September 19, 1981.
9   Howell Raines, "Reagan Reversing Many U.S. Policies," *New York Times*, July 3, 1981.
10 Heclo and Penner, "Fiscal and Political Strategy," 39.
11 For a lucid and authoritative description of the reconciliation process, see Allen Schick, *Reconciliation and the Congressional Budget Process* (Washington, D.C.: American Enterprise Institute, 1981).
12 Cannon, *Reagan*, 405, emphasis added.
13 William Greider, "The Education of David Stockman," *The Atlantic Monthly*, December 1981, 46.
14 Gains or losses in the Senate are not a good basis for comparison because only one-third of the seats are contested in a particular election year.
15 *Facts on File*, October 29, 1983, 819.
16 *Philadelphia Inquirer*, September 26, 1984.
17 I exclude Harry Truman, Lyndon Johnson, and Gerald Ford from these comparisons because they did not have full four-year first terms, because their popularity in their initial terms after succeeding to office was influenced by feelings about their immediate predecessors, and because Truman and Johnson served their full, elected terms as reelected presidents.
18 *Public Opinion*, February–March 1984, 35. See the same source for similar results in trial heats conducted by the Penn-Schoen, Harris, ABC News/*Washington Post*, and *Los Angeles Times* polls.

19   The polls in 1983-84 consistently showed that majorities of Americans agreed with Reagan on such matters as: a constitutional amendment to require a balanced federal budget; voluntary prayer in the schools; how tough the courts should be on criminals; and the sentiment that government is too big and taxes are too high. On the other hand, majorities disagreed with Reagan on such matters as: increased government spending for education, health care, and the environment; support of the Equal Rights Amendment; a nuclear arms freeze agreement with the Soviet Union; and the sentiment that the United States should *not* spend the money that would be needed to achieve military superiority over the Soviet Union. See, for example, *Public Opinion*, October-November 1983, 26-29.

20   During much of Reagan's long political career most political analysts have consistently underrated his ability and prospects. Even in 1980—after Reagan had already been twice elected governor of California, had nearly won the 1976 Republican presidential nomination, and had won it in 1980—Jimmy Carter's chief political adviser, Hamilton Jordan, said, "The American people are not going to elect a seventy-year-old, right-wing, ex-movie actor to be president." And, around the same time, political scientist Anthony King summarized the picture most Europeans and many Americans had of Reagan as a good platform performer and a nice man, but one who has no understanding of the complexity of modern public problems, who believes in his own simplistic precepts and nostrums, who is lazy and never works hard in his high public offices, who is appallingly ignorant of the facts about most of the matters with which he deals, and who relies upon his aides to tell him what to do. See Ranney, *Elections of 1980*, 212, 304.

21   These statements appear in many polls taken during Reagan's first term. See, for example: the Harris survey of May 3, 1984; the Gallup Polls of September 25, 1983; and the Gallup Poll of June 6, 1982.

22   Ranney, *Elections of 1980*, 35-36.

The Democratic Nomination and the Evolution of the Party System

1   See Nelson W. Polsby, "Party Realignment in the 1980 Election," *The Yale Review* 72 (Autumn, 1982): 41-54.

2   Max Lerner, "The Nation Shifts," *San Francisco Examiner*, November 11, 1984, sec. B10.

3   Pierre S. du Pont IV, "The GOP Isn't Doing Well Enough," *The Washington Post National Weekly Edition*, November 26, 1984, 24. See Iver Peterson, "Republicans Gain in State Legislatures," *New York Times*, November 11, 1984.

4   Commentators observe that in recent years Democratic state legislatures have rigged the boundaries of congressional districts so that small Democratic electoral majorities produce bumper crops of Democratic congressional seats. Table 2A.1, which is appended to this chapter, shows that, for whatever reasons, the Democrats have enjoyed an advantage in recent years in the conversion of votes into seats. In the Senate, an opposite result, greatly favoring Republicans, prevails. Even so, over the thirty-year period, Democrats have dominated elections for *both* houses by almost exactly the same margin. See John T. Pothier, "The Partisan Bias in Senate Elections," *American Politics Quarterly* 12 (January 1984): 89-100. Norman J. Ornstein, in "Genesis of a Gerrymander," *Wall Street Journal*, May 7, 1985, argues that turnout is characteristically lower in Democratic-held districts; consequently the charge that the Democratic majority in Congress is the result of a gerrymander is, in all probability, spurious.

5   This point is also made by Stanley Kelley, Jr., in *Interpreting Elections* (Princeton: Princeton University Press, 1983).

6 For evidence, see Nelson W. Polsby, *Consequences of Party Reform* (New York: Oxford University Press, 1983), 110–13.

7 For the most part, public opinion polls have reported minor variations in self-reports of ideological positions on a liberal-conservative scale over the past ten or fifteen years. The trend shows a drift toward conservatism. But half the respondents consider themselves neither liberal nor conservative, and that has not changed at all. For example, the CBS News/ *New York Times* poll's numbers are as shown in table 2A.2, appended to this chapter. Other polling organizations report similar results. See John Robinson, "The Ups and Downs and Ins and Outs of Ideology," *Public Opinion*, February–March 1984, 15. For 1984 data, see "Portrait of the Electorate," *New York Times*, November 8, 1984. Another piece of evidence, somewhat more volatile in character, is the fact that during the campaign the Republicans were identified as the party "best able to manage prosperity"; see the Gallup Polls reported in *Public Opinion*, December–January 1985, 38.

8 Barry Sussman, "Behind Reagan's Popularity: A Little Help from His Foes," *The Washington Post National Weekly Edition*, February 4, 1985, 37. See also David Rosenbaum, "Poll Shows Many Choose Reagan Even if They Disagree with Him," *New York Times*, September 19, 1984.

9 See table 2A.3, appended to this chapter.

10 In December 1983, an ABC News/ *Washington Post* poll asked a national sample to match three candidates with their own positions on an ideological scale. The results are shown in table 2A.4, appended to this chapter.

11 Sussman, "Behind Reagan's Popularity."

12 Ibid.

13 Polsby, *Consequences of Party Reform*, 87. Republicans, meanwhile, defected from Republican presidential voting in 1984 at a little over half their normal rate. See table 2A.5, appended to this chapter.

14 An elaborate scholarly attempt to weigh factors influencing election outcomes is Steven J. Rosenstone, *Forecasting Elections* (New Haven: Yale University Press, 1983). Rosenstone's backward glance at the 1984 election is presented in "Explaining the 1984 Presidential Election," *The Brookings Review*, 3 (Winter 1985): 25–32.

15 Polsby, *Consequences of Party Reform*, passim.

16 A highly competent summary of the Hunt Commission's work exists in the book on political parties written by the commission's executive director, David Price, *Bringing Back the Parties* (Washington, D.C.: Congressional Quarterly Press, 1984), especially 159–83.

17 Section 7D of the *Delegate Selection Rules for the 1984 Democratic National Convention* reads:

> 7.D. After the election of district-level delegates and prior to the selection of at-large delegates, each state shall elect party leaders and elected officials as national convention delegates.
>
> The numbers of these additional delegates shall be as follows:
>
> (1) A total of 400 slots for unpledged delegates to be apportioned to the states using the same formula used to compute their base delegation.
>
> (2) Additional unpledged delegate slots, if needed, sufficient to make the total allocated under (1) equal to the number of Democratic officials holding the following offices in the state: governor, U.S. senators, U.S. representatives, and mayors of cities over 250,000 in population; provided, however, that nothing contained herein shall be construed as requiring the automatic selection of any said Democratic officials as national convention delegates or conferring automatic delegate status upon any elected Democratic official.
>
> (3) Two additional unpledged delegate slots assigned to each state to accommodate its Democratic chair and vice-chair.

(4) Additional slots for pledged delegates, to be alloted to each state in the number equal to 10 percent of its base delegation.

Democratic National Committee, *Delegate Selection Rules for the 1984 Democratic National Convention* (Washington, D.C.: Democratic National Committee, March 26, 1982), 8–9.

18 Section 10A of the *Delegate Selection Rules* reads:

> 10.A. No meetings, caucuses, conventions or primaries which constitute the first determining stage in the presidential nominating process (the date of the primary states, and the date of the first tier caucus in caucus states) may be held prior to the second Tuesday in March or after the second Tuesday in June in the calendar year of the national convention. Provided, however: The New Hampshire primary may be held no earlier than seven days before the second Tuesday in March, and the Iowa precinct caucuses may be held no earlier than fifteen days before the second Tuesday in March. In no instance may a state which scheduled delegate selection procedures on or between the second Tuesday in March and the second Tuesday in June 1980 move out of compliance with the provisions of this rule.

Delegate Selection Rules, 11–12.

19 Steve Niegand, "State Democrats Look Over Seven Presidential Hopefuls," *San Francisco Chronicle*, January 5, 1983.

20 James M. Perry, "Maine's Democrats Work to Make Hay Out of a Straw Poll," *Wall Street Journal*, September 27, 1983. By the end of October 1983 the straw poll results were as shown in table 2A.6, appended to this chapter.

21 Martin Schram, "Touting Freeze, Cranston Scores Straw Poll Upset in Wisconsin," *Washington Post*, June 12, 1983. For other stories in a similar vein, see Howell Raines, "The Winners in Wisconsin," *New York Times*, June 13, 1983; Raines, "Cranston-Hart Feud Heats Up as Wisconsin Democrats Meet for Straw Poll," *New York Times*, June 12, 1983; Raines, "Candidates: A Shuffling; Presidential Race in Flux after Poll," *New York Times*, June 18, 1983; Schram, "Fair-Weather Voters Abandoned Mondale in Wisconsin's Straw Poll," *Washington Post*, June 13, 1983. A voice of sanity was provided by Donald Pfarrer of the *Milwaukee Journal*, "Candidates Act as if Straw Vote Was Golden," May 22, 1983.

22 See appendix E and table 2A.7, appended to this chapter.

23 For 1984 Florida, Illinois, Pennsylvania, Maryland, Ohio, California, New Jersey, and West Virginia adopted this type of primary (Rhodes Cook, "Shortening the Nomination Path? 1984 Democratic Party Rules Seek to Cure Past Problems but Could Create New Ones," *Congressional Quarterly Weekly Report*, August 6, 1983, 1610). Section 12A(3) of the *Delegate Selection Rules* reads:

> 12.A.(3) Direct-election primaries. Individual candidates for delegate and alternate may be voted for directly on a primary ballot, provided: (a) that such delegates and alternates shall be elected from districts no larger than a congressional district; and (b) that each delegate candidate is identified on the ballot according to his or her presidential or uncommitted preference.

Delegate Selection Rules, 14.

24 Sections 12A and 12B of the *Delegate Selection Rules* read in part:

> A. Delegates shall be allocated in a fashion that fairly reflects the expressed presidential preference or uncommitted status of the primary voters, or, if there is no binding primary, the convention and caucus participants. States shall choose *one* of the following plans for allocating delegates to presidential candidates at the district level:

(1) Proportional representation. District-level delegates shall be allocated in proportion to the percentage of the primary or caucus vote won in the district by each preference, except that preferences falling below the applicable threshold shall not be awarded any delegates.

The threshold in states holding a binding primary shall be calculated by dividing the number of delegates to be elected in the district into 100 percent, except that the threshold shall not exceed 25 percent. The threshold in caucus states shall be 20 percent.

(2) Bonus delegate plan. One delegate position per district shall initially be awarded to the primary or caucus/convention winner in that district. The remainder of the delegate positions in that district shall be allocated in proportion to the percentage of the primary or caucus vote won in that district by each preference, except the preferences falling below the applicable threshold shall not be awarded any delegates.

The threshold in states holding a binding primary shall be calculated by subtracting the bonus delegate from the number of delegates to be elected in the district and dividing this number into 100 percent, except that the threshold shall not exceed 30 percent. The threshold in caucus states shall be 20 percent.

B. At-large and pledged party and elected official delegate positions shall be allocated to presidential preferences by reference to primary or convention votes or to the division of preference among district-level delegates, as specified in Rule 9C, except that preferences falling below a threshold of 20 percent shall not be awarded any delegates at this level.

Delegate Selection Rules, 14–15.

Title 11, Section 9033.5(b) of the *Code of Federal Regulations* reads:

(b) *Insufficient Votes.* The ineligibility date shall be the thirtieth day following the date of the second consecutive primary election in which such individual receives less than 10 percent of the number of popular votes cast for all candidates of the same party for the same office in that primary election. . . ."

25 This endorsement by the AFL-CIO came one day after a similar pledge of support by the National Education Association. See Phil Gailey, "AFL-CIO Leaders Support Mondale for '84 Nomination," *New York Times*, October 2, 1983. In the November general election, 54 percent of the vote by members of labor unions went to Mondale (CBS News/*New York Times* exit poll for November 6, 1984, reported in *Public Opinion*, December–January 1985, 28). An AFL-CIO poll showed that AFL-CIO members voted 61 percent for Mondale. William Serrin, "Kirkland Stresses Solidarity on Candidate Endorsement," *New York Times*, December 2, 1984.

26 Bernard Weinraub, "Glenn Cuts Mondale Lead in Race to Fill '84 Coffers," *New York Times*, November 28, 1983.

27 Ibid.

28 Phil Gailey, "Mondale's Vital Visit," *New York Times*, September 1, 1983.

29 Ellen Hume reported in "Gays See Election as Chance for Gains; May Be Main Political Force This Year," *Wall Street Journal*, January 11, 1984, that "Mr. Mondale . . . [was] openly courting gay votes." The President of the National Organization for Women said: "The Mondale organization sought us out more assertively than anyone else . . . and we met four times with Mr. Mondale himself" ("Can Anyone Beat Fritz?" *Newsweek*, January 9, 1984, 31). The *Newsweek* story continues: "In the topsy-turvy world of 1984 politics, Mondale made the shrewd tactical decision to spend more time wooing the president of a nonpartisan group than he will probably spend winning the hearts and minds of most party leaders. The difference, of course, is that Democratic officials don't have much to offer in the way of mailing lists."

30 Rob Gurwitt, "Unions Hope Endorsement of Mondale Will Advance Labor's Legislative Grab," *Congressional Quarterly Weekly Report*, October 8, 1983, 2080–81.

31 Suzanne Garment, "The Democrats Begin Bidding for the Center," *Wall Street Journal*, November 11, 1983.

32 William C. Adams, "The Power of *The Right Stuff*: A Quasi-Experimental Field Test of the 'Docudrama Hypothesis'" (Report of the George Washington University Media Analysis Project, no date, Mimeographed).

33 See Jane Mayer, "TV is Hart's Catapult as the Networks Escalate Their Coverage of Coloradan," *Wall Street Journal*, March 9, 1984. On the same week in early March, Hart was on the covers of *Time*, *Newsweek*, *U.S. News and World Report*, and *The Economist*.

34 See "In Search of the Real Hart," *Newsweek*, March 26, 1984, 32–33, and compare with the answers in "A Talk With Gary Hart," in the same issue, 26, 31.

35 *People* magazine said: "The comparison was almost too studiedly encouraged by the candidate. It's not for nothing that Kennedy hagiographer Theodore Sorenson is a co-chairman of Hart's campaign.... [Hart] held his hand in his coat pocket just so. To make a point, he stabbed the air straight ahead with his fingers held just so. He invoked Robert Frost. He had windblown hair. And his new frontier beckoned an entire new generation yearning for new ideas" ("The Enigmatic Candidate," *People*, March 26, 1984, 32).

36 William C. Adams, "Hart Hype and Media Muscle," paper prepared for presentation at the annual meeting of the International Society for Political Psychology, Toronto, June 25, 1984.

37 The numbers from the ABC News/*Washington Post* New Hampshire exit poll are as shown in table 2A.8, appended to this chapter.

38 Rhodes Cook wrote: "Even with only a semblance of an organization, Hart decisively beat Mondale in the Nevada caucuses, was running well ahead in incomplete returns from Washington and Alaska and was narrowly leading in nearly complete returns from Oklahoma. In Hawaii, Hart did not file to compete for delegates, but Mondale still could not win. The Minnesotan finished a distant second behind 'uncommitted.'" ("Hart, Mondale Shift to Key Frost-belt Battles," *Congressional Quarterly Weekly Report*, March 17, 1984, 626).

39 Evidence from six exit polls on the second choices of Jackson voters showed Mondale very far in the lead; see table 2A.9, appended to this chapter. After the primaries, the *New York Times* reported: "Although three-quarters of the blacks who voted in Democratic presidential primaries this year voted for the Reverend Jesse Jackson, black Democrats prefer Walter Mondale to Reverend Jackson as the party's presidential nominee by a margin of 5 to 3...." (David E. Rosenbaum, "Black Democrats in a Poll Prefer Mondale to Jackson as Nominee," *New York Times*, July 10, 1984). The CBS News/*New York Times* poll on which this story was based included 411 black respondents, an unusually large number for a national sample survey.

40 Even during the most difficult period of the campaign, there was never a time when Mondale did not lead all other Democratic hopefuls in the public opinion polls. Gallup's figures are as shown in table 2A.10, appended to this chapter.

41 Mondale came in first as a vote-getter in primary elections, just ahead of Hart. See the figures in appendix D.

42 The contribution of black voters to the Democratic total in presidential elections has been calculated by Robert Axelrod. The results are shown in table 2A.11, appended to this chapter.

43 See Fay S. Joyce, "Jackson Candidacy Is Giving New Shape to Politics in U.S.," *New York Times*, April 13, 1984.

44 See Ellen Hume, "Racial Rhetoric Puts Farrakhan in Spotlight in Jesse Jackson Camp," *Wall Street Journal*, April 26, 1984. See also E. R. Shipp, "Farrakhan Statements Reflect His Background," *New York Times*, April 17, 1984.

45   A thorough discussion from the point of view of the reporter who first communicated this remark is Milton Coleman, "Eighteen Words, Seven Weeks Later," *Washington Post*, April 8, 1984.

46   See "Jesse Jackson and the Jews: A Strained Relationship," *National Journal*, March 24, 1984, 564. In the end, two-thirds of the Jewish voters supported the Mondale-Ferraro ticket; see table 7.5 in chapter 7 of this book.

47   See Ellen Hume, "GOP Views Jackson as a Plus," *Wall Street Journal*, July 11, 1984. Hume writes: "In the six months ending last April, black registration [in North Carolina] rose by 77,000, according to state election officials, but this is only about half the 145,000 increase in new white voters." Rosenstone says: "Mondale's racial liberalism cost him about four to five points in the average southern state. . . . Jesse Jackson's candidacy helped keep these issues salient in the minds of southern whites, over seven out of ten of whom cast a ballot for Ronald Reagan" ("Explaining the 1984 Presidential Election").

48   As Ronald Smothers said in the *New York Times Magazine*, March 4, 1984, "Many black elected officials, especially in those states with early primaries . . . have come over to Jackson's camp as he has gained in the polls and garnered positive news coverage. Some admit frankly that they have moved in Jackson's direction for fear that opposing him will hurt them locally." Howell Raines reported in June 1983: "Several months ago [Mayor Andrew] Young [of Atlanta], who is leaning toward endorsing Mr. Mondale, spoke out strongly against a black candidacy. But now he has 'backed off from Mondale for the time being to see what Jesse does. . . .' Some black officials worry that a Jackson candidacy could become what Representative Julian C. Dixon of California, chairman of the Congressional Black Caucus, called 'a fitness test for blackness'" ("Pressure on Jesse Jackson," *New York Times*, June 22, 1983).

49   U.S. Bureau of the Census reports on the U.S. population give information on turnout by race. Unpublished studies of these figures by John Gilmour show that significant strides had already been made by 1982 to close the gap between white and black turnout. See, for example, the figures in table 2A.12, appended to this chapter. A narrowing of the gap is especially noticeable by 1982 among younger black voters, a group especially supportive of the Jackson candidacy in Democratic primaries; see the data in table 2A.13, appended to this chapter. Finally, voting participation by blacks is higher in central cities than in suburbs, reversing the patterns observable for white voters and suggesting that, prior to the Jackson candidacy, black candidates for local public office played a part in mobilizing black voters (See Table 3 of the *Current Population Reports*, Bureau of the Census, for the elections of 1978, 1980, and 1982). See also Ronald Smothers, "Bid By Jackson is Cited in Blacks' Big Turnout," *New York Times*, March 15, 1984, for a recitation of some of the conflicting claims.

50   Elizabeth Drew, "A Political Journal," *New Yorker*, September 10, 1984, 110. Corroborative observations come from a participant in the Mondale campaign: Theodore R. Marmor, "The Lessons of Mondale's Defeat," *The Political Quarterly* 56 (April–June 1985): 153–66.

51   According to the Gallup survey of October 26–29 (1,520 respondents), 22 percent said they were more likely, 32 percent said they were less likely to vote for Mondale because of his choice of Ferraro. Three percent had no opinion and 43 percent said it made no difference. The CBS News/*New York Times* poll in November showed that favorable and unfavorable opinions of Ferraro split about evenly, whereas Vice-President Bush enjoyed favorable ratings by about a two-to-one margin. On the whole, the campaign strengthened Bush and eroded Ferraro's support. It is not entirely clear what par for this course might be. Theodore White's book on the 1968 election says of possible Republican vice-presidential candidates: "The private polls [Nixon] secretly commissioned to test names were of little help; none of the conspicuous names could add or detract more than a point or two from the test per-

centages resulting when Nixon's name was offered alone" (*The Making of the President 1968* [New York: Atheneum, 1969], 250).

52   William Cavala, "Changing the Rules Changes the Game: Party Reform and the 1972 California Delegation to the Democratic National Convention," *American Political Science Review* 68 (March 1974): 27–42.

Renominating Ronald Reagan

1   Rich Jaroslovsky, "Reagan's Optimism," *Wall Street Journal*, November 5, 1984, editorial page.

2   Quoted in "O'Neill Predicts Reagan's Defeat," *Washington Post*, May 22, 1983.

3   For a review of "Why Would Reagan Want a Second Term?" see article by David Hoffman and Lou Cannon in *Washington Post*, September 11, 1983, sec. C1.

4   Charles O. Jones, "Nominating 'Carter's Favorite Opponent': The Republicans in 1980," in *The American Elections of 1980*, ed. Austin Ranney (Washington, D.C.: American Enterprise Institute, 1981), 63.

5   Jones, "Carter's Favorite Opponent," 98.

6   Jimmy Carter, *Keeping Faith* (New York: Bantam, 1982), 88.

7   Fred I. Greenstein, *The Hidden-Hand Presidency: Eisenhower as Leader* (New York: Basic Books, 1982).

8   Dick Kirschten, "President Reagan After Two Years: Bold Actions but Uncertain Results," *National Journal*, January 1, 1983, 4.

9   As reported in Opinion Roundup, *Public Opinion*, February–March 1984, 38.

10   Everett Carll Ladd, "Public Attitudes Toward Policy and Governance: Searching for the Sources and Meaning of 'The Reagan Revolution'" (Paper prepared for conference on "Governance: The Reagan Era and Beyond," Urban Institute, Washington, D.C., December 15–16, 1983), 22.

11   Ibid., 21.

12   Fred I. Greenstein, "The Need for an Early Appraisal," in *The Reagan Presidency: An Early Assessment*, ed. Fred I. Greenstein (Baltimore: Johns Hopkins University Press, 1982), 15.

13   As reported by Lou Cannon and Martin Schram, "'Filched' Data Story Laid to Stockman," *Washington Post*, June 30, 1983, sec. A1.

14   As reported by Jody Powell, "Just a Third-Rate Theft," *Washington Post*, June 12, 1984, sec. B7.

15   For details see "House Panel Pushes '80 Debate Book Inquiry," *Congressional Quarterly Weekly Report*, July 2, 1983, 1358. It should be noted that Speaker O'Neill opposed the Albosta subcommittee investigation.

16   For details see story by Lou Cannon, "Lines Drawn between Casey, Baker," *Washington Post*, July 7, 1983, sec. A1.

17   A. James Reichley, *Conservatives in an Age of Change: The Nixon and Ford Administrations* (Washington, D.C.: The Brookings Institution, 1981), 35.

18   A. James Reichley, "A Change in Direction," in Joseph A. Pechman, ed., *Setting National Priorities: The 1982 Budget* (Washington, D.C.: The Brookings Institution, 1981), 259.

19   As listed by Reichley in ibid., 236–59.

20   Quoted in Steven Pressman, "Religious Right: Trying to Link Poll Power and Lobby Muscle," *Congressional Quarterly Weekly Report*, September 22, 1984, 2315.

21   Ibid., 2315.

22   For details, see Nelson W. Polsby and Aaron Wildavsky, *Presidential Elections* (New York: Scribners, 1984), 26-29.

23   Public opinion survey data also revealed that women tended to be more liberal than men on most issues. See Opinion Roundup, *Public Opinion*, April-May 1982, 28-30.

24   As reported by David Broder, "Pitfalls: Women See Peril to Reagan Reelection," *Washington Post*, August 8, 1983, sec. A1. See also Opinion Roundup, *Public Opinion*, October-November 1983, 38.

25   Barbara Honegger, "Reagan Has Not Fulfilled His Promise," *Washington Post*, August 21, 1983, sec. C8.

26   See report by Juan Williams, "Reagan's Aides Say Gender Gap is GOP Problem," *Washington Post*, September 19, 1983, sec. A1.

27   For details see Charles O. Jones, "A New President, A Different Congress, A Maturing Agenda," in *The Reagan Presidency and the Governing of America*, ed. Lester Salamon and Michael Lund (Washington, D.C.: Urban Institute, 1985), 261-87.

28   "It's Been a Reagan Year," *Washington Post*, December 29, 1983, sec. A17.

29   For details of the initial organization, see report by David Hoffman, "Reagan Aides Apply '80 Lessons to '84 Drive," *Washington Post*, October 16, 1983, sec. A1, and "Backing Into the Race," *Time*, October 24, 1983, 20-21.

30   Quoted in Bill Peterson, "GOP Plans Record Election Spending," *Washington Post*, February 3, 1984, sec. A6.

31   As reported by James Perry, "Reagan Campaign Hums Quietly," *Wall Street Journal*, February 29, 1984.

32   Dick Kirschten, "Reagan Conducts Clinic in How to Use the White House in Order to Hold It," *National Journal*, October 6, 1984, 1873.

33   Ibid.

34   Quoted by David Hoffman, "Reagan Fuels Public Speculation that He will Run for Reelection," *Washington Post*, May 16, 1983, sec. A3. Hoffman points out that the president and his aides were publicly hinting reelection but that the president was privately "far more reserved."

35   V. O. Key, Jr., *The Responsible Electorate: Rationality in Presidential Voting, 1936-1960* (Cambridge: Harvard University Press, 1966), 61. For a recent exposition of retrospective voting, see Morris P. Fiorina, *Retrospective Voting in American National Elections* (New Haven: Yale University Press, 1981).

36   As cited by Robert Samuelson, "Democrats Must Key on Deficit Threats," *Washington Post*, July 18, 1984, sec. D1. Tufte's principal work on this subject is *The Political Control of the Economy* (Princeton: Princeton University Press, 1978).

37   Quoted in Robert G. Kaiser, "Boom or Bust for Reagan in 1984," *Washington Post*, October 16, 1983, sec. B1.

38   ". . . With Excellent Timing . . . ," *Washington Post*, June 5, 1984, sec. A15.

39   Announced in a presidential news conference, April 4, 1984. For text, see *Congressional Quarterly Weekly Report*, April 7, 1984, 793-96.

40   Presidential news conference. For text, see *Congressional Quarterly Weekly Report*, February 25, 1984, 468-71.

41   For details, see text of Reagan's April 4 press conference, *Congressional Quarterly Weekly Report*, April 7, 1984, 793-96.

42   "The Image as Message, the Message as Image," *New York Times*, July 16, 1984.

43   "Why Criticisms Don't Stick," *Time*, May 21, 1984, 53.

44   "'Setting Out to Whomp 'Em,'" *Time*, September 3, 1984, 28.

45   "Battle Hymn of the Republicans," *Washington Post*, August 25, 1984, sec. G.

46   Quoted by David Broder and Martin Schram in "Complacency Is Only Cloud as GOP Convenes," *Washington Post*, August 20, 1984, sec. A.

47   From an interview in *First Monday* 14 (September 1984): 21. See also the article by Elisabeth Bumiller, "Setting the Stage," *Washington Post*, August 20, 1984, sec. C1.

48   Timmons is also president of a successful lobbying firm in Washington—one that does business with most of the public figures at the convention. For details, see David Rogers, "A Lobbyist's Fortuitous Position," *Wall Street Journal*, August 23, 1984.

49   The average 1984 conservative coalition support score for the 12 platform committee and subcommittee leaders from Congress was 88, about eight points higher than that for all congressional Republicans. Scores computed from *Congressional Quarterly Weekly Report*, October 27, 1984, 2820-25.

50   "GOP Platform: A Hidden Debate," *Wall Street Journal*, August 2, 1984.

51   Senator Charles McC. Mathias, Jr., in *Washington Post*, August 20, 1984, sec. A17, answering the question: "Why Should a Moderate Go to Dallas?"

52   For details on the background of delegates, see Thomas B. Edsall, "GOP Delegates Are Generally Affluent, White and Conservative," *Washington Post*, August 19, 1984, sec. A7.

53   Quoted in Harrison Donnelly, "Church and Politics: An Old Issue Returns," *Congressional Quarterly Weekly Report*, September 15, 1984, 2263.

Elected Officials

1   Anthony King, "How Not to Select Presidential Candidates," in *The American Elections of 1980*, ed. Austin Ranney (Washington, D.C.: American Enterprise Institute, 1981), 324-25.

2   Michael J. Malbin, "Democratic Rule Makers Want to Bring Party Leaders Back to the Conventions," *National Journal*, January 2, 1982, 24-28.

3   Byron E. Shafer, *Quiet Revolution: The Struggle for the Democratic Party and the Shaping of Post-Reform Politics* (New York: Russell Sage Foundation, 1983),

4   Ibid., 525.

5   See Shafer, *Quiet Revolution*; Nelson W. Polsby, *Consequences of Party Reform* (New York: Oxford University Press, 1983); and Austin Ranney, *Curing the Mischiefs of Faction* (Berkeley: University of California Press, 1975).

6   "Openness, Participation, and Party Building: Reforms for a Stronger Democratic Party" (Washington, D.C.: Democratic National Committee, 1978), 18.

7   David E. Price, *Bringing Back the Parties* (Washington, D.C.: Congressional Quarterly Press, 1984), 201.

8   This description of the Hunt Commission draws on Price, *Bringing Back the Parties*; Malbin, "Democratic Rule Makers"; and the author's personal observations as a member of the commission's Technical Advisory Committee.

9   Shafer, *Quiet Revolution*, 537.

10   Price, *Bringing Back the Parties*, 159-83.

11   Quoted in ibid., 167.

12   Quoted in ibid., 168.

13   "Report of the Commission on Presidential Nomination" (Washington, D.C.: Democratic National Committee, 1982), 8.

14   CBS News generously made available to me summaries of their delegate surveys taken just before the Democratic and Republican conventions.

15   "Mondale's Primary Weakness Bodes Ill for November Hopes," *Congressional Quarterly Weekly Report*, June 16, 1984, 1444.

16 "'Back-Room' Party Caucuses Draw Fire from Mondale Foes," *Congressional Quarterly Weekly Report*, June 2, 1984, 1315.

17 "Mondale Wins Big Among House Delegates," *Congressional Quarterly Weekly Report*, January 28, 1984, 132.

18 Quoted in Richard E. Cohen, "Congressional Super Delegates Flex New Presidential Ticket-Making Muscle," *National Journal*, July 14, 1984, 1353.

19 Quoted in ibid., 1353.

20 Mondale's successful effort to salvage his candidacy after New Hampshire was made possible by a violation of the schedule he had promoted. Had Super Tuesday (the first day of the window) come only a week after the New Hampshire primary, as provided for in the Hunt Commission plan, Mondale might not have had time to turn the tide in the South. Maine's and Vermont's decision to violate the window, and New Hampshire's subsequent response, gave him an extra week to try to break Hart's momentum.

21 Diane Granat, "Democratic Leaders Urge Hart to Withdraw," *Congressional Quarterly Weekly Report*, June 9, 1984, 1346.

22 Senate Democrats were alloted twenty-seven seats, but only twenty-five senators expressed an interest in being unpledged delegates. See "Senate Democrats Select 25 'Superdelegates,'" *Congressional Quarterly Weekly Report*, March 24, 1984, 655, and Diane Granat, "Democratic Leaders Urge Hart to Withdraw," 1346.

23 cbs News. See n. 14 above.

24 Michael J. Malbin, "The Conventions, Platforms, and Issue Activists," in Ranney, *Elections of 1980*, 135–36.

25 Quoted in Diane Granat, "Democratic Platform Writers Facing Conflicts," *Congressional Quarterly Weekly Report*, June 16, 1984, 1466.

26 Quoted in Diane Granat, "Democrats Concoct 1984 Platform in Harmony," *Congressional Quarterly Weekly Report*, June 30, 1984, 1572.

27 See, for example, Warren Weaver, Jr., "Democratic Panel Nears Completion of Fall Platform," *New York Times*, June 24, 1984.

28 Malbin, "Conventions, Platforms, and Issue Activists," 116.

29 T. R. Reid, "Platform Assails Deficit, Hails Democratic Legacy," *Washington Post*, June 24, 1984, sec. A5.

30 It is interesting to recall that as a member of the Winograd Commission, Kirkpatrick fought unsuccessfully to make all Democratic members of Congress automatic unpledged delegates.

31 Quoted in Suzanne Garment, "Can the Democrats Fly Without Their Right Wing," *Wall Street Journal*, June 22, 1984.

32 Steven Pressman, "Groups Plan Democratic Convention Assaults," *Congressional Quarterly Weekly Report*, July 7, 1984, 1631–53.

33 cbs News. See n. 14 above.

34 Quoted in David S. Broder, "Democrats Eye United Convention," *Washington Post*, June 27, 1984, sec. A1.

35 Byron E. Shafer, "Party Rules: The Long Perspective and the Short" (edited version of article published in the *Christian Science Monitor*, July 13, 1984).

36 "The Report of the Rules Committee to the 1984 Democratic National Convention" (Washington, D.C.: Democratic National Committee, June 28, 1984).

37 "Report of the Rules Committee," 7.

38 Steven V. Roberts, "Rules of Party Playing Desired Role, Poll Finds," *New York Times*, July 15, 1984.

39 Quoted in Richard E. Cohen, "A 48-Hour Shot at Political Damage Control," *National Journal Convention Daily*, July 16, 1985, 28. Weeks later, Lance left the campaign and the entire affair continued to have adverse consequences for Mondale.

40   Rob Gurwitt and Nadine Cohodas, "Hispanic-Asian Boycott: A Gesture Fizzles," *Congressional Quarterly Weekly Report*, July 21, 1984, 1733.

41   William C. Adams, "Convention Coverage," *Public Opinion*, December–January 1985, 43–48.

42   Robert J. Huckshorn and John F. Bibby, "National Party Rules and Delegate Selection in the Republican Party," *PS* 16 (Fall 1983): 660.

43   Price, *Bringing Back the Parties*, 190.

44   Shafer, "Party Rules," 2.

45   Jules Witcover, *Marathon* (New York: Viking, 1977), 475–503.

46   Malbin, "Conventions, Platforms, and Issue Activists."

47   Nadine Cohodas, "Solidly Conservative Platform Ready for Adoption by GOP," *Congressional Quarterly Weekly Report*, August 18, 1984, 2023.

48   CBS News. See n. 14 above.

49   Quoted in Alan Ehrenhalt, "Reagan-Mondale: A Polarizing Contest," *Congressional Quarterly Weekly Report*, August 24, 1984, 2067.

50   Robert Axelrod, "Communication," *American Political Science Review* 76 (June 1982): 393–96; and Everett Carll Ladd, "As the Realignment Turns: A Drama in Many Acts," *Public Opinion*, December–January 1985, 2–7.

The Campaign and the Issues

1   Dan Balz, "To Win White House, Mondale Must Sing a More National Tune," *Washington Post*, June 10, 1984.

2   David Shribman, "Mondale's Slow Start in a Very Tough Race Distresses Democrats," *Wall Street Journal*, September 7, 1984.

3   Howell Raines, "A Contrast on TV," *New York Times*, September 5, 1984.

4   Howell Raines, "Reagan Appears to Succeed By Avoiding Specific Issues," *New York Times*, September 5, 1984.

5   Robert W. Merry, "The Post Industrial Campaign," *Wall Street Journal*, October 3, 1984.

6   John J. Fialka, "Pledges By Mondale Add Up to a Big Bill, An Analysis Suggests," *Wall Street Journal*, January 24, 1984.

7   Robert Kuttner, "Revenge of the Democratic Nerds," *New Republic*, October 22, 1984.

8   "The Mondale Deficit Plan Won't Win Hearts and Minds on Wall Street," *Business Week*, October 1, 1984.

9   James P. Gannon, "Church & State Politicking: Rerun of '72," *Des Moines Register*, September 16, 1984.

10   David Rogers, "Roman Catholics Are Deeply Torn by Debate Over Religion, Politics," *Wall Street Journal*, September 19, 1984.

11   Kevin Phillips, *The American Political Report*, 13, no. 26 (September 7, 1984).

12   Joseph M. Giordano, "Facts for the President's Fables," *Los Angeles Times*, September 18, 1984.

13   William Safire, "Reagan's Desert I," *New York Times*, September 27, 1984.

14   James M. Perry and Robert W. Merry, "In Two Barometer States, the Signs Are All Bad for Mondale-Ferraro," *Wall Street Journal*, September 27, 1984.

15   David S. Broder, "Reagan Imported Tory Tactics," *Washington Post*, September 16, 1984.

16   Mary McGrory, "Fritz the Fainthearted Reinforces Doubts About His Leadership," *Washington Post*, October 4, 1984.

17   Election Extra, *Newsweek*, November–December 1984.

18   Rich Jaroslovsky and James M. Perry, "New Question in Race: Is Oldest President Now Showing His Age?" *Wall Street Journal*, October 9, 1984.

19 David S. Broder, "They're Hiding the President," *Washington Post*, October 14, 1984.

20 James Reston, "A Question for Voters," *New York Times*, October 14, 1984.

21 Thomas B. Rosenstiel, "Debate Aftermath: Media Alters View of Candidates," *Los Angeles Times*, October 14, 1984.

22 Jane Mayer, "Given Some Excuse, Media Quickly Alters Candidates' Image," *Wall Street Journal*, October 19, 1984.

23 William Schneider, "Debating the Debates," *Los Angeles Times*, October 14, 1984.

24 Ellen Hume, "Democrat Is Drawing Crowds, but Issue Is, Can She Draw Votes?" *Wall Street Journal*, September 25, 1984.

25 Bob Woodward, "U.S. Had Reliable Warnings Diplomats Were Bomb Target; Explosives Were Tracked to Lebanon," *Washington Post*, October 18, 1984.

26 Vermont Royster, "Debating the Debates," *Wall Street Journal*, October 17, 1984.

27 Thomas Oliphant and Robert Healy, "Chief Aide Tells Mondale Reagan Looks Unstoppable," *Boston Globe*, October 26, 1984.

28 Thomas B. Edsall, "New Voter Signups May Favor the GOP," *Washington Post*, November 2, 1984.

29 James M. Perry, "Whistle Stops and Waste Dumps," *Wall Street Journal*, October 18, 1984.

30 Mark Shields, "Where's His Mandate?" *Washington Post*, November 2, 1984.

31 Alan Baron, *Baron Report*, November 19, 1984.

Where's the Beef?

1 Barry Sussman, "Freeze Support Grows Slightly After War Show," *Washington Post*, November 23, 1983; Stanley Feldman and Lee Sigelman, "The Political Impact of Prime-Time Television: 'The Day After'" (University of Kentucky, Lexington, 1984, Mimeographed); and William C. Adams, Dennis Smith, Allison Salzman, Ralph Crossen, Scott Hieber, Tom Naccaroto, Richard Valenzuala, William Vantine, and Nina Weisbroth, "Before and After *The Day After*: A Nationwide Survey of a Movie's Impact," paper presented to the International Communication Association, May 1984.

2 Adams et al., "Before and After *The Day After*," 19.

3 Ibid., 5.

4 Feldman and Sigelman, "The Political Impact of Prime-Time Television," table 1.

5 Sussman, "Freeze Support Grows," 8.

6 William C. Adams, Allison Salzman, William Vantine, Anne Baker, Lucille Bonvouloir, Barbara Brenner, Leslie Suelter, Margaret Ely, Jean Feldman, and Ron Ziegel, "The Power of *The Right Stuff*: A Quasi-Experimental Field Test of the 'Docudrama Hypothesis,'" *Public Opinion Quarterly* (Fall 1985), forthcoming.

7 *Television News Index and Abstracts*, October 1983, indicates that John Glenn was the principal focus of nineteen stories. The other candidates received the following number of stories: McGovern, six; Jackson, four; Hart, three.

8 Adams et al., "Power of *The Right Stuff*."

9 Kathleen Hall Jamieson, *Packaging the Presidency: A History and Criticism of Presidential Campaign Advertising* (New York: Oxford University Press, 1984); and Edwin Diamond and Stephen Bates, *The Spot: The Rise of Political Advertising on Television* (Cambridge: MIT Press, 1984).

10 For a useful comparison among the competitive democracies, see Howard Penniman, "U.S. Elections: Really a Bargain?" *Public Opinion*, June–July 1984.

11 In the year's most adventurous ad, the Republicans used a foraging bear to symbolize the Soviet Union and a mysterious hunter to symbolize Reagan's defense program. Discussion

about the ad focused more on its subtlety than on its accuracy; the Democrats insisted that 54 percent of the people they asked did not understand the metaphor. With a lead of twenty points in the polls and plenty of money, the Republican advertising people seemed not to care about any of that.

12   Using a less systematic approach, I found the same inverse relation in the 1980 primary campaign: Bush, Reagan, Carter, and Kennedy all tended to do better, or at least as well, when spending less (Michael J. Robinson, "The Media in 1980: Was the Message the Message?" in *The American Elections of 1980*, ed. Austin Ranney [Washington, D.C.: American Enterprise Institute, 1981]).

13   Hart aside, the Jackson campaign, in and outside New Jersey, completely refutes the notion that money much determines presidential nominations. Before California Jackson had no observable paid media campaign; yet he carried Louisiana and the District of Columbia, finished second in Maryland, and won 18.6 percent of all the Democratic primary votes cast — a respectable third behind Mondale's 37.8 percent and Hart's 36.0 percent (see appendix D).

14   The ABC News/*Washington Post* poll taken three times between that Saturday and that Monday shows a decline of seventeen points in Hart's "lead" over Mondale, from a plus eight to a minus nine in three days. See David Broder, "Mondale Support Rises in Illinois Poll," *Washington Post*, March 20, 1984.

15   Martin Schram, "To Beef Up Candidates Ad Men Go from Reel to Real," *Washington Post*, May 25, 1984.

16   William C. Adams, "Recent Fables about Ronald Reagan," *Public Opinion*, October–November 1984, 9.

17   For a discussion of mediality, see Austin Ranney, *Channels of Power* (New York: Basic Books, 1983), or see my article concerning "medialities" in 1976 and 1980, Robinson, "Was the Message the Message?"

18   Michael J. Robinson and Margaret A. Sheehan, *Over the Wire and on TV: CBS and UPI in Campaign '80* (New York: Russell Sage Foundation, 1983), especially chapter 5.

19   The best of the genre are Thomas Patterson, *The Mass Media Election of 1976* (New York: Praeger, 1980); Donald Weaver, Doris Graber, Maxwell McCombs, and C. H. Eyal, *Media Agenda Setting in a Presidential Election* (New York: Praeger, 1981), and Scott Keeter and Clifford Zukin, *Uninformed Choice: The Failure of the New Presidential Nominating System* (New York: Praeger, 1983).

20   "Can Anyone Beat Fritz?" *Newsweek*, January 9, 1984, 26.

21   At the 1984 meeting of the National Capital Political Science Association, held on February 25, only one political scientist in a room of about one hundred — Byron Shafer of Florida State University — suggested that Hart might win the nomination. Everyone else, including me, seemed to assent to the conventional wisdom that Iowa meant Mondale was a shoo-in.

22   William Keyserling, "Challengers Never Had a Chance in the Media," *Washington Post*, December 25, 1983.

23   Using the *Television News Abstract and Index* for January, February, and March, I categorized each Jackson piece by its spin and its agenda. These figures reflect my best judgment about those pieces.

24   In an earlier piece Maura Clancey and I used a different, more global measure of "press," one that included information about the status of the horse race and about the topic of the piece. The measure used in this section is the most basic measure of spin, one that looks only at the interpretation the reporter offers about the quality of the candidate — his or her integrity, intelligence, consistency, credibility, accuracy. This measure fits better with my approach here. For the more global measure, see Maura Clancey and Michael J. Robinson, "General Election Coverage: Part I," *Public Opinion*, December–January 1985.

25   If reporters think not, they might simply change the nouns in these remarks and have them

address the issue of news. Change Chris Wallace's conclusions, for example, in the following way: "Protecting the ratings, the networks offered visuals and gee-whiz technology but never told us what each of the candidates was going to do in the next four years." Is that bad press about press?

26 Even when spin about the horse race is factored in, the Republican ticket got more than twice as much "cosmic" bad press as the Democrats. See Clancey and Robinson, "General Election Coverage."

27 These "favorability" measures are taken from surveys conducted by Patrick Caddell during the fall campaign.

28 This was not the case, however, when we used "approval" score as a measure of public opinion.

29 Indeed, Reagan's public opinion scores moved so little during the election campaign that any correlation analysis must be heavily qualified. There is not much meaningful variation in the public response—only in the press coverage do we see much variation.

30 Michael Robinson, "A Statesman Is a Dead Politician," in Elie Abel, *What's the News?* (San Francisco: Institute for Contemporary Studies, 1981).

31 The classic statement appears in Bernard Cohen, *The Press and Foreign Policy* (Princeton: Princeton University Press, 1963), 13. But the topic has become very popular in political science in the past five years. See Shanto Iyengar, Mark Peters, and Donald Kinder, "Experimental Demonstrations of the Not-So-Minimal Consequences of Television News Programs," *American Political Science Review* 76 (December 1982): 848–58.

32 These figures are computed from data in William C. Adams and Phillip Heyl, "From Cairo to Kabul with the Networks, 1972: 1980," in *Television Coverage of the Middle East*, ed. William C. Adams (Norwood, N.J.: Ablex, 1981), 28.

33 Michael J. Robinson and Maura Clancey, "Teflon Politics," *Public Opinion*, April–May 1984.

34 Debates ranked first as a news topic on network evening news in 1984. According to the CBS News/*New York Times* exit polling, however, only 8 percent of the public felt that debates were very important in their voting decision.

35 If Carter had not decided so melodramatically to make the hostage story *the* issue for the first six months of his reelection campaign, the media would not have done so well at setting the agenda in 1980. The hostage crisis would never have been the press story it became if Carter had not egged the press on as he did.

36 For a recent review of almost all the research on exit polls and early calls, see Percy Tannenbaum and Leslie Kostrich, *Turned On TV/Turned Off Voters: Policy Options for Election Projections* (Beverly Hills: Sage Publications, 1983).

37 William C. Adams, "Early TV Calls in 1984: How Western Voters Deplored but Ignored Them," paper presented to the American Association for Public Opinion Research, May 1985.

38 Kevin Klose of the *Washington Post* poked fun at his own newspaper, pointing out that the *Post* sent eleven reporters, three more reporters than there were candidates ("Up from Obscurity: Ratio of Journalists to Iowa Caucus-Goers Hits One to One Hundred," *Washington Post*, February 20, 1984).

39 William C. Adams, "Media Coverage of Campaign '84: A Preliminary Report," *Public Opinion*, April–May 1984.

40 David Moore, "Myths of the New Hampshire Primary," paper prepared for meeting of the American Political Science Association, Washington, D.C., August 29, 1984, 13.

41 Adams, "Media Coverage of Campaign '84," 11.

42 Martin Schram, "Surf's Up, and Hart Finds That the Airwaves Break Both Ways," *Washington Post*, March 18, 1984.

43 Adams, "Media Coverage of Campaign '84," 13.

44 Cited in Tom Shales, "What Mudd Slung," *Washington Post*, March 15, 1984.

45 William C. Adams, "Convention Coverage," *Public Opinion*, December–January 1985.

46 These figures are found in Martin Schram, "Mondale Forces Tracked Their Message in the Media," *Washington Post*, July 22, 1984.

47 Network focus on the closing ceremonies was in direct contrast with what the networks showed (did not show) of Ray Charles at the end of the Republican convention.

48 Five social scientists who tried to measure the effect of Reagan's smile found that it worked better on men than on women. Denis Sullivan, Roger Masters, John Lanzetta, Basil Englis, and Gregory McHugo, "The Effects of President Reagan's Facial Displays on Observers' Attitudes," paper prepared for meeting of the American Political Science Association, Washington, D.C., August 30, 1984.

49 ABC News/*Washington Post* poll surveys 0086–0090, October 28, 1983. See also James Dickenson, "Bombing, Invasion in Eerie Focus," *Washington Post*, October 24, 1984.

50 For a short history of the changing pattern of debate from 1976 through 1984, see John Russonello, "Beat the Odds, Beat the Point Spread" (Washington, D.C., 1984, Xeroxed). For classics, see Sidney Kraus, *The Great Debates*, vols. 1, 2 (Bloomington: Indiana University Press, 1961); Austin Ranney, ed., *The Past and Future of Presidential Debates* (Washington, D.C.: American Enterprise Institute, 1979); and George Bishop, Robert Meadow, and Marilyn Jackson-Beeck, eds., *The Presidential Debates: Media, Electoral, and Policy Perspectives* (New York: Praeger, 1978).

51 The 1984 election added one other dimension to televised presidential debating. We now refer to the debates not only by location but also by interlocutor. We tend to remember the "Donahue/Koppel" debate at Dartmouth, the "Dan Rather" debate in New York.

52 The *Des Moines Register* poll found that in the major Iowa debate Mondale impressed 54 percent of all Democrats favorably and only 8 percent unfavorably. McGovern came in second, impressing 28 percent of the Democrats favorably, 6 percent unfavorably. David Elbert, "Poll Finds McGovern Won Debate," *Des Moines Register*, February 17, 1984. The ABC News/*Washington Post* poll found Mondale was perceived as the winner of the New Hampshire by 37 percent of the New Hampshire electorate; the next closest Democrat was Jesse Jackson, at 21 percent (Barry Sussman, "Poll Sees Debate Aiding Mondale, Jackson Most," *Washington Post*, January 17, 1984, 1).

53 Mondale apparently won the second New Hampshire debate as well. See Martin Schram, "New Hampshire Debate Changed a Few Primary Voters' Minds," *Washington Post*, February 25, 1984.

54 David Moore, "Report on Survey of Democratic Party Voters" (University of New Hampshire, Department of Political Science, Durham, 1984, Mimeographed), 6–7.

55 Frederick Steeper, "Public Response to Gerald Ford's Statements on Eastern Europe in the Second Debate," in Bishop et al., *The Presidential Debates*, 81–101.

56 Clancey and Robinson, "General Election Coverage."

57 Marilyn Adams, "Poll: Reagan Bounces Back," *USA Today*, October 19, 1984.

58 Adam Clymer, "Poll Finds Debate Gave Mondale a Small Gain," *New York Times*, October 11, 1984.

59 NBC poll, October 14–16, 1983; results provided to the author.

60 Figures provided to the author by Decision Making Information (DMI). I appreciate the data that DMI was able to give me.

61 Ibid.

62 This election has even forced me to reconsider my longest-held theory about television news—that it fosters video malaise. After all, if the American people could face the frostiest relations in thirty years between the United States and the Soviet Union, a risky situation in

Central America, 7.5 percent unemployment, and real interest rates of 8 percent—and still feel good about themselves and the country—they have learned to cope with the bad-news bias in network news.

The November 6 Vote for President

1 Richard Brody and Lee Sigelman, "Presidential Popularity and Presidential Elections: An Update and Extension," *Public Opinion Quarterly* 47 (Fall 1983): 325–28.

2 *Public Opinion* (October/November 1984), 38–40.

3 Kevin Phillips, *The American Political Report* 14 (January 11, 1985): 2.

4 The exact estimate was 173,936,000. Donald E. Starsinic, "Projections of the Population of Voting Age for States: November 1984," *Current Population Reports, Population Estimates, and Projections*, Series P-25, no. 948 (Washington, D.C.: U.S. Department of Commerce, Bureau of the Census, April 1984), 6.

5 William Schneider, "The November 4 Vote for President: What Did It Mean?" in *The American Elections of 1980*, ed. Austin Ranney (Washington, D.C.: American Enterprise Institute, 1981), 215.

6 Adam Clymer, "Women and Blacks Were Keys in Voting Rise," *New York Times*, January 28, 1985. In 1984, 61 percent of women and 59 percent of men reported voting. In 1980, 59 percent of both men and women reported voting.

7 "Rise in Voter Participation: Democrats Reap the Benefits," *Congressional Quarterly Weekly Report* 40 (November 13, 1982): 2850–51.

8 Among nonvoters polled after the election, 66 percent said they would have voted for Reagan and only 25 percent for Mondale.

9 Schneider, "The November 4 Vote," table 7.2, 225.

10 Norman J. Ornstein, "Changing Congress's Course: Republicans Still in the Wings," *Public Opinion*, December–January 1985, 13.

11 Phillips, *American Political Report*, 3.

12 Arthur H. Miller and Martin P. Wattenberg, "Politics from the Pulpit," *Public Opinion Quarterly* 48 (Spring 1984): 314.

13 See William Schneider, "The Jewish Vote in 1984: Elements in a Controversy," *Public Opinion*, December–January 1985, 18–19, 58.

14 Adam Clymer's computer model of the "national primary" vote in 1984 shows Mondale's support very powerfully affected by age. He is estimated to have won only 26 percent of the vote among primary participants under thirty, 30 percent among those 30 to 44, 41 percent among those 40 to 59, and 52 percent among those sixty and older. See "The 1984 National Primary," *Public Opinion*, August–September 1984, 53.

15 Everett C. Ladd, Jr., with Charles D. Hadley, *Transformations of the American Party System*, 2d ed. (New York: Norton, 1978), 211–28.

16 See Schneider, "The November 4 Vote," 254–55.

The Elections for Congress

1 The disparity was rooted in a dispute over the winner of Indiana's Eighth District. On January 3 the House of Representatives voted to ignore the certification of Republican challenger Richard McIntyre and leave the seat vacant pending a recount, during which McIntyre and incumbent Democrat Frank McCloskey would both be paid. After a statewide recount showed McIntyre the winner, the House—under vigorous protest from the

Republicans—continued to leave the seat vacant pending its own recount by the House Administration Committee. Over the Republicans' bitter protest, McCloskey was finally seated.

2 Dale Russakoff, "Coattails Crusade Aims at Fifteen Congressional Districts," *Washington Post*, October 30, 1984.

3 *Congressional Quarterly Weekly Report*, July 2, 1983, 1349.

4 Steve Lilienthal, "The NRCC: Converting Cash into Congressmen," *The Political Report* 6 (May 13, 1983).

5 Richard E. Cohen, "The Object Is Control," *National Journal*, October 29, 1983, 2236-62; and Phil Duncan, "Wealthy and Well Organized GOP Panel Eyes 1984 Elections," *Congressional Quarterly Weekly Report*, July 2, 1983, 1349-51.

6 Cohen, "Object Is Control," and Rob Gurwitt, "Democratic Campaign Panel: New Strategies and New Friends," *Congressional Quarterly Weekly Report*, July 2, 1983, 1346-48.

7 The Democratic candidates were Colorado lieutenant governor Nancy Dick, Maine House majority leader Elizabeth H. Mitchell, Minnesota secretary of state Joan A. Growe, New Mexico state representative Judith A. Pratt, Oregon state senator Margie Hendricksen, and former Virginia delegate Edythe C. Harrison.

8 *The Political Report* 7 (March 23, 1984).

9 *Congressional Quarterly Weekly Report*, February 25, 1984, 387-88.

10 Ibid., 361.

11 *Congressional Quarterly Weekly Report*, April 13, 1984, 2581.

12 *The American Political Report* 13 (April 6, 1984).

13 "Don't Count On Coattails," *National Journal*, June 30, 1984, 1277.

14 "Senate GOP Candidates Are Not Ready to Tie Their Election Hopes to Reagan," *National Journal*, August 1, 1984, 1614.

15 Helen Dewar, "Senate Race in North Carolina is a Southern-Fried Alley Fight," *Washington Post*, July 6, 1984.

16 Ibid.

17 *Congressional Quarterly Weekly Report*, October 13, 1984, 2572.

18 Martin Tolchin, "Senate Contest in Iowa Is Taking the Low Road," *New York Times*, October 24, 1984.

19 This became an issue in the North Carolina race, and Senator Helms was forced in a televised debate to pledge to North Carolina voters that he would not accept the foreign relations position because it would require him to give up the key agriculture committee chairmanship that protected tobacco interests in North Carolina.

20 *The Political Report*, December 20, 1984.

21 Fred Barnes, "Massachusetts Race for Senate Is Close," *Baltimore Sun*, October 29, 1984.

22 James R. Dickenson, "Party Strategists Say GOP Gains in House Increasingly Likely," *Washington Post*, August 21, 1984, sec. A8.

23 Ibid.

24 *New York Times*, September 10, 1984.

25 *Washington Post*, September 24, 1984.

26 Aaron Epstein, "Democrats Keeping Distance from the Top of Their Ticket," *Philadelphia Inquirer*, September 24, 1984.

27 Ibid.

28 Julia Malone, "Debate Slows GOP's House Drive," *Christian Science Monitor*, October 11, 1984.

29 Bush's batting average was low; only one of the targeted Democrats, Joe Minish, was beaten, and one of the three vulnerable GOP incumbents, Dan Crane, went down to defeat.

30 William Robins, "Outlook in the Elections in Mid-Atlantic Region," *New York Times*, October 24, 1984.

31   *The Political Report*, October 19, 1984.

32   Ibid.

33   Ibid.

34   William E. Schmidt, "Southern Republicans Hitch Hopes to a Strong Performance by Reagan," *New York Times*, October 14, 1984.

35   *Congressional Quarterly*, October 27, 1984, 2768 and 2769.

36   *Wall Street Journal*, October 25, 1984, 64.

37   Fred Barnes, "Confident GOP Now Covets More Seats in Congress," *Baltimore Sun*, October 23, 1984.

38   Michael J. Malbin and Thomas W. Skladony, "Campaign Finance 1984," paper prepared for AEI Public Policy Week, December 2, 1984.

39   Ibid.

40   Ibid.

41   *The Political Report*, December 14, 1984.

42   *Washington Post*, August 21, 1984.

43   *New York Times*, December 4, 1984.

44   Raymond E. Wolfinger, "Dealignment, Realignment, and Mandates in the 1984 Election," paper prepared for AEI Public Policy Week, December 3, 1984. A revised version of this paper appears as chapter 9 of the present book.

Dealignment, Realignment, and Mandates in the 1984 Election

I am grateful to David P. Glass, Michael G. Hagen, and Peverill Squire for the computer work and voting record research represented in this chapter, and to Mark C. Westlye for his helpful advice about Southern politics. The data from the National Election Studies used herein were made available by the Inter-University Consortium for Political and Social Research through the State Data Program of the University of California. None of these organizations is responsible for my analyses or interpretations. An earlier version of this chapter was delivered at Public Policy Week of the American Enterprise Institute, Washington, D.C., December 3, 1984.

1   "Vote Shows Erosion of Party Loyalty," *Los Angeles Times*, November 8, 1984, 1. On page 24 of the same issue appeared the information that Ronald Reagan received the votes of 92 percent of all Republican voters in 1980 and 97 percent in 1984. This suggests that one of the two parties did not suffer from disloyalty.

2   The classic statement of this theme is in Angus Campbell, Philip E. Converse, Warren E. Miller, and Donald E. Stokes, *The American Voter* (New York: John Wiley and Sons, 1960), 121.

3   Donald R. Kinder and David O. Sears, "Public Opinion and Political Action," in *The Handbook of Social Psychology*, 3d ed., ed. Gardner Lindzey (New York: Random House, 1985).

4   Norman H. Nie, Sidney Verba, and John R. Petrocik, *The Changing American Voter*, enlarged ed. (Cambridge: Harvard University Press, 1979), 73.

5   This is the question that has been asked in the University of Michigan National Election Studies (NES) since 1952. A similar, if not identical, item is used by commercial and mass media pollsters. The Gallup Poll uses this question: "In politics, as of today, do you consider yourself a Democrat, a Republican, or an Independent?"

6   Nie, Verba, and Petrocik, *Changing American Voter*, 47.

7   William Crotty, *American Parties in Decline*, 2d ed. (Boston: Little, Brown, 1984), 28-30, 37.

8   Everett Carll Ladd, *Where Have All the Voters Gone?*, 2d ed. (New York: Harper & Row, 1982), 124, 77.

9   Gerald M. Pomper, *Voter's Choice* (New York: Harper & Row, 1975), 40.

10 My discussion of Independents is based on two papers delivered at annual meetings of the American Political Science Association by Bruce E. Keith, David B. Magleby, Candice J. Nelson, Elizabeth Orr, Mark C. Westlye, and myself: "The Myth of the Independent Voter" (1977); and "Further Evidence on the Partisan Affinities of Independent 'Leaners'" (1983).

11 These figures do not include blacks, who are much less likely to be Independents of any sort.

12 For a discussion of some political scientists' attempts to explain away these findings about Independents, see Keith et al., "Further Evidence."

13 Nie, Verba, and Petrocik, *Changing American Voter*, 41.

14 Gary C. Jacobson, *The Politics of Congressional Elections* (Boston: Little, Brown, 1983), 86.

15 Ibid., 86–101; and Thomas E. Mann and Raymond E. Wolfinger, "Candidates and Parties in Congressional Elections," *American Political Science Review* 74 (September 1980): 620–21, 626–29.

16 For evidence on the responsiveness of party identification to short-term forces, see Richard A. Brody, "Stability and Change in Party Identification: Presidential to Off-Years," paper delivered at the annual meeting of the American Political Science Association, 1977.

17 Barry Sussman, "Fragile Realignment: As the Economy Goes, So Goes the GOP," *The Washington Post National Weekly Edition*, March 18, 1985, 37.

18 "Closing the Historic Party Identification Gap," *National Journal*, June 13, 1981, 1081.

19 ABC News/*Washington Post* Poll, Surveys 0184 and 0186. The CBS/*Times* data are all in the CBS News/*New York Times* Poll, February [1985] Survey.

20 Dan Balz, "The GOP as Majority Party?" *The Washington Post National Weekly Edition*, January 28, 1985, 11.

21 See Candice J. Nelson, "The Effects of Incumbency on Voting in Congressional Elections," *Political Science Quarterly* 93 (Winter 1978–79): 665–78.

22 William Schneider, "Half a Realignment," *The New Republic*, December 3, 1984, 20.

23 Pierre S. du Pont IV, "The GOP Isn't Doing Well Enough," *The Washington Post National Weekly Edition*, November 26, 1984, 28. Democrats now control both houses of the legislature in twenty-eight states, the Republicans, although achieving divided control in several instances, did not add to the eleven states where they held complete legislative control before the election.

24 *Los Angeles Times*, November 8, 1984, 1, 24.

25 An exhaustive survey of the available data by William Schneider demonstrates the strong Jewish vote for Mondale and refutes various methodological complaints by Jewish Reagan supporters. See "The Jewish Vote in 1984: Elements in a Controversy," *Public Opinion*, December–January 1985. This outcome was a disappointment to the Reagan campaign, which, hoping to exploit resentment of Jesse Jackson and his apparent appeasement by Mondale, budgeted $2 million for efforts targeted at Jews and even displayed signs in Hebrew in the Dallas convention hall. Evidently Jerry Falwell was more disturbing than Jackson to Jews.

26 The dimensions of Carter's appeal to his native region were modest. He received equal proportions of the white vote in the North and South, and carried the South because blacks are a bigger proportion of the voting population there than in the North.

27 Richard G. Hutcheson, "The Inertial Effect of Incumbency and Two-Party Politics," *American Political Science Review* 69 (December 1975): 1399–1401.

28 The 1984 Conservative Coalition Support Scores for four of the unseated Southern Democratic incumbents were 73, 78, 83, and 88. Their Republican successors therefore are unlikely to add much to conservative voting strength in the House.

29 This discussion builds on the findings in Raymond E. Wolfinger and Robert B. Arseneau, "Partisan Change in the South, 1952–1976," in Louis Maisel and Joseph Cooper, eds., *Political Parties: Development and Decay* (Beverly Hills: Sage Publications, 1978), 179–210.

30 Laurily K. Epstein, "The Changing Structure of Party Identification," *PS* (Winter 1985): 48–52.

31 Raymond E. Wolfinger and Steven J. Rosenstone, *Who Votes?* (New Haven: Yale University Press, 1980), 90–91. These and similar findings are based on respondents' reports about turnout. Blacks are more likely than whites to claim that they have voted when they have not in fact done so; thus the cited findings may overestimate black turnout and underestimate the likelihood of increased black voting. The most thorough study of this problem reports shrinking racial differences in validated turnout by the time of the 1980 election. See Paul R. Abramson and William Claggett, "Race-Related Differences in Self-Reported and Validated Turnout," *Journal of Politics* 46 (August 1984), 719–38.

32 U. S. Department of Commerce, Bureau of the Census, "Voting and Registration in the Election of November 1984 (Advance Report)," series P-20, no. 397, January 1985.

33 Barry Sussman, "Figuring Out Young Voters' Landmark Decision to Back Reagan," *Washington Post National Weekly Edition*, November 19, 1984, 37.

34 William Schneider, "Incumbency Staved Off Disaster for Congressional Democrats in 1984 Elections," *National Journal*, December 8, 1984, 2365.

35 The same conclusion is reached if young voters are defined as those aged eighteen to twenty-four.

36 James J. Kilpatrick, "Personal Triumph for Reagan," *San Francisco Chronicle*, November 9, 1984, 50. Empirical support for Kilpatrick's interpretation can be found in the work of Steven J. Rosenstone, who shows that peace, prosperity, and a popular incumbent virtually guarantee success for the president's party. For a detailed statement, see his *Forecasting Presidential Elections* (New Haven: Yale University Press, 1983). Specific application of Rosenstone's model to the 1984 election can be found in his "Why Reagan Won," *The Brookings Review* 3 (Winter 1985): 25–32.

37 Samuel L. Popkin, "The Donkey's Dilemma: White Men Don't Vote Democratic," *Washington Post*, November 11, 1984, D1.

38 "Voters Have Endorsed His Policies, Reagan Says," *Los Angeles Times*, November 8, 1984, 24.

39 CBS News/*New York Times* release dated October 27, 1984.

40 For example, 57 percent of all voters and fully 40 percent of those who voted for Reagan agreed that the president would ask Congress to raise taxes in his second term. See the CBS News/*New York Times* postelection survey, November 8, 1984.

41 Warren E. Miller and Teresa E. Levitin, *Leadership and Change: Presidential Elections from 1952 to 1976* (Cambridge: Winthrop Publishers, 1976), 141–44, 158.

42 *San Francisco Chronicle*, November 7, 1984, 8.

43 *Los Angeles Times*, November 8, 1984, 24.

44 *New York Times*, November 8, 1984, 11.

45 *San Francisco Chronicle*, November 7, 1984, 8.

46 Quoted in Charles O. Jones, "The New, New Senate," in Ellis Sandoz and Cecil V. Crabb, Jr., eds., *A Tide of Discontent: The 1980 Elections and Their Meaning* (Washington, D.C.: Congressional Quarterly Press, 1981), 96.

47   Thomas E. Mann and Norman J. Ornstein, "The Republican Surge in 1980," in Austin Ranney, ed., *The American Elections of 1980* (Washington, D.C.: American Enterprise Institute, 1981), 293–94.

48   Jeffrey L. Pasley, "New House GOP Freshman Class Wary of Following Reagan's Budget Lead," *National Journal*, March 16, 1985, 584.

Realignment at the Top

1   Arthur M. Schlesinger, Jr., ed., *The Coming to Power: Critical Presidential Elections in American History* (New York: Chelsea House, 1972).

2   CBS News/*New York Times* exit poll, November 1984.

3   William C. Adams, "Recent Fables About Ronald Reagan," *Public Opinion*, October–November 1984, 9.

4   Ibid., 7.

5   William Schneider, "Half a Realignment," *New Republic*, December 3, 1984, 21.

6   Opinion Roundup, *Public Opinion*, April–May 1983, and February–March 1983.

7   Jeane Kirkpatrick, *The New Presidential Elite* (New York: Russell Sage Foundation, 1976), pp. 297–304.

8   Herbert McClosky, et al., "Issue Conflict and Consensus Among Party Leaders and Followers," *American Political Science Review* 54 (1960): 406–27.

9   *New York Times*, August 13, 1980.

10   *Los Angeles Times* survey, as printed in the *Boston Globe*, August 22, 1984.

11   William Schneider, "Democrats, Republicans Move Further Apart on Most Issues in 1983 Session," *National Journal*, May 12, 1984, 904–20.

12   Report of the Standing Committee on Rules to the 1984 Democratic National Convention June 28, 1984, 7.

13   Ibid., 8.

14   Samuel P. Huntington, "The Visions of the Democratic Party," *The Public Interest* (Spring 1985): 63–78.

15   Morton M. Kondracke, "Democrats' Next Chairman Must Unite Four 'Parties,'" *Wall Street Journal*, November 15, 1984.

16   John Bartlow Martin, "Election of 1964," in Schlesinger, *Coming to Power*, 468–69.

17   *National Journal*, September 1, 1984, 1610–11.

18   *Boston Globe*, July 9, 1984.

19   Quoted in Seymour Martin Lipset, "The Congressional Candidate," *Journal of Contemporary Studies* 6 (Summer, 1983): 102.

20   The central importance of schooling is shown in almost any text on public opinion.

21   *Los Angeles Times* survey, as printed in the *Boston Globe*, August 22, 1984.

22   *Public Opinion*, April–May 1981, 21–25.

Index

Contributors

ALBERT R. HUNT is Chief of the Washington Bureau of the *Wall Street Journal* and has contributed chapters to *The American Elections of 1980* and *The American Elections of 1982.*

CHARLES O. JONES is Robert Kent Gooch Professor of Government and Foreign Affairs at the University of Virginia and served as managing editor of *The American Political Science Review* from 1977 to 1981. His recent books include *The United States Congress* and *Carter and Congress.*

THOMAS E. MANN is executive director of the American Political Science Association and a visiting fellow at the American Enterprise Institute. He is the author of *Unsafe at Any Margin: Interpreting Congressional Elections* and coeditor of *The New Congress, Vital Statistics on Congress 1982,* and *The American Elections of 1982.*

NORMAN J. ORNSTEIN is a resident scholar at the American Enterprise Institute and coeditor of *The New Congress, Vital Statistics on Congress 1984-1985,* and *The American Elections of 1982.* He serves as elections analyst for CBS News and as a consultant to the MacNeil-Lehrer News Hour on PBS.

NELSON W. POLSBY is Professor of Political Science at the University of California, Berkeley, and served as managing editor of *The American Political Science Review* from 1971 to 1977. His recent books include *Consequences of Party Reform* and *Political Innovation in America: The Politics of Policy Initiation.*

AUSTIN RANNEY is a resident scholar at the American Enterprise Institute, a former president of the American Political Science Association, and served as managing editor of *The American Political Science Review* from 1965 to 1971. His recent books include *Channels of Power: The Influence of Television on American Politics,* and he edited *The American Elections of 190.*

MICHAEL J. ROBINSON is a visiting scholar at the American Enterprise Institute and directs the Media Analysis Project at AEI and the George Washington University. He has written numerous articles on the role of the mass media in American campaigns and elections and is coauthor, with Margaret Sheehan, of *Over the Wire and On TV.*

WILLIAM SCHNEIDER is a resident fellow at the American Enterprise Institute and a political analyst for the *National Journal* and the *Los Angeles Times.* He is coauthor, with Alan Baron, of the forthcoming book *The Radical Center: New Directions in American Politics.*

JAMES Q. WILSON is Henry Lee Shattuck Professor of Government at Harvard University and also Professor of Management and Public Policy at the University of California, Los Angeles. His recent books include *The Investigators, Varieties of Police Behavior,* and *Thinking About Crime* (revised edition).

RAYMOND E. WOLFINGER is Professor of Political Science and Director of the State Data Program at the University of California, Berkeley. He is the chairman of the Board of Overseers of the National Election Study and coauthor of *Who Votes?* and *The Myth of the Independent Voter.*

Library of Congress Cataloging-in-Publication Data
Main entry under title:
The American elections of 1984.
(At the polls series)
"An American Enterprise Institute book."
Bibliography: p.
Includes index.
1. Presidents—United States—Election—1984—Ad-
dresses, essays, lectures. 2. United States—Politics
and government—1981–   —Addresses, essays,
lectures. 3. Reagan, Ronald—Addresses, essays,
lectures. 4. Mondale, Walter F., 1928–   —Addresses,
essays, lectures. I. Ranney, Austin. II. American
Enterprise Institute for Public Policy Research.
III. Series.
E879.A44 1986   324.973'0927   85-24573
ISBN 0-8223-0230-6
ISBN 0-8223-0697-2 (pbk.)